Signs and Wonders in Britain's Age of Revolution

Signs and Wonders in Britain's Age of Revolution is an original collection of primary sources from the era encompassing the political, religious, and social tumult of the English Civil War.

With a focus on Britain in the seventeenth century and covering topics such as astrology, scurrilous pamphlet wars, witch-hunts and trials, and the execution of King Charles I, *Signs and Wonders* investigates published "strange and true" accounts that existed alongside more traditionally studied historical events.

Including fully edited and annotated texts of carefully selected popular pamphlets, the sourcebook is accompanied by guided introductory essays for each of the thematically divided chapters. With more than two dozen woodcut images, *Signs and Wonders* enables students to pursue in-depth primary source analysis of this rich period of history, when the supernatural was woven into the lives of those participating in or viewing the tumultuous political and religious events of the mid-seventeenth century.

In this collection of popular pamphlets, battles in the sky, witches, monstrous births, and apparitions stand side-by-side with the major political and religious events that make up the standard histories of the era, allowing a fuller perspective on these early modern narratives and their interpretation (and exploitation) by the heated presses of seventeenth-century Britain. *Signs and Wonders in Britain's Age of Revolution* is essential reading for all students of early modern Britain.

Timothy G. Fehler is Professor of History at Furman University. His previous books include *Poor Relief and Protestantism: The Evolution of Social Welfare in Sixteenth-Century Emden* (1999), and *Religious Diaspora in Early Modern Europe: Strategies of Exile* (2014).

Abigail J. Hartman (BA, Furman University; MLitt, University of St. Andrews) is pursuing doctoral work in Medieval History.

Signs and Wonders in Britain's Age of Revolution
A Sourcebook

Edited by Timothy G. Fehler and
Abigail J. Hartman

 Routledge
Taylor & Francis Group

LONDON AND NEW YORK

First published 2019
by Routledge
2 Park Square, Milton Park, Abingdon, Oxon OX14 4RN

and by Routledge
711 Third Avenue, New York, NY 10017

Routledge is an imprint of the Taylor & Francis Group, an informa business

© 2018 selection and editorial matter, Timothy G. Fehler and Abigail
J. Hartman; individual chapters, the contributors

British Library Cataloguing in Publication Data
A catalogue record for this book is available from the British Library

Library of Congress Cataloging in Publication Data
Names: Fehler, Timothy G., editor. | Hartman, Abigail J., editor.
Title: Signs and wonders in Britain's age of revolution : a sourcebook /
    edited by Timothy G. Fehler and Abigail J. Hartman.
Description: Abingdon, Oxon ; New York, NY : Routledge, 2019. |
    Includes bibliographical references.
Identifiers: LCCN 2018017674Subjects: LCSH: Great Britain—History—Civil
    War, 1642-1649—Sources. | Great Britain—History—Puritan Revolution,
    1642-1660—Sources. | Curiosities and wonders—Great Britain—
    History—17th century.
Classification: LCC DA410 .S54 2018 | DDC 942.06/2—dc23
LC record available at https://lccn.loc.gov/2018017674

ISBN: 978-1-138-49205-9 (hbk)
ISBN: 978-1-138-49206-6 (pbk)
ISBN: 978-1-351-03134-9 (ebk)

Typeset in Sabon
by Swales & Willis Ltd, Exeter, Devon, UK

Contents

4   Cavaliers and Roundheads: *'The divells agents still'*   134

5   Christian astrology: *'Amongst the celestiall hieroglyphicks'*   181

6   Sectarians and recusants: *'Recant . . . those dangerous errors'*   234

Illustrations and abbreviation

Illustrations

Abbreviation

ODNB   Oxford Dictionary of National Biography (Oxford University Press, 2004)

Preface
An age of revolution

As the astrologers spoke of the annual revolution of the world and attempted to interpret the revolutions of the heavenly spheres through the course of the 1640s (see, for instance, Chapter 5), their prognostications became ever more dramatic. Civil war, religious sectarianism, and social upheaval turned the world upside down. The political turmoil and warfare that had dominated much of the continent for over two decades was now coming to Britain. This collection of pamphlets affords an opportunity to get a sense of, if not to fully enter into, worldviews that are often jarring to a modern mindset. The extended introductory essay to Chapter 1 sheds light on the manner in which perspectives on the supernatural were woven into the lives of those participating in or viewing the tumultuous political and religious events of the mid-seventeenth century, and the opening 1638 treatise will offer the reader a starting point for interpreting prodigious events. This collection's subsequent chapters follow a similar pattern, though the following introductory essays are briefer and each thematic chapter offers the annotated text of five to seven pamphlets that deal with various types of accounts of "signs and wonders." Traditional scholarly approaches have been either to pass over such sources in silence, or else to treat them as curious, but ultimately bizarre and unhelpful, products of a superstitious worldview. While a commendable shift in scholarly interest has already led to collections of primary sources on witchcraft, there has not yet been a collection of prodigy pamphlets. In this collection of complete popular pamphlets, battles in the sky, witches, monstrous births, and apparitions stand side-by-side with the major political and religious events that make up our "textbook" histories of the era, allowing a fuller perspective on these early modern narratives and their interpretation (and exploitation) by the heated presses of seventeenth-century Britain.

Because the more standard-fare history of the English Civil War and English (or Puritan) Revolution provides the particular context for understanding these pamphlets, it is necessary to provide here a short historiographical and chronological sketch of the era.[1] However, as the traditional narratives and interpretations are so widely accessible—online and in history textbooks on Tudor-Stuart England, Early Modern Europe, or

Western Civilization—this supplemental outline highlights just a few key markers that are especially useful for the pamphlets in this collection.

As can be seen in these pamphlets, the issues behind the English Civil War have been fiercely disputed since the midst of the conflict itself. Over the past half century, however, a number of new studies have substantially reshaped the interpretive landscape regarding the origins, nature, and consequences of the revolutionary crises facing the British governments of the Stuarts during the seventeenth century. When King James VI of Scotland ascended the English throne as James I in 1603, he inaugurated an era in which the fates of those two countries would be more intricately bound than ever before. The wars that broke out in Scotland, Ireland, and England during the reign of his son Charles I, particularly the Civil War in England that culminated in Charles' execution on January 30, 1649, form a high-water mark in the political radicalism of mid century. Since the nineteenth century, the traditional historiographical interpretations of the revolutionary era often created an exclusionary English patriotic myth, portraying these conflicts as the culmination of a series of long-term political, religious, and economic developments that moved England progressively toward its inevitable future as a constitutional monarchy with a parliamentary democracy and capitalist economy. "Whig" historians emphasized the growing conflicts between the rights of Parliament (particularly an increasingly self-confident House of Commons connected with liberty and Protestantism) and an absolutist monarchy with Catholic (or "Popish") tendencies that brought about the Civil War. Marxist historians in the same progressive mold focused more on the economic conditions of a burgeoning bourgeois class (with connections to more radical religious ideas of Puritanism expanding at the time) that was in conflict with a declining aristocracy. In these accounts, a revolution was all but inevitable as rival interests clashed, and these seventeenth-century developments were thus the obvious steps that advanced England forward toward its nineteenth- and twentieth-century realities.[2]

Instead of seeing an inevitable "high road to civil war,"[3] a generation of so-called "revisionists" began to focus research on the specific, local circumstances which broke linkages between any long-brewing constitutional, religious, or socio-economic conflicts that might have erupted in the 1640s.[4] By carefully reconstructing each particular moment in the period through the eyes, experiences, and expectations of the range of participants, revisionists highlighted the role of patronage, local interests, and immediate financial, religious, and military exigencies that sparked specific crises. Revisionists, though not monolithically unified on all points, could thus, for example, see the crisis of 1640 as different from the rebellion that broke out in 1641–1642, which was separate in its causes from the revolution of 1647–1649. This new research of the 1970s both narrowed the focus into local English archives while simultaneously broadening the scope to see essential connections beyond England in both Scotland and Ireland. Broader religious, political, and financial/military realities across the British Isles—particularly the aftermath of the Scottish Bishops Wars of the late 1630s and the Irish Confederate Wars of the 1640s—have ever since been crucial to our understanding of the period. The English Civil War became one of the Wars of the Three Kingdoms and ceased to be a merely English phenomenon. Moreover, inverting causal interpretations, revisionists saw a generally ineffectual Commons and a Church of England with a broad Calvinist consensus; rather than seeing aggressive Parliament agitation against the King, the revisionists painted the critics of the King as the defenders of traditional orthodoxy in both church and state against the innovations of Charles I and his government.

In the generation after revisionism's correctives shattered the picture of progressive inevitability, historians (including many revisionists) have often re-established links between certain long-term developments and the crises of the 1640s. The political and theological consensus that revisionists pointed to before the Civil War's disruptions has once again yielded to some longer-term ideological disagreements, but now with a much richer sense of divided loyalties and interests among supporters in all camps; nuanced analysis allows for greater recognition of individuals and groups changing sides or becoming more (or less) aggressive at various points in time. The past few decades have also signaled the importance of social, economic, communication, and cultural factors and a move away from an over-emphasis on high politics.[5] Scholars have increasingly explored the interconnected roles of such factors both to help explain the causes and nature of the conflicts and to investigate the impact of the revolutionary era in the daily lives of people across the spectrum of experiences. It is onto this new landscape that these pamphlets open a fresh window.

Notes

1 Excellent summaries with which to enter into the historiographic debates over the English Civil War can be found in the Introductions of these two readers: Keith Lindley, *The English Civil War and Revolution: A Sourcebook* (London: Routledge, 1998), 1–5 (with expansions, 5–34), and Richard Cust and Ann Hughes (eds), *The English Civil War* (London: Arnold, 1997), 1–30.

2 Students who want a detailed blow-by-blow political and military history of the English Civil War of the 1640s (in the "Whig" perspective) are encouraged to see Samuel R. Gardiner's three-volume *History of the Great Civil War, 1642–1649* (London, 1896–1991; later published in four volumes). On the Marxist interpretative tradition, see, for example, Christopher Hill, *The English Revolution* (London: Larence & Wishart, 1940); also Hill's "Recent Interpretations of the Civil War," in his *Puritanism and Revolution* [1958] (New York: St. Martin's Press, 1997). Lawrence Stone's multi-causal but still highly deterministic account in 1972 incorporated social science theories of revolution and served as a catalyst for a wave of new critical scholarship that questioned anachronistic categories: *The Causes of the English Revolution 1529–1642* (London: Routledge Classics, 2017).

3 G. R. Elton, "A High Road to Civil War?" in Charles H. Carter (ed.), *From the Renaissance to the Counter-Reformation* (New York: Random House, 1965), 325–347.

4 Conrad Russell (ed.), *The Origins of the English Civil War* (Basingstoke, UK: Macmillan, 1973); John Morrill, *The Revolt of the Provinces* [1976], 2nd ed. (London: Addison Wesley Longman, 1999); David Stephenson, *Scottish Covenanters and Irish Confederates* (Belfast: Ulster Historical Foundation, 1981); Nicholas Tyacke, *Anti-Calvinists: The Rise of English Arminianism c. 1590–1640* (Oxford, UK: Oxford University Press, 1987); Kevin Sharpe, *The Personal Rule of Charles I* (New Haven, CT: Yale University Press, 1992); Conrad Russell, *The Causes of the English Civil War* (Oxford, UK: Oxford University Press, 1990). The collection of essays in Cust and Hughes (eds), *The English Civil War* has reprinted many of the landmark scholarly articles of the 1970s and 1980s; students will also find its extensive bibliography useful.

5 Selected from among numerous examples: David Underdown, *Revel, Riot, and Rebellion: Popular Politics and Culture in England 1603–1660* (Oxford, UK: Oxford University Press, 1985); idem, *Fire from Heaven: Life in an English Town in the Seventeenth Century* (New Haven, CT: Yale University Press, 1992); Mark Kishlansky, *A Monarchy Transformed: Britain 1603–1714* (London: Penguin, 2004); Ann Hughes, *Gangreana and the Struggle for the English Revolution* (Oxford, UK: Oxford University Press, 2004); Jason Peacey, *Politicians and Pamphleteers: Propaganda During the English Civil Wars and Interregnum* (Aldershot, UK: Ashgate, 2004); Richard Cust, *Charles I: A Political Life* (Harlow, UK: Pearson, 2005); Diane Purkiss, *The English Civil War: Papists, Gentlewomen, Soldiers, and Witchfinders in the Birth of Modern Britain* (New York: Basic Books, 2006); Ian Gentles, *The English Revolution and the Wars in the Three Kingdoms 1638–1652* (Harlow, UK: Pearson, 2007).

Chronology

1618   Outbreak of Thirty Years War in Holy Roman Empire between Austrian Habsburg Emperor and many of the German states; although England did not join as a formal belligerent, the dire situation in Germany was often raised as a "looking glass" for England in sermons and pamphlets.

1625   Death of James VI/I (March 27) and accession of son Charles I; marriage of Charles I and the French Catholic princess Henrietta Maria (June 23).

1628   Petition of Right brought a temporary resolution to Charles' third Parliament (June 7). Assassination of the King's chief advisor George Villiers, Duke of Buckingham (August 23).

1629   Dissolution of Charles' third Parliament and beginning of his "Personal Rule" without Parliament (until 1640).

1633   William Laud consecrated as Archbishop of Canterbury.

1637   Laud imposes a Book of Common Prayer on Scottish Church (July). John Hampden's case against Ship Money argued before Court of Exchequer (November).

1638   Initial signing of Scottish National Covenant to support Presbyterianism against episcopacy and popery (28 February).

1639   First Bishops War as Charles I raises troops to quell Covenanter turmoil; King forced to accept Pacification of Berwick (June 19).

1640   Lord Deputy of Ireland, Thomas Wentworth (Earl of Strafford), recalled to England to advise King on Scottish war; Charles I ends personal rule to deal with Scottish problem by summoning English Parliament (February 20), which sat for three weeks until Charles dissolved it in annoyance (April 13–May 5). Scottish Parliament adopts National Covenant. Second Bishops War as Scottish troops cross border, forcing Charles I to call Parliament again (Long Parliament,

November 23); House of Common impeaches Archbishop Laud of high treason (December 18).

1641 Laud imprisoned (February 15). Commons passes Bills of Attainder against Strafford (April 21) who is executed (May 12) after Charles I reluctantly signs death warrant. Habeas Corpus Act abolishes unpopular courts of High Commission and Star Chamber (July 5). Oliver Cromwell and Henry Vane the Younger propose Root and Branch Bill to abolish episcopacy (defeated in Commons, August). Irish Rebellion breaks out in Ulster as Catholic gentry seek to seize administration of Ireland from the English (October); Ulster massacres and deaths of Protestant settlers (over 10,000, though parliamentarian pamphlets reported over 200,000). Initially proposed by John Pym, Grand Remonstrance of 204 grievances drawn up by English House of Commons (November 22), presented to King (December 1), and then printed for public distribution.

1642 King Charles attempts unsuccessfully to seize the "Five Members" (including Pym and Hampden) from the House of Commons chamber (January 4). King and family leave London (January) for north (March). English Army sent to Ireland to put down rebellion; Irish Catholics form a Confederation which establishes a government at Kilkenny. King raises his standard at Nottingham against Parliament (August 22). King's 21-year-old nephew Prince Rupert of the Rhine (after three years in captivity during Thirty Years War) along with brother Maurice, arrives and is given command of cavalry, boosting royalist morale; Battle of Edgehill (October 23) marks first battle between King and Parliament.

1643 Westminster Assembly of Divines meets to restructure Church of England (July 1, 1653). Prince Rupert captures important western port of Bristol for royalists (July 26). Solemn League and Covenant lays foundation for Parliamentary alliance with Scottish Covenanters (approved August/September).

1644 King's Parliament convenes in Oxford (January 22). Parliamentarians besiege Oxford (May–June). Battle of Marston Moor (July 2) a decisive victory of the Parliamentarian army (under Lord Fairfax and Earl of Manchester) together with Scottish army (under Earl of Leven) over the Royalists (under Prince Rupert, Marquess of Newcastle, and Lord Goring). Divisions between Presbyterian and Independent factions in Parliament and army begin to appear.

1645 Parliament establishes New Model Army with Sir Thomas Fairfax as its commander-in-chief (January 6). Archbishop Laud executed (January 10). Thomas Fairfax begins second siege of Oxford (May 22); King and Princes Rupert and Maurice left (May 7); Fairfax breaks siege to pursue King (June 5) and decisively defeats Royalists at Battle of Naseby (June 14). Fairfax besieges Bristol, and Prince Rupert forced to surrender (September 10).

1646   King surrenders to Scots army camped at Newark, ending First Civil War (May 5). Parliament passes ordinance to abolish episcopacy (October). Presbyterian church settlement attempted in England.

1647   Scots army leaves England and turns Charles I over to English (January 30). Parliament attempts to disband most of New Model Army, but army agitators campaign for pay and against Presbyterianism, creating rifts within Parliament and among Londoners. The army seizes Charles I, takes him to Newmarket (June 4), and enters London (August 6). Ireton drafts the "Heads of Proposal;" army Grandees use it in an attempt to negotiate a settlement with Charles I, and Ireton promotes it as an alternative to the Levellers' "Agreement of the People" at the army's Putney Debates (October 28–November). Leveller-inspired Corkbush Field mutiny against Fairfax suppressed by Cromwell (November 15). Following escape from house arrest, Charles I imprisoned on Isle of Wight (November 11).

1648   Following failed negotiations, the Commons votes to cease further negotiations with Charles I who negotiates secretly with the Scots (January). Scots Parliament demands immediate establishment of Presbyterian Church of England (April). On the continent, long-running negotiations culminate in German treaties that end the Thirty Years War (Peace of Westphalia). Royalist riots and Scottish invasion lead to Second Civil War, suppressed by Cromwell and Fairfax (May–August). Pride's Purge excludes Presbyterians from Parliament (December 6), leaving "Rump Parliament." Charles I brought to Whitehall for trial.

1649   High Court of Justice tries Charles I as tyrant and traitor (January 8–27). Scottish Commissioners advocate against execution. After determining that there will be no successor, the regicides execute Charles I (January 30). Commonwealth declared. Scots agitate for Prince Charles' succession. English House of Lords abolished (February 6). Cromwell and Fairfax face Leveller mutiny in army (May). Cromwell and Ireton take army to Ireland (August) to begin reconquest; massacres in Drogheda (September) and Wexford (October).

1650   Prince Charles accepts Scottish demands to take Covenant (and support Presbyterianism) in exchange for acknowledgement as King Charles II (May). Cromwell quits Ireland (May 26), leaving Ireton to end remaining resistance. Cromwell defeats Scots at Battle of Dunbar (September 3).

1651   Charles slips away from Britain after Cromwell defeats his Scots army at Worcester (September 3).

1652   Act of Settlement begins formal punishment of Irish for rebellion.

1653   Cromwell dissolves the Rump Parliament (April), establishes Protectorate.

1658   Cromwell dies (September 3); succeeded by son Richard as Lord Protector.

1659   Richard Cromwell resigns (May). After struggle among factions, General Monck marches on London, restores Long Parliament, and begins negotiations with Prince Charles in exile.

1660   Restoration of the monarchy under Charles II (May 29).

1   Warning-pieces

Introduction

> Before God sends any *Plague* to a *Nation*, hee first gives them warning, sometimes by *Apparitions*, sometimes by *Visions*, sometimes by *monsterous Births*, sometimes by *Sects, Schisms,* and *devisionns*, sometimes by *Thunder* and *Lightning*, unnaturall *Tides*, &c. and innumerable ways that the LORD can use to forewarn us of an approaching *Judgment*. . .[1]

Pamphleteers of the seventeenth century evocatively called them "warning-pieces," employing the term for a signal gun fired to announce impending danger. More commonly they were known as "prodigies," which encompassed any number of unusual events and departures from the natural order. By the time this anonymous pamphleteer published his account of one such wonder in 1655, readers could have been forgiven for finding them commonplace: "What unnaturall *Tides* have we had within these few years?" the author himself asked rhetorically. "What monstrous *Fishes*. . . What lamentable *Fires*. . . What unusuall stormes of *Haile*. . . What incessant *showres* of *Raine*, whereby some of our *Plenty* is already wash'd away?"[2] And this was but a small sampling of the wonders that had proliferated in Great Britain over the preceding fifteen years of social and political turmoil. In the two decades that saw the outbreak of civil war, the execution of a king and the abolition of monarchy, the establishment of a republican government and a protectorate, and ultimately the reinstatement of a Stuart on the English throne, God's warning-pieces abounded through more than mere meteorological aberrations.

Although such providential signs were by no means an invention of the English Revolution, the British—and especially the London—press in the mid-1600s was admirably poised to both spread and exploit them. A society of increasing individual and communal literacy, in which the practices of reading aloud and of summarizing a work's contents in woodcuts allowed even the technically illiterate to share in printed intelligence,[3] generated a voracious appetite for news that was only made keener by political unrest. Unfortunately for would-be reporters, however, the Stuart government looked upon printed news with a suspicious eye—domestic especially, but also foreign, which could "reflect on British affairs, and comment unfavourably on the king's policy of non-intervention [in the ongoing European wars]."[4] James VI/I and his successor, Charles I, both sought to limit the circulation and content of the emergent periodicals of the 1620s–30s, first by an uneasy license to a single printing syndicate, then, when political pressures from abroad increased, by proscribing them altogether in October 1632.[5] For the most part, eager publishers managed to get around even these fickle censorship policies by changing the format of their publications (for instance, they printed "modern histories" instead of short newsbooks), and readers continued to follow events with keen interest.[6] Nevertheless, it was when the Star Chamber was abolished in 1641 and strictures were removed that printers were truly handed the ingredients for lucrative publishing ventures: a failure of official censorship, an eager audience, and political crises that offered intelligence worth reading. The "frantic hunger for news" was fed by a multitude of obliging printers and publishers, and 1641 to 1660 saw a dramatic rise in the number of both regular periodicals and cheap, often sensational ephemera.[7] As one later news-serial put it in its first issue, with some exaggeration:

> Wee had (some years agone) no *Diurnals* of our owne affairs in *England*. We did live then in so blessed a Time, that wee were onely curious, and desirous to heare forraigne Newes. . . And now by a strange alteration and vicissitude of Times, wee talke of nothing else, but of what is done in *England*: and perhaps once in a fortnight, we hearken after Newes out of *Scotland*.[8]

"What was done in England," however, encompassed more than troop movements and Parliamentary deliberations: and narratives of "strange and true" wonders—from witchcraft to monsters to ghostly armies observed fighting in the sky—existed without paradox alongside these more prosaic reports. Both were passed along in letters and through private news networks; both were recorded in diaries alongside writers' prayers and reflections on the state of the world. After all, wonders were "strange," and yet at the same time nothing new: to borrow Alexandra Walsham's comment regarding popular narratives of divine judgment, the prodigy genre had "a venerable heritage" that stretched back not only to the days of the early Church but to the classical pagan past as well.[9] Writers of the seventeenth century pointed to the comets and strange births that had heralded the destruction of Jerusalem in AD 70 as effortlessly as they referenced contemporary occurrences of comets and rains of blood in war-torn Germany, and the historical argument of the 1655 pamphleteer was reiterated so frequently as to become a truism: when a political or religious crisis shook a nation, and especially a nation with claims to godliness, it would be accompanied by "morbid symptoms" in nature and direct, if often puzzling, signs from God.[10]

Despite this long history, historians continue to debate how much credence early modern readers gave to the tales that appeared in the cheap "pulp" pamphlets of the wars and Interregnum. Authors typically advertised their narratives as "strange and true," stressing the number and respectability of those who had witnessed the prodigy and would even include directions to the place where readers might view it for themselves. And yet patently false reports still crept in,[11] and even the appearance of scrupulous reportage could be mere "sales talk," not necessarily credited by the buyer.[12] Some readers, indeed, may have scoffed at the idea of storms or comets as signs of divine wrath, and private sources suggest that even those who kept an eye open for such events were not always comfortable with interpreting them: Sir Simonds d'Ewes, for example, recorded many strange things in his diary, but when a lightning strike at St. James caused dire political prognostications, he sniffily observed, "I omitt these fopperyes."[13] Certainly writers themselves were quick to decry the unbelief of those who lightly dismissed their warnings; the prodigy genre abounds with authorial and editorial complaints about the hard-heartedness of their audience, who, they grumbled, too easily dismissed so-called prodigies as mere natural occurrences and failed to see in them divine warnings.

Yet this recurring grievance flows from the pamphlets' didactic purpose and must be taken with a grain of salt. It seems most probable that the majority of readers were neither entirely credulous nor wholly skeptical but, while acknowledging the validity of marvelous signs in principle, accepted the veracity of some stories and rejected that of others on a case-by-case basis. This was all the more necessary since there was no official body for the regulation and verification of prodigy accounts, and therefore truth and lies could both be published freely (a fact which writers and publishers acknowledged and occasionally denounced); it was thus down to the reader to decide for him- or herself which was which.[14]

Their credibility aside, signs from heaven abounded, and the literature surrounding them came to form a substantial portion of the 1641–1660 "print explosion." The question for scholars of early modern culture has been what, if anything, is to be made of them. Were they sensational stories designed to entertain the average (poorly educated) Englishman or woman, or sermons disguised under popular trimmings? Do they reflect a complex worldview informed by a deep belief in divine providence, or are they the product of, as one historian has argued, "unsophisticated, enchanted views of life and society" that ignored religious niceties?[15] Can they tell us anything about the intricacies of the English Revolution, or are they now, as pamphlets in general were sometimes regarded by contemporaries, "small, insignificant, ephemeral, disposable, untrustworthy, unruly, noisy, deceitful, poorly printed, addictive, a waste of time"?[16] Scholars were long inclined toward the second opinion, meaning that the popular narratives were either ignored or else marginalized as delusions, gross sensationalism, and the precursor of modern-day tabloids. Under such a paradigm, accounts of monsters, comets, apparitions, witches, and rains of blood are treated within the context of a progression from superstition to science, from the marvelous to the mundane—or, conversely, as symptomatic of a deep-rooted irrationality common to men and women of the seventeenth and the twenty-first centuries. A stage in the development of the scientific revolution, or a cousin of the magazines at the checkout counter: in either scenario, early-modern narratives of prodigies and astrological portents are not deeply studied on their own merits.

This scholarly approach has changed dramatically over the last several decades. Just as recent witchcraft studies have shifted toward an emphasis on "reconstructing contexts, searching for hidden significance, [and] respecting contemporary perspectives,"[17] so scholars of print media, the Reformation, and early modern politics are critiquing assumptions about the purpose and impact of the "pulp press" more generally and its relevance for historians today. "The objective," Malcolm Gaskill writes of his own field of research, "is no longer just to see how politics and religion help us understand witchcraft, but the reverse: the extraction of obscure strands of meaning from witchcraft and the exchanges it initiated."[18] The same could accurately be said of cheap print and providentialist literature, which is increasingly the subject of nuanced, sensitive examination by scholars who seek to elucidate the connection of prodigies to (for example) religious reformation, political controversy, and the horrors and anxieties of civil war.[19]

Without necessarily reading these works as "a transparent window" through which we can observe the mindset of early modern men and women,[20] these historians reject an anachronistic or dismissive understanding of popular print. To them, narratives of triple suns and monstrous fish were neither the direct ancestors of modern tabloids nor the last hurrah of a more superstitious age, but frequently thoughtful commentaries on the contemporary world—a world not fundamentally chaotic and unpredictable but ordered and sustained by an omnipotent God. Only within this context could phenomena like witches, apparitions, and monstrous births be "considered not merely bizarre oddities but meaningful events" worth explicating; only within a providentialist framework could the prodigy genre make sense.[21] As Walsham puts it:

> The disposition to see prodigies sprang from a theocentric view of the universe, an intensely moralistic cosmology. It rested on the premiss that the physical environment and human conduct were closely attuned: aberrations in the natural order literally incarnated the spiritual chaos and anarchy created by sin. As their etymology implied, *monstrum* and *prodigium* demonstrated and presaged divine will. The earth was one huge emblem and hieroglyph, "Gods great booke *in Folio*," and every creature "a severall page, in which wee may reade some instruction to further us in heavenly wisedome."[22]

This perspective suffused English Protestant society at all levels and was by no means limited to the poor or the uneducated—those classes which historians once considered the sole consumers of the pulp press. On the contrary, it was promulgated by elites, including pastors in their pulpits and publications, scholars in their treatises, and astrologers in their almanacs. It is thus quite understandable that accounts of prodigies were absorbed by devout men and women of very different backgrounds: one of the most famous collectors of such news items was Nehemiah Wallington, a London artisan who assiduously incorporated stories of retribution and wonders into his diary, but extraordinary events were also recorded and circulated by members of the nobility like d'Ewes and by scholars like the Cambridge-trained Joseph Mede. As discussed earlier, those who took note of signs and wonders did not all understand them in the same terms, neither were they credulous people who accepted every story that came their way; on the contrary, they often recorded prodigies with great caution. Nevertheless, many would have agreed on the principle that "strange and true" events did not occur at random; they were not freaks spawned by an uncontrolled universe but signs deliberately sent by an offended yet long-suffering God as warnings and calls for individual or national repentance. This did not mean they were always easy to interpret: prodigies could be "the Lord's riddles and conundrums," emphasizing His transcendence even in the midst of His immanence, that He was involved in the workings of His creation and yet His ways remained "past finding out" (Rom. 11:33).[23] But it was this difficulty that spurred writers on to attempt to interpret the signs, just as one attempts to work out the answer to a riddle. Even the most ambiguous phenomenon had meaning, and thus, as A.W. Bates puts it, "The early modern reader was concerned not simply with the occurrence" of such prodigies as monstrous births "but with their significance, in how they fitted into the world."[24] Popular pamphlets, no less than sermons and treatises, attempted to supply answers.

The supernatural in the English Revolution

Prodigious events, as with witch trials, were not confined to tumultuous times; they also occurred during periods of relative peace, including James VI/I's reign (1603–1625), and were advertised by writers who feared that their nation would lose God's blessings unless it repented of its many sins and underwent further reformation. Nevertheless, William Burns has noted that "an increase in monsters and monstrous births and other prodigies had traditionally been considered a sign of the coming of war, particularly civil war,"[25] and the 1640s did not disappoint.[26] As relations between the King and his Parliament deteriorated in the first months of the decade, and then increasingly after Charles raised his standard at Nottingham and symbolically began the Civil War in August 1642, the world itself seemed to mirror the disorder of the state: armies were seen in the sky, pools turned to blood, children were born without heads, and witches were discovered in the Eastern Counties. Although it would be overstating the case to say that the English people turned exclusively to the natural order for an explanation of unsettling events in the human realm, more than one pamphleteer treated these occurrences as parallel symptoms of "these troublesome and distracted times."[27] Each served to elucidate the other: prodigious events might be used to decipher the trauma of religious schisms and political rebellion, but as we shall see, more often than not it was politics and religion that were used to decipher prodigies.

To English Protestants, however, supernatural occurrences involved more than the temporal, for both canonical and apocryphal scriptures indicated that signs and wonders would precede Jesus Christ's Second Coming and the Judgment. Theologians pointed to such passages as Luke 21, which foretold "signs in the sun, and in the moon, and in the stars; and upon the earth distress of nations, with perplexity" (v. 25), and Acts 2, with its promise that the gift of prophecy and ominous wonders in the heavens would abound in the day of the Lord (v. 17–21). During the Reformation there had been "a widespread conviction" that wonders "were far more common than in earlier times, a sign of the last days."[28] The same conviction pressed upon the consciousness of many in the days of the English Revolution, from elite politicians to anonymous pamphleteers and was perhaps even heightened by the growing nationalism of the Protestant country. In a genre now called the "jeremiad" after the biblical Jeremiah, the Weeping Prophet, preachers and pamphleteers incorporated prophetic scriptures not merely as generic and universal warnings against ungodliness but as direct charges brought against an England they conflated with Old Testament Israel. Like the Israelites, the English were a people especially marked by God to be His witness, a holy nation in a corrupt world; however, some—especially those dissatisfied with the extent of reform in the Church of England since the days of Henry VIII—believed England had abdicated her responsibilities just as Israel had done millennia before. If the duties and the failings of Israel and England were the same, so the prophetic warnings intended for Israel applied equally to England—and if those warnings were not heeded, the judgments that had fallen on Israel would fall also on England. This sense of a unique relationship between God and England, a relationship England as a nation was not taking seriously enough, only increased the urgency of calls for repentance and reform that abounded in the pulp press.[29]

As Chris Durston has pointed out, tales of prodigies fed and were fed by "this apocalyptic state of mind" in a self-perpetuating cycle: millenarians sensed that the Day of Reckoning—that fearful "day of the Lord" foretold by Old Testament prophets—was near, a sense which undoubtedly increased their tendency to perceive strange wonders and which was then reinforced by the apparent proliferation of God's warning-pieces and the rise in demonic activity in the world.[30] According to Walsham, "Sermons and ephemeral literature did not always strike a discordant and contradictory note," and pamphleteers were frequently as much Hoseas and Jeremiahs calling for reformation and revival as were pastors in their pulpits.[31]

Many authors, then, shaped by their theology and worldview, were undoubtedly sincere in their interpretations of supernatural occurrences. On the other hand, it would be naïve to say that they did not also frequently impose their own beliefs about current events onto those occurrences, or that there was no manipulation of events to suit a specific agenda. The very fact that prodigies often appeared as codes demanding a cipher gave them "enormous potential as propaganda,"[32] a quality by no means lost on pamphleteers of both sides during the Civil Wars. Indeed, the Royalist John Spencer was later to complain about the use of prodigies as "mercenary soldiers" marshalled to demonize opponents or call for political and religious reform—a not entirely fair observation given that the Royalists themselves were not innocent of such activities.[33] Some of these wartime publications were relatively discreet, allowing the preternatural signs to do the talking; others were less circumspect, lashing out at those the writers perceived as enemies of the nation without the aid, or the protection, of "objective" signs and wonders. Instead, they targeted particular people or groups as malign, even demonic, influences in the body politic. As will be seen in Chapter 4, to Royalists, the Parliamentarians were hypocritical Puritans and unsophisticated, uncultured Roundheads whose spirit of rebellion aligned them, according to Scripture, with witches.[34] To Parliamentarians, who were already accustomed from the preceding decades to using the language of demonism to critique the king's advisers, it was a simple matter to continue linking key figures, such as Charles I's nephew Rupert of the Rhine, with Satan and his minions.[35] Thus, "the notion that the royalist cause was ultimately directed from Hell persisted"—indeed, arguably increased—"in parliament's wartime propaganda."[36] The language of the prodigious and the diabolic suffused the pulp press, blurring the line between the rhetorical and the literal, between calculated propaganda and sincere anxieties; indeed, it has been suggested that the focus on the Devil's activities may have been a driving force behind England's only major witch-hunt, which occurred in East Anglia between 1645 and 1647. It is this point which brings us to a field that overlaps, but is not fully coextensive, with the study of prodigies, and that requires its own brief discussion to shed further light on the documents in this sourcebook.

Witchcraft and the English Civil War

The story of the witches executed during the English Civil Wars has been an especially dark and yet also especially memorable and compelling one, symbolizing much that subsequent generations find strange, even incomprehensible, about this era. By the time the wars began, witchcraft had been a secular crime in England, with some lapses, for 100 years (since 1542), and was currently legislated against by King James' 1604 Act. The king had had personal experience with *maleficium*, or harmful magic, before ascending the English throne and had written an influential treatise on witchcraft, entitled *Daemonologie* (1597); his law appears on the surface to have been straightforward and harsh, mandating the death penalty for anyone who fed or employed an evil spirit (known as a familiar and often taking the shape of an animal) or who successfully enacted *maleficium*, as well as for anyone who was convicted of even attempting *maleficium* or divination as a second offense.[37]

Yet historians generally agree that despite James' early brush with the forces of darkness, successful witch trials were declining through the Stuart period and especially in Charles I's reign.[38] This was not the result of widespread, grassroots skepticism about the reality and power of the Devil and his agents: as Gaskill has written, "No words from on high could make people less scared of witches,"[39] and in fact these concerns suffused society in the early seventeenth century. The reason for the lack of witch executions is thus a matter of continued debate. Peter Elmer points to the role of self-perception in the Stuart court, arguing that Charles I's predilection for order and "remarkable sense of his own legitimacy and godlike status" was the key deterrent to successful trials in the 1630s. Ideologically, evidence of witchcraft was evidence of disorder in the state, a suggestion Charles could not accept of the society under his rule.[40] Historians such as Gaskill and Sharpe, meanwhile, point to the more mechanical checks placed on witchcraft prosecution by the judicial hierarchy before the war, suggesting that since accusations were typically the product of local concerns and communal tensions,[41] and since they had the capacity to prove "more disorderly than witchcraft itself" if allowed to burn into a true witch-craze, a smoothly-operating state was more likely to halt a witch panic than to encourage it.[42]

Charles I, however, was no longer in control in the mid-1640s, neither was the state operating smoothly when a witch-hunt began in the Eastern Counties in 1645.[43] The memorable figure from this moment was Matthew Hopkins, a shadowy young gentleman who, along with his associate John Stearne, felt driven to weed out the many witches he believed were at large in the towns and villages of England. Beginning in Manningtree, Essex, which Hopkins had made his home, the two began a tour of the East Anglian counties: stopping where their services were requested and accepting a small fee to interrogate and search suspected witches before handing them over to local authorities for imprisonment and execution. Their methods in pursuit of the witch's mark (given to a witch by the Devil as a sign of their contract, and from which familiars were thought to suck the witch's blood) and of confessions were unorthodox and harsh, often involving depriving the suspects of sleep until the watchers had the evidence they were looking for. Indeed, Hopkins and Stearne were not met with universal approval or welcomed into every community, and some people, such as the minister John Gaule, were especially vocal in their opposition.[44] Before the trials were ended, however, probably more than 100 people were executed as witches in the counties affected by Hopkins' and Stearne's circuit; others died in unsanitary jails, and at least 250 had had their lives and their reputations marred forever by charges of witchcraft.

The East Anglian episode has long stood out as a morbid yet fascinating aspect of the Civil Wars, one which has, somewhat ironically, spawned its own popular culture: in the late twentieth century Hopkins' story was drastically reimagined by Ronald Bassett (*Witchfinder General*, 1966), then turned into a film of the same name starring Vincent Price (1968). Thankfully, far more scholarly treatments have also appeared since, such as in James Sharpe's *Instruments of Darkness* (1996), Malcolm Gaskill's accessible *Witchfinders* (2005), and Peter Elmer's recent *Witchcraft, Witchfinding, and Politics in Early Modern England* (2016). Such works question the idea that the episode was an "aberration" in the longer history of English witchcraft[45] and instead point to the conjunction of elements that allowed beliefs about witches and the Devil—ubiquitous even when trials were at a low ebb—to boil to the surface. In addition to the breakdown of judicial hierarchies,[46] the mood of fear inculcated by local grievances and the war,[47] and the catalyzing effect of Hopkins himself,[48] they inculpate the rhetorical atmosphere fostered by print culture: as will hopefully become clear throughout this sourcebook, the language of the demonic circulated freely, used to castigate rebels and religious opponents, and it was often difficult to know where rhetoric ended and reality began.[49] Rhetoric, after all, sprang from real concerns. Thus Sharpe has suggested that, although

> [i]t is difficult to assess such matters precisely . . . it is hard not to believe that many of the justices, local clergy and parish notables of the region [East Anglia] were affected by a parliamentary propaganda which was increasingly portraying Royalists as agents of the devil, or by the tremendous fillip which the dramatic event of the war had given to the literature of apparitions and wonders.[50]

His cautious suggestion has since been demonstrated with greater and greater confidence, most recently in Elmer's treatment of witchcraft through Charles I's tumultuous reign.[51] As a useful case-study, Mark Stoyle has analyzed one issue in the Civil War press—the alleged magical powers of the Royalist commander Prince Rupert and his shapeshifting "dog-witch," Boy—to show that even pamphlets originally intended as satire likely contributed to the mentalities that produced witch-hunts.[52]

The East Anglian trials have been studied insightfully already and the key documents are reproduced elsewhere.[53] Therefore, the present sourcebook does not deal explicitly with this episode, although a few documents do make oblique references to the ongoing events. Instead, we have chosen to provide a taste of the ubiquity of charged demonological language in the press: thoughts of the Devil and of witches appear in nearly every section of this book, for far from being limited to concrete accusations, trials, and executions, they pervaded contemporary thought across the political spectrum in the 1640s. They were another kind of "sign" or "wonder;" like comets, earthquakes, and prodigies, they were a sign of the end times, as well as being a symptom of "these Times, wherein the DEVIL reignes and prevailes over the soules of poor Creatures."[54] On the other hand, just as with prodigies, it is important to note that beliefs about witchcraft were never monolithic; it engendered great debate among elites, and criticisms ranged from the methods employed by would-be witchfinders to outright skepticism about the possibility of witchcraft. These thoughts can be seen in the treatises of men like Reginald Scot (*The Discoverie of Witchcraft*, 1584), John Gaule (*Select Cases of Conscience*, 1646), and Thomas Ady (*A Candle in the Dark*, 1655), as well as in the defenses of Matthew Hopkins and John Stearne; but they may also be seen in the pamphlet wars engendered by specific trials, such as *Strange Newes from Cambridge* and its confutation, *A Lying Wonder Discovered* (1659), both included here in Chapter 6. Even in the midst of belief, contemporaries were aware that witchcraft, wonders, prodigies, and astrological portents were not neutral occurrences but very much open to both conscious and unconscious exploitation.

As the following documents may indicate, Parliamentary authors appear to have grasped this adaptability earliest and best and been most willing to report prodigies during the war decades. Following the beheading of Charles I, however, Royalists—as well as moderate Parliamentarians who opposed the execution—rallied around the martyred king with wonders of their own, while accusations of witchcraft had always been part of their rhetorical arsenal. Despite renewed censorship, the contest over the natural world continued through the Protectorate and the Restoration, and in the early 1660s became troubling enough for the new government to deploy more concerted efforts at controlling the "strange and true" narratives. To Charles II, such works were not tabloid stories to be brushed aside but seditious and dangerously influential propaganda.[55] Indeed, Burns has argued that these narratives' flexibility and use as a political tool influenced post-Restoration intellectual efforts to discredit prodigies and the providentialist worldview that gave them life.[56]

Other historians suggest that it was not official policies so much as prodigy stories' "mass circulation . . . and their manipulation by unscrupulous propagandists" during this era which "contributed to undermining the credibility of both the discourse and the genre."[57] That is, as wonders proliferated and their interpretation "became more overtly and crudely polemical" under the stresses of war, readers grew skeptical.[58] Such an argument parallels that made concerning witch-trials, where it has been suggested that the sudden peak in prosecutions in East Anglia from 1645–1647 ultimately contributed to the decline in witch-hunting in Britain, as it alienated observers and made authorities doubly cautious.[59] Nevertheless, in the shorter term (that is, over at least the following decade and a half) the problem of witchcraft seems to have gained a new lease on life: controversial trials and executions continued through the Interregnum and beyond.[60] In the same way, the belief in and reporting of prodigies did not wither and die in 1650, 1660, or even in 1661 or 1662. Further, as Walsham has observed, we should be cautious of speeding that process or of assuming that the fading of prodigies from the realm of respectability occurred because of a linear development of scientific thought.[61] The work of scholars like Burns encourages us rather to consider that slow fade in light of the very historical controversies with which the pamphlets dealt—both religious and political. When situated once more within this context, the pamphlets, like those regarding witch-trials, begin to lose their appearance of crude superstition and vulgar sensationalism and to take on greater dimensions—as moral "fables," as propaganda, and as embodiments of complex social, political, and religious concerns.

Documents in the collection

Despite the fact that ephemera were by their very nature less likely to be preserved than other, more scholarly publications, leaving us with only a portion of the works put out by the press, numerous pamphlets that deal with prodigies or demonism survive from the revolutionary decades.[62] The difficulty, as with any such compilation, was in selecting a few from the multitude of candidates. Sea monsters had to be weighed against unusual tides, haunted houses against pools of blood, prophetic infants against appearances of the Devil. Each offered points of interest, some by what they did not say more so than what they did. At the end of the day, however, the supply of unique occurrences was limited, no matter how strenuously printers claimed that nothing resembling their wonder had ever before been heard of or seen. Certain prodigies had a particularly long life—the perception of comets as portents, for example, is almost ubiquitous in history—and recurred regularly, so that far from being unique, pamphlets typically followed the tropes of their particular wonder. Accounts of monstrous births tended to have a recognizable storyline; so too did witch accusations and confessions. It was our goal to select from these often redundant narratives a few of the most representative—and, conversely, a few of those which broke the traditional mold.

Within this pool, we narrowed our selection further to those pamphlets that offer the most promise to students of the Civil Wars and Interregnum. This is not to say that all pulp literature made religious or political arguments as explicitly as those reproduced here, or even fit obviously into their larger social context; a few pamphlets leaned more heavily toward entertainment and escapism—elements of the genre which, while they should certainly not be exaggerated, should also not be ignored. However, one of our purposes for this collection is to offer a corrective to historians' tendency to dismiss *all* such works as escapist: a tendency that is far from deserved. We have therefore sought to reproduce some of the most broadly relevant pieces, ones that suggest the political and religious uses to which much, if not all, of this genre was put. The shortcoming of any sourcebook is that not everything can be represented; we have, however, attempted to indicate other documents in footnotes, and thus to demonstrate that each pamphlet existed not as an isolated text but in dialogue with its immediate competitors and with a wider literary tradition that included works both learned and popular.

After selection, the question became one of organization: especially difficult since the prodigy genre has always been diffuse. Driven not by skepticism but by a desire to keep true providential signs separate from mere "lying wonders," the Presbyterian clergyman Matthew Poole developed a scheme in the late 1650s for ordering this dangerously anarchic world; the Restoration effectively ended his project before it had even begun, but the desire to place these pamphlets into neat, understandable categories remains a powerful one.[63] In the fullest sense, however, it is impossible to wholly separate the documents from one another or to parcel them up: many feature several narratives, and most address multiple concerns. Although we have chosen to group pamphlets based on their moment or primary topic (e.g., the aftermath of Charles I's execution) rather than their subject (e.g., monsters), some still defy easy placement. *A Declaration of a Strange and Wonderfull Monster* (1645), for instance, has been put with attacks on sectarians and recusants, but it is also a piece of propaganda aimed against Royalists; notably, it is the woman's castigation of the "Roundheads," not her religion per se, that is followed by divine judgment. This document, then, could as accurately have been placed with critiques of political opponents, an ambiguity that demonstrates the all-pervasive nature of concerns surrounding religious orthodoxy in the revolutionary decades.

The categories in this collection are thus suggestions rather than hard-and-fast divisions, with overlap both expected and welcome. The current chapter introduces the reader to the prodigy genre with a short treatise by one Captain Brinckmair, whose *The Warnings of Germany* (1638), excerpts of which are also included in Chapter 2, collected some of the wonders reported during the ongoing wars on the Continent. While the body of the work features straightforward connections between prodigies and their fulfillments, many lifted directly from reports in newsbooks, in the preface the author adopts a more philosophical, learned tone as he explains the definition of a prodigy, the biblical justification for examining them, and the ways in which they ought to be understood and used. Brinckmair thus provides a rationale and a framework for understanding the discussions of signs and wonders in the sections that follow.

The next part of the book is also concerned with setting the stage, but chronologically rather than theoretically. While the outbreak of Civil War in the summer of 1642 certainly provided impetus for the perception and publication of prodigies, the documents in Chapter 2 demonstrate that unusual events were not lacking in the preceding decades: English readers heard of monstrous births and rains of blood on the Continent from newsbooks and collections like *The Warnings of Germany*, while pamphleteers reported anxiously on such domestic prodigies as earthquakes and apparitions right up to the eve of Civil War. In keeping with the current laudable emphasis on repositioning Britain and its Civil Wars within an international framework, this portion of the sourcebook is intended to provide context to the following chapters and offer a glimpse into the larger political milieu within which prodigy reports operated.

The documents in the next two chapters deal, broadly speaking, with the political side of the Civil Wars. Those in Chapter 3 are concerned with national judgments and are less overtly propagandist—although not necessarily less partisan—than those in Chapter 4, which features some of the more vicious and satirical attacks of "Roundheads" against "Cavaliers" and vice versa. The documents in this latter chapter are examples not only of the demonizing theme of propaganda but also of that propaganda's amorphous nature and of the blurred boundary between the rhetorical and the literal that we have discussed earlier. Chapter 5 turns to look at the world through the more formalized lens of judicial astrology. English astrologers were well versed in classical, Arabic, and recent continental astrology, and especially as the political upheaval broke out, they took to the press frequently with their predictions and mathematical analyses of heavenly movements and unusual events. From here, we turn in Chapter 6 to pamphlets that display most transparently the concerns that swirled around religious nonconformists in seventeenth-century England—not only around Catholics, linked with such national alarms as the Spanish Armada (1588) and the Gunpowder Treason (1605), but around radical Protestant groups who questioned or rejected Anglican traditions. Such sects tended to be the subject of judgment narratives, especially those featuring a "monstrous birth;" anxieties about heresy and blasphemy, however, also spilled over into concerns about the dangers of witchcraft, as illustrated in *A Relation of a Strange Apparition in an Ale-house* (1641) and *Strange & Terrible Newes from Cambridge* (1659) (and its companion piece of the same year, *A Lying Wonder Discovered*).

The final chapter of the book returns to explicit political concerns, this time dealing with the execution of Charles I in 1649 and its reverberations through the following decade. Many of these are attacks on the regicides, indicating, perhaps, the growing ability of Royalists to exploit the prodigy genre. Yet several of the pamphlets reproduced here demonstrate that Royalists were not the only ones who saw apparitions and that even Parliamentarians had their anxieties during this decade. As always, while prodigies and portents could be obvious, they could also be, and frequently were, flexible and vague. Indeed, it is their openness to competing interpretations, and thus their usefulness as an ideological battleground, that is increasingly being recognized by historians of the English Revolution: though they be but little, these pamphlets are fierce. The purpose of this collection is to make the small but powerful documents available to a wider audience, as indeed they would have been when they were first published.

Thus reproduced, they may continue their already substantial contributions to a deeper understanding of—and appreciation for—the ways in which the events of a remarkably heady time were interpreted, presented, and often exploited, within a providentialist worldview, by the burgeoning press of seventeenth-century Britain.

Notes on the illustrations, transcriptions, and editorial conventions

In numerous pamphlets and newsbooks, graphic woodcut illustrations provided an additional avenue of engagement beyond the text for those reading the news of the day or listening to it read by others. Many of the pulp press pamphlets included woodcuts on their title pages, which often summarized in visual form the content of the narrative to follow. We have included thirteen such title pages in this collection, as well as the illustrations that accompanied the prodigy accounts within the longer collections of Brinckmair's *The Warnings of Germany* and Vicars' *Prodigies & Apparitions*. These works frequently contained complex imagery that makes their reproductions here valuable for further analysis and interpretation, supplementing the textual analysis. Not only can the woodcut enhance or complicate the story in a text but occasionally stock images seem to have been used that bear little resemblance to the account in the pamphlet (see, for instance, Figure 4.5, which appears to be a re-purposed sixteenth-century woodcut).[64] Readers are thus encouraged to "read" the illustrations closely as well as the texts and to note the common iconography and symbols used in the images (Figures 6.2 and 6.4 offer an opportunity to analyze the re-appropriation of a woodcut in different news accounts).

In our transcriptions we have maintained original spelling and punctuation, with the following general exceptions: we have modernized the interchangeable u-v and i-j (and vv into w, and the long ſ into s). To attempt to modernize or "correct" the irregular spelling, capitalization, and punctuation throughout the pamphlets would rob the texts of much of their character. The conclusions of sentences frequently lacked periods, and we have left the original colons or semi-colons that often mark sentence-end. When necessary to facilitate smoother comprehension, we have added missing letters and punctuation in square brackets [ ]. Where we have corrected obvious printing errors, inverted letters, and unusual (even for the period) spelling, we have indicated the original spelling in a note. Several pamphlets include Latin or Greek phrases; we have furnished translations in the notes unless the author immediately follows with a translation or paraphrase of his own. We begin each pamphlet's transcription with the text of the title page bolded and in its original layout, except for variations in font size, which can be compared in the cases of the number of included illustrations. Within each transcription we have included the original pamphlet page numbers in square brackets (also indicating that some pamphlets were unnumbered or had unnumbered prefatory pages or blank pages).

———◆———

THE
WARNINGS
OF
GERMANY.
BY
WONDERFULL SIGNES,
and strange *Prodigies* seene in
divers parts of that Countrey of
GERMANY, betweene the
Yeare 1618 and 1638.
Together with a briefe relation of
the miserable Events which ensued.
LUKE 21. 25. &c.
And there shall[ ]be signes in the Sunne, and in the
Moone, and in the starres, and upon the Earth
distresse of Nations with perplexitie. &c.
All faithfully collected out of credible
High Dutch Chronicles, and other *Histories*
by *L. Brinckmair* Captaine.
As also a learned & Godly Sermon preached
before the Lords the States at *Norrimberg.*
Anno. 1638.[65]
LONDON.
Printed by JOHN NORTON, for JOHN
ROTHWELL, and are to be sold at the
Sunne in *Pauls* Church-yard. 1638.

[p. 1 of unpaginated prefatory material]

A BRIEFE DISCOURSE OF *PRODIGIES*, by way of *Preface* to the *Treatise* following.

§ 1

Most divine is that *Axiome, God and nature do nothing in vaine.*[66] Nature is that constant order of being and working, which God hath appointed for the creatures. Where there is *order*, and that order *constant*, and both *determined by an infinite wisdome*, there must necessarily be some good end propounded by the *Ordainer*, and all motions effectuall for accomplishment. Yet the course of Nature is subject to many alterations, because there is a *God above nature*, who hath set bounds for the [p. 2] creatures, but none for him[67] save *the counsell of his will. Whatsoever the Lord pleases, that doth hee in Heaven above, and in the Earth beneath* (Psalm 135:6).

§ 2

Hereupon it followes, That even those things which come to passe according to the course of nature, are very considerable: because they are effected according to Gods ordination. *His invisible power and Godhead may be seene in them* (Romans 1:20). Nothing is so small, but his providence extends to it. *Præsentemque refert quæ libet herba Deum.*

> In every tender grasse
>
> God may be seen as in a glasse.

Divine præscience were far from being, as indeed it is, *all Infinite*, did it not extend it selfe to every accident.[68] Nothing *is* or *moves*, or *suffers* in any kinde, but in subordination to Gods eternall decrees, that his wise purpose may be effected. And what is it which we see or heare of in any of the creatures, which affords not some morall and divine use? The world is Gods great booke *in Folio*. Every creature is a severall page, in which wee may reade some instruction to further us in heavenly wisedome. The *Occasional Meditations* of such as are piously [p. 3] devoted, give us sensible demonstration of this. Prophane then, and irreligious are they that looke on the ordinary course of Gods providence, but never looke up to God in holy meditation. Whereas everything wee see is like *Jacobs Ladder* [Genesis 28:12]. The foote of it is in earth, but the top is in Heaven. We should therefore looke beyond our senses, and use them as a prospective glasse, to see God through, that he may be brought nigh our hearts, though wee be farre from his glorious presence. That Philosopher seemés to have had some secret inspiration from the almighty, who being asked wherfore man was made, answered, *coeli contemplandi gratiâ.*[69] For God indeede made us to study himselfe, and minde things above. Why was *Adam* put in *Paradise*? Onely to till the garden without taking other care, or pleasure? rather, that by imploying himselfe about the creatures, he might more distinctly meditate of every one to inflame his affections toward God. And what is it which affords no instruction? Toades, and such like, seeing man fly from them presently. A lively Emblem of lapsed mankinde, which cannot indure Gods presence, we being conscious to our selves that we are worthy of his hatred. Seeing poore wormes made by God in such a condition, that every foole[70] may tread on them, and them without meanes to revenge or resist that hurt, we should [p. 4] hence learne humilitie, patience, and all subjection to the will of God. Every Cocke crowing is a lesson of Repentance. Every sound of a trumpet an Alarum to the last Judgement. And every puffe of breath a *Memento mori.*[71] For *what is our life? it is even a Vapour, appearing for a little time, then vanishing.* Jam[es]. 4. 14.

§ 3

This supposed, it followes further. Those things which are more rare in the course of nature, *divers, contrary,* or *above,* are more then ordinarily to be thought upon.[72] For of every such thing it may be said, *Digitus Dei est hic*,[73] God hath an immediate hand in them, they are for speciall use. Having therefore in the Treatise following *the wonderfull things of God* reflected to us as in a glasse,[74] by an historicall gleaning together of some remarkable Prodigies which of late Yeares have happened in *Germany*, with the Events which followed them, it will not bee superfluous to take something along with us in reading them, touching the nature, ends, and use which is to be made of such like, according to the Scripture. The rather because they are in themselves like the writing on the Wall in *Beshazzars* Palace (Daniel 5:8), which *Sooth-sayers*, *Astrologians*, and *Chaldeans* could neither understand nor [p. 5] reade. Who can reade Gods riddle, but they who plough with his Heifer? None know what use to make of his workes, but they who meditate of them, according to his word, with the helpe of his spirit. Hence it is though some are carefull in observing them, yet few have the happinesse to profit by them. Most men profanely disregard them, being of *Gallio's* temper, carelesse of such matters. Some suspitiously[75] abuse them. Many onely gaze, and wonder. Few know what they meane, and therefore skip them over as unskilfull readers use to doe sentences of *Greeke* and *Latine* which they understand not. To remedy this in some part, Here is my indeavour in hope of Gods blessing. *The worke of the Lord is great, sought out of all them that have pleasure therein* Psalm. *111. 2.*

§ 4

If the question be what Prodigies are, the answer may be, Signes and wonders wrought by God immediately, or by others at his appointment, to signifie his pleasure aforehand touching some speciall mercy or judgement ensuing.

The Treatise cals them Prodigies, that is *prædictions* or forewarnings. So much the word implyes.[76] In Scripture phrase they are cal- [p. 6] led σημεῖα καὶ τέρατα[77] signes and wonders, Joel (chap. 2. v. 38.) calls them wonders, St. Luke, [(]chap. 21. 11) calls them *fearefull sights, and great signes.*[78] St. *Peter* tearmes them, *wonders in Heaven, and signes in Earth.* Acts. 2. 21. Of signes some are to represent, Some for commemoration, Some to assure, Others to prognosticate, whereof some be ordinary, others extraordinary. *Prodigies be extraordinary prognosticating signes.* They are also called wonders, not because they are all *miracles in propriety*; but because they seeme to bee, unto such as know not the causes and effects of them, and therefore cause wondring. *A miracle is that which happens besides the order of all nature, particular, and general*[.][79] For a stone to moove upward when it is throwne, is contrary to the particular nature of a stone, yet no miracle, because all things give way to violence. The hanging of Mahomets iron tombe in the Ayre (if it bee, as it is reported) is no miracle, because it may be drawne up by vertue of some Loadstone above it. But every thing is a wonder, whose cause we know not, or at least which wise men know not. Admiration alwaies rises out of some degree of Ignorance. There is therefore

a difference betwixt a miracle and a marvell:[80] under the tearme of wonder;
3 Severall things be comprehended.

[p. 7] 1 Speciall rarities in the course of nature, and in the actions and
affaires of men.[81] Secondly, miracles properly so called. Thirdly, whatsoever it is which makes the wiser or greater part of men to admire, as wel
as fooles, however it be called. Alwhich are here included under the name
of prodigies.

§ 5

Having briefly notified the meaning both of the name and thing in hand, the
next thing most necessary is to consider of the author, who gives being to
things prodigious, and appoints their use.[82] That must needs bee God, who
is the onely Alpha and Omega; The center from which all lines are drawne,
and the circumference wherein they are terminated. All predictions, whether
they bee naturall or supernaturall, must needs originally issue from him,
that decrees things from eternity, and causes them to exist in time in all
circumstances according to his appointment. This hath alwaies been out of
controversie, not onely among Christians, but also among the Philosophers,
yea even amung the very Vulgar heathen. But though all have reference to
God, yet not all alike. Some things hee either doth immediately, or at least
wise seemes to doe, for both *God, and nature are often clouded.* Many
things are effected by the Ministery of the Angells. Some proceed [p. 8]
from me, and the course of nature, yet not without God. Those things
which are most common in the course of nature, are to bee counted Gods
workes, and therefore much more those which are strange. God puts these
Questions to Job (Job 38:28–19). *Hath the raine a Father? or who hath
begotten the drops of dew? Out of whose wombe came the yce? and the
hoary frost of heaven, who hath gendred it?* The answer to bee made
is this, God giveth being to al these things according to his pleasure,
what then shall be thought of raining bloud, Fire, and such like? No
otherwise then according to that, The Lord rained upon *Sodom* and
Gomorrah, fire and Brimstone from the Lord out of Heaven (Genesis
19:24). He threatens such aforehand, and he alone hath power to effect
them. Therefore when we see or heare of any such thing, we can doe no
lesse then acknowledge in the *Psalmists* words, This is the Lords doing,
and it is marvellous in our eyes. Psal. *118. 23.*

§ 6

But how is it that signes and wonders are said to be wrought by false
Prophets? for so Moses intimates (Deuteronomy 13:1) And our Saviour
sayes expresly, *There shall arise false Prophets, and false Christs, and shall
shew great signes and wonders* (Matthew 24:24)[.] And to like effect Paul
speakes of Antichrist, [p. 9] 2. Thess. 2. 9. We read also that many signes

done before *Pharaoh* by *Moses*, were also done before him by the Magitians of *Ægypt* (Exodus 7:11).

No doubt but Satan and his Instruments are permitted to doe great things for the triall of Gods Church and children, but in all they doe they are no more but instruments. Therefore that Fire wherewith Jobs sheepe and servants were consumed, is fitly called the *Fire of God*, though the *Prince of the Ayre* was in that the Incendiary and the bellowes, and added oyle to the flame (Job 1:16). But Gods wonders and Satans differs very much. Oftentimes in the thing it selfe.[83] Satan seemes to worke miracles, but God workes miracles indeed.

Satan also makes a shew of doing many things which indeed hee doth not, deluding the outward senses and the the the Phantasie. He alwayes lies against God or nature. Therefore well saith *Moses, Who is like unto thee O Lord among the Gods? who is like unto thee? glorious in holinesse, fearefull in praise, doing wonders* (Exod. 15:11). But in the ground and end there is alwayes a vast and manifest difference betwixt the one and the other. All that Satan does, is out of hatred, envy and malice, to God and man. But all that God doth is in mercy or Justice. The plot which the Devill prosecutes in every particular, is to rob God of his glory, to make his [p. 10] word of none effect, and to frustrate the salvation intended for the Elect. Gods immutable purpose is to glorifie himselfe, to fulfill his word in all the promises and threatnings, and to save those whom he hath chosen in Christ. The one intends nothing but fraud and mischiefe, the other to approve his goodnesse even to them that wilfully perish. Satan labours to bring men into Heresie, superstition, and Idolatry, to blind their eyes, harden their hearts, and wholly to corrupt them in all their wayes. God would have all men come to the knowledge of the truth that they might be saved (I Timothy 2:4), if any desire to know how it may be knowne, which wonders be wrought by God especially, and which by Satan, let them consider, This is needlesse for us curiously to inquire after, and fruitlesse to bee knowne. Our duty is to looke upon all good and evill as coming from God, as Job did, saying, *The Lord, hath given, and the Lord hath taken, &c. Shall wee receive good from the hand of the Lord, and not evill?* [Job 2:10] And though some Prodigies be but rarities in nature, yet are wee to ascribe all to God, in as much as nature is his handmaid, and even of naturall things there is more to be made then a naturall use.

§ 7

As for the matter wherof Prodigies consist, that is worthy to be considered of, but warily to be deter- [p. 11] mined. A confused Notion that some things are prodigious, without knowledge of the particulars, and whether it be good or evill that is portended, hath bred and nourished much curiositie and superstition, needlesse feares in some, fond hopes in others, there have anciently beene a sort of men who have made it their study and profession to teach what is ominous, and of what: such were the Soothsayers,

Astrologians, Chaldeans, and the like. But the light of the Gospell hath made all these seeming[84] starres to vanish. And yet still pride, curiositie, infidelity, like bitter rootes growing in the heart of mankinde naturally, leade them much what in the same way. Hence it is that almost every accident is by some counted a signe of good or evill lucke, according to our common phrase. To reckon up particulars in this kinde, would be both tedious and ridiculous.

But it must be granted that some things are *Prodigious*: true. And that some things are so in reference to particular persons, and families. Some to Countries, Nations, and whole States. This also cannot be denied. What[ ]is then the rule to know them by? No vulgar conceit, no nor every pretended reason. Nor yet all manner of experience, so far as wee are to regard *Prodigies.* The Scripture is a sufficient rule. Therein we have multitude and varietie of examples that [p. 12] teaches us to count of sinne as a certaine forerunner of divine vengeance, unlesse[ ]repentance intercept. And to take Repentance, Faith, Obedience, Piety, Justice, and Charity for assured pledge[s][85] of Gods love and purpose of blessednes in every kinde. According unto these we are to regulate our hopes and feares. *Humility is a speciall token of honor ensuing, and pride a forerunner of destruction.*[86] He that goes on in an evill way shall not prosper at the last, *though the Sun, Moon and Starres should seeme to fall downe and worship him*, as they did sometime to *Joseph.*[87] And he that feareth God, and escheweth evill may be confident that all shall worke together for the best, though Hell were for the present let loose upon him. Yea, though God himselfe should make a but[88] of him to empty his quiver in. Foure hundred Prophets may say to *Ahab, Goe up to Ramoth Gilead and prosper.* Yet *Ahab* falls there, for he had sold himselfe to worke wickednesse. *Romes* merchants will not believe her fall, but they shall certainly see and lament it[.][89] *Babylon* says *I am, and none else besides me. I shall not sit as a widdow, neither shall I know the losse of children. But these two things (saith God) shall come to thee in a moment in one day, the losse of children and widdowhood, they shall come upon thee in their perfection,* &c (Isaiah 47:8–9).

[p. 13] In sinning there be some circumstances which are more immediate harbingers of judgement, and so likewise many particular sinnes. Backsliding, as in *Solomon.* Presently hereupon God stirred him up adversaries. Rashnesse in things which require a waighty consultation, as in *Rehoboam.* Selfe-will, as in *Josias.* Impudency, as in *Absolon.* But I had rather leave particulars to the studious Readers observation.

So on the other side humility, wisedome, patience, importunity in prayer, diligence in well doing doe more especially demonstrate Gods purpose to manifest his especiall mercy. But those prædi[cti]ons[90] which we have now especially to consider, are of another sort.

§ 8

To speake more fully of the *Matter* of *Prodigies*, in general; I conceive it is some speciall accident happening by the providence of God. The things about which such accidents happen are diverse, and according to the difference thereof wee may count of 3. kinds of *Prodigies, Naturall, Morall* and *Divine,* κατ᾽ ἐξοχῆν.⁹¹

Naturall are those speciall accidents which fall out in the particular or generall course of nature. Of which some are *Celestiall*, some *Elementarie*. *Celestiall* I call those which happen [p. 14] about the heavenly bodies. As about the Sunne, Moone or other Starrs. By Elementary I meane those which happen in the Elements themselves, or those things which are compounded of them. *Morall Prodigies* are those which consist in the affections, passions, words, or actions of men. *Divine* I call those wherein (τὶ θεῖον)⁹² some divine impression is more conspicuous or necessarily to be acknowledged.⁹³ For each of these kinds there is mutiplicity of Instances to be had almost in all *Histories,* but it shall suffice me to particularise in some few out of Scripture.

That extraordinary Eclipse which happened at our Saviours passion (Mat. 27:45), at which the greatest *Philosophers*, that then were, much admired. The plague of darknesse in *Ægypt* (Exod. 10:21), and the apparition of Angells and heavenly visions, whereof we often read in Scripture, were *Prodigies* Celestiall. Of Elementary we have more variety of examples, The Fire which consumed *Nadab* and *Abihu* (Leviticus 10:2), That which fell from heaven on the Captaines and their companies, sent by *Ahaziah* to *Elijah* (2 Kings 1:10), The pillar of Fire which was for safe conduct to the Israelites in the night time (Exod. 13:21). The fire & brimstone which fell on *Sodom* and *Gomorrah* (Gen. 19:24). The *Cherubims* and flaming Sword which God placed before paradice (Gen. 3:24).

[p. 15] The cloudy pillar which was Israels guide by day. The *Manna* wherewith they were fed in the wildernesse [Exod. 16]. The plague of Haile in *Egypt* [Exod. 9:23]. That on the army of the Five *Canaanitish* Kings in *Joshua's* time (Joshua 10:11).

The dividing of the red Sea [Exod. 14].

And of *Jordan* [Josh. 3].

Christs walking on the water [Matt. 14:25].

Water issuing out of the rocke [Exod. 17:6],

And out of the Jaw bone of an Asse [Judg. 15:19].

Bitter Water becomming sweet by casting in Salt [2 Kings 2:21–22].

Earthquakes, Famine, Extraordinary fruitfullnesse, Excessive multitude of Birds, as of Quailes, among the *Israelites* [Num. 11:31–32], or of *Flyes, Beasts, or creeping things,* as among the Plagues of Egypt [Exod. 7–11], The strange peregrination of Creatures, from their wonted habitation, as the comming of the creatures into the *Arke* [Gen. 7:8–9].

These and many such like particulars are counted Prodigies, and for distinction sake naturall, because some thing in it selfe naturall, is the subject
of them.

As for morall *Prodigies* that which is passed in the former *Section* shall
suffice, because it is but a schedule that I have to write, and not a volume:
for divine prodigies, so called in a more [p. 16] especiall manner, these following are most apparent.

The *Sun* and *Moone* standing still as in *Joshua's* time [Josh. 10:12–14].
The shadowes going backe 10 degrees on *Ahaz* his Diall in *Hezechiahs* time
(Isaiah 38:8). The new starres appearing at our *Saviours* birth [Matt. 2:2].
The rending of the vaile of the Temple, and the resurrection of dead bodies,
at the time of his crucifying [Matt. 27:51–53]. &c.

These are sufficient to shew us what is to bee counted prodigious, and what
not. For all particulars we have no instance. Things new and strange may daily
happen as God sees cause to conclude this part of the matter in hand, let this
note suffice. Whatsoever happens extraordinarily and rarely to us or to any of
the creatures, hath more or lesse of the nature of a Prodigie in it. Such was the
strange fighting in the wombe of *Rebekah* [Gen. 25:22], *Nebuchadnezzars*,
Pharaohs, and *Pilates* wives dreames [Dan. 2, 4; Gen. 41; Matt. 27:19]. The
carriage and speech of *Baalams* Asse [Numb. 22:21–33]. The falling off of
the Chariot Wheeles of the *Egyptians*, as they drave in the red *Sea* [Exod.
14:24–25]. *Dagons* prostrating before the *Arke* [1 Sam. 5:3–4].

§ 9

Sufficient being spoken of the *Matter*, the next [p. 17] thing necessary to
be touched is the forme, to shew what makes any speciall accident to be a
Prodigie, that is (as I conceive) the aptitude which such accidents have in
themselves, or by divine institution to portend the futurition or manifestation of something as yet not existent, or not knowne. As for example,
Bloud happening extraordinarily in raine, in sweate, or in the use of bread
or otherwise, doth fitly betoken warre, murther, execution of malefactors,
or persecution. But how comes the *Rainebow* to be a signe the world shall
never be overflowne againe by an Universall Inundation, whereas naturally
it signifies raine. This it could not doe if God had not appointed it for such
an use. It may be demanded what I thinke of experience. If it be found by
observation from time to time that after such an accident in one kind, such
an event in another followes, may not that accident thenceforth be taken for
a certaine signe of such an event to ensue? *I answer*, God is unsearchable
in his wayes. No observation whatsoever will inable us to trace him. *As the
way of a ship in the Sea, or a Bird in the Ayre, so are Gods waies.* Experience
therefore is but an uncertaine guide, because the course of Gods providence
is a perfect maze or Labyrinth. There is indeed no variance nor shadow of
turning betwixt his will at one time, and [p. 18] his will at another. *(I speake
of his absolute will[.])* Neither is there any difference betwixt his *will in*

decree, and his will in deed, and hee often doth the same things over againe, *for kind*. Yet there is so much variety for circumstances, that its impossible by al observation to conclude for certaine, from that which doth happen in one kind, to that which shall happen in another. This notwithstanding the argument from existence of the signe, to the futurition of the thing signified, concluding onely probably and indefinitely, cannot justly bee gainesaid: for instance, Thus to reason is very usefull. After a Comet or blazing starres appearing and vanishing, some great personages doe commonly expire.

This experience out of many Histories confirms, Therefore such a comet now appearing, its likely some of the Gods of the Earth shall dye like men, and all of them have just cause more then ordinarily to prepare for death, especially such as *Herod*. But other matter calls me to it.[94]

§ 10

Touching the finall cause of prodigies, that is divers in divers respects. The common end is that God may be glorified by us in beholding his works, [p. 19] and spelling out of them his infinite wisedome, power, and goodnesse, whereunto prodigies conduce no little, because they minister matter for an invincible argument against an Atheist or Epicure;[95] and strongly prove both God and providence. The proper end of them is either *neare* or *remote*; That which they serve for more immediately is in generall, to intimate some change in the condition of them, to whom they have reference: But sometimes they serve to bring to light that which was hid, or to make that knowne which was secret; as when *Satan* appeares for a time where some body lies buried in secret, and then vanishes, or when extraordinary trouble of minde falls on some, that thereby they may be brought to disclose some secret sin, the revealing whereof may tend to Gods glory. Some of them doe more especially serve for comfort, some for terror.[96] Some serve to terrifye for a while, as the burning Bush, but leave comfort in the issue, as that did. And the Angells wonderfull behaviour in the presence of *Sampsons* parents: some serve to strengthen the faith of Gods children in time of great discouragement; or when they are called to some special service: some serve to invite and call all, of all sorts, to repentance and amendment of life.

Those which serve to this end are in a more peculiar manner The *Prodigies*, [p. 20] and such are those which are instanced in, in the following History. Comfortable ones may happen to the wicked, and terrible to the godly, to harden the one, and humble the other. That the one may prepare for correction and profit by it, the other in Gods just judgement perish everlastingly. If the Question be when fearefull Prodigies happen in a Countrey where there be two contrary sides of different professions in religion, how it may be knowne whether of them they concerne. I answer, the only necessary thing is, for each private person of what sort soever, whose abode is in such place, to take it to himself, and to examine his heart, wayes, and spiritual estate, that he may reforme himselfe according to the word of God, lest hee also perish. Many are too prone to cry woe unto others, but at last are forced to say (with him mentioned by *Josephus*, where he speakes of the lass destruction of *Jerusalem*.) *woe unto mee also.* God is not wont to send generall judgements, till all flesh more or lesse have corrupted their way: and therefore it behoves all of all sorts, howsoever different in the profession of religion to humble themselves, and study reformation really, not in pretence.[97] If they of *Germany* doe so, and then send out a dove from their Arke, she is likely to return with an Olive branch in her mouth [Gen. 8:11]. In the meane while so long as every one looking on his neighbour saies, Truth is on [p. 21] my side, Thou art an hereticke, and therefore the destruction threatned is to thee, but I shall escape: God that is no respecter of Persons findes just matter of offence in both, and on which side peace and Victory will rest, as touching sence is yet uncertaine. But wee know who they are that cry peace, peace, to themselves: that for temporall things dreame of a *fifth Monarchie*,[98] and for Church affaires would faine force all to doe as they doe, that is, to put their Noses under the Popes girdle. And though here I digresse a little, I hope it will be pardoned.

§ 11

As for those particular *Prodigies* which the History at hand makes mention of, the Reader may well admire at them, and happily revolve these questions in his minde. Whether there were such things as are here related. Whether they are truly Prodigious or no. Whether those Events here adopted to them were portended. Whether the like things have not happened elsewhere[99] without like effects or consequences, with more of like[ ]nature, if hee bee either cautious, or scrupulous, to alwhich I have onely this to answere. If any credit may be given to such Histories of *Germane* affaires, as commonly fall into the hands of the learned, from *Mercurius Gallo-Belgicus*;[100] it is certaine that *Africa* was not antiently more famous for Mon- [p. 22] sters then *Germany* hath for many yeares been of *Prodigies*. The particulars hereafter mentioned make not a fourth part of what might be collected in like kinde. And if *Prodigies* be taken in a large sense, as they are here to be understood, the matter doth well answer the title. But this must needs be granted, this or that single prodigie may happen, and yet no remarkable judgement follow. For God may shake his rod often, before he strike once. And many times he threatens, but to try. But when Heaven and Earth, Sea, and Land did all make one outery, and strike up an *Alarum*, no other could be expected, but that God should march on apace in fury after. It is but a generall intimation of this or that Judgement, that Prodigies doe make necessarily. But what else could bee expected but shedding bloud on earth, when it rained bloud from heaven. Battailes in the Ayre were most lively pictures of the same to bee on earth. So that wee may truly say, God wrote his minde in most lively Characters, and hath punctually fulfilled what hee threatned. It seemes they were confident of longer peace, or else God needed not to have reade them so many Lectures of bloud: what particular Judgements are signified by particular *Prodigies* may wel be guessed by the Prodigies themselves: for my owne part *I beleeve, admire,* and *adore,* and shal wonder at him that can doe [p. 23] lesse. I doe every day expect the like and greater, because our Saviour hath so largely prophesied in this kinde in reference to our times, which all the Evangelists have recorded. The latter dayes shal bee short beyond expectation, and Christ come sooner then we are aware, and therefore the signes of his comming must needs bee expected, whereof strange Prodigies are one.

§ 12

And[101] now hopeing this may satisfie such as have any candor; its high time to draw the Arrow to the head, and hit the marke I shoote at, which is to point out the Christian use which godly feare and reverence teaches us to make upon the knowledge of these dreadfull things. To which end there are some cautions to be premised.

I[.] Seeing God is the author of Prodigies, wee must religiously observe them, and by prayer seeke from him instruction and grace, to fit us for a holy improvement of them to his glory and our own benefit; Saying as *Paul,* when Christ spake to him in a vision out of Heaven, *Lord what wilt thou have mee to doe* [Acts 9:6]? And with prayer wee must joyne all diligence in studying of his holy word, for thence it is that al necessary instruction is derived. Be we sure to make use of Prodigies according to this rule, and light will come out of darkenesse, comfort out of feare.

[p. 24] Secondly we may not bee too curious in searching after the particular evills which Prodigies foreshew, much lesse to know their circumstances, when, where, and how they shall happen. It is enough for us, and great mercy from God, that we have, aforehand, so much as the noise of his comming to aflict. In the state of Israel, God was wont to threaten in the Fathers dayes those Judgements which hee purposed to their posteritie, and yet upon those threatnings, he expected present repentance. And surely that *Memento* given by Christ unto the Angell of *Sardis,* is necessary for every Church and state to apply unto[102] themselves in these dayes: *Remember how thou hast received, and heard, and hold fast and repent. If therefore thou shalt not watch, I will come on thee as a thiefe, and thou shalt not know what houre I will come upon thee* (Revelations 3:3).

A third caveat is that, which God himselfe gives by the Prophet Jeremy, *Learne not the way of the heathen, and be not dismaied at the signes of heaven. For the heathen are dismaied at them* (Jeremiah 10:2). Where 2 things are forbidden. The one is learning the heathens way, that is, to worship the creatures themselves, or to use any part of their Idolatrous service: The other is excessive feare upon the sight of all unpleasant aspects in the heavenly bodies, without any true feare of God who [p. 25] causes them, and in whose hand it is to hasten or prolong, increase or diminish, or totally remove all threatned evils. The grosser sort of antient Idolaters[103] thought the Sun, Moone, and other starres to be Gods,[104] and Eclipses and such like to be signes of their anger, whereupon they feared exceedingly unto astonishment, and addicted themselves by divers rites and ceremonies to pacify them. Many times the *Israelites* were much subject to like Idolatry, against which God there instructs them. This place therfore does not condemne all feare upon the sight of prodigies, as unlawfull, but the abuse of feare, when it is placed on the creature, not on God, and leades not to true piety, but to will worship. Or when it so captivates, that we thinke it in vaine to seeke God by repentance, and doe hereupon despise him, and harden our hearts, and commit all iniquity with greedinesse. Of all things such a feare is most to be feared. As for such whom a lively faith hath incorporated into Christ, and a true feare of God in his judgements, made penitent and obedient according to Gods word. Prodigies should rather comfort them, then otherwise. Joel having said in one verse, *The Sunne shall bee turned into darknesse, and the Moone into blood, before the great and terrible day of the Lord come*, saith immediately in the next[105] *verse, It shall come to passe that who soever* [p. 26] *shall call upon the name of the Lord shall be saved. For in Mount Sion and in Jerusalem shall be deliverance* [Joel 2:31–32]. Our Saviour speaking in like manner of the Prodigies which shall happen partly before the destruction of Jerusalem, but especially before the end of the world, and of the feare which shall be in many, said to his disciples, *When these things begin to come to passe, then looke up and lift up your heads, for your redemption draweth nigh*, Christ the accomplisher & finisher of it (Luke 21:31). Thus much for caution.

§ 13

Now for the uses themselves, who will not hereby be assured of a generall judgement comming on apace, seeing these forerunners of it. I speake both of the Prodigies, and of the things which follow and accompany. The order of the signes of the latter day is this. First false Prophets. Many shall be deceived. Iniquity shall abound. Secondly, persecution, and by meanes thereof Apostacy in some, great misery to others. Then Warres, Famine, Pestilence. *Prodigies*, interchangeably, till false Prophets, and al deceived by them be rooted out of the earth. And as touching warrs, judgement must begin at the house of God. Therein false Prophets arise, as *Paul* saies, *from among your selves* &c. (Acts 20). Their rising is like the opening of Pandoraes box, the original of al[ ]evil. And certainly the churches negligence in not convincing them by doctrine, and suppressing them by discipline in the particular Churches wher- [p. 27] in they first appeared is the corner stone of all, and therefore it is fit gods churches should be first in the course of Judgement, who are first in the course of sinning. The third course of signes which are now most conspicuous shall continue till the first error be discovered and amended, and that evill which it hath brought in be removed, I meane particular Churches be rightly stated, and faithfull in administration of all publicke Ordinances, &c.

§ 14

In the meane while, *for a second use*, let every one of us learne hence, *To search and try our waies, and turne unto the Lord our God*, lest our securitie prove prodigious unto us. Be we more carefull to know Gods will, and to professe that we know, and live according to our profession; in one or other of these specialties we all faile. Yea wherein is it that we faile not? see the state of the seven Churches of *Asia*, as St. *John* describes it, and I feare whatsoever is reproved in all them together will be found among us, but little of that which they are commended for [Rev. 2–3]. Were it not that God is jealous of his own honour, and (in his own phrase) *feares the wrath of the enemie, lest our adversaries should behave themselves strangely, and say, our hand is high, the Lord hath not done this* (Deut. 32:27), we also ere this time had felt the effect of many prodigies which have beene among our selves. But I hope God will shortly stirre up some in a more especiall manner, to bring Gods [p. 28] wonders among us in remembrance. This for the present may serve something to awaken us. And if we regard neither the voyce of God on earth, by his *Ministers*, nor the voyce of God from heaven by his wonderous workes, *though Noah, Job, and Daniel were among us, they shall deliver but their owne soules* [Ezek. 14:14]. God must deny himselfe, or we perish if we continue impenitent, The name of reformation which we have in our mouthes, will no more helpe us then the *Jewes* crying. *The Temple of the Lord, We be Abrahams children.* In many abuses there is not so much as a colour of reformation, as in the matter of sacriledge for one. It was after *Josiah* had reformed many things, that his heart was tender, and smote him upon hearing of the Law. Perceiving thereby there were yet more abuses in the Land than he at first was ware of [2 Kings 22]. Antichrist had made all places like *Augean* stables.[106] They doe therefore surely neede a continuall clensing. The God of all grace fill us according to our measure with wisdome and zeale, that we may grow from beauty to beauty in his eyes.

§ 15

And seeing God is so gracious, as by all meanes to manifest himselfe and his intended judgements, he hath not left himselfe without witnesse, but we [p. 29] are altogether without excuse. Let him have the prayse which is due unto his name, who abounds toward us in all meanes of grace, whereby we might be made wise unto salvation. Thy Word, O Lord, is sufficient of it selfe to warne all the World. Thy Workes are the utmost that we can aske or thinke: what shall we say of thy wonderous Workes from day to day! Oh thou holy one of *Israel*. All this is *that thou mightest be justified in thy sayings, and overcome when thou art judged* (Rom. 3:4). It will be thy glory that thou hast shewed us signes in Heaven above, and wonders in Earth beneath; But it will be our misery if we regard them not, or if regarding we doe not blesse thee the Almighty, or if blessing thee in words we repent not and amend. Of our selves we are able to doe none of all this. Let it not alwayes be said of us as it was sometime of thy people *Israel, Yet the Lord hath not given you a heart to perceive, and eyes to see, and eares to heare unto this day* (Deut. 29:4). For thy Annoynteds sake powre upon us thy spirit, give us hearts according to thine owne heart, and cause us to walke in thy wayes. Truth Lord, thou mayst leave us to our selves, and let us perish: if thy Grace were not free for thee, to bestow or not, it were no grace. If thou sayest, I have no pleasure in you, doe to us as seemeth good in thy sight. Yet be pleased to remember thy Covenant. And for his sake who hath sealed it [p. 30] with his bloud poure out his spirit among us. Worke knowledge in our minds, submission in our wills. Yea sanctify us we beseech thee throughout. Oh love us, and cause us to love thee, and then wee know assuredly that all things shall worke together for the best, Amen.

If any thing offend thee Christian Reader in this Prologue, consider herein I tread an unbeaten path, wherein it is easie to erre. The way it selfe is rough, my spare houres for such imployment few. Importunity of others, and arguments drawne from the publicke good, have stollen mee from my selfe to doe others service in this businesse. If it seeme strange I make so much a doe to usher in a small Pamphlet, consider not the book, but the subject. In Prodigies God comes in, as riding on a Cherub, and flying on the wings of the wind [Psalm 18:10]. *How then can just exceptions be taken at one for co[m]ming before to cry* Bow the knee?[107] *my boldnesse pardoned I am content to beare all other blame.*

In Magnis est voluisse Satis.[108]

Notes

1 *A Warning Piece for the World, or, A Watch-Word to England* (London: Printed for Robert Eeles, 1655), 4.
2 *A Warning Piece*, 5.
3 Alexandra Walsham, *Providence in Early Modern England* (Oxford University Press, 1999), 36.
4 Joad Raymond, *The Invention of the Newspaper: English Newsbooks 1641–1649* (Oxford: Clarendon Press, 1996), 10; see also Andrew Pettegree's discussion of early English news ventures in *The Invention of News: How the World Came to Know about Itself* (London: Yale University Press, 2014), 194–200.
5 Raymond, *Invention of the Newspaper*, 10. After war broke out in Scotland in 1638 over the imposition of a Book of Common Prayer, this legislation was amended to allow for an official foreign-news periodical (p. 12–13).

6 Raymond, *Invention of the Newspaper*, 12.

7 Joad Raymond, *Pamphlets and Pamphleteering in Early Modern Britain* (Cambridge: Cambridge University Press, 2003), 162. For a helpful depiction of the estimated output of the English press between 1588 and 1690, see Raymond's graph on p. 164.

8 Thomas Fawcett, *The Exchange Intelligencer* (Number 1: May 15, 1645), (London: Printed according to order for T. Forcet, [1645]), 1.

9 Walsham, *Providence*, 96.

10 For a discussion of prodigies as "morbid symptoms," see Julie Crawford, *Marvelous Protestantism: Monstrous Births in Post-Reformation England* (Baltimore, MD: Johns Hopkins University Press, 2005), 13–16. Crawford examines accounts of deformed or "monstrous" births—one staple of the prodigy genre—within the context of sixteenth- and seventeenth-century religious controversies, arguing that "for almost all early modern people the birth of a monster, a morbid symptom, signaled a crisis in the reproduction of religious and social norms and institutions" (13).

11 For one example, see Walsham's discussion of the printer John Trundle, who concocted a story about a Sussex dragon (*True and Wonderfull. A Discourse Relating a Strange and Monstrous Serpent (or Dragon)*, 1614) and received much heat from other writers for his falsehood: *Providence*, 45–47.

12 Walsham, *Providence*, 40.

13 Simonds D'Ewes, *The Diary of Simonds D'Ewes (1622–1624): Journal d'un étudiant Londonien sous le règne de Jacques I*er, ed. Elisabeth Bourcier, Publications de la Sorbonne Littératures 5 (Paris: Didier, 1975), 146.

14 William E. Burns, *An Age of Wonders: Prodigies, Politics and Providence in England 1657–1727* (Manchester, UK: Manchester University Press, 2002), 3. For one example of writers commenting on their own genre and the difficulty of separating truth from lies, see *The Wonderfull Battell of Starelings* (1622), whose "To the Reader" expresses a hope that greater censorship would put a stop to the profusion of fictional accounts reaching the market.

15 Jerome Friedman, *The Battle of the Frogs and Fairford's Flies: Miracles and the Pulp Press During the English Revolution* (New York: St. Martin's Press, 1993), xii.

16 Raymond, *Pamphlets and Pamphleteering*, 10.

17 Malcolm Gaskill, "Witchcraft, Politics, and Memory in Seventeenth-Century England," *The Historical Journal* 50 no. 2 (2007), 291.

18 Gaskill, "Witchcraft, Politics, and Memory," 291.

19 See, e.g., Walsham, *Providence* and Crawford, *Marvelous Protestantism*, for prodigies within the framework of religion in society. For a more political slant in an English context, see the work of William Burns, as in *An Age of Wonders*. For the link between prodigies and crisis in early modern Europe, see, e.g., Jennifer Spinks' studies of prodigies in the midst of war, including "Civil War Violence, Prodigy Culture and Families in the French Wars of Religion," in *Disaster, Death and the Emotions in the Shadow of the Apocalypse, 1400–1700*, ed. Jennifer Spinks and Charles Zika (London: Palgrave Macmillan, 2016), 113–134, and Holger Berg, *Military Occupation under the Eyes of the Lord: Studies in Erfurt during the Thirty Years War* (Göttingen, Germany: Vandenhoeck & Ruprecht, 2010), esp. chap. 4.

20 Walsham, *Providence*, 37–39, quote at 37. Friedman, *The Battle of the Frogs*, is one example of a problematically literalist approach to such sources.

21 Burns, *An Age of Wonders*, 1.

22 Walsham, *Providence*, 169.

23 Walsham, *Providence*, 179.

24 A.W. Bates, *Emblematic Monsters: Unnatural Conceptions and Deformed Births in Early Modern Europe* (New York: Editions Rodopi B.V., Amsterdam, 2005), 12.

25 William E. Burns, "The King's Two Monstrous Bodies: John Bulwer and the English Revolution," in *Wonders, Marvels, and Monsters in Early Modern Culture*, ed. Peter G. Platt (London: Associated University Presses, 1999), 188.

26 Raymond, *Pamphlets and Pamphleteering*, 117.

27 *Irelands Amazement, Or the Heavens Armado* (London: Printed for John Thomas, 1642), title page.

28 Lorraine J. Daston and Katharine Park, "Unnatural Conceptions: The Study of Monsters in Sixteenth- and Seventeenth-Century France and England," *Past & Present* 92 (1981), 34. Daston and Park quote a 1562 English ballad that helpfully encapsulates the apocalyptic beliefs of the early modern era: "The Scripture sayth, before the ende / Of all thinges shall appeare, / God will wounders straunge thinges send, / As some is sene this yeare. // The selye infantes, voyde of shape, / the calues and pygges so straunge, / With other mo of suche misshape, / Declareth this worldes chaunge."

29 Walsham discusses the "Israelite paradigm" of sixteenth- and seventeenth-century sermons in chap. 6 of *Providence in Early Modern England*, 281–325. It was not a paradigm limited to England, however; John Thiebault analyzes the role of similar, German works in his essay "Jeremiah in the Village: Prophecy, Preaching, Pamphlets, and Penance in the Thirty Years' War," *Central European History (Brill Academic Publishers)* 27, no. 4 (1994), 441–460.

30 Chris Durston, "Signs and Wonders and the English Civil War," *History Today* 37 no. 10 (1987), 22.

31 Walsham, *Providence*, 32.

32 Durston, "Signs and Wonders," 23.

33 From Spencer's *Discourse Concerning Prodigies* (1665); quoted in Durston, "Signs and Wonders," 28.

34 1 Samuel 15:23—"For rebellion is as the sin of witchcraft, and stubbornness is as iniquity and idolatry"—was a frequently-quoted passage in the Royalist camp. For further discussion, see Chapter 4.

35 Mark Stoyle, *The Black Legend of Prince Rupert's Dog: Witchcraft and Propaganda during the English Civil War* (Exeter, UK: University of Exeter Press, 2011), 40.

36 Nathan Johnstone, *The Devil and Demonism in Early Modern England* (Cambridge: Cambridge University Press, 2006), 229.

37 Fuller analysis of the 1604 Act is offered in *Witchcraft and the Act of 1604*, ed. John Newton and Jo Bath, Studies in Medieval and Reformation Traditions 131, series ed. Andrew Colin Gow (Leiden, the Netherlands: Brill, 2008).

38 James Sharpe, *Instruments of Darkness: Witchcraft in Early Modern England* (Philadelphia, PA: University of Pennsylvania Press, 1996), 126–127; Malcolm Gaskill, *Witchfinders: A Seventeenth-Century English Tragedy* (Cambridge, MA: Harvard University Press, 2005), 32 and "Witchcraft and Evidence in Early Modern England," *Past & Present* 198 (2008), 44.

39 Gaskill, *Witchfinders*, 32; cf. Peter Elmer, *Witchcraft, Witch-Hunting, and Politics in Early Modern England* (Oxford: Oxford University Press, 2016), 69.

40 Elmer, *Witchcraft*, 74–78, quote at 75.

41 A point stressed by Keith Thomas, *Religion and the Decline of Magic: Studies in Popular Beliefs in Sixteenth- and Seventeenth-Century England* (London: Weidenfeld & Nicolson, 1971; reprint Penguin Books, 1991), 698, and which informs such studies as Robin Briggs' *Witches & Neighbors: The Social and Cultural Context of European Witchcraft* (New York: Viking, 1996).

42 Gaskill, "Witchcraft and Evidence," 34–35 (quote at 34); cf. Sharpe, *Instruments of Darkness*, 30 ("There were, simply, too many checks and balances in the English system to allow a witch craze to develop"). The argument regarding the reluctance of states to sponsor full-blown witch-hunts is made in Brian P. Levack, "State-Building and Witch-Hunting in Early Modern Europe," in *Witchcraft in Early Modern Europe: Studies in Culture and Belief*, ed. Jonathan Barry, Marianne Hester and Gareth Roberts (Cambridge: Cambridge University Press, 1996), 99.

43 Overviews of the East Anglian witch hunt may be found in Malcolm Gaskill's introduction to *English Witchcraft 1560–1736*, Vol. 3: The Matthew Hopkins Trials (London: Pickering & Chatto, 2003), xi–xxix and in chapter 5 of Sharpe, *Instruments of Darkness*. A fuller exploration of this episode is offered in Gaskill, *Witchfinders*; but see also Elmer, *Witchcraft*, 114–138, which offers an expanded take on some of Gaskill's emphases, including the role of religious zeal and the influence of the demonological rhetoric prevalent at the time.

44 Gaskill, *Witchfinders*, 74, 221–224. Gaule preached against the so-called "witchfinders" and published a treatise attacking their methods, *Select Cases of Conscience Touching Witches and Witchcraft* (1646), which may have occasioned defenses by Hopkins (*The Discovery of Witches*, 1647) and Stearne (*A Confirmation and Discovery of Witchcraft*, 1648). All three of these works are reproduced in Gaskill, *English Witchcraft 1560–1736*, Vol. 3.

45 Gaskill, "Witchcraft and Evidence," 36–37 and *English Witchcraft 1560–1736*, Vol. 3, xiv; Sharpe, *Instruments of Darkness*, 131; Elmer, *Witchcraft*, 114–115.

46 Sharpe, *Instruments of Darkness*, 140; Gaskill, "Witchcraft and Evidence," 46.

47 Diane Purkiss, *The English Civil War: Papists, Gentlewomen, Soldiers, and Witchfinders in the Birth of Modern Britain* (New York: Basic Books, 2006), 385–386.

48 Gaskill, *Witchfinders*, 273; Sharpe, *Instruments of Darkness*, 142; Purkiss, *English Civil War*, 381.

49 Stuart Clark, *Thinking with Demons: The Idea of Witchcraft in Early Modern Europe* (New York: Oxford University Press, 1997), 87–88 and 533–537.

50 Sharpe, *Instruments of Darkness*, 142. Also quoted in Stoyle, *Black Legend*, 150.

51 Elmer, *Witchcraft*, chap. 3.

52 Stoyle, *Black Legend*.

53 Malcolm Gaskill, *English Witchcraft 1560–1736*, Vol. 3: The Matthew Hopkins Trials (London: Pickering & Chatto, 2003) reprints facsimiles of the key pamphlets related to the confessions of the accused witches, the treatises of the witchfinding-opponent John Gaule, and the defenses of the witchfinders, Hopkins and Stearne, and several "tangential" pamphlets that are transcribed in the present sourcebook (*A Most Certain . . . Discovery of a Witch* [1643] in Chapter 4 and *Signes and Wonders from Heaven* [1645] in Chapter 3).

54 *The Lawes against Witchcraft . . .* also, the *Confession of Mother Lakeland* (London: Printed for R.W., 1645), title page. For the perception of both witches and prodigies as signs of the end times, see Clark, *Thinking with Demons*, chap. 24.

55 Burns, *An Age of Wonders*, 20.

56 Burns, *An Age of Wonders*, 186.

57 Walsham, *Providence*, 221; see also Durston, "Signs and Wonders," 28.

58 Walsham, *Providence*, 220.

59 Gaskill, *Witchfinders*, 279; Sharpe, *Instruments of Darkness*, 146.

60 Sharpe, *Instruments of Darkness*, 146; see also Elmer's discussion of witchcraft from 1649 to the Restoration in *Witchcraft*, chap. 4. It is useful to keep in mind that the 1604 Act was not repealed until 1736, and even this did not put an end to accusations of witchcraft and the illegal perpetration of violence against suspected witches; Thomas, *Religion and the Decline of Magic*, 696–697.

61 Walsham, *Providence*, 221–222.
62 Walsham found about 250 extant works from c. 1560–1640 and traced lost pamphlets through stationers' records (*Providence*, 33 n.122). The percentage of ephemera that survived likely increased after 1640–1641, when interested readers such as the bookseller George Thomason began assembling pamphlet collections. Thomason continued to build his up until the Restoration, and it ultimately comprised over 22,000 documents; we have consulted his collection in the course of most of this compendium's transcriptions.
63 Poole's proposed tactics are discussed in Burns, *An Age of Wonders*, 12–19.
64 Authors, of course, could be at the mercy of their printers in the imagery. For instance, parliamentarian astrologer William Lilly (see Chapter 5 this volume) later recounted his discontent over one of his first pamphlets (*Supernatural Sights and Apparitions seen in London June 30*, 1644) that was printed without the imagery he wanted: "indeed, if I could have procured the dull stationer to have been at charges to have cut the *icon* or form of that prodigious apparition, as I had drawn it forth, it would have given great satisfaction." *William Lilly's History of His Life and Times, from the Year 1602 to 1681. Written by Himself in the Sixty-sixth year of his Age, to His Worthy Friend, Elias Ashmole (Published 1715)* (London: reprinted for Charles Baldwyn, 1822), 106.
65 Not included in the text of *Warnings* itself, nor in this transcription, the supplemental work was a sermon on Isaiah 64:11 preached at Nuremberg in April, translated and reprinted as *Lacrymae Germaniae*, or *The Teares of Germany* (London: Printed by I. Okes . . . sold by H. Overton and John Rothwell, 1638). The English copy of this sermon began with a letter to the reader that presented the once-glorious Germany as "a Looking-glasse" in which other "Kingdomes of *Christendome* may see . . . the fearfull and horrible issues of sins;" "what the Richest of them is," it warned, "*Germany* was; what she by her Impieties is, they may be" (2–3, unpaginated preface). A second edition of *Warnings* of the same year, printed by J[ohn] N[orton] for Rothwell, advertised on the title page the further addition of "a bloody battell fought betweene Duke Saxon Weymar, and Duke of Savelly, and Gotze." This new pamphlet had its own title page, *A True and Brief Relation of the Bloudy Battell* (London: Printed by E.G. for Henry Overton, 1638).
66 Marginal note: "Beda inter axiome. Philos. ex Arist."
67 Corrected in Errata to "for himselfe."
68 Marginal note: "Virtutis est maxima, pertingere quam remotissima." It is the greatest power that reaches what is most remote.
69 Marginal note: "Apud [. . .] Arist. de an." Aristotle is said to have replied that "man was made to contemplate the heavens."
70 Note in Errata: "for foole r[ead] foote."
71 Marginal note in Greek: Σκιᾶς ὄναρ ἄνθρωπος. Pind. "A human being is the dream of a shadow." Pindar, *Pythian* 8, line 96–97.
72 Marginal note: "A minori ad maius." From the lesser to the greater.
73 The finger of God is here.
74 Marginal note in Greek: τὰ μεγαλεῖα τοῦ θεοῦ. "The wonderful things of God." Acts 2:11.
75 Corrected in the Errata to "superstitiously."
76 Reference in text, but no marginal comment.
77 Signes and wonders; Mark 13:22, John 4:48, Acts 4:30, Acts 14:3.
78 Marginal note: "Prodigia, quod porro dicant, id est, futurra p[r]ædicant. Au[gustine]. De Civ[itate]. Dei. lib. 21. cap. 8[.] Omnia quippe portenta contra naturam dicimus esse: Sed non sunt idem." "Prodigies, as they are called; that is, they predict the future." And: "We say as a matter of course that all portents

are contrary to nature; but they are not." This and all subsequent renderings of Augustine are adapted from the translation by Henry Bettenson (Penguin Books, 1972, 2003).

79 Reference with marginal note: "Zanch[ius]. de operib[us]. Dei. lib. 3. cap. 18." A reference to Hieronymus Zanchius, the Latinized name of Girolamo Zanchi (1516–1590), an Italian Protestant reformer who wrote on, among other things, the attributes of God.

80 Reference with marginal note: "Inter miraculum & mirum." Between miracle and marvel.

81 Reference with marginal note: "Quæ sunt rara ipsa sunt mira. Aug[ustine]." From *De Civitate Dei*, Book XXI, chap. 8: "It is rarities that arouse wonder."

82 Marginal note: "Novis omnia plena. [V]irg[il]." But, per the Errata: "*Jovis* omnia plena." All things are full of Jove.

83 Reference with marginal note: "Martinus Biermanus, de Magicis Actionibus." Martin Biermann wrote a treatise "on the actions of magicians," first published 1590.

84 Original: "see ming."

85 Corrected from "pledge" per the Errata.

86 Reference with incomplete marginal note: "Pro[verbs 16:18?]."

87 The marginal note cites Gen. 27:9, a misprint for Gen. 37:9.

88 "butt" – a target for archery practice.

89 The original citation reads "Rom. 19," corrected in the Errata to "Revel. 19." Brinckmair is referencing Rev. 18:11, where the "merchants of the earth" bewail the fall of Babylon; such passages were widely regarded by Protestants as references to Rome and the papacy.

90 Corrected from "prædions" per Errata.

91 Preeminent, par excellence; Acts 25:23.

92 Something divine; Plato, *Gorgias* 242e2.

93 Reference with marginal note: "Qui portentorum numerat multitudinem quæ historia gentium continentur. Aug[ustine]." From *De Civitate Dei*, Book XXI, chap. 8: "Who can count the enormous number of portents which are included in pagan histories?"

94 Marginal note: *Vide Alstedium in Chronol. Cometarum.* A reference to work of the Calvinjst minister, polymath, and encyclopedist Johann Heinrich Alsted (1588–1638) on comets.

95 Marginal note: "Ipsa nomina indica finem rei. Monstra sane dicta perhibent a monstrando. &c. Aug[ustine] quo supra." This is also from *De Civitate Dei*, Book XXI, chap. 8; compare to n.14 above. "The name itself indicates the purpose of the thing. The name 'monster,' we are told, evidently comes from *monstrare*, 'to show.'"

96 Reference with marginal note: "Cum Deus puniturus est gentem vel orbem prodigiis, id prius solet significare. Herod[otus]." When God is going to punish a nation or the world, he is accustomed first to signify his intention through prodigies.

97 Reference with marginal note: "De cultoribus etiam Dei duæ partes interibunt et tertia quum fuerit Probata, remanebit. Lact. instit. lib. 7. cap. 16." From the *Divine Institutes* of the church father Lactantius (c. 250–c. 325), "On the Blessed Life": "And of the worshippers of God, two parts will perish and the third part, when they have been tested, shall remain."

98 The last kingdom foretold in the Book of Daniel, understood in the seventeenth century as the coming millennial reign of Jesus Christ. "Fifth-monarchy man" was also used to refer to someone who believed Christ's physical kingdom was imminent and was to be brought in through violence on the part of faithful believers.

99 Original: "elseuhere."

100 An influential Latin newsbook that began to be printed in the late sixteenth century and had a readership throughout Europe. English newswriters gathered much of their information about continental events from this work and often reprinted verbatim translations in their own newsbooks and modern histories.
101 Original: "Aud."
102 Original: "uato."
103 Original: "Idolalaters."
104 The note alongside this sentence references Ezekiel 8; the citation goes with the following sentence.
105 Original: "uext."
106 The fifth labor of Hercules was to clean the stables of King Augeas, who owned thousands of cattle, in a single day; he accomplished the feat by diverting two rivers through the stables.
107 The marginal reference is misprinted as Gen. 44:43; correct citation, 41:43.
108 In great things, it is sufficient to desire to do well.

2 Prelude to war
'Fore-runners of destruction'

Introduction

Even to contemporaries, 1618 was a year of historic and apocalyptic significance. While the Three Kingdoms of England, Ireland, and Scotland were experiencing a period of calm under James I/VI, who "affect[ed] the name of a King of Peace, and Peace-maker, as his chief glory,"[1] affairs on the Continent were less than idyllic: there was conflict in the Holy Roman Empire over the religious policies of the Hapsburg emperors, tension between Catholics and Huguenots in France, and the prospect of renewed war when a truce between Spain and the Protestant Dutch Republic would expire in 1621. Into this mix was thrown a rebellion in Bohemia, where in May 1618, Protestant lords showed their displeasure with the Emperor by throwing his representatives out of a window. This Second Defenestration of Prague, however, could not be seen immediately as the herald of a war that would engulf Europe for the next thirty years; more portentous to many observers, at least in retrospect, was the comet that blazed across the late-autumn skies that same year.[2]

Although the scene was far removed from their own shores, the British were nevertheless deeply interested in Continental events on both the political and the personal level. Politically, the Bohemians had accepted the son-in-law of James I, Frederick V of the Palatinate, as their king in place of the Holy Roman Emperor, which raised immediate questions about English military involvement. Privately, while the European conflict was far from a black-and-white religious controversy, many English Protestants saw it as their duty to support their co-religionists on the Continent. "We are all members of one and the same mysticall body, whereof Christ is head," one divine wrote in 1638. "Our peace and security is in great measure bound up in theirs."[3] Yet while Englishmen and Scotsmen crossed the Channel to fight, the Stuart monarchy remained reluctant to take up the cudgels, preferring in general the path of diplomacy to that of full-scale war.

Throughout the 1620s and 1630s, then, the subject of England and the European war was a sensitive one—a point reflected in the relationship between the crown and the burgeoning news trade. Capitalizing on interest in German events, publishers in 1619 had begun producing corantos and newsbooks, derived from Continental sources, that traced the political machinations, military engagements, economic upheaval, and natural (and unnatural) disasters occurring across the Channel. Such works were subject to sporadic bans depending on the shifting policies and needs of the English court; for the majority of these two eventful decades, however, readers were able to satisfy their curiosity in the natural and the supernatural through the pages of periodicals and "modern histories." This "culture of active and conscientious reading," Jayne E.E. Boys has argued, "was a way of searching for signs of God's work in the world,"[4] signs which could as easily be wonderful as mundane. Reports of bloody pools and strange suns thus cropped up alongside those of treaties and troop movements, sometimes accompanied by a skeptical caveat or explanation, at other times allowed to stand on their own.

Yet such news, if not absolutely apolitical, was at least low on political content, with prodigies appearing more as curiosities or symptoms of a troubled land than as vehicles for a particular agenda. Some observers, however, saw a different message in these alarming occurrences, one not limited to the German territories. "God strikes some that others might take warning"[5] became a commonplace of English popular literature and jeremiads in the first two decades of the Thirty Years War, with pamphleteers and preachers urging their audiences to recognize that "the seedes of all their [Germany's] evills are sowne in our fields" and only swift and sincere repentance would save England from the same fate.[6] These authors were quick to point out the blessings currently being enjoyed by the Three Kingdoms, paralleling their situation with that of Israel under Solomon: "And Judah and Israel dwelt safely, every man under his vine and under his fig tree, from Dan even to Beersheba, all the days of Solomon" (1 Kings 4:25).[7] Nevertheless, they saw that peace as not only fragile but increasingly threatened by the sins of the nation—sins which ranged from idolatry to licentiousness to frivolity in dress. God was "hang[ing] out his white Flag of mercy," as one preacher put it, but would soon "[hang] out his red Flag of utter defiance;" He was firing "his warning Peeces, before his murdering Peeces."[8]

It was thus with a sense of urgency and alarm that writers directed attention toward both foreign and domestic upheavals in the 1620s–30s. War, famine, and plague, God's "three arrows,"[9] were ominous signs enough, and it was these three which became the focus of two pamphlets published by John Rothwell in 1638—the one a recapitulation of the German battles (*The Invasions of Germanie*), the other a graphic delineation of local atrocities (*The Lamentations of Germany*). Yet while prodigies were less standard judgments, they made a forceful supplement to the others, and the 1638 series was rounded off with a collection of prodigy accounts entitled *The Warnings of Germany*. All three works pulled from newsbooks, but in this new venue their message was more direct: England desperately needed to learn from the sufferings and signs of her sister nation if she wished to continue on her path of peace.

In this tense atmosphere, the Three Kingdoms were not lacking in warning-pieces of their own: they too experienced earthquakes, celestial apparitions, terrifying storms, and ominous flights of birds. As with foreign news, pamphleteers who produced narratives of these events and recipients who noted them in diaries or letters typically saw them as having either a political message, a spiritual message, or both. Thus, the London artisan Nehemiah Wallington wrote in his journal about a pool near Oxford that had turned to blood in 1623 and added the cryptic note that this, along with other ominous events, "happened when the Prince *Charles* was in *Spain* [pursuing a match with the Catholic Infanta]."[10] (Needless to say, Wallington was no great supporter of the attempted match.) For 15 February 1622, Sir Simonds d'Ewes noted down a recent appearance of three suns in Shropshire, "the like of which was in Richard the seconds time," and prayed, "God forbid the like consequents as succeeded them," i.e., civil war.[11] In print, however, political commentary was muted, and censors would find little that was objectionable in pamphlets like *Motus Medi-terraneus* (1626) and *Looke Up and See Wonders* (1628), which mingled domestic and foreign alarms to encourage reflection on one's mortality, the nearness of judgment, and the need for personal repentance—especially in light of current events.

By the eve of civil war, signs and wonders had become even more alarming as focus shifted from relatively distant Germany to Scotland, where war broke out in 1639 over Charles I's attempted imposition of a Book of Common Prayer, and then with even greater horror to Ireland, when the native people rebelled in 1641. Atrocities reportedly enacted by Irish Catholics against Protestants were detailed in blood-curdling pamphlets like John Cranford's *The Teares of Ireland* (1642), printed, like the 1638 Germany publications, for John Rothwell; prodigies also appeared, including the apparition of an army in the sky and the unusual flurry of birds at Dublin that were printed in *Irelands Amazement* (1642).[12] The Continental struggles were a message to England, a preacher observed, but:

> God speaks now more neerly to us, by the bloudy rebellion that is in *Ireland*; The sword that is there drawn, is like the Comet, that for a whole yeer hung over *Jerusalem*, in the likenesse of a fiery flaming sword.[13]

God's judgments were increasing in number and proximity to England— and no wonder, poet John Vicars noted pessimistically, considering that England had failed to heed the "fore-runners of destruction" God had shown her through Germany for so long.[14] Unless at this eleventh hour she acknowledged her sin, she would have to experience the same bloodshed, the same famines, the same plagues, and the same horrific signs of a disturbed world as the lands she had observed with so much curiosity and anxiety for twenty-four years. Hindsight allows us the ease of knowing already how the story ended, that England did join other European countries in the experience of civil war. During the first three decades of the seventeenth century, however, this was no foregone conclusion. It was, rather, a possible future, one that might still be avoided—although by the time *Irelands Amazement* appeared, that must have seemed very unlikely indeed.

———————◆———————

MOTUS MEDI-TERRANEUS.
OR,
A TRUE RE-
LATION OF A FEAREFULL AND
PRODIGIOUS EARTH-
QUAKE,
WHICH LATELY HAP-
PENED IN THE ANCIENT
Citie of COVENTRIE, and some other
places of the Kingdome, to the great amaze-
ment of the Inhabitants.
With a touch of some other occurren-
ces, as well Forraine as Do-
mestique.

LUKE 21. & 11.
Great Earth-quakes shall bee in divers places, and Famine, and Pe-
stilence, and fearefull things, and great Signes shall there bee from
Heaven.

Printed for HE: HOLLAND. 1626.

[p. *1 of unpaginated prefatory material*]

To THE WORSHIPFULL MY worthy Freind [sic], *T. S.* Esquire, of *B.* in Hertford-shire.

SIR,

IT is not many Moneths since you accepted from my hands, at the second hand, my mournefull Meditations compiled in the late memorable Mortalitie of the Plague: And heretofore for this good while, I have constantly sent, and imparted unto you, all manner of *Forraine* Newes and Novelties of moment; [p. *2, unpaginated*] whereof you have beene, and are desirous and studious, and the rather because of your sedentarie life at home, and sel-dome or never stirring abroad, for divers yeeres past; So now, I pray, give me leave to impart unto you this domestique Newes, and most true Relation of a fearefull Earthquake, which happened lately in the Citie and place of my Nativitie: within a few dayes after I had been there, to visite my neer-est and dearest friends; who now are witnesses of the same, from whom (as also from others) I have the certaine information of it. I doubt not but you received the severall Pamphlets I lately sent you by your trustie servant *R. H.* And, it being your condition now to be so farre remote from *London,* (in a fresh Aire and sweet soyle,) where [p. 3, *unpaginated*] Novelties are the more welcome unto you; It hath rather induced mee to Inscribe unto you, at the first hand, this small Pamphlet of a prodigious Accident: For other matters, I hope I shall not forget still to send you, knowing your earnest desire after them: and I cannot mervaile thereat, considering, *Est natura hominis Novitatis avida:*[15] I must leave to enlarge my selfe further unto you by way of Epistle, because the thing it selfe is, I say, but a Pamphlet: Only, With your pleasant situated Place, *I* wish and pray for your health and welfare in soule and body: And so *I* take my leave.

HALLELUIAH.

[p. 4, *unpaginated*]

To the Reader.

SIR, If you bee courteous, you will give me the publisher hereof thankes for my paines, and thinke your two pence or three pence, at the most, well bestowed: But if you be censorious, you will haply object at the Introduction, and say, it is larger than the Relation it selfe: If not with the introduction, then haply you will finde fault with the Enlargement, application, and conclusion: To both which, I must before-hand answer you; It hath beene the laudable custome in all Ages, upon the publishing of any *Prodigie*, or *extraordinarie worke of God*, not to let it passe without *Introduction* and *Application*, to the end, that men may bee stirred up the better, to make good use of the Almighties handy-workes: which are never sent, but for our *Instruction*, And for the truth of the Relation it selfe, I trow no understanding man can, or will make any question, when he hath read the Contents. And so farewell.

[p. 1 *of unpaginated text*]

A TRUE RELATION
of a fearefull and prodigious Earthquake, &c.

OF the naturall causes of Earth-quakes many Philosophers, both ancient and moderne have written largely and learnedly: and of those latter Writers, the *Paire* of most learned Germanes, *viz. Bartholomew Keckerman* and *John Magirus*,[16] in my judgement (yea, it is the judgement of the learned) have written best & most profoundly: and therefore it shall suffice me to write but a word for the better understanding of the common reader, as followeth: In the caves and concavities of the Earth [p. 2] there is some times conceived and bred, a vaporous Winde, which searching to breake forth, doubtlesse is the first naturall cause of Earthquakes, &c. But our Saviour Christ (TRUTH it selfe,) in the Gospell, when he speaketh of the Signes before the last judgement Day, and better informing us than all the Philosophers in the world have done, He tells us, *Wee shall heare of Warres and Seditions; Nation shall rise against Nation, and Kingdome against Kingdome*: and with *Famine and Pestilence, and other fearefull things and signes from Heaven*, he tells us plainely wee shall have *great EARTH-QUAKES,* and those *in divers places, &c* (Luke 21).

Now, that wee that live in this latter and sinfull Iron-Age of the World may a little awaken and rouse up our selves from the Cradle of Securitie, wherein wee have beene long rocked asleepe: hath not God caused the whole Christian World to ring a lowd Peale of *Warres and Rumours of Warres* (Matthew 24:6)? witnesse fertile *France,* spacious *Germanie,* the *Netherlands, Bohemia, Italy,* [p. 3] *Valtolin, Switzerland, Savoy,* and what Countrie, Kingdome, or State witnessing not the same? Yea, and though wee in this faerie Iland, through the admirable blessing and long-suffering of God, have not the sounding of the Trumpet, and beating up of the Drum in our eares, further than for *exercise* and *preparation*: and blessed bee God for his Mercie our Peace, and his Lieutenant, our gracious King and Peacemaker. Yet, we are not I say without those *Rumours of Warres* abroad, and have a fellow-feeling of our Neighbouring Countries Calamities therein, and wee are alreadie engaged in their just Quarrells, for our owne better securitie and safetie. Amongst other signes and fore-runners of the latter day, I remember our Saviour tells us of *false Cprists,*[17] *false Prophets,* and *Heresies* that shall arise, where, without doubt hee includeth, false Professors of CHRIST: And are wee without such? how comes it then to passe, that each Head of the *Hydra*-headed balefull Beast of Heresies, and [p. 4] Schisme striveth, of late, so much for superioritie; amongst us here in this Nation, to goe no further than our owne: Certes, the ugly Head of *Papisme* hath striven for place; the rotten Head of *Arrianisme* hath also striven for place, the mis-shapen and ill-lookt Heads of old *Pelagianisme* & new *Arminianisme* have laboured to be reconciled, & *Janus*-like, to be joyned together, & so to take place: It is not my purpose to meddle with the small Heads of Schisme, they being easily suppressed: They are those *foure Heads* before-named, that trouble the Peace of the Church: the two former; they doe openly disclaime the Doctrine of the Church; the two latter, a little more cunningly; they (forsooth) would intrude themselves into our Church, that so they might the better afterwards bring in the whole body of the BEAST her selfe (Titus 3:11): But leaving these Heads of Heresies to be suppressed, cut off and damned, by GOD, and the King, with the helpe of his Reverend Orthodox Clergie-men: And not to [p. 5] enlarge my selfe further in the Introduction to a small Relation, heare and understand as followeth:

About the middest and Centre of this Land, is situated and standeth the ancient Citie of COVENTRIE, a Countie of it selfe, though within the compasse of Warwickshire: And in this Citie, on Munday the twentie seventh day of March last past, 1626. about one of the clocke after dinner, unlookt for, and on a sudden, happened this fearefull and prodigious shocke of Earth-quake, to the great amazement, and almost astonishment of the Inhabitants; which was sensiblie felt and observed throughout the Citie, shrewdly shaking the Houses, making the glasse windowes about the houses, the Pewter and other materialls in the Houses to clatter: the Beds (wherein some lay sicke) to shake under them, and all in a most terrible manner; and to make it more strange, fearefull, and prodigious, it yeelded forth at the instant an hideous noise and roaring, [p. 6] as it were, in the Aire: which noise and roaring was like betwixt the noise of Thunder, and the roaring of the Sea: The Inhabitants and beholders hereof, (especially the better sort) betaking themselves to their best meditations and devotions, and humbly submitting themselves under Gods hand and handie-workes: Though, blessed be Almightie God, there was no great hurt done thereby throughout the whole Citie: albeit therin are many goodly Houses and buildings, two large and faire Churches about the heart of the Citie,[18] and with those Churches two loftie Pyramidall Spire-steeples of stone-worke, and not farre from them a Crosse of stone also in the Market-place: either of which three Monuments will hardly yeeld inferioritie to any others in the Kingdome.

Now, that this Earth-quake or Prodigie, did not containe it selfe in *Coventrie* alone, but by credible information, it was also sensibly observed in divers other pla- [p. 7] ces of the Countrie, even as farre as *Bristoll*: And what this prodigious Accident may portend, in the Counsell of GOD, I must leave it: But thus much I dare bee bold to say, and pray, GOD grant us quietnesse upon the Land, for doubtlesse the Earth was much shaken within.

If any list to bee so censorious, as to make question of the truth of this fearfull Earth-quake, let them repaire unto the publisher and printer hereof, who hath divers Letters from sundrie grave, learned, religious, and judicious people, for confirmation thereof: which shall be produced, if need require: And if this late Earth-quake seeme strange or incredible unto them, I wish them have recourse unto that more admirable worke of the Omnipotent, even in ours and our Fathers remembrance, in Hereford-shire: and recorded by our best Historiographers:[19] when as, *In the yeere of Christ Jesus*, 1571. *Marcley Hill in the East of the shire,* [p. 8] *rowzed it selfe out of a dead sleepe, and with a roaring noise removed from the place where it stood, (for ought wee know, from the Creation, or the Deluge at the least,) and for three dayes together travailed from her first Site, to the great amazement and feare of the beholders. It began to journey upon the seventh day of Februarie, being Saturday, at sixe of the clocke at night, and by seven in the next morning had gone fourtie Paces, carrying with it Sheepe in their coates, hedge-rowes and Trees; whereof some were overturned, and some that stood upon the Plaine, are firmely growing upon the Hill, those that were East are turned West; and those in the West, were set in the East: In which remove, it overthrew Kinnaston-Chappell, and turned two Highwayes neere a hundred yardes from their usuall Paths formerly trod. The ground thus travelling, was about twentie six Acres, which opening it selfe with Rockes and all, bare the Earth before it, for foure hundred yardes without any stay, leaving that which was Pasturage in the place of Tillage, and the Tillage* [p. 9] *overspread with Pasturage. Lastly, overwhelming the lower parts, mounted to an Hill of twelve fathomes high, and there rested her selfe, after three dayes travell: remaining His Marke that so laid his hand upon this Rocke, whose Power hath poysed the Hills in His Balance* (Job 28:9, Isaiah 40:12).

But leaving Hereford shire and *Marcley* Hill, where God hath now placed it, and not to speake of divers other inferiour Eearth-quakes; which since and before, wee and our Fathers may remember, and our Chronicles make mention of them: And to come more neere to these present times, (though somewhat further from home,) Wee may remember, that about the very time of the Apparition of that most memorable Comet or Blazing-Starre, which appeared in *Aarctophylax, Anno* 1618. In *Italie*, a Towne called *Pleurs*, was by a fearefull and prodigious Earthquake, (the ground opening it selfe,) cleane swallowed up, Houses, Inhabitants and all: not one [p. 10] soule in it left alive, nor so much as any Monument of it remaining to be seene:[20] And a while after the subversion of it, divers neighboures that repaired thither, would needs attempt to digge into the ground, that they might see what they could finde: Among other things that they found, GOD directed them to *a Stone*, which when they had taken up, they saw something written upon it in *Hebrew Letters*, as if (like the *Tables of Stone* that were given to MOSES in *Mount Sinay*) it had beene graven with Gods owne finger [Exod. 31:18]. Miraculous it was: and the writing this; (Read and tremble; Reade and wonder,)

Thus saith the LORD; My Word is like fire, and like an hammer breaking the Rockes: Goe out of Babylon, and every one looke to the saving of his owne soule. Let none winke at his sinnes, for the vengeance will come, and all shall be rewarded according to their wickednesse. Immediatly after that most memorable Prodigie, followed the [p. 11] Death of Great Princes and Potentates; to wit, the Emperour MATTHIAS and Empresse his wife; his two Brethren, both Arch-Dukes of *Austria*;[21] then, Queene ANNE of Great *Britaine*, his Sacred Majesties Mother, (of famous Memorie:) then PHILIP the third, King of *Spaine*, (and since that, King JAMES, of blessed Memorie:)[22] then also began the Broyles and Warres in *Bohemia*, the *Palatinate*, and other places, the wofull Consequences whereof wee daily see and heare of; In so much, as that wee have I say, (as our Saviour Prophesieth) *Warres, Seditions*, and almost nothing but *Rumours of Warres*; Yea, I may further say the RED HORSE of WARRE, hath and doth trample all over Christendome, with a fearefull and most lamentable havocke, embrewing his feet especially in the blood of Saints, the professours of the Gospell: And to passe from Warre: Hath not God caused the BLACK HORSE of PESTILENCE [p. 12] to play his part more neere us? yea, even here amongst us in and about this famous Citie of *London*, where hee hath trampled to death since this time twelve-moneth above 55000. soules, besides what have died in other Cities, Townes, and places in this Kingdome: And now for the LEANE and Pale HORSE of FAMINE, although wee must thankfully confesse, that God hath wonderfully restrained him, yet other Countries have felt and doe feele his weight, with *cleanenesse of Teeth* and *emptinesse of Belly*: yea, and wee our selves have had a fearefull Glympse of Him: and how soone God may permit him further to appeare amongst us, for our manyfold sinnes, wee know not, but may doubt, and ought to pray against Famine.

To draw to a conclusion; If *Warres* and *Seditions, Pestilences, Famines*, and *Earth-quakes*, bee speciall Signes and Fore-runners of the last Judgement, as our Saviour CHRIST hath prophesied they are: [p. 13] and certes, *Heaven and Earth shall passe, but his words shall not passe* (Matt. 24:35): It behoveth us, except we will be wilfully blinde and stupid, to take the Premisses into consideration, and not slightly to passe by without observation, and good use making of this *Earthquake*; such, being I say (once againe) one of our blessed Saviours Signes of his comming to judgement. And however, hee in his wisedome have concealed that Yeere, day, and houre; that hee will come, (though some too to pragmatically and petulantly have gone about to define the Yeere, to bee nigh at hand:) yet it much behoveth us to meditate thereon; and prepare therefore, that so wee may take all these fore-runners to be so many fore-warners of us particularly to turne to God by a true Conversion: whereupon will ensue all other Graces needfull for Salvation: And the rather wee ought to take all Gods judgements to bee warnings unto us of the last Day; because, [p. 14] be it whensoever it shall please God, every particular mans death is unto him as the day of Judgement; for as wee die, so shall wee rise: Now, what is more certeine than Death? and what more uncertaine than the day of Death? and it being so, *what manner of men ought wee to bee? Good Lord, therefore give us grace to turne unto thee by true Repentance, that so we may say ingenuously, and heartily wish, Thy will be done*; And, *Come Lord Jesu, Come quickly*.

HALLELUIAH

DEO UNITRINO GLORIA.[23]

Amen.

FINIS.

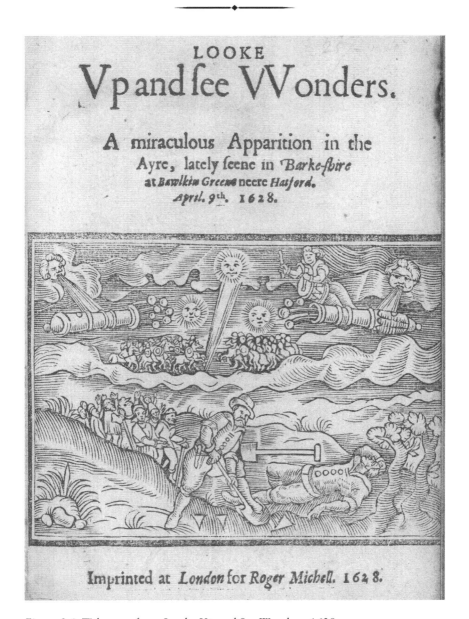

Figure 2.1 Title page from *Looke Up and See Wonders*, 1628.
Source: RB 31532, The Huntington Library, San Marino, California.

LOOKE
Up and see Wonders.
A miraculous Apparition in the
Ayre, lately seene in *Barke-shire*
at *Bawlkin Greene* neere *Hatford.*
April. 9th. 1628.
Imprinted at *London* for *Roger Michell* 1628.

[p. *1 of unpaginated prefatory material*]

To the Reader.

As thou doest Reade, so practise to Understand, and make use of thy Labour: Let not this Knowledge vanish away like a Dreame, but keepe it as a Monument ingraven in Brasse or Marble. This is a strange Chronicle, written by a strong hand: The best Antiquary in the World hath set it downe, for God himselfe puts his owne Name to it: A few leaves of his Filling, are an ample Volume: Every small Epitome[24] Written by him, is a Booke in Folio. Here thou shalt finde no great number of Lines, but much more Matter comprehended in them, then the Words seeme to carry. This is but a Picture of a Battaile fought in the Aire: A naked Description of a terrible Fight; fearefull no doubt to the Standers by; but it may be [p. 2] Comfortable to thee, if heereby thou getst thy selfe Arm'd to Combate with thy sinnes, for questionlesse uppon some such occasions grew this Quarrell;[25] which may easily be taken up, if thou (and every one of us) submit our selves, confesse wherein wee are faulty, and so plead for Attonement.

Nothing is here presented to thine eyes, to fright thee, but to fill thee with Joy, that this Storme fell so farre off, and not uppon thine owne Head. Yet beware, for the same Hand holds a Rod to strike every one that deserves punishment. Pray to Heaven to free Thee from it; and so wishing thee the strong heart of a true Christian, to beare with Patience, what thy Selfe shalt feele, and to pitty others, I bid thee farewell.

[p. 1] Looke Up,

And

See Wonders.

So Benummed wee are in our Sences, that albeit God himselfe Holla in our Eares, wee by our wills are loath to heare him. His dreadfull Pursivants[26] of *Thunder*, and *Lightning* terrifie us so long as they have us in their fingers, but beeing off, [p. 2] wee dance and sing in the midst of our Follies. So blinde are wee in the understanding of Heavenly matters, that wee cannot see our way to Goodnesse, but runne head-long into the Pathes of our owne everlasting undoing. Dangers have not the skill to fright us; Death onely is the Man, that can doe good upon us: And yet, though Death knockes at our very Doores, nay; albeit wee see him sit at our Bed-side, yet the hope of Life, playes her idle, vayne, and wanton Musicke under our Windowes.

Into what a miserable Sea of calamities does a man then throw him-selfe, when in this his earthly Navigation, hee sayles he cares not how, nor knowes where to finde a safe Landing-place.

Wee had neede therefore to make much of understanding, wise, and skil-full Pilots, for the best of us all is an ignorant Marriner. Apt enough [p. 3] we are, to run upon Rockes and quicksands; but an excellent Sea-man is hee, that in all weathers can beare up Sayle, and by the vertue of his good Compasse, is able to avoyde such mortall Dangers.

The foure Elements have beene Preachers to us, yet wee get (or at least, shew) little amendment by the Doctrin, they have Read unto us. The *Earth*, (once fruitfull) hath of late yeares felt the curse of *Barrennesse*: Her wombe hath beene the devourer of many thousands of her owne Children; shee has not playd the part of a Mother, but a Step-dame, for insteed of strong wines, shee hath bin drunke with bloud.

How hath the other Element of water beene troubled? What Monsters hath the Sea brought forth? The sonnes of Murder, Rapine, Fury, and Pyracy. As for *Fire*, it hath denied of late to warme us, but at unreason-able rates, and extreame hard conditions. But what talke [p. 4] I of this earthy nourishment of *fire?* how have the *Fires* of Heaven (some few yeares past) gone beyond their bounds, and appeared in the shapes of Comets, and Blazing Starres? The *Aire* hath bin infected, and millions have dropd into Graves, by sucking in her mortall poyson. The *Aire* is the shop of Thunder and Lightning: In that, hath of late bin held a Muster of terrible enemies, and threatners of Vengeance, which the great Generall of the Field, who Conducts and Commands all such Armies, (*God Almighty, I meane*) avert from our Kingdome, and shoote the arrowes of his indignation some other way, upon the bosomes of those that would confound his Gospell.

Now, albeit that these foure great quarter-masters of the World (*the foure Elements*) have in former times, and in this of our owne, bin in civill Warres one against another, and bent their Forces at the Heart of this Kingdome; [p. 5] yet how happy are we, to eate our bread in Peace, and to drinke our wholesome and sweete Waters? No *Nation* beneath the *Sunne* hath more cause to sing Prayses to *God*, and send up Thankes to Heaven then ours.

The Drum beates here, but the Battailes are abroad: The Barbed Horse tramples not downe our Corne-fieldes: The earth is not manurde with mans Bloud (as it was in the Warres of the Barons; and those of the two Royall con-tending Families, of *Yorke* and *Lancaster*.[27]) Here we presse Souldiers; but other Countries beare the burthen of their Armies. Heere they kindle their Match, but the fire is not given, till they come into Forraigne Kingdomes.

This Security yet must not bee suffered to rocke us fast asleepe; and so with *Sampson*, to have our strength cut from us, by the Strumpet of our carelesnes [Judges 16]: For albeit, our Gates have no Canons [p. 6] planted agaynst them[;] Nor no scaling-ladders set to the Walls of our Cities; yet there are Whole Ambushes of enemies lurking in our private Bosomes; And those are our sinnes, which daily lay traynes of powder, to blow us up, and confound us.

For these, there is an Eye open, which day and night doth over looke our actions; and if milde and gentle chidings cannot call us home, let us thanke our selves, and the stubbornnesse of our hearts, if wee groane under the stripes of correction.

Let us turne to *God*, and *God* will not turne his Face from us: Say thy sinnes were as blacke as Hell; yet *Repentance* shall make them like the Winges of a Dove, cover'd (*as the Kingly Prophet sings*) with silver, the Wings bearing the colour of yellow Gold. *Repentance* is able to make the soule as white as the snow in *Zalmon*; and *Gods* mercy like the mountaine of *Bashan*.[28]

[p. 7] *Repentance* is a golden Key, which opens Heaven, and lookes up to *Gods* anger. *Repentance* wins him to smile upon us, and to say thus; If thou still art climing up this Hill of *Repentance*; Blessed shalt thou be in the City; and Blessed in the Field: Blessed shall be the fruite of thy Body; and the Fruite of thy ground, and the fruite of thy Cattle: The increase of thy Kine; and the Flockes of thy Sheepe: Blessed shall be thy Basket, and thy Dough: Blessed shalt thou bee when thou commest in; and blessed also when thou goest out.

Thy Land-Souldiers (*O England*) shall not stand in feare of any *Italian Spinolaes*;[29] nor thy Navy Royall of any *Spanish Armadoes*: For, thine enemies that rise agaynst thee, shall fall before thy face; they shall come out against thee one way, and flye before thee seaven wayes.

His word that speakes this, may be taken better than any Kings in the [p. 8] World; and therefore hold out both thy hands, under this Tree of Blessings, and catch the golden Apples, when so freely they are shaken downe into thy lappe[.] But if thou trample these gifts under thy feete, and spurnest at Gods Favours bestowed uppon thee; New quivers of punishments will then be opened, and other strange fearefull arrowes be shot at thy bosome. Heaven shalbe turned to Brasse; earth to Iron; dust and ashes be given for Raine; our Wives shall have others lye with them; our great houses shall have others dwell in them, our Vineyards to bee planted, yet we shall never taste them: Our sheep to bee given to our enemies; and our sonnes and daughters to be led into Captivity.[30]

If therfore with *Naaman*, thou wouldst be cleansed from thy Leaprosie of sinne, thou must obey *Elisha*, and wash thy selfe seaven times in *Jordan*:[31] Weepe seaven times a day; nay seaven times an [p. 9] houre, for offending thy mercifull Father: Whosoever with *Ahazia*, the King of *Samaria* falleth sicke, and sendeth for recovery to *Baal-zebub* (the God of *Ekron*) and not to the true God indeede, he shall not come from his bed, but die the Death [2 Kings 1].

For, wee sinke to the bottome of the waters, as the Carpenters axe did (*in the second of the Kings* [2 Kings 6:4–7],) but, though never so iron-hearted, the voyce of an *Elisha* (the fervency of Prayer, and praysing God) can fetch us from the bottome of Hell, and by contrition make us swim on the top of the waters of life.

Stand therefore at the Gates of Gods mercy still; begge still; knocke still; and knocke hard: For *Hannah*, was barren, yet being an importunate suiter, her petition was heard, and signed: She was fruitfull, and had three Sonnes and Daughters [1 Sam. 1–2]: So, when we are barren in *Repentance*, in Thanksgiving[,] in Charity, in Patience, in Goodnesse, let us unfeig- [p. 10] nedly pray to Heaven, we shalbe fruitfull, and these five shalbee our Sonnes and Daughters. By this meanes our *Mara* shall change her name to *Naomi*, and our bitternesse be turned into sweetnesse (Ruth 1:20).

Have we not great cause then to magnifie him, who Crowneth the yeare with plenty, and whose steppes drop fatnesse (Psalm 65): Have we not reason to tremble at his Threatnings, who covereth himselfe with Light, as with a Garment, and spreadeth the Heavens like a Curtaine? who layeth the beames of his Chambers in the Waters, and maketh the Clouds his Chariot, and walketh uppon the wings of the winde? This Almighty Thunderer, hath Spirits attending upon him, for his Messengers are flaming fire to runne of his errands: If he but lookes uppon the earth in anger, it trembles: If hee but touch the Mountaynes, they smoake, and are consumed (Psalm 104): So that if wee fall not on our [p. 11] knees, to doe him reverence. If we open not our lips, to glorifie his Name: If we fall not flat on the Earth, at the sound of his dreadfull voyce; woe be to us, we are lost for ever, undone for ever: His blessings (if we receive them not with the right hand) are to us, as messes of meate set upon a Grave[.] What then are his chastizements? O[!] they are terrible and not to be indurde. Many windowes hath he set open in Heaven, to shewe what Artillery hee has lying there, and many of our Kings have trembled, when they were shewne unto them. What blazing Starres (even at Noone-dayes,) in those times, hung hovering in the Aire? How many frightfull Ecclipses both of Sun and Moone? What apparitions of battailes? How many times have Armies fought against Armies, in the disturbed upper Regions?

It is not for man to dispute with God, why he has done this so often, nor rashly to pronounce judgement uppon any [p. 12] thing, it pleaseth God to accomplish now; but, with feare and trembling casting our eyes up to Heaven, let us now behold him, bending his Fist onely, as lately he did to the terrour and affrightment of all the Inhabitants, dwelling within a Towne in the County of *Barkshire*.

Looke up therefore now; and see a New Wonder.

The name of the Towne is *Hatford* (in *Barke shire*) some eight miles from *Oxford*. Over this Towne, upon *Wensday* being the ninth of this instant

Moneth of *April* 1628. about five of the clocke in the afternoone. This miraculous, prodigious, and fearefull handy-worke of God was presented, to the astonishable amaze- [p. 13] ment of all the beholders, Men, Women, and children, being many in number.

The weather was warme, and without any great shewe of distemperature,[32] only the skye waxed by degrees a little gloomy, yet not so darkned but that the Sunne still and anon, by the power of the brightnesse, brake through the thicke clouds, and made them give way to the Majesty of his beames.

A gentle gale of wind then blowing from betweene the *West* and *Northwest*; in an instant was heard, first a hideous rumbling in the *Ayre*, and presently after followed a strange and fearefull peale of Thunder, running up and downe these parts of the *Countrey*, but it strake with the loudest violence, and more furious tearing of the *Ayre*, about a place called *The white Horse hill*,[33] than in any other. The whole order of this *thunder*, carried a kind of Majesticall state with it, for it maintayned (*to the affrighted Beholders seeming*) [p. 14] the fashion of a fought Battaile.

It beganne thus: First, for an on-set, went on one great *Cannon* as it were of *thunder* alone, like a warning peece to the rest, that were to follow. Then a little while[ ]after, was heard a second; and so by degrees a third, untill the number of 20. were discharged (or there abouts) in very good order, though in very great terror.

In some little distance of time after this, was audibly heard the sound of a Drum beating a Retreate[.] Amongst all these angry peales, shot off from Heaven; this begat a wonderful admiration, that at the end of the report of every cracke, or *Cannon-thundering*, a hizzing Noyse made way through the *Ayre*, not unlike the flying of *Bullets* from the mouthes of great Ordnance: And by the judgement of all the terror-stricken witnesses, they were *Thunderbolts*. For one of them was seene by many people, to fall at a place called [p. 15] *Bawlkin Greene*, beeing a mile and a halfe from *Hatford*: Which *Thunderbolt* was by one Mistris *Greene*, caused to be digged out of the ground, she being an eye-witnesse amongst many other, of the manner of the falling.

The forme of the *Stone* is three-square, and picked in the end: In colour outwardly blackish, some-what like Iron: Crusted over with that blacknesse about the thicknesse of a shilling: Within, it is soft, of a gray colour, mixed with some kind of minerall, shining like small peeces of glasse.

This *Stone* brake in the fal: The whole peece is in weight nineteene pound and a halfe: The greater peece that fell off, weigheth five pound, which with other small peeces being put together, make foure and twenty pound and better.

At the hearing of this horrid *Thunder*, all men (especially about *Sheffington*) were so terrified, that they fell on their knees, and not onely thought, but [p. 16] sayd, that verily *the day of Judgement was come*. Neyther did these feares take hold only of the people, but even Beasts had the selfe-same feeling and apprehension of danger, running up and downe, and bellowing, as if they had bin mad.

It is in the Countrey credibly reported, that some other *Thunder-stones* have bin found in other places: But for certainty, there was one taken up at *Letcombe*, and is now in the custody of the *Shriefe*.

Many do constantly affirme, that the shape of a *Man, beating of a Drum*, was visibly seene in the *Ayre*, but this wee leave to proove.

Others report that he, who digged up the *Stone in Bawlkin Greene*, was at that instant stricken lame, but (*God bee thanked*) there is no such matter.

Report in such distractions as these, hath a thousand eyes, and sees more than it can understand; and as many tongues, which being once set a going, [p. 17] they speake any thing. So now a number of people report there were three *Sunnes* seene in the *Element*; but on the contrary side, they are opposers against them, that will affirme they beheld no such matter, and that it was not so. Admit it were, how oftentimes have three *Sunnes*, foure; nay five, and sometimes more appeared in the *Ayre*, both in *England*, and other Countries round about us? They who out of their Astronomicall judgements write of such apparitions, alleadging, and prooving by strong arguments, that such disturbances in the Cælestiall bodies of the *Sunne*, *Moone*, and *Starres*, do more often from Naturall causes, than Supernaturall.

Howsoever, it is not fit that any man, should take uppon him, to write too broad and busie Comments on any such Textes as these[.] Let us not be so daring as to pry into the closet of *Gods determinations*. His *workes are full of Wonders, and not to be examined*: Let us not be so foolish, as turne *Almanacke-makers*, [p. 18] and to *Prognosticate, Prophesie, Foredoome*, or *Fore-tell*, what shall happen, faire weather or foule, to our owne *Kingdome*, or any other; scarcity, or plenty, Warre, or Peace, for such giddy-brayn'd *Medlers*, shoote their arrowes beyond the *Moone*.

The *Heavenly designes* are of a higher Nature, than to hold any correspondence, commixture, or conjunction with the phantasticall compositions of *Humane* frailty. Gods Bookes are not so easily opened: *Mans* eyes are too weake-sighted, too dull-poynted to looke into his *Voluminous*, and *Misterious Wonders*. The *Learning* of all the *Universities* in the World, is meere *ignorance*, to the *Almighties understanding*.

Lay by therfore thy *Jacobs* staffe,[34] thou that art too *scrutinous*, to looke into the *Thunderers* treasury; forbeare to take the height of these false imaginary *Sunnes*; and fright not thy *Countrey* with thy over-daring, foolish, and vaine glorious *predictions*. I speake not this to *Arme* a- [p. 19] ny *Man* with *security, negligence*, or *misbeliefe*; or to make him thinke, that *God* when he shewes us such *signes*, such *rods* from Heauen, (doing so but seldome,) does it to no purpose; But let not us be too inquisitive what that purpose is: the wranglings of Schooles, is not so unpleasing, to ignorant standers by, as our *contentions* and *quæres* about this businesse, should be to God.

Enough it shalbe for us *to see, and feare; to heare*, and *not meddle*; to *apprehend* what our *weaknesse* can, and to admire the *depth* which we cannot *read*.

The *Master* of the *houshold* being *angry*, it is the *duty* of us his *servants*, to doe our best to please him, keepe him *quiet*, and not to provoke him to a higher indignation, least in his just *fury*, which every day (every houre,) we are apt to run in. to [*sic*], he utterly *confounds* us, and bring us to nothing. Which, the *Almighty* for his owne *mercies* sake, *forbid[,] forget,* and *forgive our sinnes*. Amen.

FINIS.

---◆---

Prodigies of Germany
excerpts from L. Brinckmair, *The Warnings of Germany* (pamphlet's
more theoretical preface is included in Chapter 1)
[p. 1]
DREADFULL, AND
PRODIGIOUS ASPECTS WHICH
have happened, and appeared in the
Ayre, Water, and on Earth, beyond the common course of nature, in diverse parts of
Germany, since the beginning of these late bloody-
broyles in that Country, from the yeere of our Lord, 1618.
to this present time; together with briefe
observations of the issues, and *Consequences ensuing after them.*

Among the many troubles, and turmoyles (*Courteous Reader*) which have
long time roved, and raged not onely in *Bohemia,* but also in divers other
places of *Germany,* there appeared a terrible Comet with a great blazing
tayle, which was as terrible as visible.

It appeared first, October, 26. 1618. in the signe of *Scorpio,* and the tayle
thereof was extended betwixt the *Spica virginis,* and *Arcturus,* to- [p. 2]
wards *Polus Septentrionalis.* Afterwards it tooke its progresse in *Signo Libræ,*
continuing its course from the *Ecliptica* to *T[r]opico Cancri,* from East to West,
or Northerly. It was to be seene, often in a cleare Skie, in the East: In *Bohemia*
and *Austria,* it appeared, at first, with red; in other places with a Saturnish
pale-red colour, for the space of 27. dayes, and in some places longer. This
fearefull, & ominous Link or Torch the Omnipotent *Jehovah* had constituted,
and ordained in the Pulpit of the Heavens to bee a Preacher of Repentance;
that sinfull man might see, and discerne, that for incorrigible sinne he was
resolved to plague and punish them if they timely prevented not the threatned
danger, by seeking grace, and speedily flying from sinne the sole cause thereof.
For in as much as the secure, and hood-winckt-World had long despised, and
neglected the gracious reclaming voyce of his sacred Word, in the publike
preaching thereof by his vigilant and diligent Ministers, and refused to heare
those charmers, charmed they never so wisely, running on in their accustomed
course of sinne, and transgression, refusing to be reclamed, and living all their
dayes in sensuall impenitence, as if God regarded not their doings, and tooke
no notice of their desperate rebellions; Therefore the Almighty Lord God, as
mercifull, as just, sent forth these his prodigious signes, in the Sunne, Moon,
and Starres of Heaven, as certain fore-runners of his wrath, and of imminent,
and eminent Plagues and punishments on them, if not speedily prevented, thus
(if it were possible) to awaken men from thei[r] [p. 3] even dead sleepe of
sin, to timely repentance, and true reformation of life; but otherwise to shew

and assure them that he would come suddainly, and severely upon them, and bring all those evills, and miseries on them, which those hideous, and horred signes did portend unto them. Of which his proceeding in former ages manifold examples are extant, both in the sacred Scriptures, and in other various, and voluminous Histories, which, for brevities sake, I heere of purpose pretermit.[35] This Comet herein mentioned hath bin indeed a certain harbinger, and fore-runner of the Lords high indignation, and future punishments, wherewith (since it appeared) the secure world hath bin soundly whipped, and severely corrected: yea the great Miseries and Calamities, which poore dilacerated[36] *Germany* hath, since its appearance, felt and found, are as unspeakable, as deplorable, hardly to bee lively delineated by mans tongue or pen. For that is now compleatly (if not too fully) effected, which is spoken of in Comets, that never did a Comet appeare, which was not accompanied with much evill and miserie. And *Claudianus* the Poet writ thus of their operations.

> —*Bella[ ]canunt, ignes subitosq[ue] tumultus,*
> *Et clandestinis surgentia fraudibus arma,*
> *Civiles etiam motus, cognataq[ue] bella*
> *Significant.*—Thus englished.

They shew fierce wars, fire, sword & sudain broyles,
    And by clandestine craft, fast springing toyles,
    Uncivill-civill jarres, and home-bred flames
    They signifie, &c.

> [p. 4] *Pontanus* also writes thus of them.
> *Ventorum quoq[ue] certa dabunt tibi signa Cometæ*
> —*Etiam belli motus, feraq[ue] arma minantur;*
> *Magnorum & clades populorum, & funera Regum.*

Comets are certaine signes of future things
    Threatning fierce Wirres, much blood, and death of Kings.

Of the estate, & conditio[n] of this our present Comet ancient Astrologians have thus written.

> *Verba docent, et signa monent, et pœna probabit,*
> *Ni subitò in melius vitam convertimus, actum est.*

Words teach, signes preach, and punishments make plain,
    That want of true *repentance* proves our bane.

Which altogether the following yeers being fulfilled & verified, is notable to all the Christian world to take warning by: and to declare the misery w[hi]ch (after this appearing blazing Comet) *Germany* felt, would require many volumes.[37]

How many fruitfull Countries, Dominions, and Territories are through these last warres totally ruinated; the Cities, Towns, and Villages therein spoiled, and made pillars of fire and smoke; the Churches lying desolate, the woods being cut down, the earth untilled, and lying waste. The bloody and cruell dealing of inhumane souldiers, especially of the *Crabats*,[38] in many goodly Townes and Cities, is scarce credible, which furiously have plundered the places, torturing the Inhabitants most barbarously; ravished women even to death; powred dunghill-water and vineger into the throats of men and women; tyed chains and cords about their heads, and have twisted them so hard, that they have fallen down dead upon the ground; some are hanged up by the privy members[,] [p. 5] sawed off the legs of some, rubbed off the flesh from the legs of others to the very bones; tyed the armes of others backwards, and so hanged them up by those distorted parts; drew many through the streets of the Cities starke naked, brake and wounded them with axes and hammers, and generally used them with such barbarous cruelty, that many begged to be shot or slain instantly, rather than to live, and be partakers of such misery. Some they have rosted alive, and sacked the Cities miserably, that they spoiled what they could not carry away. All the corn and provision of victuals, have they taken away with them, and left the places so bare, that many of the best rank, for the space of 8. dayes after, saw not one bit of bread, but were glad to feed upon roots and water: spoiled the Inhabitants of their garments, exposed them to that nakednesse, that neither man, woman, nor childe have had clothes to put on. No man indeed can be ignorant of the miserable condition of all *Germany*. No man can think of it without a sorrowfull heart: none that hath not put on the Stoicks stupidity, can heare it without compassion. Such civill warres were never without strange prodigies, and this as in the beginning it was threatned by this said Comet, so in the continuance the uncouth condition thereof was still made apparent by those strange things, which happened out of the common course of Nature, which I shall endeavour to declare, as followeth. . . .

[End of p. 5 through p. 13 omitted. Brinckmair reports a river turning to blood in Hungary (1619) prior to skirmishes in 1620–1621; a "great blazing Starre" and two celestial armies fighting over Groningen (1619), followed by a battle between Christian IV of Denmark and General Tilly (1626); water turning to blood in a ditch at Wien in Austria, along with the appearance of three rainbows and three suns (1619), followed by a battle the same year; a rain of blood in Poland (1620); two armies fighting in the sky in Austria (1621), as well as two swords and two armies appearing over Lintz (1621) prior to a siege (1626); three suns and three rainbows at Prague and Heidelberg (1622), with a battle and a siege at Prague (1632 and 1634) and a siege at Heidelberg (1622); and trees dropping blood in Darmstadt, followed by battles (1622)]

[p. 15] *Anno.* 1623. about Midsommer many bloody signes and aspects appeared in divers Countries, and places. In *Bohemia* in the County of *Podybrat* a well for some dayes was turned to blood. At *Tursin* a Towne 3.

Figure 2.2 "At Minefeld and Malants the Shikles were seene bloodey [&] Men
drew there hands out bloodey when they Cut the Corne," from *The
Warnings of Germany* (1638), page 14.

Source: RB 60364, The Huntington Library, San Marino, California.

or 4. leagues from *Egra*, in a Citizens house, the table, the wall of the parler, and the chaires sweated blood, in so much that it began to runne in
the parler. What bloody encounters happened in the next, and other yeeres
in those places, is too well knowne: where 4000. of the *Bohemians* under
Count *Mansfeld*[39] were slaine: some 300. of the Imperialists not long after
lost their lives also by the Sword: 5. troopes of the Elector of *Saxonies*
Horses, lying then at *Rakonick* in *Bohemia*, were at once knockt downe
by the Imperialists; scarce 120. of them escaping with their lives. What if
we should remember the bloody tragedy acted by the Imperialists at *Egra*,
where the Imperiall Generalissimo Duke of *Fridland* himselfe,[40] with 4.
others chiefe Commanders, was murthred, and massacred the 25. of
February, Anno. 1634.

   In the Territories about the *Rhine*, and *Hossen Darmstad* in this 1623.
yeere, in divers Townes, and Villages, were seene bloody signes and tokens,
on houses, stones and walls: how prodigious this hath beene at *Mingelheim*,
where 2000. of the Imperialists were put to the Sword by Count *Mansfeld*,

the wayes side by the River *Rhine* towards *Germersheim* being strewed with their dead bodies. Also next yeere following in a Battell at *Wimpfen* betwixt Generall *Tilly*,[41] and Marquis of *Durlech*,[42] 5000. were slaine upon the place. In [p. 16] the moneth of *January, Anno* 1632. the *Swedish* Generall *Rhinegrave* taking the Towne of *Kinchberg* by assault, put to the Sword 147. Imperialists, and *Spanyards* therein. Not long after the *Rhinegrave* in another occasion lost 300. of his men by the *Spanyards* Sword.

About *Meyenfild* and *Malantz*, the Sickles, and the hands of the labourers in the Medowes were seene bloody. What cruelty, and shedding of blood by the invasion of the *Spanyards* in those places afterwards hath beene, would require a large relation; where the Inhabitants, without respect of Sex or condition, have beene miserably massacred. This is notable amongst other cruelties there committed; The *Spanish*, and Imperiall Army comming from the *Rhine*, passed by *Gall* into those parts, *Anno* 1635. where the Catholikes to secure themselves from being made a prey unto them, marked their dwelling houses with the signe of the Crosse, then thinking themselves as secure from injury from that Army, as *Rahab* was by hanging the scarlet thread at her window, from the victorious Sonnes of *Jacob* at *Jericho* [Joshua 2]; or *Israel* by striking the blood of the pascall *Lambe* upon their posts, and lintels, from the destroying Angell [Exod. 12]. But as the grounds of their hopes were most different; So the issue was most unlike. These were the first which felt the effects of their insolency, being pillaged, and murthered without distinction of age, sex, calling, or place; men and women in religious orders being forced in their Monasteries, and an Agent sent unto them from the States of the Province, preci- [p. 17] pitated by them from an high Rock.

In the Dukedome of *Wirtemberg* at *Herbrechtingen* and *Hermeringen*, the 16. of *July, Anno* 1622. it rayned so much blood, that it fell upon the hands, and cloaths of the labouring men, and was to be seene upon Trees, Stones, and other places in the fields. How many thousands of the Inhabitants of that Dukedome in those last warres, and especially after the Battell, and in the Battell of *Norlingen* have lost their lives, is too well knowen to the Christian World: in which bloody Battell how many thousands on both sides were slayne, no man had certainty of it. Amongst which were many brave Colonels, and chiefe Commanders, as the Marquesse of *Anspach*,[43] 5. Colonels, divers Captaines, and Officers all dead in the bed of honour. *Anno* 1634. the 24. of *Aug*.

The 26 of *December, Anno* 1624. for the space of 10. or 11. houres it was observed in *Bohemia*, that the Sunne was changed first in divers colours; at the last fiery beames came forth out of the Sunne, which for a time held their opposition against the Sunne, then they went away, and vanished like a smoake in the Ayre, and at last fell downe with a noyse like Rackets. Two dayes before, in *Silesia* happened an horrible prodigie, as if two Armies in the ayre continued a great fight and skirmish against one another. How many skirmishes and conflicts have fallen out in these two Countries the yeers following, is needlesse to remember: remarkable alone is the siege of the Citie of *Franckford* upon the borders of *Silesia*, which the King of *Sweden*[44] took in by assault, *Anno* 1631. [p. 18] to the terrour and slaughter of 2000. Imperialists, which were cut in pieces upon the place, besides those that were drowned, and others found dead in Cellars, Chambers, and elsewhere, as many more perchance. 300. *Swedes* also there slaine, and 100. hurt. At *Lansbergen* in the front of *Silesia*, 300 *Swedish* souldiers, over-confident of their valour, were put to the sword by the *Crabats*: which Town the King the 15. of *Aprill* took in by assault, with slaughter of 300. Imperialists: but of his own men no lesse then 600. lost their lives. In this time at *Cressin* in *Silesia*, 200. Imperialists attempting the recovery of the same Towne, were slain by the *Swedes*. . .

[Remainder of p. 18 through p. 23 omitted. Brinckmair reports in detail a celestial apparition in Anhalt, involving an army dressed in Hungarian uniforms, followed by a comet and then a second army bearing a red cross; around the same time, blood had rained in Bohemia and in Silesia (1624),

Figure 2.3 "Multitudes of Crowes killing Each other the baskits of them were Caried into the Citie in Selesia 1625," from *The Warnings of Germany* (1638), page 24.

all of which prodigies were followed by battles in the coming years. He then reports a strange, damaging storm at Regensburg (1624), followed by a siege (1634); and a "prodigious Fruit" discovered at Frankenthall (1625), foretelling the widespread destruction of the Palatinate as well as local fighting (1631–1632).]

[p. 25] Neere *Troppaw* in *Silesia*, in the Moneth of *February, Anno.* 1625. a great multitude of little Crowes (*Corniculæ*) appeared in the Ayre, which fought as it were in a set Battaile, and skirmished so eagerly, killing many amongst themselves, that the Boores[45] gathered some sacks full of them dead, and transported them unto the City. The yeere after, *Anno.* 1626. fell out a hard and sharpe fight, betwixt the Imperialists, and the *Weinmarish* Forces in this place. The Imperiall Commanders *Schaffgotch, Dona, Colorede,* and *Hexted,* with an Army of some 1000. men of Horse, and many Foot, attempting to assault the *Weinmarish* troupes in their Camp neere *Troppaw,* were still repulsed; and in the end 7. Compaines of the *Weinmarish* sallying out of the Campe, slew and rowted the Imperialists, 4000. dead corpes being found of them upon the place, and many Officers slaine; and so the *Weinmarish* got an happy victory of their enemy, although they were more in number. Another, but more bloody, conflict fell out few Leagues from this place the 3. of *May, Anno.* 1634. where the *Saxonian* Army, under the command of field-Marshall *Arnheim* obtained a memorable Battell, and brave successefull victory against the Imperialists: where the onset, and first shocke of the Battell was hot and fiery, continuing with great obstinacy, and bloody opposition, for the space of 6. houres: the *Saxons* Canons being three times lost to the Imperialists, and three times with much slaughter recovered againe from them by the *Saxons.* The *Curassiers,*[46] [p. 26] and *Crabats* did shew much valour and resolution for the most part of the Battell, till in the end the victory enclined to the *Saxon* side. Of the Imperialists were slaine upon the place of Battell above 5000. amongst whom were two Generall Majors, 1. Colonell, 1. Colonell Lieutenant, 4. other Officers of account: *Coloredo* the Generall, *Trost* and *Winse,* both Colonels, were grievously wounded; and most of the Captaines of the Foot forces were slaine. Of the *Saxons* party slaine about 400. whereof 2 Ritmasters,[47] 5. Cornets,[48] and 4. Ancients,[49] and 100. of them hurt: 36. Ensignes, 9. peeces of Ordnance, 27. Cornets won in the field.

[Remainder of p. 26 through p. 29 omitted. Brinckmair covers storms damaging churches in Silesia (1625, 1627) and an abnormally large moon accompanied by sounds like cannon-fire observed over Breslau (now Wrocław) (1628), which he links to a battle (1632).]

[p. 31] This 1628. yeare was full of portentuous prodigies, which were seen in many and divers places. At *Sunderbory* in *Pomerland,* the Heaven being open, an Army appeared comming from the Northern parts, the Avantguard thereof being Pioners and Muskettiers; hereupon did follow great peeces of Cannons and Ordnances: the reere was concluded by Cavallery or horsemen. Another Army came forth on the other side against the first, where began a fiery, and hot skirmish betwixt them: but the victory

Figure 2.4 "At Sanderborn in Pomerland Appeared a great Army and the northern side prevailed" and "At Broge in Selisia came a greate thunderboulte and brake downe a Church and slew many in it," from *The Warnings of Germany* (1638), page 30.

enclined to the Northern Army. At last a right fiery beame followed upon the Northren [*sic*] Conquerour, which beame put forth fiery rayes or beames, and continued thus prodigiously for the space of some houres. A prediction of a great Astronomer of the *English* Nation, and his judgment upon that great conjunction of *Saturne* and *Jupiter, July,* 18. *Anno* 1623. is this; That the effect of that conjunction would bee felt in the North, and North-East parts of *Europe* in particular: and in generall over all. That it would produce Warres, Famines, Plagues, &c. Places subject to this he nameth, *Italy, France, Bohemia, Silesia,* and *Germany.* Of Provinces he nameth *Prusia, Brandenburg, Stiria, Hassia,* and *Saxony*: yea, he descends to Cities; naming *Rome, Prague, Magdenburg, Coblenz* betwixt *Mentz* and *Cullen, Vlin, Brunswick, Augsburg,* &c. He sayes it is likely to goe hard with the *Romane* Empire, Clergy, Jesuites: he speakes of a King of a true Religion that should doe all this, and much happinesse that should succeede it. How this observa-[p. 32] tion hath even now been verified, we neede not feede the humour of the times: true it is, and cannot be denyed, that in the yeare 1630. following, *Gustavus Adolphus* King of *Sweden,* having conquered many Townes from the King of *Poland,* both in *Prussia,* and *Livonia,* came with an Army of some 12000. men out of the Northern corner of the world, and landed first in *Pomerania,* not very farre from *Sunderborg,* where the fore-said prodigy was seene: where he first beate out the whole Imperiall Army, nor ever returned he out of them, but with the Olive Branches, the emblemes of Victory. But these Northern trophes upon his next neighbours, as they had much of glory; so have they much of credit in them: but chronicle, and beliefe, must straine hard to make his Germane conquest any thing probable with posterity: and were they not written in the times of doing, and acknowledged by his enemy, scarcely would the legend be more apocryphall. For what beleefe (not easily to be abused) could perswade it selfe, that two third parts of *Germany* could (and by him that entred with 12. or 11000. men) in two yeares, and 4. months space, be wrested from so puissant an Emperour? A might[y] Empire and a potent, formidable for its greatnesse, confident upon the power of its colleagues, and upholders: vast in extent, terrible for its armes and Captaines, renowned for its conquests, beyond expectation successefull in all its enterprises, and that knew no bounds but the *Alpes,* and the *Ocean.* And yet this Empire, with its Armies [p. 33] or Garisons, that did hold so many Princes at a bay, was it selfe constrained to take the yoake, which *Swedens* Gantlet put upon it. In lesse then 2. yeeres and a halfe this Northern Lyon did all this: what might he more have atchieved, had hee gon on another yeare, and two moneths, and filled up the time of that malicious and false prediction, which the *Jesuits,* had cast abroad of him? They comforted their credulous Novices with his being *Antichrist*; and that he should raigne 3. yeares and a halfe, and no longer.

[Remainder of p. 33 through p. 41 omitted. Brinckmair covers the monstrous birth of two conjoined girls near Strasbourg (1628), presaging the atrocities committed in that city by soldiers; powerful storms and lightning strikes at churches in two Silesian towns (1628), which he links to battles

At Madenburke a Captaines wife dieing in Childbed desired to be ripte vp shee had a Child as bige as a child of 3 yeares old on his hind a head pe ace and a brest plate Gret bootes and a bag at his side

At Frawenstein 6 miles from Dres den a woman haueinge bought bread and goeing to cut it thereout I shewed bloode

Figure 2.5 "At Madenburke a Captaines wife dieing in Childbed desired to be ripte up shee had a Child as bige as a child of 3 yeares old on his head a head peace and a brest plate Gre[a]t bootes and a bag at his side," from *The Warnings of Germany* (1638), page 42.

Source: RB 60364, The Huntington Library, San Marino, California.

(1632, 1634) and depravations in the region; a soldier sweating blood at Geismar (1630), which he links to atrocities committed in Hesse by Imperialists; a strange fire at Coburg (1630), followed by the city's capture (1632); and bloody water at Halle (1631), linked to the city's sufferings in the wars.]

[p. 43] In the time of the siege of *Magdeburg* a City Captaines wife dying in child-bed, desires to be ript: the child was found, a boy almost as big as one of three yeeres old. He had an headpeice and an iron breast-plate upon him; great bootes of the french fashion: and a bag by his side, with two like musket-bullets. This horrible prodigy hath doubtlesse portended the deplorable destruction, and dire abodement unto the same City; which fell out the 10. of *May, Anno* 1631. when a generall assault, by the Imperialists was made upon the Towne; the walls were in a trice mounted, the Towne entred, and the Souldiers fell to killing. *Falckenberg* the *Swedish* commander therein, after valiant resistance was slaine with a shot, the administrator hurt and taken. Whilest all thus goes to wrack, a mighty fire breakes out (how none knowes) it being a great windy day, all was on the sudden become one great flame: the whole Towne was in twelve houres space, wholly turned to cinders, excepting few fisher houses. Six goodly Churches are burnt: the Cathedrall was by the Monkes, and Souldiers diligence preserved. Twenty thousand people at least were herein killed, burned, and smothered: six thousand being observed to be drowned in the River *Elve. Tilly, Wallons,* and *Crabats* never use to give quarter, or beg any: So that all were killed. 2. dayes after *Tilly* came into the Towne, and finding some hundreds of women and children in the Church, he gives them their lives, and some bread to maintaine them.

[p. 44] How inhumane a devastation of this so ancient and goodly *Hanse* Towne, the County of *Tilly*, and *Pappenheim*[50] had then made, no Pen can expresse it. The cruelty of which fury, no man can discover one halfe to the world, that a[ ]goodly City should be reduced to such ruines: as if *Hannibal* had done it, and not *Tilly*; *Hannibal* who had the art by fire and vinegar, to moulder away, the Rocks and Mountaines into crumbles; for the forcing of his owne passage.

[Remainder of p. 44 through the first line and a half of p. 47 omitted. This section covers two armies that fought in the sky over Ashersleben (1631), followed by a great battle between the Swedes under Gustavus Adolphus and the Imperialists under Pappenheim; and the Battle of Leipzig (1631), with a pre-battle flight of birds that seemed to augur victory for Gustavus (although he "had a better presage then a flight of Birds, God with us" [46]).]

[p. 47] Few yeares before the long, cruell and bloody Battell was fought at *Lutzen*, the water in the Towne ditch of *Lutzen*, was turned to blood, which prodigy was fullfilled upon the 6. of *November, Anno* 1632. wherein the bloody encounter in continuall exercise lasted from 9. in the morning untill night; in which the *Swedes* did overthrow the whole Imperiall Army with slaughter of 9000. men upon the place: many a brave man dyed of the anguish of his wounds miserably; who might otherwise have beene cured. The King of *Swedens* Majesty himselfe, (as was sayd) out of the greatnesse and heate of his courage, having made a charge upon the Imperiall curassiers,[51] was there over-laid with a number of men, and did receive a shot in the left arme, which he scarce feeling at first, would needs have led on still. But perceiving by and by his royall blood to gush out abundantly, in his retreate was shot thorow the body. Whose death indeed is never enough to bee lamented, and so this dying Conquerour did seale the Religion, and liberty of the *Germans* Nations with his blood; and to whom the more ingenuous Imperialists at *Prague*, were heard to give this honourable Testimony, that he was the bravest enemy, and the best Captaine, that ever was in Christendome. And so the *Swedes*, and protestants Army found themselves to have gotten but a dolefull and a wofull victory; losing that incomparable Conquerour who was, alone, [p. 48] worth 2. Armies. But he is dead; and that as heartily bemoaned of the *Germanes* (to speake of him no more) as of his owne subjects, who yet professe their losse to be unspeakeable. And in both their Chronicles shall his Sacred memory be made famous, and his Name shall live in their mouths, and be honored. About the death of this glorious King of *Sweden*, some singular, and miraculous Prodigies happening also, had affrighted the people in *Swedland*: amongst others, in the selfe same houres and times, when this Battell of *Lutzen* was fought appeared just over the Castle, and Royall Seate of *Stockholm* a Virgin or Damsel at night, holding in one hand a burning Candle, in the other a white Handkercher, which she cast about. Besides it was noted and observed, that all the doores in Castle, although they were shut and lockt, three severall times did open themselves. A River not of small account in *Swedland*, lost the same time his water, insomuch that all the day long a man might goe thorow with a drie foot. In *Smaland* a Province of that Kingdome, the Bells without helpe of man began to sound, with great dishartning and terror of the Inhabitants.

[Remainder of p. 48 through first half of p. 57 omitted. Brinckmair reports a double rainbow and a loaf of bread emitting blood at Frauenstein (1632), followed by the town's brutal subjugation and atrocities committed by Imperialists (1632); a monstrous birth at Kempten (1632), a town subjected to several sieges (1633, 1634); blood in a pool near Altenburg (1633), symbolizing atrocities; swords in the sky over Biberach (1633), followed by battles and sieges; apparitions in the sun and moon at Dresden (1634), the sun morphing into the shape of a crown and then a feather, which he parallels with the ominous effects of the 1618 comet; a rain of blood and brimstone at Berlin (1634) and of blood at Itzehoe (1635), linked to such conflicts as a battle in 1637; and an apparition of a scepter in the sky at Melnik (1634), linked to local atrocities.]

[p. 57] Man and beast, and Fowles of the Ayre, all seemed now to be at an irreconciliable difference, and *Germany* must be the stage whereupon they played their prizes: at *Hessen*, in the moneth of *March, Anno* 1635. there met together two Armies of strange Birds, which fought, as it were,

Within the image:

Multitudes of Strange dogges fought so
Eagerly and slew each other that the
Gouerner of Ratisbone sent
4 Companies of Muskets
against them and 9 of
the men were slaine
by the dogges

The Conduit at Isenach rane blood
for 2 houres together 1637

Figure 2.6 "Multitudes of Strange dogges fought so Eagerly and slew each other
that the Governer of Ratisbone sent 4 Companies of Muskets against
them and 9. of the men were slaine by the dogges" and "The Conduit at
Isenach rane blood for 2 houres together 1637," from *The Warnings of
Germany* (1638), page 59.

Source: RB 60364, The Huntington Library, San Marino, California.

in a set Battaile: and neere *Straubinge*, upon the *Danubie* multitudes of Dogges had their randevouze, which fought so eagerly, that the whole vicinage was not onely affrighted by the Prodigy, but, as if they would not admit of any agreement, but such as themselves liked of, when the Governour of *Ratisbone* had sent out against [p. 58] them 4. companies of his Garrison, with Muskets and other Military instruments to assault and slaye them, they left their hostility, a strange Enemy comming upon them, set upon the Souldiers, and in despite of their shot and weapons devoured nine men.

[p. 60 – blank]

[p. 61] Strange Prodigies terrifying the hearts of the people, while the Princes and peeres were in their jollitie in the Dyet at *Ratisbone*: *Mars*, and *Saturne* reigned abroad, and warre with his grim attendants, Famine, Pestilence, Fire, and destruction also raging abroad in the *Romane* Empire. What might happen by the fault of a carelesse or unskilfull Mason, not well bedding or cementing the stones, at the building of a new Steeple at *Vienna*, was by the construction of the vulgar sort counted ominous. The spire of *Shotten* lately built fell downe suddenly the 19. of *December*, *Anno* 1636. about the time of the Coronation of the new King of *Romanes* at *Ratisbone*,[52] and demolished the new builded Church: and that was made portentous, the rather, being accompained with another of the same time at *Rome*; where a great blazing Starre, called by the Naturalists *Cometa Crinitus*,[53] appeared for a space, and then vanished away suddenly over S. *Pauls* Church with a noyse: and diverse Monuments, placed in the Church, fell downe, and were defaced utterly. Now it would relish of over much boldnesse to peepe into the Arke of the Divine Secrets, nor can we conclude any particular consequences to have been portended by the accidentary fall of the aforesaid new Steeple at *Vienna*; yet doubtlesse the comet, though caused by the meeting of secundary and naturall causes, was the [p. 62] significator of what ensued about that time, and not long after. Within the space of a moneth the Emperour *Ferdinand* the second, who had long been sickly at *Ratisbone*, and then removed to *Vienna*, exhaled his last spirit, *February* the 5. *Anno* 1637. betwixt 8. and 9. of the clock in the morning, to the great griefe of the Court and City.

[Remainder of p. 62 through p. 66 omitted. Brinckmair continues to discuss his subjects' grief at Emperor Ferdinand's death, and then mentions unnerving prodigies that occurred during the Diet of Regensburg, including three carved eagles falling from a house in Lintz; this is followed by an observation that to treat these events as omens would be "superstitious," the product of "Distracted wits" (63). He also reports the conduit at Isenach gushing blood (1637), followed by clashes between the Imperialists and Swedes and general misery in Saxony, such that "Peace, the benefits whereof have not for many late yeeres been sensibly discovered to the *Germans*, was now. . .the generall desire of the people" (64).]

Figure 2.7 "A woman at vienna appeared Crying Nothing but woe unto you woe unto you," from *The Warnings of Germany* (1638), page 68.

Source: RB 60364, The Huntington Library, San Marino, California.

[p. 67 – blank]

[p. 69] *Anno* 1637. the water at *Weimar* againe turned to blood. A strange Worm in the shape of a man, with perfect Lineaments, and a golden Crowne upon his head, was found in a sallad at an Herbwomans shop at *Coblentz*, and which (if not prestigious) was most terrible, A woman appeared in a mourning habit, in *Stephens* the Cathedrall Church-yard at *Vienna, June* the 18. 1637. which, with an accent of sorrow, from 11. to 12. at night yelled out woe unto you, woe unto you; often repeating those words, and nothing else: the Bells without helpe of man rung sodainly, to the great affrightment of the people, who descanted upon the *Omen*, doubting such horrid consequences would ensue it, as presented themselves to their severall fancies. A new time of trouble began then, fire and sword raging in the most and best part of *Germany*, not only casually, but by the arbitrement and will of such as used that devouring element, to the damage of those with whom they were at enmity.

FINIS.

————◆————

IRELANDS
Amazement,
Or the Heavens
ARMADO.
Being a true Relation of two strange and
prodigious wonders or Apparitions, which was
seene over the City of *Dublin*, the one *Decemb.*
24. and the other *Decemb.* 30. 1641.
Which appeared in the Heavens like to an host of Ar-
med men with great Ordnance as it were giving fire, and
all other furniture for warre, with other fearefull signes.
Which strange Visions put the City and Inhabitants
into great astonishment and feare.
And may serve as a warning peece for *England* in these troublesome and distracted times:
London, Printed for *John Thomas*, 1641.[54]

[*p. 1*] *Dublins* warning Peece,
OR,
The Heavens Armado, with a Spurre to Repentance.

IT hath been reported from Antiquity, and our Fathers have foretold
us concerning the impious and nefarious imaginations of the Children
of the age to come[,] the which being verified in these present times, we
ought to take into our serious consideration the present and now imminent danger ordained by the direfull wrath of the just and Almighty God;
True it is, that we have like *Icarus* (scorning the Counsell of our all creating Father God) soared so high with the waxed wings of our humane
and mortall invention, that we are almost fallen into the surging Ocean
of this our present misery, and the wings of our vaine and selfe-conceited
inventions are Sun-burnt with the hot and melting Sunne of Gods wrath.[55]
The prodigious Apparitions in the Heavens doe shew and forewarne us
from proceeding into our daily vices and hainous iniquities; As lately for
Example sake.[56]

[p. 2] Upon the 30. day of *Decemb.* last, *Anno*, 1641. There did appeare
in the sight of the Inhabitants of the City of *Dublin* a prodigious Apparition
in the Firmament, the similitude whereof I shall truely demonstrate in this
present Declaration; There appeared a great host of Armed men in the likenesse of horse and Foot, and according to humane supposition they seemed
innumerable, when especially were notified to the eye of the aforesaid
beholders of the City of *Dublin*, a traine of Artillery with great Ordnance
and Field peeces, as necessary for Battell, where also was presented to the
amazement of the beholders, Gunners giving fire in direfull and hideous

manner, that the very likenesse of the flames thereof, strooke the beholders with great astonishment and admiration.

Oh is it not time therefore for *Israell* to repent and call to the Lord that he would reforme her wicked wayes? Oh it is the vengeance of the Lord, not that we are in erroneous and false Doctrinall Religion; But by reason that we forget to worship God our Creator.

Did not the Lord suffer the *Philistins* to vanquish and overcome *Israel*, because they gave themselves over to all vice and carnall delights of the flesh, and running headlong after strange Gods, forgetting the Lord Almighty, that conducted them out of the Bondage of Pharoah, and the slavery of the *Egyptians* [Judg. 10:6–8].

Oh let us with *Peter* mourne and lament for the deniall of Gods true Worship [Luke 22:61–62]; Oh let the eyes of our Repentance, like the Rocks of *Marah* power forth the abundant and flowing streames of Repentance,[57] [p. 3] that our God, the God of infinite mercy, may withstand the hand of those mercilesse and irreligious *Caitiffes*[58] of the blood-sucking Rebels of *Ireland*, under whose Tyranny our Protestants lye groaning; Oh that the Lord would unite our hearts in the true and fervent prayer of *Manasses*.[59]

Oh that we might have a *David* sent from the Lord to slay the vaunting *Golia[t]h* of those daring Rebels [1 Sam. 17], then should *Israel* see manifold blessings, the blessings of the Lord, and learne how to praise God her Maker, If the tares of blind superstition and Idolatry were rooted out and clensed from the good Seed of the pure Gospell; Then should wee know, how to praise the Lord and rejoyce in his Holy Name.

A strange Wonder.

GREAT are the wonderfull workes of God, and innumerable are the Signes and Wonders, by which he expresses & foretels his judgements, striving by that meanes to deterre mankind from sinning.

And that this Miracle may not be esteem'd fabulous, and vaine, (too many hearts being hardned with unbeliefe, which vainely thinke that such things are occasioned by chance, and not by divine providence) [p. 4] therefore I have thought good to give you some testimonies in the like nature, which have hapned on other Countries, which have found by sad experience, the effect of those dismall, and amazing Apparitions.

> *In Silesia at Trappa, Crowes fought a mortall Battell, Feb. 1625.*
>
> *At Hessen likewise flights of Birds fought and kild each other, March 1635.*[60]
>
> *Many other Signes and Wonders I could relate which were the forerunners of desolation and destruction.*
>
> *A neerer Testimony I can give you which hath lately happened at Worsop in Nottinghamshire on the 16. day of Novemb. last, 1641.*[61]

A certaine Maid lay dead the space of 20. houres, afterwards she came to life againe and made a strange and wonderfull Prophecie, fore-telling strange and wonderfull alterations in these Kingdomes, without speedy repentance, declaring how neere Gods Judgements were at hand, and ready to fall upon our heads.

Likewise at *Dublin* on Christmas Eve last, 1641. was a true information sent to an Alderman of *London* fro[m] his Factor in *Ireland*,[62] of a strange wonder seen on the same day about 4. of the clock in the afternoon it growing dark, such an incredible number of Sea Guls, Ravens and Crowes assembled together, fluttering, croaking, and pewling over our heads in so strange a hideous manner, that they astonished all the Inhabitants, and thus continued till 6. at night, being an houre especially at this time of the yeare, that Fowle seldome are seene or heard abroad, nay the shooting of many Muskets, and of divers pieces from the Ca- [p. 5] stle could not affright or scarre them away, nay we in my very conscience were more affraid of them, then they of us, what it should meane I cannot divine, but the oldest man in *Dublin*, either English or Irish never saw the like, but by this wee have cause to conjecture, that God by those Apparitions fore-tels his judgements in Signes and Wonders, which without speedy Repentance, wee have cause to feare will suddainly fall upon us, God I beseech him avert them, and give us penitent hearts, so that we may truely loath our sinnes and turne to the Lord our God.

FINIS.

---◆---

A STRANGE
WONDER,
or,
The Cities Amazement.
Being a Relation occasioned by a wonderfull and unusuall accident that happened in the
River of *Thames*, Friday, Feb. 4. 1641.[63]
There flowing two Tydes at *London*-Bridge, within
the space of an houre and a halfe, the last comming with such
violence and hideous noyse, that it not onely affrighted,
but even astonished above 500. Water-men
that stood beholding it, on both
sides the *Thames*.
Which latter *Tyde* rose sixe foote higher
then the former Tyde had done, to the great admiration of all men.
LONDON, Printed for JOHN THOMAS, 1641.

[p. 2] True Newes from Heaven,

IT hath been manifestly shewne how in all Ages for these 700. yeares, ever since the Conquest,[64] dismall chances, and heavy events, have ever attended such unnaturall and undue motions of the Ocean; beseeching God Almighty that it may be his mercy in Christ towards us, that it may not misse of it[s] wonted course and that no sad distasters or judgements follow or ensue it[ ] hereupon, all good people of this Kingdome are desired to lay away dispute, and embrace devotion[,] to surcease[65] contention and strifes, and embrace charity in peace, and quiet, with humility, and thus disposed to pray day and night, with unanimous consent; for the joyfull[66] Union, and prosperous harmony between King and Parliament, wherein consisteth the onely hap-pinesse of this Kingdome.

Not long since was printed an idle Pamphlet, entituled *Newes from Hell*, a pasquill[67] onely intended for mirth and pastime not so seasonable for these dayes of publike distraction, and severall discontent; if *Salomon* may be heard, who saith, that there is a time for all things under the Sunne [Eccles. 3:1].

But see the chance, no sooner was that breviary of tales and collection of idle falsitie, publike, extinct and quenched, men having both seene and read their fill. But behold comes *Newes from Heaven*, true Newes I warrant you, for God we know as the God of truth, so he delights in nothing lesse then falshood, that being as opposite to him as light unto darknesse, good unto evill, no questioning therefore any thing done by God for matter of Fact, because he doth them for the most [p. 3] part so publickely (as who dares stand to and avouch them) that many times Kingdomes and Nations, at the least multitudes of persons are forced, will they take notice of them, nay more if the world is so either stupid or Sottish, that it will take no notice, nor give any heede to Gods newes, (which are his signes and Tokens, appearing either in Skye, Earth or Water contrary or above the ordinarie steerage of nature) what time I say men shall spare to take speciall regard, and to slight the prodigious ensigns, if not ominous harbingers in their addresse, and appearing, it is altogether a knowne certainty that they will take notice of him by their determinate working: God saith, that the very Snow and raine shall not returne without the accomplishment of that for which they were sent [Is. 55:10–11], which are the ordinary affects of naturall causes very familiar with us, and shall we thinke that his wonders stand for Cyphers, that his extraordinary workes (that sometime the world is not acquainte with all once in an age,) shall dye speechlesse, that his terrible Apparitions should depart empty, leaving no effects, no prints behind them, surely[68] no, they are of greater consequence then so, and in all Ages they have by wofull instance, that have followed them compelled the world to be of another beliefe, the Heathen Phylosophers that had nothing but the glimmering of nature to helpe them, and some roving guesse at naturall causes, that Blazing Starre of our[ ]time, the deaths of great Princes, and Potentates, immoderate Windes[,] Plague and Pestilence, intemperate Raines[,] Rot, Murren[69] among Beasts and Cattell, the unexpected suddaine and causelesse swelling of Rivers, Dearth and Famine, the disorderly and changeable ebbing and flowing of the Tyde, blood[,] and discention, if the Heathen by the Candle of nature could not onely perceive [. . .] but [. . .] Gods notable Messengers, and partly tell their arrant; shall Christians that live in the day of the Gospell descrye nothing by them, but take them to bee as dombe in effect as some of them are in sound, especially when [p. 4] God himselfe cryeth, *my Wonders shall fill the Earth*,[70] which is understood so much with their number, as their operation, if then Gods extraordinary Heralds, I meane his dread and unacquainted predictions have ever had some undoubted designe, then this of ours that happened *Februarie*. the 4. being last Fryday, ought not to be passed over, as not worth the marking or observing, The strange tokens which GOD from Heaven, the day above-said, shewed amongst us, was this, *Fryday Februarie* 4. 1641. [1642] it was high Water at one of the Clocke at noone; a time, (by reason so accommodated for all imployments,[71] either by Water or Land) very fit to afford witnesse, of a strange and notorious accident, after it was full high Water, and that it flowed its full due time as all *Almanacks* set downe, and Water-men the unquestionable Prognosticators in that affaire, with confidence mainetaine it stood a quiet still dead Water, a full houre and halfe, without moving or returning any way never so lit[t]le, yea the water-men flung in Stickes to the streame, as neare as they could guesse, which lay in the Water as upon the Earth, without moving this way, or that, Dishes likewise and Wodden [*sic*] Buckets they set a swimming, but it proved a stilling for move they would not any way by force of stream or water, so that it seemed that the water was indeed asleepe or dead, or had changed or borrowed the stability of the Earth, the Water-men not content with this evidence would needs make the utmost of the tryall,[72] that they might report[73] with the more boldnesse the truth of the matter, and with more credible confidence they tooke their Boates and la[u]nched into the streame or very Channell: the Boates that lay hailed up upon the shore moved as much, except when they used their Oares, nay (a thing worthy the admiration of all men) they rowed under the very Arches, tooke up their Oares and slept there [. . .] or at least lay still an houre very neare [p. 5] their Boates not so much as moved through any way, either upward or downeward: the water seeming as plaine, quiet, even, and stable, as a pavement, under the Arch, where if any where in the Thames, there must be moving by reason of the narrownesse of the place, in this posture stood the water a whole houre and halfe or rather above by the Testimony of above five hundred Water-men on either side the *Thames*, whom not to believe in this case were stupiditie, not discretion.

At least when all men expected its ebb, being filled with amazement that it stood so long as hath been delivered, behold a greater wonder, a new Tyde comes in, a new Tyde with a witnesse, you might easily take notice of him, so lowde he roared, that the noise was guessed to be about *Greenewich* when it was heard so, not onely clearly but fearefully to the Bridge, and up he comes tumbling, roaring, and foaming in that furious manner that it was horror unto all that beheld it, and as it gave sufficient notice to the eare of its comming, so it left sufficient satisfaction to the eye, that it was now come, having raised the water foure foote higher then[74] the first Tyde had done, foure foote by rule, as by evident measure did appeare, and presently ebbed in as hasty confused unaccustomed manner, see here reader a wonder, that (all things considered the oldest man never saw, or heard of the like, what God would signifie unto us by it, especially in these not well setled times) we must leave to him that in such cases teacheth and instructeth by the event, but for our parts let it worke this good effect in us (knowing that in all ages from the Conquest hitherto, if we will believe our owne Chronologers the Feoffees in trust of the passed times, this unusuall, sudden, unnaturall [p. 6] returne of the Tyde, hath in this Kingdome been evermore followed with continuall dismall heavie issues, either of deaths of unmatchable and Peerelesse personages, of Battaile, sicknesse, or Famine (as by sixe and forty mournfull instances we are able to make it appeare:) this effect I say let it worke, let it end, or at least qualifie our dissentions & uncharitable disputes, let it worke in us a hate of Popish Idolatry, yet alone unto the men, to doe well as we say well to endeavour to joyne true charity towards our neighbour with true piety toward God, to couple true sincerity with true humility, to lincke true amity toward my friend, with true and unfained Loyalty toward my Soveraigne.

To pray day and night for a perfect Concord, and unanimous consent, undivided Union betweene King and Parliament, wherein consisteth the onely permanent happinesse of this Kingdome.

FINIS.

Notes

1 John Rushworth, *Historical Collections of Private Passages of State*, Vol. I (London: Printed by Tho. Newcomb for George Thomason, 1659), 1.
2 Perceptions of the comet were undoubtedly colored by subsequent events, but it was also recognized and variously interpreted at the time. The astrologer John Bainbridge quickly produced a pamphlet on this prodigy, and while he ended his prognostication with the desire that "Whatsoever evill this new Comet may presage, the signe be to them that hate us" (42), yet he seemed to vacillate between being "an ominous Scrich-owle" and a "Halcyon of calme serenitie" (29). Moreover, his attempts to highlight the positive events that had followed earlier comets appear somewhat meager in light of the more common belief that comets heralded war, plague, and famine. John Bainbridge, *An Astronomicall Description of the late Comet from the 18. of Novemb. 1618. to the 16. of December following* (London: Printed by Edward Griffin for Henry Fetherstone, 1618).
3 Philip Vincent, *The Lamentations of Germany* (London: Printed by E. G. for John Rothwell, 1638), 6 of unpaginated preface.
4 Jayne E.E. Boys, *England's News Press and the Thirty Years War* (Woodbridge, UK: The Boydell Press, 2011), 270.
5 *The Invasions of Germanie* (London: Printed by I. Norton, for I. Rothwell, 1638), 2 of unpaginated forward.
6 Vincent, *Lamentations*, 7 of preface.
7 See, for example, Vincent, *Lamentations*, 2 of unpaginated "To the Reader" and 1 of unpaginated preface. John Vicars uses the same language in *Prodigies and Apparitions* ([London?: n.p., 1643]), 12; pointedly, however, he limits this time of Solomonic peace to the days of James only.
8 Edmund Calamy, *Englands Looking-Glasse* (London: Printed by I. Raworth, for Chr. Meredith, 1642), 11.
9 Based on a repeated passage in the book of Jeremiah, such as in chapter 15, these judgments were widely regarded as the three main weapons in God's arsenal. See for example William Gouge, *Gods three arrowes plague, famine, sword, in three treatises* (London: Printed by George Miller for Edward Brewster, 1631).
10 Nehemiah Wallington, *Historical Notices of Events Occurring Chiefly in the Reign of Charles I*, Vol. I (London: Richard Bentley, 1869), 5.
11 Simonds D'Ewes, *The Diary of Simonds D'Ewes (1622–1624): Journal d'un étudiant Londonien sous le règne de Jacques I*er, ed. Elisabeth Bourcier, Publications de la Sorbonne Littératures 5 (Paris: Didier, 1975), 65.
12 For other wonders, including a comet and an infestation of frogs, see *The Lord Osmonds overthrow* (London: Printed for John Greensmith, 1642). Ethan Howard Shagan offers an analysis of the reaction to the Irish revolt in the English press, including a discussion of this pamphlet, in his essay "Constructing Discord: Ideology, Propaganda, and English Responses to the Irish Rebellion of 1641," *Journal of British Studies* 36 (1997), 4–34.
13 Calamy, *Looking-Glasse*, 16. The sword-shaped comet over Jerusalem was recorded by Flavius Josephus in his *Wars of the Jews* and was regularly referenced by early modern prodigy writers.
14 Vicars, *Prodigies and Apparitions*, 8–12.
15 It is the nature of man to crave novelty.
16 Marginal reference: "*Keckerman de Terrae motu. Magiri Phys:*[.]" The author refers to the natural philosophers Johannes Magirus (c. 1560–1596) and Bartholomäus Keckermann (c. 1572–1608).
17 Christs. A reader has blotted the "p" and written an "h" over it to correct the error.

18 Marginal note: "S. Michaels / Trinitie."
19 Marginal reference: "*Speed*, in his Geography. *pag*. 49." That is, John Speed, *The Theatre of the Empire of Great Britaine* (Imprinted at London: [n.p.], 1611 [1612]), Book I chapter 25, p. 49.
20 Marginal reference: "1619. *Gallobelgicus* B. of *Londons* Sermon at the Crosse. *I. Leech* his Militarie Sermon." *Mercurius Gallobelgicus* was a Continental news periodical; the "Militarie Sermon" is a reference to Jeremy Leech's sermon *The trayne souldier* (London: Imprinted by J. B. for Nathanaell Newbery, 1619), 51–55. The event (without the discovery of the tablets) was also reported in *Newes from Italy* (London: Printed by N. O. for Nathaniell Newbery and John Pyper, 1618).
21 Marginal note: "*Maximilian; Albertus*."
22 The Habsburg Holy Roman Emperor Matthias died in March 1619; his consort, Anna of Tyrol, had died three months earlier. Matthias' brothers Maximilian and Albert died in November 1618 and July 1621, respectively. Anne of Denmark, consort of James VI/I, died in March 1619. Philip III of Spain died in March 1621. The death of James VI/I in March 1625 was the most recent of these royal deaths from the perspective of this pamphleteer.
23 Glory to the triune God.
24 A summary or abstract.
25 Original: "Qnarrell."
26 "pursuivant" – a messenger.
27 The two Barons' Wars fought in the thirteenth century between the nobility of England and the monarch (first John, then Henry III), and the fifteenth-century Wars of the Roses between the houses of Lancaster and York.
28 The marginal note cites Psalm 67; the correct reference is to Psalm 68, in which the psalmist praises God for saving Israel from its enemies: "Though ye have lien among the pots, yet shall ye be as the wings of a dove covered with silver, and her feathers with yellow gold. When the Almighty scattered kings in it, it was white as snow in Salmon. The hill of God is as the hill of Bashan; an high hill as the hill of Bashan" (v. 13–15).
29 Ambrogio Spinola (1569–1630) was born in Genoa but served as a general in the Spanish army in the Netherlands and Germany; he had left the field for Spain earlier in 1628.
30 The marginal note beside this paragraph cites Deuteronomy 20, but this and the preceding two paragraphs draw from the blessings and curses in Deuteronomy 28.
31 The marginal reference is to 2 Kings 5:41, but should be 5:14 (there is no forty-first verse in the chapter).
32 Unwholesomeness.
33 The Uffington White Horse, a prehistoric chalk design on one of the hills of the Berkshire Downs.
34 An astronomical instrument for measuring the sun's altitude.
35 Leave out, omit.
36 Torn in pieces.
37 Many of the following atrocities were recounted in newsbooks and collected in Philip Vincent's *The lamentations of Germany* (London: Printed by E.G. for John Rothwell, 1638).
38 The Crabats or Croats were a military group formed in 1625 that fought for the Catholic League and earned a reputation for particular brutality toward Protestants.
39 Ernst von Mansfeld (c. 1580–1626), a mercenary general who fought for the Protestants during the Thirty Years War.

40 Albrecht von Wallenstein (1583–1634), a self-made man who commanded the armies of the Holy Roman Emperor, Ferdinand, and whose power was feared by many in the Empire; he was assassinated by officers of his own army.

41 Johann Tserclaes (1559–1632), Count of Tilly, commanded the forces of the Catholic League.

42 George Frederick (1573–1638), Margrave of Baden-Durlach and a member of the Protestant Union. He was defeated at the battle the writer mentions here.

43 The Battle of Nördlingen was a sweeping Imperialist victory, at which Frederick III (1616–1634), Margrave of Brandenburg-Ansbach, was killed.

44 Gustavus Adolphus (1594–1632), King of Sweden, entered the German war in 1630 in opposition to the Holy Roman Emperor and was lauded as the divinely-appointed champion of the Protestant cause. English newsbooks and pamphlets followed his progress with great enthusiasm; for one example, see *The New Starre of the North, Shining Upon the Victorious King of Sweden* (London: Printed by Augustine Matthewes for Robert Milbourne, 1631), which argued that the king's successes on the Continent had been foretold via a comet recorded by Tycho Brahe in 1572 (pp. 22–23, esp.).

45 Peasant farmers.

46 Cavalrymen so called for the "cuirass" they wore, a breast- and back-plate buckled together.

47 Title borne by captains in cavalry regiments.

48 The officer in a cavalry troop who carried the standard, or a full company of cavalry.

49 A standard bearer (ensign).

50 Gottfried Heinrich (1594–1632), Count of Pappenheim, an Imperialist field marshal.

51 Cavalry soldiers wearing a cuirass or breastplate.

52 Ferdinand III (1608–1657) was elected Holy Roman Emperor upon the death of his father, Ferdinand II; his coronation took place on December 22.

53 A "long-haired comet."

54 The final digit appears to be a 2 superimposed over a 1, reflecting contemporary confusion over the dating system. Beginning the new year on January 1, the pamphlet was published in early 1642.

55 In Greek myth, the craftsman Daedalus constructed wings for he and his son Icarus to escape their imprisonment on Crete. When Icarus ignored his father's warning not to fly too near the sun, the wax on his wings melted and he plunged into the sea.

56 Probably a printer's error for "take." An ink blot may be accidental, or it might be an annotator's addition of a crossbar to correct the offending letter.

57 The author conflates Ex. 15:23–25, in which Moses casts a tree into the bitter waters of Marah to make them drinkable, with Ex. 17:1–7, in which Moses strikes a rock in Horeb and water comes out. Moses calls the place in the second passage "Meribah."

58 Cowards.

59 Manasses/Manasseh was a king of Judah who practiced idolatry and consorted with witches; after being captured and imprisoned by the Assyrians, he repented and was restored by God to his throne (2 Chronicles 33:1–19).

60 These two avian battles, drawn from news publications, were included in L. Brinckmair's *The Warnings of Germany* (London: Printed by John Norton, for John Rothwell, 1638), 25 and 57.

61 The narrative of this resurrection and prophecy was also published by John Thomas, either in late 1641 or early 1642; see *The Wonderfull Works of God Declared by a Strange Prophecie of a Maid* (London: Printed for John Thomas, 1641 [1642?]).

62 The following is a slightly embellished version of an account of "A strange and wonderfull thing by Fowles" included in the pamphlet *The state of Dublin, as it stood the 27. of December* (Printed at London for Nath[aniel] Butter, 1642).
63 Based on the Old Style calendar, which begins the new year on March 25. The author's February 1641 would be our February 1642, placing this pamphlet about a month after Charles I's removal from his capital.
64 The Norman Conquest of 1066.
65 Stop; leave off.
66 Original: "joysull."
67 A lampoon or libel.
68 Original: "furely."
69 Carrion or diseased flesh.
70 A paraphrase of Acts 2:19 and Joel 2:30.
71 Original: "imploymeuts."
72 Original: "rryall."
73 Original: "teport."
74 Original: "highert hen."

3 Civil war

'These troublesome and distracted times'

Introduction

In 1642, the publisher John Hammond printed a satirical poem by John Taylor entitled *Mad Fashions, Od Fashions, All out of Fashions, Or, The Emblems of these Distracted Times*. A classic example of the frequent interplay of text and imagery in early modern print, its six pages of verse served to explicate the woodcut on the title page: a "Monstrous"[1] and "preposterous"[2] picture that graphically depicted Taylor's opinion on the contemporary situation. In the center stood a man with his feet in a pair of gloves, his doublet on his legs, his breeches on his torso, and his hands stuck into spurred boots. A church and a candlestick floated upside down in two corners and a fish swam across the sky, and in the background a horse drove a cart and a wheelbarrow pushed a man, while around the central man's feet a rat pursued a cat and a rabbit a dog. Even without the accompanying text, it was not difficult to guess that all this inversion reflected Taylor's belief that, as he put it in his poem, "The world's turn'd upside downe, from bad to worse, / Quite out of frame, *the cart before the Horse*."[3] It has become an iconic depiction of the English Revolution: a time of social and religious chaos, during which nothing and no one knew his place and where time-honored institutions were flung on their heads.[4]

This characterization of the 1640s and 1650s should not be made uncritically: Taylor's is the perspective of a firm traditionalist who opposed the proliferation of religious sects such as those which will appear in Chapter 5 and whose wartime literary career was in large measure built upon decrying current affairs through passionate, vicious harangues. Nevertheless, there is much in the following pamphlets to indicate that he was not the only one to sense the abnormal, even the absurd, nature of society in the mid-seventeenth century. Indeed, it was not a new sentiment, and although Taylor concerned himself with England, it was not even limited to the Three Kingdoms. Chapter 2 has already demonstrated how pamphleteers opined that theirs were especially bloody, anxious times in the world at large, despite their own relative freedom from military conflict, and interest in foreign affairs did not entirely dry up after August 1642. Some periodicals and pamphlets continued to print news from beyond Britain's borders: *Sad Newes from the Eastern Parts* (1647), for instance, dealt primarily with apparitions in the Eastern Counties, but ended by relaying prodigies from the Netherlands and linking England's trials with those across the Channel. Britain did not cease to be part of a European context because she was at war within herself, and her trials could still be seen as part of a more wide-spread disorder.[5]

Nevertheless, attention certainly turned inward in the 1640s–50s, for it was no longer imperative for London printers to look far for signs that all was not right with their nation's soul. In the political climate as much as in the natural world, the pamphleteers represented in this section saw evidence that these were "troublesome and distracted,"[6] "not well-setled,"[7] and "sad and monsterous"[8] times. In response, it was natural for them to employ the same prodigy-narrative format as they had done for decades, only now to lament the strife and divisions into which their own country had fallen more so than those of their neighbors. At the same time, these examples of the prodigy genre tended to avoid overt assignments of blame. This does not mean that these pamphleteers were merely lamenting change as change, or that they desired a return to the *status quo ante bellum* on any terms: it is possible to find hints of Parliamentarian sympathies in such works as *A Great Wonder in Heaven* (1643), which described apparitions over Edgehill following Parliament's "glorious victory over the Cavaliers,"[9] and *The New Yeares Wonder* (1643), a rather garbled, sometimes unintel-ligible version of the same events. Although it primarily expressed anguish over the bloodshed, and although it was far more slapdash than *A Great Wonder*, the latter pamphlet went so far as to say that the King needed to be "inlighten[ed]" and to put away his evil advisers before the country could have peace.[10] Two years later, *The Most Strange and Wounderfull Apparition of Blood in a Poole at Garraton in Leicester-shire* (1645) spoke more subtly of the King being reconciled to his Parliament rather than the other way round, while also delivering a harsh critique of the local Royalist lord who stole and murdered in Charles' name.[11]

For the most part, however, these were not works of scurrilous propa-ganda (like those to be found in Chapter 4); rather, these authors were concerned with nationalizing and internalizing the blame for England's cur-rent state of affairs—turning the reader's attention to the ways in which he or she was responsible, and in which he or she might, humanly speaking, affect the future. The average person could not hope to change Charles I's attitude toward Parliament, for instance, but he or she could pray for such a change. And while it might have been simpler to dismiss calamities as the result of someone else's sin, or of leaders' foolish decisions, these pamphlets warned each individual to search his or her own heart: "it is [n]ot only for one mans sins, but it is for every ones sins that the Lord hath caused the sword to be drawn amongst us,"[12] and thus all were called to repent and avert God's anger.

This was the hope held out in these pamphlets, as it had been in the works printed before the war: that the nation might respond to the host of terrible wonders, from unusual tides to ghostly battles to monstrous births, and that God might in turn be pleased to restrain His judgment. The prodigies, after all, were no less warnings sent to save Britain from a worse fate than the wonders in Brinckmair's *Warnings of Germany* had been, for all that they were closer to home. They were, to put it in terms of Ebenezer Scrooge's question to the Ghost of Christmas Future, "the shadows of the things that May be," but not necessarily "the shadows of the things that Will be."[13] These pamphlets encouraged all to repent as Scrooge would in Dickens' nineteenth-century novel and by so doing, in the inscrutable will of God, to bring an end to the present troubles and distractions. However, whether that meant an end to the kind of inversion Taylor had in mind and the restoration of Charles I to his throne, or whether it meant that Charles laid down his arms and submitted to the authority and privileges of Parliament, was not necessarily agreed upon by all who wrote or read these works.

Figure 3.1 Title page, John Vicars' *Prodigies & Apparitions*, 1643.

PRODIGIES & Apparitions
Or
Englands War[n]ning Pieces
Being a Seasonable Description
by lively figures & apt illustration
of many remarkable & prodigious
fore-ru[n]ners & apparent Predictions of Gods Wrath against
England, if not timely prevented by
true Repentance.
Written by J. V.

Are to be sould by
Tho Bates in ould Baily
& by, Ralphe Markland
neere the Conduitt[14]

[p. 1] PRODIGIES and APPARITIONS,
OR,
ENGLANDS Warning-Pieces.

HISTORIES doe report and make mention of *Tamberlane*,[15] that famous Warriour, and great scourge of the Turke, (as he was termed) that in his battels, especially in his intended siege and assault of a City or Towne, his custome was, first, to hang out a white flag or banner, in the sight of the Besieged; thereby intimating to them his tender[16] of mercy and favourable-quarter to them, if they would instantly yeeld and submit to his mercy. But if that would not serve, but that they resolved to stand it out against him, and put it to the hazard of warre; then hee hung out a red flag, in token, that now [p. 2] there was nothing but death and destruction to be expected upon their refusall of his profered favor and mercy to them. Even so Almighty God, the great and supreme Sovereigne of all Nations and Kingdomes, and the most terrible heart-tamer and wonder-working-King of all Kings, who with the word of his mouth and breath of his nostrils, is able to subdue the mightiest Kings, Kingdoms and people, and to cast down al strong holds and mightiest mountaines before him, as those Heathen Kings, *Nebuchadnezar* and King *Darius* freely confessed.[17] Yet, I say, though he be so mighty and terrible a God, when hee is provoked to wrath by the sinnes and transgressions of a nation or people, he never punisheth, but he first admonisheth; and heerin like this foresaid *Tamberlane*, before hee intends the ruine of a Nation or a Kingdome, he first holds out the white flag of his profered grace and mercy, [p. 3] on their true repentance and hearty reformation from their evill courses and conversation, but if this will not worke kindly on them, but they wil obstinately and stubbornly stand out and refuse his mercy and proffered grace and favour, then at last, he hangs out his red-flag of wrath and confusion and sodainly consumes his proud and rebellious opposers, all insolent and incorrigible sinners, who have thus made themselves uncapable of mercy and compassion, and are so become as combustible stubble in the presence of a terrible and angry God, who as a consuming fire, devoures them, as in a moment (Heb. 12:29). For, as the Prophet sayes, who is able to stand before, or to dwell with everlasting burnings? (Is. 33:14) Now, this mercifull course of our mercifull God in thus hanging out first this white-flag of favour and mercifull premonitions (which is the thing mainly intended to be described in these following figures [p. 4] and ocular-Emblemes of prodigious portentious [*sic*], and apparitions) before he inflicteth severe punishments on his sinning Servants: The Lord useth to manifest unto them divers waies, but most especially and most remarkably, these two waies. Either by his Prophets and faithfull Preachers, declaring his word and will to his people; as *Jonas* in Ninevie, and all the Prophets else to the people of Israel, in their constant proclaiming mercy to Penitents, but judgement and wrath to obstinate sinners and refractorie[18] transgressours: Or else, by sending prodigious signes and wonders among them, either by fearfull apparitions in the ayre, monstrous births, heart-frighting-voyces and exclamations, oftimes unknowne from whence or by whome uttered, and such like. And this last course, the Lord hath also frequently taken, with a provoking and impenitent people in all ages and times. And this is the thing which in [p. 5] this little Treatise is mainly intended to be declared and insisted upon.

Namely, to shew, that even of late also, in these our modern times (as well as in former and ancient ages) we, being by our sins and transgressions, a greatly provoking people, incensing and exasperating the high indignation and wrath of the Lord against us; yet he hath among us also shewn himself to bee God that changeth not, full of compassion and slow to wrath; bending his bow, whetting his sword, holding up his arm, ready to let it down, yet loath to strike, that so by these preparations to the blow before it falls heavie upon us, we might see and shun and avoid it by our true and cordiall repentance (Ps. 7:12–13). Now in the first place, I shall very briefly give you a taste and sight of what God hath done in this nature and kinde in former ages and times, and so passe on succinctly to our [p. 6] owne times, which I say is here mainly intended.

And, first, to begin with him who is the beginning and end of all things, even the Lord Jesus Christ,[19] our most pretious and deare Saviour, the authour and finisher of our faith (Heb. 12:2), that glorious Lord of life, and Prince of peace; who being born into the world in the dayes of an Emperour of peace, *Augustus Cæsar*, then Emperour of Rome, yet bringing into the world not onely peace, but a sword also (Mat. 10:34–35); peace to penitent and broken-hearted beleevers, and a sword of variance and revenge to proud and impenitent sinners: Therefore at his birth, what a most admirable and unparalel'd Starre was seen in the East? so great and so miraculous a Starre as hath puzled and posed the greatest and most learned Astronomers and

Mathematicians of the world. A white Flag of mercy indeed, yea of ever-lasting redemption from Sin, Death and Hell, if [p. 7] graciously accepted with firm faith, and sound universall obedience (John 3:16). But a red Flag of wrath and confusion; yea of horror and perdition, if obstinately rejected, or lazily neglected by sin, and ignorance, and infidelity (Heb. 2:2–3). Again, a little before the destruction of that great and most magnificent Metropolis of the whole world, Jerusalem, I mean; what fearfull and prodigious fore-warnings were sent to that Citie, to foreshew them the wrath to come? As, first, a fearfull blindnesse and stupidity of minde, or hardnesse of heart (the most fearfull fore-runner of wrath toward them, of all the rest) not to see or beleeve those wonderfull fore-warnings, which God then sent among them. Secondly, a Comet, like a sword, and a bright shining light, in their Temple, round about their Altar, in the midst of the night. Thirdly, a Cow, (which should have, then, been sacrificed) that brought forth a Lamb, [p. 8] in the midst of the Temple. Fourthly, the great and massie[20] brasen gate of the Temple, which opened of itself. Fiftly, fearfull and hideous sights and apparitions in the aire, of mighty companies of Chariots and armed men in an hostile manner. Sixtly and lastly, a voyce was heard in the Temple crying out, *Let us goe hence.* With other such like, mentioned by *Josephus* in his famous history of the Jewes, page 738.[21]

But, to come neerer to our own times. Are not the fearfull apparitions and signes in the heavens, and prodigies on the earth, often seen in Germany, by the inhabitants thereof in many places, notable fore-runners and predictions of Germanies succeeding miserie, still fresh in the memory of many yet living? who have been both eye and eare witnesses of the manifold and most lamen-table distresses and destructions which have befallen; and, even to this day, lye still very heavy on that (once) [p. 9] most famous and flourishing Eden of the whole Christian world, now, made a desolate desart, and bare and barren wildernesse.

But, all this while, that we have only heard that our neighbours houses have been so fearfully on fire; what use have we of England made thereof? How have we endeavoured to keep the flame off from our own houses and habi-tations? Certainly, wee have not made that holy and humbling use thereof as we might and ought to have done, considering our meanes of grace and reconciliation, wherewith we have been, even lifted up (like Capernaum) to heaven (Mat. 11:23); far beyond our neighbours round about us. We have not been wise by other mens harmes, as meer humane and worldly wisedome might have taught us to be: But have, contrariwise, drunk wine in bowles, as the Prophet complaines, and stretched our selves on our beds of Ivory,[22] none of us hardly [p. 10] being grieved for the afflictions of *Joseph*, in the aforesaid Germany, and now also of late and lamentably bleeding *Ireland*. Wherefore the Lord hath (and that most justly) come neerer home to our owne doores, and begunne to make us (who were only supine[23] spec-tators of others miseries) now, unhappy spectacles to others of imbred and homebred devouring destructions.

Nor yet, I say, in all these our selfe-procured sorrowes, can we justly taxe the Lord in the least measure, with any more harsh or hasty proceedings heerein, with us, then with any of his other servants in by-past times, but have been, every-way wholy left without excuse. For, hath not the Lord for these many yeares together both called upon us by by [*sic*] his faithfull and painfull[24] Preachers of the word fore-warned us to flie from the wrath to come? Have they not frequently and fervently cried out and told us, that except we repent we also should [p. 11] perish?[25] Yea, when *this one* great and maine meanes of reclaming us his people from our sinnes, would not serve, hath not the Lord used *that other* more terrible and heart-frighting course (heer, mainly intended in this treatise) of Prodigies, Signes and Apparitions in the ayre, and other most degenerating, unnaturall and wonder-striking contingents amongst us here at home? As now I intend more exactly and particularly to set forth and shew to the Reader whereby wee shall easily discerne and discover to our owne hearts (if we will not bee too wilfully blind, which as I shewed before, was the first and worst signe of smart and sorrow in Jerusalem, and more then marble-hearted) most apparent prints and even visible footsteps and impressions of Gods highly conceived indignation and provoked patience, turned into enforced furie by our constant and unconscionable sinning against him, and now resolved to exe- [p. 12] cute the utmost severitie of his wrath upon us, if now at last wee hasten not most heartily to prevent and divert it, by true and timely repentance and reformation.

And now, I say, that we may no longer looke abroad into forreigne parts, nor many yeeres past, for examples of this sort, I shall desire the Reader to remember what yet may be fresh in memory among us: That in the Reigne of King *James*, that so peacefull a Prince, who so much delighted in the name and worke of Peace, both at home and abroad, that hee had this Motto given to him, *Beati Pacifici*, Blessed are the Peace-makers. And so successefully had he prosecuted his affections therin, that (as heere you may see in this Embleme, or following Figure) Every man sate under his owne Vine, and under his owne figge tree, even from Dan to Beersheba, all the dayes of the sayd King *James*, our so peacefull King; as it

[p. 13 – Figure 3.2; p. 14 – poem[26]]

[p. 15] was said of King *Salomon* also, that Prince of Peace.[27] But this peace, being but a meer externall and sensuall peace, and so the mother of Luxury, Libertinisme and prophanenesse (whereof the whole Kingdome did then, and so all along, to this very day) too rifely and rankly abound, together with all kind of sinfulnesse; Piety being then turned into Court-Policy, and sincerity into outside and Diabolicall hypocrisie. The Lord therefore, even about the yeere 1618. *November* 18. sent a visible demonstration of his just wrath and displeasure; namely, a great Comet or Blazing Star (as there also you have it in the Embleme) with seven streames, which continued to the 16. of *Decemb.* following, rising every morning about three or foure

Figure 3.2 "Every man Sitting vnder his vine & vnder his owne fig gtree,
enjoying all good things, in the days of King James. But, on the
18th of November 1618 A great Blazing-starr, with 7 long streames
appeared, much damping mens hearts," from John Vicars' *Prodigies &
Apparitions*, 1643, p. 13.

of the clocke, and so continued shining most cleerly and bright, till day light appeared, the streames of it blazing upwards. Now what this Comet or Blazing Star might portend [p. 16] and prognosticate, hath been evidently seene and known amongst us, by reall and sensible experience, ever since; not only over all Christendome in general, as in Germany, Rochel in France,[28] and still fresh bleeding and lamentably dilacerated[29] and forlorne Ireland; but even within our owne bosomes in England also, as in the death of Queene *Anne*, and of King *James* also himselfe, not long after; yea and many most eminent Peeres and Nobles of this Land, suddenly taken away, but by what stroke is not yet fully discovered, though greatly suspected; as, the Marquesse of *Hamilton*,[30] the Duke of *Richmond*,[31] and the Lord *Belfast*,[32] &c. all eminent Common wealths men, fierce and furious warres also and rumours of warres, Nation against Nation, and Kingdome against Kingdome. And (as I toucht before) wee now see our too secure Kingdom must also share in these common calamities, now fallen upon the [p. 17] earth, England having sinned, and done very foolishly, England must also come under the lash of Gods justice and greatly incensed indignation against it, as well as Germany, Rochell and Ireland.

Before I can leave the blazoning of this Blazing-star, I must give the Reader one more remarkable note and observation on it. Namely, that at the first appearing of this Star, wee were all in peace, and (seeming) serene tranquility, but indeed (as was fore-mentioned) such a peace as justly rendred us setled on the lees of carnall security. Even as if this Star had been sent among us in speciall to fore-warne us of our present too loose security, and therefore future ensuing infelicity, if not speedily prevented by true and unfained repentance. For, it first appeared, as I said, the 18 of November, the day after the annuall memoriall of Queen *Elizabeths* (of ever most famous memory) most [p. 18] happy inauguration to the Crowne of England, the day when we began to enjoy the liberty of the Gospel, and deliverance from that former most formidable yoke of Romish Egyptian bondage and slavery, under bloody Babylonish and terrible conscience-curbing task-masters, and which so blessed liberty, we have now in a good and great measure enjoyed, at least, these three-score yeares. And this, I say, seemed most particularly to bee delineated out unto us, by this notable Comets appearing just on the next day to the 17 of November, as if the Lord would, thus, have expostulated with us.[33] O England, ungratefull and unfruitfull England, thou hast, now, these sixty yeares by my free favour and bounty, enjoyed my Gospel of pure peace, together with the sweet and amiable peace of this my Gospel, but hast beene, all the while but little the better (if not far the worser) by it. Well, though I [p. 19] confesse I know not what I could have done more for England, my choyce vine, my pleasant plant, then I have done, having so hedged, digged and dressed it; yea, and watered it with the dewes and drops of heaven: and now that I expected it should have brought me forth sweet grapes of faith and pure obedience, it hath contrariwise brought forth the wilde grapes of sin and rebellion;

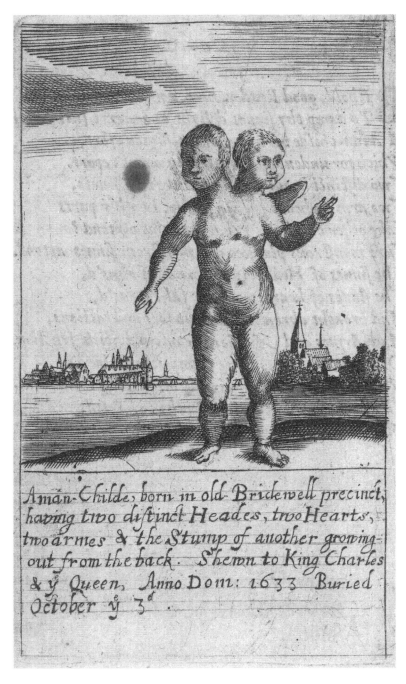

Figure 3.3 "A man-Childe, born in old-Bridewell precinct, having two distinct
Heades, two Hearts, two armes & the Stump of another growing-out from
the back. Shewn to King Charles & y^e Queen, Anno Dom: 1633 Buried
October ye 3^d," from John Vicars' *Prodigies & Apparitions*, 1643, p. 21.

Source: RB 148141, The Huntington Library, San Marino, California.

though, I say, it deserves (like the fruitlesse Fig-tree[34]) to be cut down, and not suffered to encumber the ground any longer: yet, out of my meer mercy and indulgence to England, I will let it alone one yeare of patience more, and onely shake my rod over it, with this prodigious apparition, and celestiall signe of my just displeasure, as a premonition thereof to move it to repentance, which if it cordially fall upon, well and good; if not, whereas, all this while, I have been severely whipping and scourging other neighbour-nations, e- [p. 20] specially her sister Ireland, to make England (if it might be) wise by others woes, my leaden-heeles of long-sufferance, patience, and compassion, shall be found to have Iron-hands of wrath without remedy; and then I will doe my work, my strange worke, and bring to passe my act, my strange act (Is. 28:21); and when I begin, I will also make an end (1 Sam. 3:12). The Lord, timely, open the eyes of Englands understanding, that shee may see (yet) in this her day, the things that concern her eternall peace; lest, hereafter they bee everlastingly hid from her.

A second warning-piece (worthy our serious notice) of Gods gracious longanimity[35] and patient forbearance, toward us, notwithstanding our pertinacious provocations, and refractory rebellions towards him, may be this. A prodigious-birth, and monstrous Man-childe, borne in Old-bride-well, about October 3. 1633. having two heads, two

[p. 21 – Figure 3.3; p. 22 – poem[36]]

[p. 23] hearts, two armes, and a stump, beside. This childe was borne of poor parents, inhabitants in that precinct. Which foresaid Birth, being so marvellous and prodigious a Monster in nature, was carried and shewed to King *Charles* our Soveraigne, and his royall consort, the Queen, who greatly astonisht at the sight thereof, most graciously and charitably sent the poore woman, the mother of it, five pieces, to refresh her in her present poverty and weaknesse.

Now, whereas, peradventure, some may here object and say; Why doe you count this such a wonder which is (as the Naturalists and Philosophers affirme and write) but a deficiencie and weaknesse of nature?

Whereunto I answer, This is an objection indeed, but of a meere naturalist and carnall man, who is willing only to look upon externall and secondarie causes, not considering the wonders and operations of Gods hands. *David* [p. 24] could say, that a man in his ordinary, naturall, and well-composed generation, is fearfully and wonderfully made;[37] how much more terribly and wonderfully, when the Lord is pleased to frame such a fearfull and wonder-striking birth in the womb of his creature, so contrary to nature? And did not the Lord Jesus Christ himselfe, the fountaine of wisedome and understanding, (yea far more wise then all the Naturalists and Philosophers that ever were or will be) tell his Disciples, who curiously questioned the cause, why that man (mentioned in the Gospel) that was borne blinde from his mothers wombe; was so made by God, that the Lords mighty power might be manifested in him?[38] And although it cannot be denied but that sometimes such monstrous births are produced by defect of nature: yet its as true that frequently the Lord is pleased to cause such monstrous productions from his [p. 25] creatures, as predictions and forerunners of some fearfull judgement to come for sinne. For otherwise, God could have given power (as in an ordinary way he does) to have brought forth to perfection.

But tis confest clearly, by that wise and famous Historian *Josephus*, fore-mentioned at the beginning of this Treatise, who there, brings in that strange and unnaturall birth of the Cow which brought forth (in the Temple of Jerusalem) a Lamb instead of a Calfe, and which he there introduceth as one of the fearfull forerunners and signes of Jerusalems ensuing misery and desolation; to which prodigious birth, this also, me thinkes, may fitly be a paralell, and justly be taken for a fearfull prediction of wrath to come, if not prevented by timely repentance.

And why may wee not yet farther consider, even with particular application, this monstrous birth, to this effect? [p. 26] That God, by these two heads, two hearts, two armes, and a stump of another in this child, might let us now see his hastning judgements and wrath on our Kingdoms of England and Ireland, wherein hath beene too manifestly seen to our sorrow, such divisions; by two heads, the King and this renowned Parliament, some siding with the one, and some with the other: by two hearts, Papists and Protestants, or Malignant and well affected Christians, some standing for Truth, and some for Errour; some for Christ, and some for Antichrist; some for Gospel and a holy Reformation, and some for beggarly Ceremonies and Romish trash and trumpery; two armes or armies for just defence in England and Scotland, and a miserable and monstrous stump of an arme in lamentably torne and mangled Ireland. And this use, I remember our brethren in New England, not long since made of another most prodigious [p. 27] and mishapen and monstrous birth, brought foorth by a Gentlewoman of that New Plantation, who had beene a maine fautrix,[39] if not originall broacher of very many most wicked, dangerous, & damnable opinions in their Church: God having declared his high displeasure therat, by her so fearfull monstrous and mis-shapen birth, which, as a godly Minister there related, had as many externall and corporall deformities in its body, as she maintained diversities of most dangerous opinions. Which was all of it, I say, testified for most true, by some of the most learned and godly Pastours and people amongst them.[40]

Againe, have we not had many most remarkable warnings and fearfull forerunners of Gods displeasure against us for our sinns and transgressions, by most hideous and horrour-striking-thunder-claps, and spirit-affrighting-Lightnings, doing much and most fearfull hurt, bur- [p. 28] ning, defacing and spoiling our very materiall Churches and houses in this Kingdome, most manifestly giving us to understand that something, surely, is much amisse even in our Churches and worship and service of the Lord our God (as I shall afterward more particularly and truly shew) in our most sumptuous and superfluously huge built Churches and Cathedrall Minsters,

Figure 3.4 "A most prodigious & fearefull storme of winde lightning & thunder, mightily defaceing Withcomb-church in Devon[shire] burning and slayeing diverse men and women all this in service-time, on the Lords day Octob: 21. 1638," from John Vicars' *Prodigies & Apparitions*, 1643, p. 30.

indeed farre more like Heathen Temples then Christian Churches. And as an undoubted testimony of Gods displeasure heerein, take first that most memorable and terrible, yea never to bee forgotten example of Gods wrath & deep indignation manifested by thunder and lightning, against super-stitious superfluous and idolatrous impieties in our Churches of England, which God was pleased to manifest upon the Parish Church of *Withcombe* in Devonshire,[41] (besides divers other Churches in other places, much about the same time [p. 29] also, which is the more remarkeable) being a very faire Church, and but then newly trimmed, having a very fayre Towre with great and small pinnacles, and reported to be one of the fairest and most famous Church steeples in all the Westerne parts of England; which I have heere described and set foorth in this Figure and Embleme for the Readers better content and satisfaction.

Which said faire Church and steeple was most fearfully and furiously assaulted with most hideous thunder and lightning on the 21. day of *October* 1638. (which also was so much the more admirable, being in the Winter season) which was the Lords Day, and in the time of their Church Service or Evening Prayer (still the more observable) in the midst of the performance of which duties, I say, on a sudden there was heard most fearfull & heart-damping claps of thunder, much like the roaring noise or ratling reports of great

[p. 30 – Figure 3.4; p. 31 – poem[42]]

[p. 32] Canons, and musket shot discharged; upon which, presently fol-lowed a most fearfull Fog, and almost palpable darknesse all over the Church, and a most strong and almost stifling Stygian[43] stink and loath-some smell of brimstone, together with a most boysterous and blustering blast of wind and clap of thunder, which strucke in at the Northside of the steeple or towre, and tearing through a strong wall came into the Church through the highest window, and bare before it sheere away, a great part thereof, and with a mighty power it also strook away the Northside wall of the Church, and violently battered and shook it very much, passing on toward the Pulpit, and in the way tooke with it the lime and sand from off the wall, grating the wall much and mightily defacing it, it having been but lately new whited and trimmed, as aforesaid. It tore away also most fiercely the side Deske from the Pulpit, colouring [p. 33] the pulpit it selfe of a black hew, and leaving it as moist as if it had been newly washed over with inke. In which time there was also a most terrible and heart-astonishing light-ning, which did both mightily affright the people, and even scald their skin with the extreame heat thereof; insomuch as the greatest part of them fell prostrate, some on their faces, and some on their knees, and some one upon another, screeking and crying out in a most pittifull and patheticall manner.

The Ministers wife, there present, had her Ruffe and Linnen next her body, burnt off, and her body it self grievously scorched. One Mistresse *Ditford*, sitting in the seat with her, had her Gowne, two Wast-coats, and her linnen next her body also grievously scorched. Another woman frighted with this fearfull spectacle, running out of the Church, had her cloathes set on fire, her body scorched, her flesh torne [p. 34] on her back in a most grievous manner. One Master *Hill*, a Gentleman had his head smitten against the wall, and died the very next day of it. Sir *Richard Reynolds* his Warriner[44] had his head cloven, his skull rent in three pieces, whereof two fell in the next seat, the other fell down in the seat where he sate: his braines fell entirely whole into the next seat behinde him, his blood dasht against the wall; some of the skin of his head, flesh and haire, to the quantity of an handfull, was carried into the Chancell, his body left in the seat, as though he had been alive, sitting asleep, and leaning on his elbow resting on the desk of his Pew, with the fore-part of his head and face whole. O most terrible and fearfull power of the Lord! A man that sate before him, in the same seat, was scalded and burnt all over on that side next the said Warriner. In the second seat behinde the Warriner, a man was in a most grievous manner [p. 35] burnt and scalded all over his body, so as he was all over like raw flesh, and lived in great misery about a week after, and then died. A Dogge neere the Chancell doore, was fiercely whirled up three times, and the last time fell down dead. Some seats in the body of the Church, were torn up, and overwhelmed up-side-down; yet they that were in them had no harme, notwithstanding that they were thereby throwne out of them into other seats foure or five pewes higher. About the number of eight boyes sitting about the railes of the Communion Table (heere wee may observe what a superstitious Church it was, like, almost all the rest of our Churches in these miserable daies) were all of them taken up by the violence of this so terrible a storme, and throwne on heaps within the railes, but had no hurt at all. A beame was broken in the midst, and fell downe between the Minister and his Clerke, but [p. 36] neither of them hurt thereby. The Church was also very much defaced and torn in many parts of it, and a great stone neere the very foundation, was torne up and removed thence. Other stones were violently throwne out of the tower, as thick as if there had been an hundred men throwing them, some stones of them of such a weight and bignesse, as no one man was able to lift. One of the Pinacles of the Tower was tumbled downe into the Church. A man sitting on the Church-beere, at the lower end of the Church, had the said beere torne in pieces under him, and himself thrown into a seat by the wall, but had no other hurt. A great stone was throwne about an hundred yards from the Church, and sunke into the ground so deep and so fast, that it could hardly be seen afterward. A Bowling-alley also neere the Church-yard, was strangely turned into deep pits; and a Wine-Taverne nere the Church, had [p. 37] the side thereof next the Church torne up, and the top or covering broken and caried off, and one of the rafters broken into the said house.

And was not heere a most terrible and almost an incredible print and impression of Gods threatned wrath and indignation against both the internall and externall vanity and impiety of such profuse and superfluous Church-buildings, vaine and needlesse, I say, now under the Gospel, though in the time of the Leviticall Law, most requisite and lawfull in most gorgeous maner to be set out, as typifying Christ Jesus in all his excellencies and graces; and therefore these fearefull examples may serve as a remarkable caution and fore-warning of Gods displeasure heerein. But because tis likely, our super-stitious Cathedralists will bee apt to object in their carnall incredulity, that one Swallow makes not a Summer, and so one single testimony is not suf-ficient to con- [p. 38] firme so weighty a conclusion and inference as I would fain gather from these fearefull premises. I shall therefore in the next place give the Reader other remarkable examples of Gods semblable[45] undoubted displeasure with the vanity and impiety of our Churches and Church gov-ernment, and services too long exercised among us to the high indignation of the Lord [(]especially now of late, since our Prelats began so grosly to tyrannize over the consciences of Gods people) and then say, whether thou canst not easily be induced to beleeve with me, this truth, which I have hence collected, and which the Lord by these feareful examples, seems most plainly to have indigitated[46] and demonstrated to us. And therefore to cry out with the Prophet in holy admiration and trembling, Who would not feare thee, O King of Nations, to whom it belongeth justly to punish sinners (Jer. 10:7)?

In January also then next ensuing, [p. 39] there was very great hurt done, in and upon divers other Churches, in other parts of this Kingdome, by thunder and lightning, and mighty stormy weather, to the great and terrible astonishment of the inhabitants and beholders. As namely upon the 14. day of the aforesayd month, about five of the clock at night, three Churches were wasted and defaced with fearefull thunder and lightning, and most violent windes; the one was *Micham* in Kent, also *Greenhith* and *Stone-Church*, both in the sayd County of Kent. And upon Whitsunday 1640. in the Parish Church of *S. Anthony* in Cornewall, great hurt was done by terrible thunder and lightning, the people being then in the Church at their Sabbath dayes exercises.[47] As heer thou seest it summarily and briefly deline-ated in those following Figures or Emblemes.

[p. 40 – Figure 3.5; p. 41 – poem[48]]

[p. 42] Now all these considered together, with the time of the yeere, the Winter season, and the day whereon they fell, the Lords day, and (that, which is so much the more remarkable) in the time of their Sabbath dayes duties; tell me, can any man be so Atheistically minded and blindly or obstinately opinionated as to thinke that these so fearfull and formidable affright-ments immediately from heaven, can bee meerly casuall or contingent by naturall concurrences only, and not rather immediate demonstrations and fore-runners of Gods high indignation for the great sins and provocations of our Clergy and Prelaticall Church-government. Certainly it were meere madnesse, or at least grosse carnall security, if not diabolicall delusion,

Figure 3.5 "3 or 4 Churches more, as namely Micham and Greenhith in Kent also Stone-church, all fearefully defaced with lightning and thunder, the Ianuary following And St Anthonies Church in Cornwall, Anno Dom: 1640," from John Vicars' *Prodigies & Apparitions*, 1643, p. 40.

Source: RB 148141, The Huntington Library, San Marino, California.

to say, or thinke otherwise. For, if we looke on our late most intolerable superstitious and idolatrous times, not silently-creeping, but audaciously running, and (with the Romish-whores un- [p. 43] blushing face) breaking out upon us, and impudently and too frequently practised among us by crossing and Jesu-cringing, altar-worship, rayling in of our Communion-tables turned into altars, Popish, sumptuous and superstitious adornation and bedawbing of Churches with crucifixes & other Popish pictures, apish gestures, vestures, and such like beggarly-rudiments and ceremonies, as the Apostle cals them (Gal. 4:9, Col. 2:20); making more, by farre, of the meere wals, and dead stones of their Churches, than of the living stones of Gods House and Temple. What other thing could be discovered by all these, but a most disloyall apostacy, and almost a generall backsliding and defection from our first love the Lord Jesus Christ, and from his sound faith, to Antichrist, Arminianisme, and Atheisticall profanenesse, both in Priest and people.

And may we not then justly conceive and beleeve that the Lord, by these so [p. 44] fearfull, and I dare say unparallel'd examples of wrath on (even) these materiall Churches, might truly indigitate and point-out unto us his holy purpose to ruinate this Romish-rubbish, to purge his holy Temple and worship, from these out-side formalities and fopperies, and to set up and establish a more pure and powerfull, a more precious and glorious inter-nall, spirituall, simple, and plaine unmixed-worship to himselfe, and such faithfull and fruitfull worshippers, as should worship him in spirit and in truth, in plaine simplicity and singlenesse of heart (John 4:23); for, such worshippers, now under the Gospel, hath hee chosen to himself, as our Saviour Christ Jesus himselfe assures us, whose infallible heavenly author-ity I choose rather to beleeve, then the best and most reverend (pretended) antiquity of primitive Fathers, and humane authorities, so urgently and instantly pressed upon us by our late Romish-hearted Prelates, and [p. 45] Pontifician Doctors whomsoever.

What a most notable warning-piece also did the Lord make visible unto us by Sea, about the moneth of September, 1640. namely, that Spanish Fleet which came (without controule) most audaciously upon our English coasts, with many and mighty Vessels full fraught and furnished with armes, ammunition, and many thousand Souldiers (almost such another formidable and affrighting Armado, as that was in 1588[49]) thinking then also to have swallowed us up, and to have found us and our brethren of Scotland together by the eares, that so they might with the more ease have unresistibly set firme footing, and securely have landed on our English shore, and so have stept in betweene both parties, and have made up their mouthes with a fat and full prey of three rich and royall Diademes at once; which, indeed, hath beene the long expected prize of the Spaniards [p. 46] most greedy appetite and hungry hope to have made up his long dreamed of universall Monarchy; as here you see it set forth and described in this next Figure or Embleme.

Figure 3.6 "A second Spanish-Armado, much like that in, 1588 hovering about our
English – Sea's near Deale & Dover, hoping to have made England thier
[*sic*] pray & to have found us fighting with our brethren of Scotland;
but beaten back and destroyed by Van Trump and his Dutch Fleet An:
Dom: 1642," from John Vicars' *Prodigies & Apparitions*, 1643, p. 47.

Source: RB 148141, The Huntington Library, San Marino, California.

[p. 47 – Figure 3.6; p. 48 – poem⁵⁰]

[p. 49] But it pleased the Lord to direct the Dutch Fleet, at that time abroad at Sea, under the command of *Van Tromp* their Admirall, to meet with them, and (before Deale and Dover) to fight with them for us, when wee little thought of fighting for our selves, though ready to be made a prey to this devouring Spanish-Leviathan.⁵¹ Here, I say also, did the Lord, by them, ring us such a peale of thundring Canon, as it were knocking at our doores to awaken us out of our marvellous Lethargy of ease and carnall security, or of blockish stupidity, as might have beene thought sufficient to have made us recollect our thoughts, open our eyes and looke about us, and see the hand of God lifted up against us, yet loath to let the stroke fall so heavily upon us, to our irrccoverable ruine and destruction, as our sinnes most justly deserved, had hee in his justice so dealt with us.

On Thursday also, August 4. 1642.⁵² [p. 50] about 5. of the clocke in the afternoone, at a Towne called Alborough in the County of Suffolke, there was heard in the ayre, and evidently seene, a mighty sound of drummes beating very loud, after which was also heard at the same time, a long and fierce peale of small shot, as of Muskets and such like, and then as it were a discharging of great Ordnance in a pitcht field; all this continuing about an houre and a halfe, and then there was a mighty and terrible report or noise of them all together: At the ceasing whereof a blacke stone was as it were shot out of the skye, being about eight inches long, and five or sixe inches broad, and about two inches thicke, which was taken up by two men which stood by and heard the foresaid noise, and the whistling of the stone over their head as it past by them (but they could not see it) they found it by meanes of a little dogge, who followed it by the s[c]ent, and ran barking to and [p. 51] fro, till they following the dogge, were brought to the place where it lay, covered with earth and grasse. The men that found it brought it to London, and presented it to a Burgesse of Parliament, upon whose ground it was found, and by him was shewne to divers others. One Captaine *Johnson*, and one Master *Thompson*, men well knowne in those parts of Suffolke, being at a Towne called Woodbridge, hearing of this marvellous noyse toward Alborough, verily supposing that some enemy was landed, and had made some sodaine onset or invasion upon the Town, took horse and rode hastily homeward, the rather because they heard of the battaile louder and louder, and being on their way neare Alborough, they met with the greatest part of the townsmen, who were generally run out of their houses, round about, much amazed with such an uncouth noise of war. But after all this, there was, for certaine, sodainly [p. 52] heard a most joyfull noyse of sweet musicke, and of sundry rare musicall instruments sounding in a most melodious manner, for a good space together, and at last it all concluded with a most harmonious noise, as it were of delicate ringing of well-tuned bels.

Figure 3.7 "A most terrible representation of a great fight in the Ayre at Alborough in Suffolk, drum's beateing; Can[n]ons and Musketts-shooting, a black stone shooting out from the cloudes found by a dogg, on the ground, but all, at last, ending with most melodious musick, and ringing of belles as an triumph of some victories Aug: 4. 1642," from John Vicars' *Prodigies & Apparitions*, 1643, p. 53.

Source: RB 148141, The Huntington Library, San Marino, California.

[p. 53 – Figure 3.7; p. 54 – poem⁵³]

[p. 55] Now this Tragi-Comicall Warning-piece (for so methinkes I may fitly call it) which we have here described and set forth, as well as a figure and expression of that nature might be; beginning so terribly, and concluding so sweetly, did far transcend, in prognosticating comfort, in the issue, all the fore-mentioned marvellous prodigies and predictions, either in Jerusalem, Germany, or elsewhere among us; and may therefore (surely) serve as a soveraigne antidote against our too much fainting and affrighting feares. The Lord our good God seeming hereby to foreshew us (as blessed Mr. *Brightman* also, that famous Divine, and faithfull servant of the Lord, in his most bright and learned revelation of the Revelations of Saint *John*, hath even prophetically written⁵⁴) that Englands terrible storme of woes and warres now begun in it, by Papists, Atheists, and profane Malignants, whom God hath stirred up to disturb [p. 56] its abused peace and plenty, and as a just punishment of Englands great sins and enormities, though for a while it may seeme sharp, yet shall be short, and prove sweet in the issue, fanning away the chaffe, and burning up the drosse thereof, and making way for a glorious peace and perfect reformation, and for the setting up of Christs Throne, and advancing of his Scepter, in the power and purity of holy ordinances, in the issue and conclusion.

It is our part therefore, in faith, patience, and prayer, to possesse our souls, and to wait on the Lord for the happy performance of the same in his due time, and by that way which is best pleasing to his most wise providence. And the Lord in mercy perfect our expectation thereof in his appointed season. Amen and Amen.

I have made no mention all the while, of the many strange, fearfull, and unaccustomed Eclipses of the Sunne and [p. 57] Moone, which have been seen from yeare to yeare both in other parts, and also in our owne English Horizon; which also by the judgement of the best Astrologers and Mathematicians, have and doe prognosticate and declare unto us, many notable changes and overtures of States and Kingdoms; as also that late and memorable conjunction of *Saturne* and *Jupiter* among us in February last, 1643. which hath been written of long before it fell out; and which (with all the rest) doth prognosticate and demonstrate unto us (as so many Warning-pieces) the great alteration and vicissitude of Kingdoms, Countreyes, times and things in Church and State; especially, I say, this late and great conjunction of those two celestiall Planets as Mr. *Booker* in his Prognostication for this instant yeare 1643. doth most notably declare and manifest unto us.⁵⁵

But of these, and some other such [p. 58] like strange apparitions in the aire, I shall desire (with wise King *Solomon*) all my Christian brethren and friends) [sic] to take holy and wholsome counsell which the Spirit of God prompts the children of wisedome to embrace and follow, *viz.* A prudent man fore-sees the evill (or approaching storme) and hideth himself from it. And what better, nay what so safe a hiding-place as the clifts and holes of the Rocks, even the wounds of the Lord Jesus Christ, that immoveable and everlasting Rock of our Salvation [Ps. 95:1], and under the holy and heavenly wings of the Sunne of Righteousnesse [Mal. 4:2]; where onely (as the Prophet sayes) is true and infallible Soule-healing comfort indeed, to all truly penitent, and conscience-wounded sinners, who with godly sorrow, and unfained repentance and reformation, by faith in prayer, seeke and sue unto him; which, the Lord give us all wisedome and grace so to doe. Amen.

FINIS.

◆

A Great
WONDER
IN
HEAVEN:
SHEWING
The late Apparitions and prodigious
noyses of War and Battels, seen on *Edge-Hill*
neere Keinton in Northampton-shire.

Certified under the hands of *William Wood*
Esquire, and Justice for the *Peace* in the said
Countie, *Samuel Marshall* Preacher
of Gods Word in *Keinton,*
and other persons of
qualitie.

LONDON,
Printed for THO. JACKSON,
Jan. 23. Anno Dom. 1642.[56]

[p. 3] A great wonder in HEAVEN:

Shewing the late Apparitions and Prodigious noyses of War and Battails
seen on Edge-Hill neer Keynton in Northampton-shire.

THAT there hath beene, and ever will be *Larvæ*[57] [,] *spectra,* and
such like apparitions, namely, Ghosts and Goblins, have beene the opinion of all the famousest Divines of the Primitive Church, and is (though
oppugned[58] by some) the received Doctrine of divers learned men at this
day, their opinion being indeed ratified and confirmed by divers Texts
of Scripture, as the Divells possessing the Swine [Mat. 8:28–34], and the
men possessed with Divells in the *Acts* of the Apostles, that came out of
them, and beat the Exorcists [Acts 19:13–16], by which it is evidently
confirmed, that those legions of erring angels that fell with their great
Master, *Lucifer,* are not all confined to the locall Hell, but live scattered
here and there, dispersed in the empty regions of the ayre as thicke as
motes in the Sunne, and those are those things which our too superstitious ancestors called Elves and Goblins, Furies, and the like, such as
were those who appeared to *Machbeth* the after King [p. 4] of *Scotland,*
and foretold him of his fortunes both in life and death.[59] It is evident,
besides, that the divell can condense the ayre into any shape he pleaseth;
as hee is a subtill spirit, thin and open, and rancke himselfe into any
forme or likenesse, as Saint *Augustin, Prudentius, Hieronimus,*[60] *Cyril,*

Saint *Basil* the Great; and none better then our late Soveraigne King *James* of ever-living memory, in his Treatise *de Dæmonologia*, hath sufficiently proved: but to omit circumstance[61] and preamble, no man that thinkes hee hath a soule, but will verily and confidently believe that there are divels, and so consequently such divels as appeare either in premonstrance of Gods Judgements, or as fatall Embassadours to declare the message of mortality and destruction on offending Nations; and hath in *Germany* and other places afflicted afterwards with the horror of a civill and forraigne warres notoriously manifested.

But to our purpose *Edge-Hill* in the very confines of *Warwickeshire*, neere unto *Keynton* in *Northamptonshire*, a place, as appears by the sequele, destined for civill warres and battels; as where King *John* fought a battell with his Barons,[62] and who in the defence of the Kingdomes lawes and libertie was fought a bloody conflict betweene his Majesties and the Parliaments forces, who under the conduct of his Excellence the Earle of *Essex*, obtained there a glorious victory over the Cavaliers at this *Edge-Hill*, in the very place where the battell was strucken, have since, and doth appeare, strange and portentuous *Apparitions* of two jarring and contrary Armies, as I shall in order deliver, it being certified by the men of most credit in those parts, as *William Wood* Esquire, *Samuel Marshall* Minister, and others, on Saturday, which was in Christmas time, as if the Saviour of the world, who died to redeeme mankind, had beene angry that so much Christian blood was there spilt, and so had permitted these Infernall Armies to appeare, [p. 5] where the corporeall Armies had shed so much blood; between twelve and one of the clock in the morning was heard by some Sheepherds, and other countrey-men and travellers, first the sound of Drums a far off, and the noyse of Soulders, as it were, giving out their last groanes; at which they were much amazed, and amazed stood still, till it seemed by the neernesse of the noyse to approach them, at which too much affrighted, they sought to withdraw as fast as possibly they could, but then on the sudden, whilest they were in these cogitations, appeared in the ayre the same incorporeall souldiers that made those clamours, and immediately with Ensignes displayed[,] Drums beating, Musquets going off, Cannons discharged, Horses neyghing, which also to these men were visible, the alarum or entrance to this game of death was strucke up, one Army which gave the first charge, having the Kings colours, and the other the Parliaments in their head or front of the battells, and so pell mell to it they went; the battell that appeared to the Kings forces seeming at first to have the best, but afterwards to be put into apparent rout; but till two or three in the morning in equall scale continued this dreadfull fight, the clattering of Armes, noyse of Cannons, cries of souldiers so amazing and terrifying the poore men, that they could not believe they were mortall, or give credit to their eares and eyes, runne away they durst not, for feare of being made a prey to these infernall souldiers, and so they with much feare and affright, stayed to behold the successe of the businesse, which at last suited to this effect: after some three houres fight, that Army which carryed the Kings colours withdrew, or rather appeared to flie; the other remaining, as it were, Masters of the field, stayed a good space triumphing, and expressing all the signes of joy and conquest,[63] and then with all their Drummes, Trumpets, Ordnance and Souldiers vanished, the poore men [p. 6] glad they were gone, that had so long staid them there against their wils, made with all haste to Keinton, and there knocking up Mr. *Wood*, a Justice of Peace, who called up his neighbour Mr. *Marshall* the Minister, they gave them an account of the whole passage, and averred it upon their oaths to be true. At which affirmation of theirs, being much amazed, they should hardly have given credit to it, but would have conjectured the men to have been either mad or drunk, had they not knowne some of them to have been of approved integritie; and so suspending their judgements till the next night about the same houre, they with the same men, and all the substantiall Inhabitants of that and the neighbouring parishes, drew thither; where about halfe an houre after their arrivall on Sunday, being Christmas night, appeared in the same tumultuous warlike manner, the same two adverse Armies, fighting was as much spite and spleen as formerly: and so departed the Gentlemen and all the spectatours, much terrified with these visions of horrour, withdrew themselves to their houses, beseeching God to defend them from those hellish and prodigious enemies. The next night they appeared not, nor all that week, so that the dwellers thereabout were in good hope they had been for ever departed; but on the ensuing Saturday night, in the same place, and at the same houre, they were againe seene, with far greater tumult fighting in the manner afore-mentioned for foure houres, or verie neere, and then vanished, appearing againe on Sunday night, and performing the same actions of hostilitie and bloud-shed; so that both Mr, *Wood* and others, whose faith it should seeme was not strong enough to carrie them out against these delusions, forsook their habitations thereabout, and retired themselves, to other more secure dwellings; but Mr. *Marshall* stayed, and some other, and so successively the next Saturday and Sunday the same tumults and prodigious sights and actions were put in the state and condition they were formerly. The rumour [p. 7] whereof comming to his Majestie at Oxford, he immediately dispatched thither Colonell *Lewis Kirke*, Captaine *Dudley*, Captaine *Wainman*, and three other Gentlemen of credit, to take the full view and notice of the said businesse, who first hearing the true attestation[64] and relation of Mr. *Marshall* and others, staid there till Saturday night following, wherein they heard and saw the fore-mentioned prodigies, and so on Sunday distinctly knowing divers of the apparitions, or incorporeall substances by their faces, as that of Sir *Edmund Varney*,[65] and others that were there slaine; of which upon oath they made testimony to his Majestie. What this does portend, God only knoweth, and time perhaps will discover; but doubtlessly it is a signe of his wrath against this Land, for these civill wars, which He in his good time finish, and send a sudden peace between his Majestie and Parliament.

FINIS.

————————◆————————

THE NEW
YEARES
WONDER.
BEING
A most cernaine [*sic*] and true Relation of the disturbed
inhabitants of *Kenton*,

And other neighbouring villages neere unto *Edge-
Hil*, where the great battaile betwixt the kings
army, and the Parliaments forces was
fought.

In which place is heard & seene fearfull and strange
apparitions of spirits as sounds of drums, trumpets,
with the discharging of Canons Muskies, Carbines pettronels,[66] to the terrour and amazement, of all the fearfull hearers and
behoulders.

Certified under the hands of *William Wood*, Esquier,
and Justice for the *Peace* in the said Countie,
Samuel Marshall, Preacher of Gods
Word in *Keynton*, and other
persons of qualitie.

Printed for Robert Ellit, lodger neer the
old Rose in Thames-street, who was
an eye witnesse unto this.[67]

[p. 2 – woodcut of five soldiers, with the regimental drum, pipe, and banner]
[p. 3] THE NEW
YEARES
WONDER.
BEING
A most cartain and true Relation, of the disturbed inhabitance of *Kenton*,
and other neighboring villages neere *Edg-Hill*.

NOT altogether disalowing of old folkes similys and saying that winters
nights, thunder[68] presageth events[69] of sumars [i.e. summer's] strange wonders, which is greatly to be feard & doubted if it begin before sumar and
ushers in the new yeare amoungst us with such care terour and strange eye
[p. 4] optick appearance, as is by divers affirmed and related.

To which avoydance therefoer, wee ought every hopefull and belee[v]ing christian to put on new obedience unto Heaven, and begin with the new yeare, a newnesse of life & conversation, with the endevr of continuance till the nihgt [*sic*] of our death comes.

With love feare & obedience contineu [*sic*] in prayers to Almighty God, that he would be pleased to call back his destroying Angell from amongst us, and with the hand of his mercy sheath up the sword of his venganc[e],[70] which his wrath by our multiplying sinns caus'd him [to] draw against us, unto our feares and terours.

Still apearing a prodigious meteor or [i.e. over] the fearefull head of this distracted Kingdome, and that this little Ile that was but late the admiration of larger[71] Christend[o]me, for selfe accomodation and comerce for plenty and for every thing besides, with such a largnes of abundancy that it almost needeth noe affinity with any neighbouring nation but its owne.

And now to see the change times heere hath made, and with it made us a la[u]ghter to the world to see our selves divided against ourselves, doing ourselves that ill, which forain nations would but could not doe.

Which Heaven of his mercy grant a period that both the offended sides no more may sheath their wraths in one another, but be freinds, and brandish palmes insted of polaxes and that these apparitions I am entring in Relation of, beget no farther Sumer [p. 5] feare amoungst us.

As famine from evasion and utter reuine that may enter in that gap we open our selves, and that no more such fields as *Kenton*, may be fought nor *Edge-Hill* sharpened to cut us more.[72]

Whose troubles peete of earth plastred with English goare and turned unto[73] a golgotha[74] of bones is now become the plot of feare and horrour, whose earth now groning with the weight of lives whose last beds there were maid to sleepe upon, rests in[.]

Whose dying grones a second time revives[75] breking the caverns of the covring[76] earth, and sends both feare and horour round about to terifie the living with dead soules, which first amasing wonder began his shadowing apparitons on the first of *January*, as neere as the relatours gest [i.e. guessed] in the afternone betwixt three and foure of the clocke which was beheld by three Countrymen rideing a long the way in the likenesse of a Troope of horse posting up to them with full speede, which caus'd the Countrymen to make a stop as fearfull of their events.[77]

But coming neer unto them they of a sudaine sunke into the earth which turned to their more greater feare and amaizement then at there first advancing.

But seeing some certain heards-men atending on cattell in the fields they rode up to them who related the same story which thay were eye witnisses [p. 6] unto them[;] the horsemen at the heards[78]-mens confermation of what themselves had seene[79] ware so affrighted that they resolved[80] to goe no farther then *Kenton* that night, where the on[e] being glad of eithers human sosiety a companyes each other.

Where having taking up there nightly habitation they began to relate it unto the Townesmen, the on[e] confirming the words of the other both strangers and there townes dweling heardsmen, which soone was spred abroad[81] but few or none that had belife unto't.

On the morning the strangers departed & thouhgt [though] al the towne heard the relation of it, yet they made slight of it, this passed on till the forth of *January* nothing more heard or seene, which made the poore heardsmen the more derided for it[.]

But the forth of *January* being come many of the towne went to [the place where] the heardsmen grased there cattell, jeering the poore men, when should they heard more wowders [*sic*] from them[.]

But the day being spent, and all the Towne at rest within there beds, about the midle season of the night, that which apeard to them rediculus, gave them a Testimony of their owne belife.

For why the dolfull and the hydious groanes of dying men were heard crying revenge and some againe to ease them of their paine by friendly killing them, this waked many in the towne, and sent they [i.e. them] trembling agues in there beds, [p. 7] But their to amplifie the noyse of Drumes[82] and Trumpets sounded a sudaine alarum as if an enimye had entred in their towne to put them to a sudaine exicution and plunder all their estates.

Some hid themselves in corners, some over-head and eares lay sweating and halfe smothered in their beds, and some of better courage looke through the winddowes where they to there apearing visibly saw armed horseman riding one againe the other and so vanisht all.

Many women['s] feare made them miscary, and the stoutest hearted man amoungst them all could not denye but that then he feared death.

Next night they set strong watch every where and from there neighbouring townes gathered more assistance[;] the crosse heyway and every place besides was strongly warded neither would women or children that were able keepe either house or beds.

But they [*sic*] expected houer of twelve being come, Drumes and Trumpets gave againe to sound a larum[83] to fight and all the spirit horse and foot appeared and stood in battleray, the foot againe the foot and horse against the horse discherging of M. peetternell[84] and Carbines the one againe the other, falling to the ground on either side apace, and Ordinance playing on against the other as plainely visable to the behoul[d]ers view as if the reall action had bin there.

All night it lasted in this hidious[85] maner, but at the break of day all as they formarly in the twinkling [p. 8] of an eye did vanish.

But since hath no more bin seene which caus'd the Inhabitants of *Kenton* to forsake their Towne and get new ha[b]itations for themselves.

But some learned men have since delivered their opininons [*sic*], that there may be yet unburied ka[r]ckasses found, so dilligent search hath bin made, and found it so.

Which God of his mercy cease these warrs and blesse our Land with peace.

Mr. *Marshall* the Minister of *Kenton*, went to *Oxon* [Oxford] to the King, and did informe him of the apparitions of all the aforesaid proceedings of the spirits.

THE King presently sent to *Edge-Hill* Colonell *Lewis Kirke*, Captaine *Dudly*, Captaine *Winman*, and three other Gentelmen of worth who heard of this sad fearful and hidious sight which[86] Mr. *Marshall*, related to his Majesty and then departed wonderous fearfull amaized and affrighted, & saw divers to their apperance that were there slaine as Sir *Edmund Varney*,[87] with divers others: Thus have you heard the sad relation of the apperance of these ugly fiends[.] Upon which was made oath to his Majesty, which the Lord in His mercy inlighten his Majestys heart, that those eveill councelares whhich[88] are about him may be put ever far from him and that wee may have peace. Amen.

FINIS.

Figure 3.8 Title page, *Signes and Wonders from Heaven*, 1645.
Source: RB 16199, The Huntington Library, San Marino, California.

Signes and wonders from Heaven.

With a true Relation of a Monster borne in *Ratcliffe High-
way,* at the signe of the three Arrows, Mistris *Bullock*
the Midwife delivering her thereof.
Also shewing how a Cat kitned a Monster in
Lombard street in London.
Likewise a new discovery of Witches in *Stepney* Parish.
And how 20. Witches more were executed in *Suffolke* this last
Assise. Also how the Divell came to Soffam to a Farmers
house in the habit of a Gentlewoman on horse-backe.
With divers other strange remarkable passages.

Printed at *London* by *I. H.*[89]

[p. 1] Signes and wonders from heaven.
WITH
A true Relation of a strange Monster born in *Ratcliffe* High-way: Also a
Cat kitning a monster in *Lombard* street, &c.

IT is a knowne thing to all Christian people which are capable of understanding how that the sinnes of the world have in a high degree offended
the worlds Maker, and provoked the Lord to anger, yet hath the Divel so
blinded the eyes, and hardned the hearts of many men and women, that they
cannot or will not see nor take notice of their owne iniquities, but rather
seeme to excuse themselves of those errors which they every day runne into.
One will say, What though the Lord hath laid his punishing hand upon the
Kingdome, is it my fault? I am no swearer, nor drunkard, no covetous person, no prophaner of the Lords Sabbath: and yet peradventure he that thus
justifies himselfe is guilty of all these, and more then are here named.

Another will be apt to say thus: If it be sinne that hath brought the sword,
or the plague, or any other judgement upon us, 'tis not for any sins of mine, tis
long of[90] such a Lord, or long of such a Magistrate that the Lord hath punished
the Land.

Others have said, Tis long of the King that the whole Nation is so grievously troubled, for, say they, if the King had staid with his Parliament, we had
beene all at peace and quiet. And thus doe many people flatter themselves,
and lay the blame on others. But of this I am certainly perswaded that it is not
only for one mans sins, but it is for every ones sins that the Lord hath caused
the sword to be drawn amongst us. [p. 2] Furthermore I observe that the Lord
had decreed a separation betweene the King and his Parliament before the
wars began in England for the sins of the whole nation. That the Lord is angry
with us every one; for our sins doe appeare in this: Doe we not see that the
bloody wars doth more and more increase in our three Kingdoms[,] whereby
every mans heart e[v]en trimbles to thinke what shall become of them.

Doe we not know that the plague of Pestilence doth daily annoy our Cities, Townes, and Countries: and what great numbers have dyed in *Bristoll, Abington,* and many places more.

Doe we not heare continuall claymour ring in our ears? how that famine[91] will follow after the sword, except the Lord will in mercy stay the rage of our enemies: It is said, that Pestilence, the Sword and Famine, are the searchers, wherwith the Lord drawes blood of sinners: is there then any particular man or woman amongst us all, but either at one time or other hath felt the smart of one, if not all of those forenamed scourges: no, no, there is none alive but hath smarted in one degree or other; even from the King to the Begger, *Ergo,* we are all sinners: to make it further appeare, that the Lord is angry with us for our sins. Have there not beene strange Comets seen in the ayre, prodigies, fights on the seas, marvellous tempests and stormes on the land: all these are eminent tokens of Gods anger to Sinners[,] yet thats one all: Have not nature altered her course so much, that women framed of pure flesh and blood, bringeth forth ugly and deformed Monsters; and contrariwise[,] Beasts bring forth humane shapes contrary to their kind.

Have not the Lord suffered the Devill to ramble about like a roring Lyon see[k]ing to devoure us: have not a crew of wicked Witches, together with the Devils assistance done many mischiefes, in *Norfolke, Suffolke, Essex,* and other parts of our Kingdome, whereof some were executed at *Chensford* in Essex last to the number of fourteen, and many more imprisoned to this day, and by the voice of people there are some in *Stepney* Parish now in question about witchcraft, [p. 3] being persons of eminence: their names must as yet be concealed, but time will bring truth to light: one thing more of the Witches which have not beene yet printed, was thus: on wednesday last, *July,* 30. being Fast-day at a Towne called *Soffam* in Norfolke, at the House of *Peter-Smith,* about 4, a clock in the afternoone came a woman seeming to be some great gentle woman or Lady on Horse-back who knocking at the dore desired to come in, there being in the house no body but one servant Maid, who told her, that her Master and Dam with the rest of the Houshold were at the Church, and that she durst let in no body, till such time the Sermon was done, whereat the Gentlewoman commanded her to fetch her some of the best Beer in the House: the Maid replyed, that there was but one sort of Beer in the House, and that shee would not meddle with till her Master came from Church, the Gentlewoman bad her to give her some of the Bacon, that was boyling in the pot, whereat the Maid began to tremble, and withal marvelled much how she should come to know what meat was in the pot, and therwithall lift up her hands crying, *The Lord deliver me from all witches:* said the Gentlewoman, see thou look well to thy Beer, & thy Swines flesh presently seem'd to mount her Horse over the top of the Barne and so vanished: When the man[92] and his servants were come from the Church, they found the Maid trembling and quaking in a mighty sweat, being not able to speake to them for the space of two hours, but having recovered her strength & speech, she told them how the Gentlewoman had talkt with her, & what answer she made, & of her sudden departure, and of her going into the Sellar for Beer the Casks were broken, and all the Beere about the Roome: Then the Maid remembred, how that the woman bad her have a care of her Beer, and Swines flesh went streight-way into the Barten,[93] where she found three of her Masters fat Hogs, crying, and laying out their tongues, and so they dyed.

[p. 4] *July* 30. *Soffam,* a knowne witch in *Suffolke,* not above 2. miles from *Clare,* met with a woman great with childe comming from the Bake-house with a Cake under her arme, said the witch, Give me thy Cake: the woman broke it in the middle, and offered her one part, which the witch refused, and said, As she had broken the Cake, so should the childe be broken in her body. And immediately the woman went home, and was delivered of two lumps of flesh.

It is likewise certified by many of good quality and worth that at the last Assises in *Norfolke* there were 40 witches araigned for their lives, and 20. executed: and that they have done very much harme in that Countrey, and have prophesied of the downfall of the King and his Army, and that Prince *Robert*[94] shall be no longer shot-free:[95] with many strange and unheard of things that shall come to passe.[96]

These and many more such like evils have of late beene done in the Countrey, as is affirmed by good sufficient Authors, as shall be related here-after. And now will I returne and tell you of some strange newes neerer home.

July 28. at a place called *Ratcliffe High-way* neere unto *London,* at the signe of the three Arrows, dwelt a woman named Mistris *Hart,* who lived and was well beloved of her neighbours, she was religiously given, honest in behaviour, courteous in her speech, and well qualified in her actions: This woman being with childe, would oftentimes say that she was mightily troubled with what she bore in her wombe, as well she might be: for on the 28. day of *July* last, about 6. of the clocke in the morning she fell strongly in labour, and therewithall sent for the Midwife, whose name is Mistris *Bullock,* and other of her neighbours to come to her labour, who through Gods assistance brought her to a safe delivery. The Infant being brought into the world, the Midwife and the rest of the women having [p. 5] taken a view of it, perceived it to be the strangest misshapen Monster that ever they lookt on, or heard tell of. It was both hee and shee, borne without a nose, without hands and feet or legs, one eare, and that grew in the neck, and where the legs and armes should have beene, there grew pieces of flesh, and no bones nor joynts. This deformed Monster was borne alive, but it lived not long: the woman is yet living.

Thus doth the Lord daily send wonders into the world, thereby to put us in minde of our sinnes, and move us to repentance.

One strange Relation more I have to mention, and so conclude: and that is this:

In *Lombardstreet* in *London* in a Goldsmiths house, a Cat brought forth a monstrous Kitnen, which was partly shapen like a humane creature, and the other part Monster like. The manner of the forme was thus: It had eight feet upon one body, and two tayls, his pawes were like a childes hands, and never a head, but one great eye placed in the body where the head should be.

Thus have I related unto you such news which is known to be as true as strange: God in his mercy give us all a sight of our sins, and grant us grace to acknowledge them, and amend our lives.

FINIS.

The most
STRANGE
AND
WOUNDERFULL
apperation of blood in a poole at
GARRATON
In Leicester-shire, which continued
for the space of foure dayes, the rednesse of the colour
for the space of those foure dayes every day increasing
higher and higher, to the infinet amazement of many
hundreds of beholders of all degrees and conditions, who have dipped their handketchers in this
bloody poole, the scarlet complection of the
linnen will be a testimoniall of this wonderfull truth to many succeding generations.
AS ALSO
The true relation of a miraculous and prodigious birth
in *Shoo-lane*, where one Mistris *Browne* a Cuttlers wife
was delivered of a monster without a head or feet,
and in stead of a head had a hollow out of which
a child did proceed, which was little but
lovely, perfect in all but very spare
and leane.
AS ALSO
The KINGS sending to his Parliament for hostage
for the security of his person to come unto London
and to sit with his parliament for the composing the diffirences in the Kingdome.
Printed at *London* by I. H.[97]

[p. 2] The most strange and wounderfull apperitions of blood, in a Poole
at Garraton in Leicester-shire, which continued for the space of foure
dayes, the rednesse of the colour for the space of those foure dayes every
day increasing higher and higher, to the infinet amazement of many
hundred beholders of all degrees.

WHOSOEVER shall consider these sad times, wherin not onely the sonne
riseth against the father the brother against the brother, and the spirit of
dissention and warre is spread over the whole face of the earth but such
prodigious and wonderfull things have apheared as no age before have ever

seene or heard of[,] he must confesse that he liveth now in the evening of
time, and in the last age of the world, wherein all things do begin to suffer
a change.

I will not trouble you with any thing which in this nature hath heretofore
beene delivered to you: The Sword at *Plaisto* flourishing without hands, and
the great Stone clambring up the staires and whatsoever there is strange or
wonderfull are but sluggish miaclous [i.e. miracles] compared to this, which
doth the raither prefer it self to your observation, because in the buisnesse
of *Plaisto* there are as to be seene for the most part but some knavish lights
and as it were the *Hocus Pocus* of a spirit[,] but in this which now shall be
represented unto you the immediate anger of God in great Characte[r]s of
blood is most appearently to be read.[98]

At *Garraton* a Towne in *Leicester*-shire, not far from *Loughborough* is a
great pond of water, which for many generations [p. 3] hath beene knowne
to be there time out of mind, it is above an Acre on the length, and about
an Acre in the bredth. It was made at first to satisfie the thirst of the Cattle,
which from the commons and pastures there abouts did daily resort unto it
and sometimes it allayed the drought of the poore and thirsty travailer, but
now (as if it were another element,) it altread [i.e. altered] both its nature
and complexion, for the beasts did refuse to drinke thereof and some few
dayes afterwards being passed they would not come neere the water, which
the Countrymen and Inhabitants who were owners of the Cattle thereabouts perceiving they repayred to the pond to see what the[99] reason of this
strange thing should be.

Being come unto the pond they found the colour of the water changed,
for it began[ ]to looke red, and the substance thereof, was thicker then
before, amazed at the novelty of this sight they departed from the place, they
make a relation of it to their friends and one neighbour brings in another to
behold this wonderfull chance.

The noyse is spread over all the Country, and in thronging numbers
they make haste to see it. The water which at the first began to looke but
reddish, doth now looke higher and higher, and as the people came in it
did increase[100] in colour. This continued for the space of foure dayes, the
Country farre and neere (who had notice of it) comming in to be spectatiors
of it. It waxed more red the second day then it seemed at the first, and farre
more red the third day then it did of the second, and on the fourth day it
grew a perfect sanguine.

There is no wonder in this nature[101] but carrieth some divotion in it[,]
the people stand round about the bankes of the pond, and from looking on
the water they look up to heaven from whence they believe that the wonder
came; with reverence they discover this miracle of the water turned into
wine, but of the water turned into blood they never heard of that wonder
before. Some of them more hardy then the rest would undertake to taste
of it, to understand[102] if it were already as much in taste as in complection,
but they were severely charged by those that did stand by them, and were

told that they might follow the more [p. 4] wise example of the beasts, for since the Cattle refused to drink of the water by so doing they would now shew themselves more brutish then the Beasts.

The water still continueth in its bloody colour and had all one standing face of blood, and with all it seemed so thick that if a high wind had blown it is believed that it would very hardly at all[,] or else very gently have moved[.] Every day brought[103] in new observers to behold this admirable poole, and who had but seene it the day before could not be content with one dayes, wonder, but must come the next day to behold it againe.

It was the object of all the eyes thereabouts, and on their returne home-wards the subject of all their discourse. The Knights[,] the Gentlemen, and the Ladies[,] the Peasants, and their Families stood all closse together round about it, and being overcome with the amazement of the sight there was [no?] regard unto degrees or distinction of persons, and it seemes they learned this instruction from the Pond which they now made use of. *That they were all but one blood.*

From the observation of the blood they fall into the consideration at last of the bloody times, wherein they live, and being so neere to *Loughborough* they grow in discourse of how much blood hath beene spilt by the Lord of *Loughborough*[104] his meanes[,] who being there the great Agent for the King hath robbed many housekeepers in those parts of their goods and their treasure and which is far more deare to them many of their Childrens lives.

Report in the way is made how many families hath he robbed of their fathers, and how many he hath left without their children, they report from the beginning all the skirmishes that have beene made in those parts, and all the battles that have beene fought and all the sieges that have bin laid and raised[,] and passing from one devouring buisnesse to another, they do curse the proceedings of the civill warre.

The true narration of this water turned into blood may be put into suc-ceding calanders, and it may be printed in its owne rubrick, in our dayes did this prodigious sight appeare and afterwards the crimsin colour of the pond did begin to change, and [p. 5] every day to looke paler and paler untill at length[105] it by degree[s] turned unto its first complection of water the bloody substance sinking downe, and by its owne weight settling it selfe in the bottome of the pond. In the meane time the rumor of this flying up and downe the Country, there being above one thousand witnesses to jus-tifie the truth of it, one Master *Neale* a Gentleman of good account living at great *Leake* in *Nottingham-shire*, being travailing on his occasion unto *London,* and hearing the report of it to be commonly spoken as he did ride upon the way[,] thought [i.e. though] it was foure miles out of the ro[a]d, he resolved to see it[,] and making haste he easily overcome the lenght of the way, out of a desire to in enjoy [sic] the novelty of the sight being avived [i.e., arrived] he sat a long time on horseback at the entrance into the Pond musing and looking on it, (for it was just at that time) when the water did begin to returne to its first complection and perceving the red substance in the nature of a filmy body to descend towards the bottome, he did put spurres unto his horse who did fling back and snorted and was unwilling to goe into the Pond, but after he had forced him to enter alittle way into it, and stirred towards the bottome of the water with his Cane he percei[v]ed clots as it were of congealed blood in great abundance to rise up and having stayed upon the top of the water for alittle space to descend afterwards by degrees againe.

Not able to satisfie himselfe with any reason from whence this wonder should arise, he departed but the Country people resolving to examine and dive into the cause[106] thereof, they had a meeting amongst themselves for that intent and concluded at it to have the pond dreyned: It being beleeved that the enemy had throwne some Carcasses into the pond to stayne the water, and to bring thereby some suddaine distruction upon the Cattle.

This beleeve being entertained, the sluce is opened and now the water comes trumbling forth as if it were glad of its liberty, and was afraid to stay any longer in the portentous place where before it was in a swift to rent it made good its passage as if one part were emulation to overtake the other, and the latter strove with the former for the honour of proceeding. And to perfect the worke wherein some deeper places of the pond, the water [p. 6] stood still, and could not disadvantage it selfe into the chennell, the Countrymen some with scoopes and some with pailes did carry forth the water, with many hands they overcame the task which seemed at first almost impossible. And the pond being drayned and found nothing but fish of which in divers kinds there were great store, & those fish seemed still to be very good and nothing the worse for that miraculous accident which had made red the water. We may learne by this what God can doe who in a most wonderfull way can expresse his power without the least dammage to the Creatures.

Howsoever the pond being drayned dry which may increase the wonder, the blood in many places was discovered in extended degrees to be like so many scarlet Carpots on the bottome of the poole, to the unspeakeable amazement of the beholders, and indeed they may well put wonder on, for though in our owne Chronicles & in other Histories we have read sometimes of Clouds that have rayned dropes of blood, which though it is very wonderfull, yet because Phelosophers have undertake[n] to give a naturall reason for it, it substracteth some thing from the greatnesse of the wonder; but this as no cause can be assigned for it, so no story that I remember can example it, but being as farre beyond nature as example it sheweth it selfe to proceed from the immediate power and the hand of God.

I will not presume to give you the interpretation of it nor say it is suitable to the present condition of these bleeding times, neither will I be so hardy as to affirme that the foure dayes wherein the water every day seemed to increase in the rednesse of its colour doth signifie the foure[107] years of the war which now are already or neere expired and that as the water every day for the foure dayes exceeded one another in the desines of its sanguine dye, it looking every day redder then before, so the warre for these foure yeares hath every yeare beene one yeare more bloody then the other, surely it will prove good newes could I from hence assure you that as after the foure dayes being ended, the water did begin to returne in its first genuine colour, so the fourth yeare of this war being expired, the Kingdome shall againe returne to its ancient blessing and habit of peace, and that [p. 7] as the water bringing its first cleanes the blood did sinke downe and vanish away, so now the crying sins of blood shall be washed away from this Kingdome by the cleanes[s] of a new life and by the teares of true repentance.

There were many of the towne of Garraton both men and women, and of the inhabitants of the Country thereabouts who dipped their hand-kechers in this pond when it was of a bloodly colour, and the linnen retayning the complection of blood, it will be a testimoniall to succeeding times of this most strange and wonderfull accident and of the truth of what we write.

But to give you a good pond[108] to all these wonderfull events, we have received intelligence and it is confidently reported that the King having of late received so many overthrowes, and losse upon losse and despairing of any[109] successe by Armes, hath now sent unto the Parliament at Westminster to desire hostages for the security of his person, that he may come and sit among them to compose the differences of the Kingdome.

It is[110] the desire of many thousands that His Majesty may continue in this happy resolution, and that after so many deffi[c]ulties and dangers past, and so much blood spilt he might at lenght by the mercy of God returne and be reconciled to his Parliament, and to this there is no good Subject (unlesse he be a desperate Malignant or some arch Papist) but will say Amen.

In these sad dayes when the voyce of Gods wrath are poured forth on the face of the whole Earth wonders were never more frequent. Every day almost bringeth forth some new Miracle.

In Shoolane London, on Tuesday September sixteene there was a monstrous and prodigious Birth of which the good-woman was delivered with infinet paine and danger. It seemed to be as it were two children the one arising from upper monstrous part of the other, the first child out of which the other did proceed had neither head not feet, but was onely content with thighes and two stumps for leggs, neither had it any armes but two imperfect branches came from the shoulders of it which had no hands at all.

The nailes both for the hands & foot in a formidable length and shapenesse did grow out of the hipps on each side to the [p. 8] great amazement of the beholders: It had no head, but in stead thereof there did arise from the neck a great and hollow lumpe of flesh, and from thence did proceed another birth in the shape of a man child, and perfect in every limb, it was but little but very lovely to behold, spare and leane and its feet were fastoned in the hollow trunke which grew about the neck of the other monster out of which it doth appeare the whole body doth proceed, it is crediable that it received its originall and the beginning of its growth from the imperfect ruines of the other which (as I have said) having neither head nor feet, receive perfect shapes in all other parts the armes onely excepted, and it was very plumpe and fat, and (as it seemed) designed by nature a female. These births do carry with them remarkable observations, sad and monsterous times must labour still with sad and monstrous births and this (as it was still-borne) was exposed unto publick[111] veiw to the infinet amazement of the beholders, and to the great griefe of the Parents.

FINIS.

———◆———

SAD
NEWES
From The
Eastern Parts,
OR,
A true and perfect relation of the strange
Spectacles and Signes, both seen and heard in the
Eastern Association. Distinctly setting forth,
the Names of the Townes and Places
where *Englands* Warning-Piece late-
ly appeared.

As also, the description of a most wonderfull Sight (or Cloud) which appeared over the
famous, and chiefe City, the Hague in
Holland.

Whereunto is annexed,
Severall Observations, and Remarkable
Passages, plainly setting forth the signification of
Gods Signes and Tokens to *England* and
Holland.

These are printed by by [sic] the Originall Papers, and perused by
the English and Dutch Copies, and now published according to Order.

London, Printed by *B. Alsop*, July 14. 1646.

[p. 1] A more full and distinct
RELATION
OF
The strange Spectacles and Signes both seen and heard as well in *England*,
as in the *Netherlands*, upon the same day, to wit, *May* 21. 1646.

FIRST, there were heard in the Ayre in severall places in the Easterne
Association in *England*, by divers persons of very good credit, such strange
Military noises and sounds, as seeme to pretend wars and not peace.

As first there was heard in Marshland not farre from Kings-Linne in
Norfolk, by those who could judge of such sounds, the beating as of a whole
Regiment of Drums, which did beat a perfect call.

[p. 2] Near unto Cambridge the same day were heard by divers sober,
and credible persons; first, the sound of certain Pieces of Ordnance, as at
the beginning of some Battell, and the noise of many Muskets shot off,

as in the time of fight. The like sound of Musket shot was heard also in Suffolk the same day.

Secondly, there were sundry strange sights and apparitions seen in the severall Countries and Places of the Eastern Association upon the same day, as followeth:

First, there were seen at Combarton neer Cambridge by many persons assembled at a Muster there a Spire Steeple with swords about it, neere unto New-Market towards Thetford: there was a Pillar of a Cloud obscure to ascend from the Earth, with the hilts of a great Sword in the bottome of it, which Cloud fashioned it self into the forme of a sharp steeple, which was encountred by a Pike or Sphear coming down point blanck from Heaven, and threatned by another Lance or Pike, with very sharp points descending out of the Skye, standing ready to interpose, but did not engage it self. The first of these Sphears being afterwards elevated, and drawn up a little higher; the Spire Steeple which came from the Earth followed after it, and encountred with it a second time. This continued neere upon two hours and was seen by many.

The like Spire Steeple with a Lance or Pike descending from above, and encountring it as before, was beholden by many persons, Inhabitants at Brandon in Norfolk, and by others who travelled those parts at the same time, lying betwixt Cambridge and Botsam, there was seen a broach or sharpe steeple ascending out of a Cloud like a Church which removed from place to place: This steeple afterwards did split it selfe into three parts, of three distinct colours; the one red; the other yellow; and the third blew: one of which being highest sunck down lower, and out of it went forth a great Ball of fire towards the two Townes in Cambridgshire, the one called Sopham, the other Sop- [p. 3] ham Bullbark, scorching and sing[e]ing the grasse and the grain as it went, and left a very hot and strong scent of Brimstone behind it; The sight of which fire, with the smoak which it caused, was so terrible to the Inhabitants of both the said Sophams, that they caused their Bells to be rung backwards, as fearing a judgment, or firing of their houses from Heaven: Which sight was also terrible to many more; but they of Sopham Bullbark were the rather possessed with this feare, because that not above two years since, a Chappell there, and part of the Mannor house were set on fire from Heaven.

These Apparitions of a steeple in severall places thus assaulted with Swords and Pikes, seemes to fore-warn us of further troubles in or about the Church and Church Affaires.

Yet the said Ball of fire when it had run his circuit or course, returned and re-entred into the steeple or forme of a Distellatery, out of which it first issued. There was thunder that afternoon in many places, with very great store of Rain, and Haile-stones of a strange bignesse, and of extraordinary forms: many of the said stones being bigger then Pigeons Egges, and some of them were round and hallow like rings, and were taken up and put upon mens fingers.

At Brandon, besides the Spire Steeple opposed from heaven by a Pike, was a great Fleet of ships presented in the Ayre, all of them under sayle, and with their Flags hanged out: of which spectacle there were many beholders and witnesses: The same day there was a Navie of ships seene in the Ayre by some persons of understanding and repute at *London*, as they passed over the *Thames*, and might have been observed by many more, if they had regarded how the Ayre was affected. This fore-tells us, that we are like to have conflicts by Sea as[ ]well as by Land; yea, that our Country may be assaulted, and invaded by Forraigners.

Lastly, betwixt New-Market and Whitford bridge, three men appeared in the Ayre grappling together, and haling [p. 4] or tugging each other; wherof one at the first had a sword. This number of the three Combatants & the steeple which was split or divided into 3 parts, or lesser steeples, seemes to threaten further divisions in the three Kingdoms if not hostility, among three sorts of religious men. The Lord grant that the Inhabitants[112] of the three Kingdoms, & more especially those of the English Eastern Association may so speedily and throughly turn to the Lord, and to cleave to him that by his Spirit of Truth and Unity, they may bee made one new people, serving the Lord in the Truth and Unity of his Spirit and may be made subfirment[113] to each other in love and peace, through Christ Jesus, *Amen.*

But whatsoever our future sufferings may be, we are not likely to be scourged, exercised, or tryed alone; for upon the same day of *May* according to their old stile & account there were many fights,[114] no lesse strange and terrible seen at the Hague, the chiefe City of the Court of Netherlands or the Low Countries, as followeth:[115]

1   There appeared betwixt twelve and one of the clock in the afternoon, in a very cleere and bright day, a round circle about the bignesse of a round table, of the colour of gray paper, which seemed to be the Theater of the Spectacles and Sights afterwards presented.

2   There appeared there without a Lyon and a Dragon which fought fearfully[116] against each other, and the Dragon did terribly spit or spew forth much fire upon the Lyon, but in conclusion the Lyon over-came the dragon, and so the dragon vanished leaving the Lyon behind him in that place.

3   There were incontienly[117] seen with the Lyon a great multitude of Souldiery or Warlike people, and there appeared a Dragon like the former with a great Army or hoast likewise as[ ]well horse as foot, every Troope & Company of which Army, had a Trumpeter before them who were perfectly seen to set their Trumpets[118] to their mouths which Armies began to troope and march, and so warred [p. 5] against the other side, that it was doubtfull to the Spectators who should have the day or get the victory, all which forces afterwards vanished, the two Generals the Lyon and the Dra[gon] still abiding in fight.

4   There appeared a King with three Crowns upon his head sitting upon a royall throne & having many attendants round about his throne who afterwards disappeared leaving the Lyon and the Dragon still in view.

5   There appeared a great heape of mens hands, and in another place were seene a great company of mens bodies, which were headlesse, which also afterwards vanished, but the Lyon and the Dragon continued still in fight.

7   [*sic*] There appeared a very great Fleet of Ships from the South West, which moved towards the South East neer unto the Lyon and the Dragon, where the fight had been. There were many men with their bodies seen above board or upon the Decks of the ships, who handled their tackling, or were observed to hoyse[119] up their Sayles. These ships did drive one against, or thorow another, as in a Sea-fight. After this, all stood still, and was quiet, and the Lyon and the Dragon embraced each other, and so fell off, or disappeared.

Lastly, there appeared a great Cloud, which was not there before, and continued for a space, but a wind came, and drove that away; so all was silence and cleare again.

This was seen (saith the Dutch Copy) by many hundreds at the same time, but the signification thereof is known to God.

Yet that God[,] who caused all this to be seen, intended to signifie therby what he is about to do especially in those parts; And we hope it shall neither offend his Majesty, nor displease any sober and judicious persons to make a wholesome application of these things, with probable and [*sic*] conjectures and observations thereupon.

First the Lyon and the Dragon cannot represent our blessed Saviour, and his grand Adversary the Divell, for they can'never [*sic*] be reconciled as the Lyon and Dragon were in conclusion. Therefore in all probability, these with the rest of the spectacles in this eminent and remarkable Apparition, must represent the future actions, and transactions of some illustrious persons and States now upon the Earth, and shortly to be accomplished.

[p. 6] There have been of late some passages and predictions of future jars, yea war to break forth betwixt the States of Holland who give the Lyon,[120] and the Kingdom of France who are yet in league together; but what relation the Dragon hath to France is to me unknown.

It is well known, that not onely the Elector Palatine, but the States of Holland, yea most Princes in Europe give the Lyon one way or other; so that the Lyon may concern all Europe in generall, though it may reflect upon Germany in speciall, and the States of the Low-Countries more particularly. The Dragon may signifie the Turk, yet an enemy of[ ]Christ, the Lyon of the Tribe of Judah, who makes great and hostile preparations against our Christian Europe. The King with three Crownes seemes to represent the King of England, who may joyn in assistance of the German

European Lyon, or come in to desire the States. In the first fight the Dragon will be overcome, but afterwards he will conquer his forces, and great wars will ensue.

The heads upon an heap fore-tells what will ensue; perhaps the Turk offended with his Generall, his Admirall, or some great Agent, may cut him off with many more. However it is too too probable, that there will be great civill executions, and cutting off persons, by way of dicollation or beheading them, who have been thought the Authors of the wars, or unfaithfull in their places of Trust, The horseman who shot himself thorow is some great undertaker by hand, as it seemes, who shall but work his own overthrow, by his own enterprises.[121]

The Fleet from the South-West may be a Navie from France and those parts, or rather a Fleet from Europe to encounter the Eastern Enemy and Turkish Navie. Whatsoever these great Warriors be, they shall in the end embrace peace, and each other therein; The Turk may be converted and become a christian Brother. The Cloud now seen, and not before, in a sad presage of the great sorrow which shall remain for a time after so much blood-shed and calamity caused by these wars.

The winds that dispierced the Cloud seemes to be the sweet Gayle of Gods Spirit, which through the Gospell shall quiet and comfort all again. *Come Lord Jesus*, Amen.

FINIS.

Notes

1 John Taylor, *Mad Fashions, Od Fashions, All out of Fashions, Or, The Emblems of these Distracted Times* (London: Printed by John Hammond, for Thomas Banks, 1642), 1 [unpaginated]. The woodcut and poem (with slight modifications) would be reprinted under another title five years later, likely by Taylor again, and this later version became the better remembered of the two. T. J., *The world turn'd upside down: or, a briefe description of the ridiculous fashions of these distracted times. By T. J. a well-willer to King, Parliament and Kingdom* (London: Printed for John Smith, 1647).
2 Taylor, *Mad Fashions*, 3.
3 Taylor, *Mad Fashions*, 3.
4 Perhaps mostly notably, the title of T. J.'s pamphlet was used by Christopher Hill for his 1972 intellectual history *The World Turned Upside Down: Radical Ideas During the English Revolution.*
5 *Wee have brought our hogges to a faire market* (London: [s.n.], 1648) is an example of an English pamphleteer's perspective on his country's situation following the Peace of Westphalia, which brought an end to the Thirty Years War on the Continent. For a historian who presses especially hard for resituating England's political struggles throughout this century within a more solidly European framework, see Jonathan Scott, *England's Troubles: Seventeenth-Century English Political Instability in European Context* (Cambridge: Cambridge University Press, 2000).
6 *Irelands Amazement, Or the Heavens Armado* (London: Printed for John Thomas, 1642), title page.

7 *A Strange Wonder, or, the Cities Amazement* (London: Printed for John Thomas, 1641 [i.e. 1642]), 4.

8 *The Most Strange and Wounderfull apperation of blood in a poole at Garraton in Leicester-shire* (Printed at London: by I. H., [1645]), 8.

9 *A Great Wonder in Heaven* (London: Printed for Tho[mas] Jackson, 1642 [1643]), 4.

10 *The New Yeares Wonder* ([London]: Printed for Robert Ellit, [1643]), 8.

11 *The Most Strange and Wounderfull apperation*, 7, 4.

12 *Signes and Wonders from Heaven* (Printed at London: by I.H., [1645]), 1.

13 Stave Four of Charles Dickens, *A Christmas Carol* (Philadelphia, PA: J.B. Lippincott Co., 1915), 133.

14 A copy from the British Library has "(1643)" added to the title page in the collector's hand.

15 Timur or Tamerlane (1336–1405), a Turkish warlord who established an empire encompassing Central Asia and India and intruding into the Middle East. Vicars' portrayal of his simultaneously violent and magnanimous character is drawn from Christopher Marlowe's play *Tamburlaine the Great*. "Your tents of white now pitched before the gates," Tamerlane is told in Act III, "and gentle flags of amity displayed, / I doubt not but the Governor will yield, / Offering Damascus to your Majesty." "So shall he have his life, and all the rest," Tamerlane replies. "But if he stay until the bloody flag / Be once advanced on my vermilion Tent, / He dies, and those that kept us out so long." Christopher Marlowe, *Tamburlaine the Great: Part One and Two*, ed. by Mathew R. Martin (Peterbrough, ON: Broadview Press, 2014), 138.

16 Offer.

17 Author's gloss cites Daniel 3:26 (correct citation, v. 29) and 6:26–27.

18 Obstinate.

19 Marginal note: "A Jove omne principium." Every beginning is from Jove.

20 Solid, weighty.

21 Book VII, chapter XII of Flavius Josephus' *Wars of the Jews*. See *The Famous and Memorable Works of Josephus* (London: Printed by J[ohn] L[egat] for Andrew Hebb, 1640), 738.

22 Author's gloss: "Amos 6:6." Vicars' reference encompasses at least Amos 6:1–7, if not the full chapter.

23 Morally lax; lazy.

24 Diligent; careful.

25 Gloss cites Luke 1:33; misprint for 13:3.

26 Here, every one sits under his owne Vine,
All, under their-own Figtrees sup and dine,
In Pleasures, Treasures, and all joyes encrease,
In pleasant Plentie, amiable Peace.
But, whiles this Peace and Plentie brings forth Pride,
Luxurie, Loosnes, and all sinnes besides;
Gods wrath is kindled, Heav'n therwith offended,
Lets England see his judgements sore, intended.
By a strange Blazing-starre, which every day,
Betimes ith'morning did bright beames display;
Which, as a Warning piece, the Lord thus sent
To rouze-up England, timely, to repent,
And to prevent his judgements, thus, foreshown,
Lest (still) secure England be overthrown.
See, here, th'indulgence of a gratious God,
Who, ere he strikes, first, shewes and shakes his Rod.

27 Gloss cites I Kings 4:23; correct citation, v. 24–25.

28 La Rochelle, a coastal city in western France, was a Protestant stronghold during the seventeeth-century Wars of Religion and the center of several Huguenot rebellions against France's Catholic monarchy.

29 Torn apart.

30 James Hamilton, 2nd Marquesse of Hamilton (1589–1625), courtier to James VI/I, died of a fever but was suspected to have been poisoned (*ODNB*).

31 Ludovick (or Ludovic) Stewart/Stuart, 2nd Duke of Lennox and 1st Duke of Richmond (1574–1624), served James both as King of Scotland and as King of England. Intriguingly, given Vicars' own strong Presbyterianism, Richmond was often "accused of lukewarm adherence to protestant doctrine" and "was openly suspected of Catholicism on a number of occasions." He died of apoplexy in February 1624. *ODNB*.

32 Arthur Chichester, 1st Baron Chichester of Belfast (1563–1625). As Lord Deputy of Ireland from 1605–1616, Chichester attempted to establish English control by buttressing the Protestant Church of Ireland and rooting out Catholicism— tactics that would likely have earned Vicars' commendation. Chichester died of pleurisy in February 1625, less than two weeks before Hamilton. *ODNB*.

33 The following section to the end of the paragraph paraphrases Isaiah 5, a song of God's judgment upon his people Israel for their wickedness. Vicars, who cites the passage in his gloss, replaces Israel with England and applies God's words to his seventeenth-century context.

34 Author's gloss cites Luke 13:7; Vicars is paraphrasing the full parable, v. 6–9.

35 Longsuffering.

36 Behold, good Reader, here, a monstrous birth,
To damp thy sinnes delight, and marre such mirth,
A Man-childe born in most prodigious sort,
Which for undoubted truth thou mayst report.
Two distinct heads it had, and eke two hearts,
Two arms, whence grew a stump. In other parts
Like other children. What may this portend?
Sure monstrous plagues doe monstrous sinnes attend.
The sinnes of Heads, in government abus'd,
The sinnes of hearts, opinions false infus'd,
And broacht abroad to raise up foes and factions,
And Armes and Armies to confound with fractions,
Dis-joynted States (like stump-like Ireland)
Whiles brothers thus 'gainst brothers lift their hand.
This (surely) God seemes hereby to foretell,
That having Plagues must hideous Sinnes expell.

37 Marginal gloss cites Psalm 139:24; correct citation, v. 14.

38 Author's gloss cites John 19:3; misprint for 9:1–3.

39 Feminine form of *fautor*, meaning an abettor or instigator.

40 Vicars refers to Mary Dyer, who gave birth to a deformed infant in October 1637 in the Massachusetts Bay Colony. The event occurred in the midst of the colony's Antinomian Controversy, a religious conflict in which Dyer's friend Anne Hutchinson (who also suffered a "monstrous" birth) was especially prominent, and thus it attracted a great deal of attention from those who saw it as a graphic sign of Dyer's and Hutchinson's illicit theological views. John Winthrop, governor of the colony, discussed the birth in a report sent back to England, and news of it spread quickly; for instance, it was relayed along with other such monstrous births in the pamphlet *Newes from New-England* (London: Printed for John G. Smith, 1642).

41 The destruction of this church had been recounted in *A True Relation of Those Sad and Lamentable Accidents . . . in and about the Parish Church of*

Withycombe in the Dartmoores (London: Printed by G. M. for R. Hartford, 1638), which was expanded in a subsequent pamphlet, *A Second and Most Exact Relation of Those Sad and Lamentable Accidents . . . in and about the Parish Church of Wydecombe neere the Dartmoores* (London: Printed by G. M. for R. Hartford, 1638). These publications included a generic call "to search our hearts and amend our waies" (*A True Relation*, 2), but no mention of "superstitious superfluous and idolatrous impieties" in the church.

42 Here, Reader, ope thine eyes and ears and heart,
   Consider what this figure doth impart.
   Behold, and tremble to behold and see,
   How Christ, Gods Lambe, a Lion fierce can be:
   When Sin doth patience into passion turne,
   And make sweet favour, like fierce fury burne.
   When Bethel is a baudie-Babel made,
   God will his fair Jerusalems invade.
   When, for pure worship of his sacred name,
   We, Idol-Altars, Popish-Rites will frame:
   O, how the jealousie of God doth burn!
   All Idol-worship, quite, to over-turne.
   Shall England (thus) pretend a reformation,
   And, yet, uphold Romish abomination?
   Surely (as here) God will let England know,
   If these continue, God will angry grow.

43 The adjectival form of the river Styx in Greek mythology, but can be used of the underworld more generally. Vicars is probably thinking of the smell of brimstone, or sulfur, biblically associated with Hell.

44 An officer who watches over the game in a park or preserve.

45 Similar.

46 Pointed out.

47 The Cornish storm was recounted in the pamphlet *The Voyce of the Lord in the Temple* (London: *T. Paine* for *Francis Eglesfield*, 1640).

48 And, here, againe, that All may clearly see,
   False-worship, and Idolatry to be
   The sin of England: God, in other places,
   More Houses of such worship, much defaces,
   With fearfull storms, lightnings, fierce claps of thunder,
   Churches and Steeples rends and cleaves asunder.
   Though many other sins doe England staine,
   Yet, this, of all the rest, is dy'd in graine.
   Idolatry and Superstition base,
   The Lord will not endure in any case.
   And therefore shewes, by so many examples,
   With how great wrath under his feet he tramples
   Such Romish-trash, and all Wil-worship vaine,
   And, only, will unmixed Truth maintaine.
   Be warned, then, betimes, England take heed,
   Lest wrath, without redresse, does make thee bleed.

49 The Armada of 1588, sent by Philip II of Spain to remove Elizabeth I from the throne, was destroyed before it could transport the Spanish invasion force to English shores. Its failure became a fixture in English literature, representing both the dangers of Catholics and God's providential care for Protestant England.

50 And, here, another Warning-piece we had,
   A frighting Storme, by Sea, t'have made us sad,

Had not Heav'ns wisedome, power and providence
Prevented it, and beene our strong defence.
A Spanish Fleet, floating upon our Seas,
Hopefull to land upon our Land with ease;
To finde us fearlesse, or engag'd in fight,
With Scotland, through intestine d[e]epe despite.
But, whiles they hovered about Deale and Dover,
Watching occasion us to triumph over,
Whiles we-our-selves dreadlesse of danger were,
So neare our ruine, yet, so void of feare,
The Lord a Fleet of Dutchmen to them sent,
To pay their pride, their mischiefe to prevent.
This Warning-piece we, therefore may admire,
Preserv'd thus strangely from destruction dire.

51 At the Battle of the Downs (which was fought, not in September 1640 but on
October 21, 1639), the Dutch Admiral Maarten Tromp won a decisive victory
over a Spanish armada in neutral English waters. Contrary to Vicars' implica-
tion, the Spanish were not launching an invasion of England but rather sailing
to reinforce their armies in the Netherlands as they attempted to put down the
long-running Dutch revolt; neither was the English government thankful for its
"salvation," since by attacking the Spanish in the anchorage of the Downs, the
Dutch had violated England's neutrality. See C.V. Wedgwood, *The Thirty Years
War* (London: The Folio Society, 1999), 377.

52 This battle in the sky was recounted in *A Signe from Heaven, or, A fearefull and
terrible noise heard in the ayre at Alborow* (London: Printed by T. Fawcet, Aug
12, 1642).

53 Of all the Warning-Pieces to us sent,
See here a Master-piece of wonderment.
A mighty battell fought (as 'twere) in th'aire,
Which Alb'rough Townsmen mightily did scare:
For first, they heard Drummes beating loud alarms,
Great Canons shooting, as in fields of Armes,
Thick and quick vollies of small shot; likewise
A stone most black breaking forth from the skies,
Which whistling through the air, did pierce the ground,
And (by a Dogge) where it fell down, was found.
But suddenly this frighting feare was past,
And, by melodious musicke turnd at last
Into much joy and great alacrity,
Bells (as 'twere) ringing most harmoniously,
As if the Lord would hereby let us see
His gracious love at last to set us free
From all our fore-felt feares, and terrors great,
To crown us with a conquest most complete,
Shown in this figure Tragi-comicall:
Heav'n say Amen to this. So pray we all.

54 A reference to the posthumously published commentary on Revelation by
the Presbyterian minister Thomas Brightman (1562–1607), *A revelation
of the Apocalyps* (Amsterdam: Printed by Iudocus Hondius & Hendrick
Laurenss, 1611).

55 John Booker's prognostication for February 1643: "Great Starres conjoyn'd,
do shew great alterations / In many Kingdomes, Countries, nay all Nations /
Shall suffer change, so saith th'Astrologer / For in this Moneth Saturne with
Jupiter / And all the Planets one another viewing / By severall Rayes, great

Wonders are foreshewing." In Booker, *M.D.C.XLIII. almanack et prognosti-con, sive, Speculum anni à nat. J.C.* (London: Printed by F.K. for the Company of Stationers, [1643]), 10.

56 By the New Style calendar, this would be January 1643 (after the Battle of Edgehill on October 23, 1642).

57 A disembodied spirit; a ghost, hobgoblin, or specter.

58 Questioned, doubted.

59 The encounter between Macbeth and the Three Witches, made famous by Shakespeare's *Tragedy of Macbeth*, was drawn from Raphael Holinshed's *Chronicles of England, Scotland, and Ireland*; see Volume II of *The first and second volumes of Chronicles* (London: Printed [by Henry Denham], [1587]), 170–171.

60 Jerome.

61 Original: "circnmstance."

62 The First Barons' War, fought between King John and his nobles from 1215–1217.

63 Original: "conqnest."

64 Original: "atrestation."

65 Sir Edmund Verney (1590–1642), the king's standard-bearer, raised the standard at Nottingham in August 1642 and died two months later at the Battle of Edgehill.

66 A large carbine used especially by cavalry.

67 No publication information, but the Thomason copy adds "Jan 27" and "1642" to the title page. As with *A Great Wonder in Heaven*, however, the collector has used the Old Style calendar, which does not begin the new year until March 25; by the modern calendar this would be January 27, 1643, after the Battle of Edgehill in October 1642.

68 Original: "thuuder."

69 Original: "enents."

70 Original: "venganr."

71 Original: "lergar."

72 The sense of this and the following sentence is unclear.

73 Original: "vuto."

74 Greek, from the Aramaic, meaning "place of the skull." Golgotha was the place at which Jesus Christ was crucified, more commonly known in English as Calvary.

75 The second letter transcribed here as a "v" is a "u" in the text; "revives," rather than "reviues/reviews," seems to be the intended meaning.

76 Original: "couring."

77 Original: "euents." The more logical word would seem to be "intents."

78 Original: "heatds."

79 Original: "senee."

80 Original: "resouled."

81 Original: "abrond."

82 Original: "Drnmes."

83 A call to arms.

84 A large pistol or carbine, often used by cavalry.

85 Original: "hidiour."

86 Original: "wihch."

87 Sir Edmund Verney (1590–1642) carried the Royal Standard and was killed in the Battle of Edgehill.

88 There is a space between wh and ich and what appears to be part of another h in the gap above the other letters.

89 Annotation on Thomason copy adds "Aug: 5," but no year; internal evidence places the pamphlet in 1645.

90 Due to.
91 Original: "famiue."
92 Original: "mau."
93 Possibly a misprint for "Garten" (garden).
94 Prince Rupert of the Palatinate (1619–1682), Charles I's nephew and com-mander of the Royalist cavalry, was known as "Rupert" and "Robert" in the English press.
95 Bulletproof.
96 A Parliamentarian newsbook reported this information in its July 21–28 issue, forcing a paragraph onto the final page after its martial news: "But that I want room, I should have told you of the late tryall of the *Norfolke* Witches about 40. of them, and 20. of them already executed, and what strange Prophesies some of them had before their death of the downfall of the Kings Army, and that *Prince Rupert* should not now longer be shot free, and much more but of this I conceive I have already said more then most will have faith to believe, though it be never so true, however by the next, if I be not prevented by oth-ers, I will give it you all at large, and from unquestionable Authority." As the pamphleteer does not elaborate, it seems likely he got his information from this newsbook. See Samuel Pecke, *A Perfect Diurnall of Some Passages in Parliament* (Number 104: July 21–28, 1645), ([London]: Printed for Francis Coles and Laurence Blaikelock, [1645]), 830.
97 Annotation on Thomason copy: "7bre [September] 30th" and "1645."
98 The anonymous *Strange and Fearfull Newes from Plaisto* (London: I.H., 1645) had been published slightly earlier in 1645, also by "*I. H.*" of London, to alert readers to a recent string of strange occurrences at the house of a silk-weaver in Essex. Among other incidents, a sword flew about a room "no hand touching of it," a massive stone from the yard rolled up the staircase of its own accord, and an evil spirit threw objects about, beat the residents, and ruined their silk-work. The author was unable to inform his readers of the reasons for these bizarre events, merely suggesting that they might be related to the many witches in Essex and its neighboring counties. Unlike the present pamphlet, *Plaisto* offered no commentary on current political events, although it may reflect growing concerns about the danger of witchcraft in the face of the newly-initiated witch-trials in the Eastern Counties.
99 Original: "tht."
100 Original: "incrcase."
101 Original: "natnre."
102 Original: "nnderstand."
103 Original: "bronght."
104 Henry Hastings, 1st Baron Loughborough (1610–1667), was appointed high sheriff of Leicestershire by the king in 1642, in which capacity he worked to maintain Royalist control of the Midlands and raise arms for Charles.
105 Original: "lenght."
106 Original: "canse."
107 Original: "fonre."
108 Perhaps a mistake for "end," which would make far more sense.
109 Original: "and."
110 Original: "it."
111 Original: "buplick."
112 Original: "Inhabitanis"
113 Probably a misprint for "subservient," if the author is paraphrasing Ephesians 5:21: "Submitting yourselves one to another in the fear of God."
114 This may have been intended as "sights," although in the context of celestial battles, either word could make sense.

115 See also the accounts of these apparitions in *Good Newes from Oxford* (London: Printed by Jane Coe, 1646), 4–5 and *Severall Apparitions Seene in the Ayre, at the Hague in Holland* (London: Printed by T. Forcet, 1646).

116 Original: "ferafully."

117 From "incontinently:" straightway, immediately.

118 Original: "Trumptes."

119 Raise, hoist.

120 Likely a reference to the lion depicted on the Dutch *Leeuwendaalder,* or "lion dollar."

121 This item should have been sixth in the list but is missing from the account due to a printer's error. See *Good Newes from Oxford*: "There appeared also a man sitting upon a horse who kills himselfe and falls backward" (p. 5).

4 Cavaliers and Roundheads
'The divells agents still'

Introduction

If the pamphlets in the previous section took a bird's-eye view of Britain's affairs, universalizing rather than centralizing blame for the national crisis, then the following documents paint a picture of current events from the ground. The perspectives were not necessarily incompatible, but while the former emphasized the role of God in judging a sinful nation, the latter pointed primarily to the part played by certain groups and individuals in turning England upside down. Partisanship and polemic thus became more overt, for, as William Burns notes, "Monsters were not simply accompaniments to or signs of civil strife; they were also weapons in it. All sides in the political conflicts of the 1640s used charges of monstrosity against their opponents."[1] It served a double purpose: by demonizing the other side, authors not only evoked hatred and fear of that party in their readers but professed their own party's allegiance to true religion and just government.

In this war of words, Parliamentarians were more experienced than their opponents; it was critics of the government who had first popularized the "play-pamphlets" that criticized elites in satirical, often obscene dialogues.[2] Indeed, it was once thought that Parliamentarians reigned supreme in the popular press, while Royalists eschewed such propaganda as vulgar and therefore unworthy to be associated with the monarch's cause. This is, however, clearly an untenable position, for Charles I's wartime capital of Oxford produced both newsbooks and popular ephemera and there were many prominent pamphleteers and editors who supported the King. Royalists were not slow to use print media. Laura Lunger Knoppers has suggested rather a difference in *style* between Royalist and Parliamentarian rhetoric, with the former taking its cues from the masques so popular in the Caroline court: "In royalist satire," she argues, "the antimasque figures of Stuart court drama moved into the world of popular print, no longer expelled by the appearance of the king and queen, but presumably to be run off the public stage by popular derision and laughter."[3]

The role of laughter as a weapon is important to bear in mind when approaching these pamphlets, whether Royalist or Parliamentarian; yet it is also important not to make too fine a distinction between the camps' rhetorical approaches. On the contrary, they were often quite similar. Both deployed the language of witchcraft and demonism, as well as of immorality and hypocrisy, to castigate opponents, and the Devil was a common feature in their pamphlets and woodcuts. Both had serious arguments to make; both also used satire to devastating effect, as illustrated—to take one instance among many—by the pamphlet exchange in 1642 between Henry Walker, a Parliamentarian tradesman turned bookseller and preacher, and John Taylor, a deeply traditional waterman whose career had been linked to the court and who eventually fled London to join the Royalists at Oxford. The episode is an example of the "polemical mud-slinging"[4] common in the wartime press, and its tone on the Royalist side is exemplified by the first document reproduced here, *The Devils Last Legacy* (1642). Although the work does not admit to being written by Taylor, its attack on "a Round-headed Ironmonger," an allusion to Walker, underscores the fact that it was written within the context of this literary battle. Moreover, its unsubtle linkage of the Devil and the Roundheads, as well as its salacious accusations concerning religious sectarians, were mirrored in works like Taylor's *A Devil Turn'd Round-head* (1642) and many others of this year and beyond. In these pamphlets, Roundheads were objects of derision, as indeed was the Devil himself—but they were also, of course, sources of evil.

Naturally, Parliamentarians did not accept this charge, but instead turned it against the Royalists. In some cases, this meant highlighting the wickedness of the "Cavaliers" and illustrating the harsh fates to which they would come—a technique that fit neatly within the well-established trope of the "judgment narrative," best exemplified by Thomas Beard's *Theatre of Gods Judgements* (1597).[5] Several pamphlets recounted judgments that had fallen upon Royalists, both high-ranking leaders and petty soldiers: in one, for instance, a boy was kidnapped by the Devil and conducted on a tour of Hell to witness the torments prepared for Royalists like Sir Richard Grenville, Baron George Goring, and Lady Anne Dalkeith.[6] Equally vicious, though, were works like *The Kingdomes Monster* (1643) and *The Devills White Boyes* (1644), which presented the King's forces not being punished by the Devil but working with him to bring about the downfall of the nation. Such pamphlets and broadsheets made a point not much different from those written by Royalists but tended to be more serious: there was black humor in a work like *The Devills White Boyes*, but the Devil and his agents seem, on the whole, far less amusing.

How much of this hellish rhetoric was intended literally? Concerned by the uncontrolled nature of the wartime press, one observer noted in 1642 that "what we laugh at, our children may believe."[7] But it may have been as difficult for contemporaries as for modern historians to know when to laugh and when to frown. Mark Stoyle has demonstrated this of the pamphlets concerning Charles I's nephew, Rupert of the Palatinate, and his allegedly diabolical dog Boy, arguing that the inciting text, *Observations upon Prince Rupert's White Dog* (1643), was a satire rather than a serious report by a Parliamentarian spy.[8] Nevertheless, this did not stop the pamphlet from engendering other works; Rupert's supposed sorcery and his dog's powers became a recurring element in the press, culminating in one of the texts transcribed here, *A Dog's Elegy* (1644), after Boy was killed in the Battle of Marston Moor. Another, earlier text, *A Most Certain, Strange, and True Discovery of a Witch* (1643), may have grown out of the same milieu and raises similar questions about the line between rhetoric and reality. Is it a serious elaboration of a news report,[9] or does the final comment that "This Book is not Printed according to Order" open the possibility that this, too, was tongue-in-cheek?[10] Likewise, are we to understand the author of *The English Devil* (1660) to be claiming that Oliver Cromwell had literally employed a witch to convince Parliament to execute Charles? Or is this a rhetorical device, a means of linking the prophecies of the controversial Lady Eleanor Davies and the predictions of the astrologer William Lilly, and thus Parliament itself, with the powers of darkness? The idea of bewitchment was widespread among Royalist commentators, providing a helpful explanation for the political turmoil engulfing the nation and especially for the execution of the divinely-ordained monarch; after the Restoration, it also helped excuse collaboration with the Interregnum government. But where did "rhetorical flourishes" end and true belief begin, or was there any distinction?[11]

Perhaps readers at the time were not always certain. As we have seen, it has been suggested that the originally satirical accusation regarding Rupert furthered honest fears about witches and helped inspire the East Anglian witch-hunt from 1645–1647, where some of the Devil's agents were linked with the King's cause.[12] For charges of witchcraft and the language of the demonic were not limited to the popular press: they were also explicated in serious works, such as the sermon Nathaniel Bernard preached in Oxford in June 1644, *A Looking-Glasse for Rebellion*.[13] Taking as his text 1 Samuel 15:23, "For rebellion is as the sin of witchcraft," Bernard expounded upon the similarities between the two crimes while taking explicit jabs at the Parliamentarians—in particular, for promising many benefits but in reality bringing ruin upon the country. His point was mainly metaphorical, but he left it an open question whether Parliament used *actual* witchcraft, especially when he suggested that, like witches, the rebels were able to know whatever happened secretly in the King's council in Oxford.[14]

Bernard did not reference the press, but his sermon was preached in the midst of the Rupert/Boy pamphlets (*Observations* was published the previous year; *A Dog's Elegy* would appear the following month) and may further demonstrate the interpenetration of "high" and "low" literary culture. Certainly it demonstrates the pervasiveness of concerns about the diabolic and the occult and the hard lines being drawn by the two sides in the Civil Wars. While each party charged the other with wickedness and saw the Devil at its back, there could be compromise. Thus, pamphlets like those in the following section did their part to fuel the conflict, providing moral vindication to the author's compatriots and promising the downfall of their opponents. For, as *The Kingdomes Monster* observed: "there's a God that will at last regard // Our sufferings, and give them their just reward."[15] It was the duty of the righteous ones to stand firm and fight until that final vindication came.

---◆---

THE
DEVILS
LAST
LEGACY:
OR,

A Round-headed Ironmonger,[16] made
Executor to *Pluto*.

Wherein is shewed, The Discent of
the Round-heads.

AS ALSO,

The Round-heads great desire of a Crown, and to
sway a Scepter, although it be but *Pluto* his
Crown and Scepter.

Composed by W. K. *first a Turke, and now
turned Roundhead.*

London, Printed *Anno Domini*, 1642.

[p. 2 – blank]

[p. 3, unpaginated] *The Devils Last Legacy:*

Pluto,

ALL haile my deare Adopted Sonne, thou alone art he that is my onely
joy and hope, at whose sight my soule is filled with fatnesse, and the pleasure I take in thee runneth like to a Julop[17] in my veines: come on brave soule,
be couragious, for this I know, thy impudence it is so great, that the whole
World is not able to out-face; leane close to me, and I will be as willing to
entice, as thou to follow; leave me not, for then I shall not know to whom
to leave my Kingdome and immortall Scepter. Thou art the Heire and only
he, be faithfull to my Kingdome, bend neither one way nor other, end as
thou hast begun, and none shall more reward than I: my youngest Sonne
Amimius[18] hath quite left me, his too much yeelding made him fall off; goe
on as thou hast begun, and I will reward thee.

> *Both my Scepter and my Diodem,*
> *I leave to th' Rounheads, and to none but them.*

Roundhead. Great King and Prince of darkenesse, whatsoever thou shalt
command, no sooner spoke but done, I am as ready for to doe, as you to

speak, and you not fuller[19] of enticements, but I twice as full of actions, yet fuller of Words, perhaps it may seem difficult to your understanding, but thus to doe good, I say much, but doe little, for I never in all my life knew how to doe good; I am the Heire, and delight to overtop men in wickednesse, I am presently desperate if I see any more wicked then I, yet cunning to the World: beare a faire show, and have the Devill Printed in my Heart, and strive to be the Prince of darkenesse Sonne: it is the height [p. 4] of my ambition to get his Crowne, and though all the world should bid farewell to Pluto and his Pallace, and sound a retreat from his damnable designes, I would stand as fast as Mountaines.

> *My seates to shew, who can be at all fearefull,*
> *To whom Grand Pluto saies, my Son be cheerfull.*

Pluto. Brave resolution Son, but in the way take some of my damnable devices, and what ever thou dost here on Earth, shall presently in my black pallace be innacted for a Statute: thou hast performed the duty of a Son in executing my decrees that I left with you at the last Conventicles,[20] where I wish I had not been with you, for I think I have got my last, from a Cobler, who in villany exceeded even his Father great Pluto. I having not long life, enact thee overseer and chiefest Executor of my last Will and Testament, doe what in it is commanded, and I will in one houre bring thee to my Acaronticall[21] Pallace, where nothing shall be too much for him that acknowledgeth me, hot scalding Lead, dear Son, shall be thy Nactar, thou shalt quaffe[22] off whole boules of teares [Psalm 80:5] to thy secconders, each sence with a greedy appetite shall have its fill, and the whole Man shall taste my best pleasures, Musick thou shalt delight in much and heare a quire of Cerberuses and the Syrens of Hell;

> *In this performance have but Argus eyes,*
> *For Musick, black zantes, and the Stigian[23] cries.*

Roundhead. Ever honoured Prince, if a Son may have the permission and boldnesse to speak to a Farther, let what designe from you be spoken, my power in your service extends it selfe so far that I will effect.

> *And think it done, what ever you command,*
> *I'le perpetrate the thing I take in hand.*

[p. 5] *Pluto.* Upon my death-bed Son, I enjoyne thee that thou seest my will compleatly performed, let not a Bishop in the Land have power, neither let the Churches stand, pull down all and abolish the light, that we may live in darknesse, a tub is sufficient for any one to Preach in: I would have my kingdome flourish that it may be said, tis *Pluto's* Kingdome, that is the chiefest Throne.

Thou art an Ironmonger, and though thou hast broke here, I have Chaines and old Iron for to set thee up again; thou hast almost quit thy selfe, witnesse thy last Sermon of *Toby and his Dog*,[24] and the *Tale in a Tub*:[25] To change a trade it is no shame, from an Ironmonger to a Cooper, and the best trad[e], for if thy zeale should strike the bottome out, then might thou exercise a faculty and turne Cooper, Cobler, and Tinker, I teach thee a way to thrive; some of thy Brethren are horned heads as well as Roundheads, turn, Grafier and make one Branch two, that our Sect may the better be noted;

> With *Famialists*,[26] *all things are lawfull Son,*
> *Performe* [. . .] Round-head *what thou hast begun.*

Roundhead[.] I will [ende]avour to the utmost, dread Soveraigne, in any thing by you commanded, and though I be cract[27] in trade, I will not neglect your affaires, and be discouraged in your occasions; I will also crack my braine before I will leave unperfected, what you command me.

> *Some call me little-Wit, but tis no evill,*
> *For I have spent it all, to please the Devill.*

Pluto. This is my Will, deare Son, the first thing specified is this: I leave one hundred pound *per Annum*, for our Conventicles.

2. I leave my Braines, Head, and Hornes to all the rest of [p. 6] our Brethren, for wickednesse and that which is naught they want not I am sure.

3 And thirdly, I leave my Scepter and Kingdome to thee, and onely thee, deare Son: I cannot live, the Doctor specified so much to me the other day, but doe these things and I will helpe thee at all times, do any thing, nothing shall hinder thy course to my blacke Pallace, therefore disturbe me not, but goe about it, and I will betake me to my more serious considerations.[28]

> *I am a dying thus to him I say,*
> *But for to punish,* Round-heads *live alway,*
> *And this alone shall be my Round-head than*
> *Which is a Brownist*[29] *and a Knave,*
> *But seemes an honest Man.*

An Oration of the Round-head, a crackt Ironmonger, new made Executor to the Devill.
Roundhead,

BRETHREN, it is the fortune of Knaves and Fooles to have the best lucke: I make no question but it is well known to you all, that our Father *Pluto* hath given over trading, and hath made me supervisor of his last Will and

Testament; tis a fortune beyond the Moone, and though I be both Knave and Foole, yet I thought the Proverbe would have crost it selfe in me; and seeing I am so chosen and predestinated, I will have an eye to all his entreaties, and execute the part of an adopted Son; he hath given me charge over your *cum cura animarum*,[30] therefore deare Sisters and Brethren, I must performe the part of the Devils Viccar and Curate of Hell, [p. 7] therefore lets follow him, and our Service-Clarke set the Song.

Clarke, Lets sing this Song to the tune of *Old Sir Symon the King*; 'tis a New Dittie, ellevate you voyces.

> *GRAND* Pluto *he is dead,*
> *Lets sing in this very Day,*
> *That he hath left his Throne*
> *Unto the* Round-heads *sway.*
> *And Old Sir* Symon *the King,*
> *And Old Sir* Symon *the King,*
> *We'll have a thred-bare Coate, and a mamsey Nose,*[31]
> *Sing hey ding ding a ding ding.*
> *The Ironmonger Rules,*
> *The Cobler also Preaches,*
> *The Tinker he Cornutes,*
> *The Weaver sometimes teaches.*
> *And Old Sir* Symon *the King.*
> *The Sisters pratles much,*
> *Canarie-Birds imitating,*
> *The Baker gets a Tubs,*
> *And never holds his prating.*
> *And Old Sir* Symon *the King.*
> *We stuffe our guts with Capons,*
> *Devotions but very small,*
> *The World we thus can flatter,*
> *And say Devotions all.*
> *With Old Sir* Symon *the King.*

[p. 8]

> *To Westminster we trudge,*
> *Each Man with a Bilbo blade,*[32]
> *At Night to Conventicles,*
> *And ride like Hackney-Jade.*[33]
> *And Old Sir* Symon *the King.*
> *The Miters from the Prelats*
> *We will pull away,*
> *No Man dare contradict,*
> *Or once against it say.*

Then Old Sir Symon *the King.*
The Divell hath left us his,
What is it we want at all,
Be stedfast sister deare,
Although that Round-heads *fall.*
Then Old Sir Symon *the King,*
Then Old Sir Symon *the King,*
Wee'l have a thred bare Coat, and a Mamsie Nose,
Sing hey ding ding a ding ding.

Clarke, Peace and put out the Candles, you have gone a Note too high, lie all the Sisters downe, and straine lower, *procreandi causa*.[34]

FINIS.

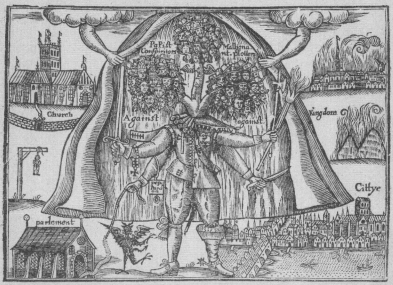

Figure 4.1 Full broadsheet, *The Kingdomes Monster Uncloaked from Heaven*, 1643.
Source: © The British Library Board 669.F.8.(24).

THE
KINGDOMES MONSTER
Uncloaked from Heaven:
The Popish Conspirators, Malignant Plotters, and cruell Irish, in one Body
to destroy Kingdome, Religion and Lawes: But under colour to defend
them, especially the Irish, who having destroyed the Protestants There, flye
hither to defend the Protestant Religion Here.
Printed in the Year, 1643.[35]

O England looke upon this monstrous Thing,
That would our Kingdome unto ruine bring,
'Tis framed and composed of three parts
Which are all joyned both in heads and hearts:
Doe not behold it with a carelesse eye,
This Monster brings this Land to misery:
This Monster following its forefathers hate,
Seeks to destroy the Kingdome and the State:
While Church and Kingdom should oppressed lie
Subjected to their blinded Popery:
Long time it walked muffled in a cloak
Till *Straffords*[36] head was cut off, then it broke
Out of the cloud, but Heavens holy hands
Hath now uncloak'd it, so that now it stands
In a full figure as this Picture here
Doth make it lively to your view appeare,
And in fit Emblems to your sight presents
His shape, his postures, and his blacke intents;
So that if you behold it round about
You shall see how this Monster is set out;
His Spanish Ruffe, and Jacket shew him here
To be halfe Papist, and halfe Cavalier;
His left side Popish is, which on his breast
Is by the figure of the Crosse exprest;
Besides his Beads and Popish pardon be
Emblemes that speak his love to Papistry:
So on the left side Popish heads are got
Together ready to conspire and plot
Unfathom'd mischiefe, and lest they should want
Brain to be wicked, and should so be scant
Of knowledge how they might undo this land,
Plotting malignant heads against them stand:
The winged cluster of heads do discover
That Papists Rebels from Ireland flye over:
These to make strong their party, do combine

While in one body they together joyne,
Which in this Monster of the times exprest,
And to shew that there lodges in his breast
Nothing but cruelty, while 'tis his desire
To kill the Protestants, and their houses fire:
His double hands a sword, a knife containes,
A match, a Poleaxe, and a torch that flames;
Thus arm'd you may aske what he means to do,
Alas! his dayly actions this doe shew;
He doth intend to change the Churches coat,
That masse may be sung through a Friars throat;
And that the Protestants true Church may grow
Catholicke, and unto the Pope may owe
Supremacie, while Popery that hath bin
Long purged out, may be brought in agen;
In hope whereof, they oppose the Parliament,
Which Papists once to blow up did consent,
As here the match in hand doth represent,
While the blacke fiend did further their intent;
Besides this monstrous Body here compact
Of Papists, Irish and malignants act
Most horrid cruelties where they do approach,
Set out here by the sword in hand and torch;
Firing both Towns & houses where they come,
As they of late to Brimidgham have done;[37]
And like unthankfull wretches have no pity
Neither upon this Kingdome nor this City,
But *Nero* like would laugh while it did burn,
And would massacre such as would not turn
To their Religion, robbing them of life,
Described by the hand armed with a knife:
Thus under sword and fire this Kingdomes lies
Bleeding, and is this Monsters sacrifice;
While Papists, Irish, and Malignants are
Drawne all into the body of a war,
Who breath[e] destruction, and would ruinate
Church, Kingdome, City, Parliament, and State,
Therefore this Picture here set out may be
Called the Kingdomes Map of misery.
But there's a God that will at last regard
Our sufferings, and give them their just reward;
Let them take heed, here on the side we see't.
They and the gallows at the last shall meet.

FINIS.

Figure 4.2 Title page, *A Most Certain, Strange, and True Discovery of a Witch,* 1643.

A MOST
Certain, Strange, and true Discovery of a
WITCH.

Being taken by some of the Parliament Forces, as she was
standing on a small planck-board and sayling on
it over the River of *Newbury*:

Together with the strange and true manner of her death, with
the propheticall words and speeches she used at the same time.

Printed by John Hammond, 1643.[38]

[p. 3] A
TRUE RELATION OF THE
WITCH
in the Army.

MANY are in a belief, that this silly sex of women can by no means attaine
to that so vile and damned a practise of sorcery, and Witch-craft, in regard
of their illiteratenesse and want of learning, which many men have by great
learning done, *Adam* by temptation toucht and tasted the deceiving apple,
so some high learnd & read by the same temptor that deceived him hath
bin insnared to contract with the Divel; as for example, in the instancing
a few, as, *English Bacon* of *Oxford*, *Vandermast* of *Holland*, *Bungy*[39] of
Germany,[40] *Fostus* of the same,[41] *Franciscus* the *English Monke* of *Bury*[,]
Doctor *Blackleach*, and [p. 4] divers others that were tedious to relate of, but
how weake women should attain unto it many are incredible of the same,
and many too are opposite in opinion against the same, that giving a possibility to their doubtings, that the malice, and inveterate malice of a woman
entirely devoted to her revengefull wrath frequenting desolate and desart
places, and giving way unto their wished temptation, may have converse
with that world roaring lion, and covenant and contract upon condition, the
like hath in sundry place[s], and divers times been tried[42] at the Assises of
Lancaster, Carlile, Buckingham, and else where, but to come to the intended
relation of this Witch[43] or Sorceresse, as is manifest and credibly related by
Gentlemen, Commanders, and Captains, of the Earle of Essex[44] his Army.
   A part of the Army marching through Newbury some of the Souldiers
being scattered by the reason of their loytering by the way, in gathering
Nuts, Apples, Plummes, Blackberries, and the like, one of them by chance
in clambring up a tree, being pursued by his fellow or Comrade in waggish[45]
merriment, jesting one with another, espied on the river being there adjacent,
a tall, lean, slender woman, as he supposed, to his amazement, and great terrour treading of the water with her feet, with as much ease and firmnesse as
if one should walk or trample, on the earth, wherewith he softly calls, and

beckened to his fellowes to behold it, and with all possible speed that could be
to obscure them from her sight, who as conveniently [p. 5] as they could they
did observe, this could be no little amazement unto them you may think to see
a woman dance upon the water, nor could all their sights be deluded, though
perhaps one might but coming nearer to the shore, they could perceive there
was a plank or deale[46] overshadowed with a little shallow water that she stood
upon, the which did beare her up, anon rode by some of the Commanders
who were eye witnesses, as well as they, and were as much astonished as they
could be, still too and fro she fleeted[47] on the water, the boord standing firm
bou[l]t upright, indeed I have both heard and read of many that in tempests
and on rivers by casualty have beene shipwracked, or cast over board, where
catching empty barrells, rudders, boards, or planks have made good shift by
the assisting providence of God to get on shore, but not in this womans kind
to stand upon the board, turning and winding it which way she pleased, making it pastime to her, as little thinking who perceived her tricks, or that she
did imagine that they were the last she ever should show, as we have heard
the swan sing before her death, so did this divellish woman, as after plainly it
appeared make sport before her death, at last having sufficiently been upon
the water, he that deceived her alway did so then, blinding her that she could
not at her landing see the ambush that was laid for her, coming upon the
shore she gave the board a push, which they plainly perceived, and crossed
the river, they searched after her but could not find her: she being landed the
Commanders beholding her, gave order to lay [p. 6] hold on her and bring
her to them straight, the which some were fearfull, but some being more
venturous then other some, boldly went to her & seized on her by the armes,
demanding what she was? but the woman no whit replying any words unto
them, they brought her to the Commanders, to whom though mightily she
was urged she did reply as little: so consulting with themselves what should
be done with her, being it so apparently appeard she was a *Witch*, being loth
to let her goe, & as loth to carry her with them, so they resolved with themselves, to make a shot at her, and gave order to a couple of their Souldiers that
were approved good marks-men, to charge and shoot her straight, which they
prepared to doe: so setting her boult upright against a mud banke or wall;
two of the Souldiers according to their command made themselves ready,
where having taken aime gave fire and shot at her as thinking sure they had
sped[48] her, but with a deriding and loud laughter at them she caught their bullets in her hands and chew'd them, which was a stronger testimony then the
water, that she was the same that their imaginations thought her for to be, so
resolving with themselves if either fire or sword or halter were sufficient for to
make an end of her, one set his Carbin close unto her brest: where discharging, the bullet back rebounded like a ball, and narrowly he mist it in his face
that was the shooter: this so enraged the Gentleman, that one drew out his
sword & manfully run at her with all the force his strength had power [p. 7]
to make, but it prevailed no more then did the shot, the woman still though
speeechlesse [sic], yet in a most contemptible way of scorn, still laughing at
them, which did the more exhaust their furie against her life, yet one amongst

the rest had heard that piercing or drawing bloud from forth the veines that crosse the temples of the head, it would prevail against the strongest sorcery, and quell the force of Witchcraft, which was allowed for triall: the woman hearing this, knew then the Devill had left her and her power was gone, wherefore she began alowd to cry, and roare, tearing her haire, and making pitious moan, which in these words expressed were; And is it come to passe, that I must dye indeed? why then his Excellency the Earle of Essex shall be fortunate and win the field, after which no more words could be got from her; wherewith they immediately discharged a Pistoll underneath her eare, at which she straight sunk down and dyed, leaving her legacy of a detested carcasse to the wormes, her soul we ought not to judge of, though the evills of her wicked life and death can scape no censure.

FINIS.

This Book is not Printed according
to Order.

A
DOGS ELEGY, 17
OR
RVPERT'S TEARS,

For the late Defeat given him at *Marston-moore*, neer *York*, by the Three Renowned
Generalls, *Alexander Earl of* Leven, *Generall of the Scottish Forces*, Fardinando *Lord* Fairefax, *and the Earle of* Manchester *Generalls of the* English *Forces in the North.*

Where his beloved Dog, named *B O Y*, was killed by a Valiant Souldier, who had skill in *Necromancy.*

Likewise the strange breed of this Shagg'd Cavalier, whelp'd of a Malignant Water-witch; With all his Tricks, and Feats.

Sad Cavaliers, *Rupert* invites you all ⎫ Close-mourners are the Witch, Pope, & devill,
That doe survive, to his Dogs Funerall. ⎭ That much lament yo'r late befallen evill.

Printed at *London*, for *G. B.* July 27. 1644.

Figure 4.3 Title page, *A Dogs Elegy*, 1644.
Source: © The British Library Board E.3.(17.).

A
DOG'S ELEGY,
OR
RUPERT'S TEARS,
For the late Defeat given him at *Marston-moore,* neer *York,* by the Three Renowned
Generalls; *Alexander Earl of* Leven, *Generall of the Scottish
Forces,* Fardinando *Lord* Fairefax, *and the Earle of* Man-
chester *Generalls of the* English *Forces in the North.*

Where his beloved Dog, named *BOY,* was killed by a Val-
liant Souldier, who had skill in *Necromancy.*

Likewise the strange breed of this Shagg'd Cavalier, *whelp'd of a Malignant*
Water-witch; *With all his Tricks, and Feats.*

Sad Cavaliers, *Rupert* invites you all
That doe survive, to his Dogs Funerall.
Close-mourners are the Witch, Pope, & devill,
That much lament yo'r late befallen evill.

Printed at *London,* for *G. B.* July 27. 1644.

[p. 3] *A Dogg's Elegie,*
Or
RUPERT'S Tears.

LAMENT poor *Cavaliers,* cry, howl and yelp
For the great losse of your *Malignant Whelp,*
Hee's dead! Hee's dead? No more alas can he
Protect you *Dammes,* or get Victorie.
 How sad that *Son* of *Blood* did look to hear[49]
One tell the death of this shagg'd *Cavalier,*
Hee rav'd, he tore his Perriwigg, and swore,
Against the Round-heads that hee'd ne're fight more:
Close couch'd, as in a field of *Beanes* he lay,[50]
Cursing and banning all that live-long day;
Thousands of Devills Ramme me into Hell,
Or may I live and die an Infidell,
The Day's quite lost, wee are all confounded,
And made a prey to ev'ry paltry *Roundhead;*
 Just Heav'n had so Decreed, as it fell out,
The *Cavaliers* receiv'd a finall Rout.
Manchester, Leslie, Fairefax weares the *Bay.*[51]

And *Crumwell* crown'd chief Victor of the Day;[52]
While thousands weltring in their blood, did lie
Weary of life, and yet afraid to die.
    But for to tell of this Black *Water-witch*,[53]
That puppy'd was of a Malignant *Bitch,*
Or *Hagge,* so cunning in her Art, that shee
Walk'd under earth or in the aire could flie,[54]
Sell windes she could, command the Ebb or Tide,
Raise Foggs, give Spells or on the Clowds could ride,
For Magick, Sorcery, Charme or Evill,
She well might [be Schoolmistress?] to th' Devill.
    [p. 4] This Witch one night, late, picking banefull Drugs,
Meeting grim *Brenno*, us'd to suck her duggs,[55]
In shape of a young stripling *Dammy Blade,*
For Whoredome, Murder, and for Rapine made,
For all the world, some say, just such another
That used to call Prince *Maurice* brother:[56]
Thus shee Accoasted him, What Forme is this
Thou hast assum'd *Brenno?* By the *Abysse,*
My blood rebells more powerfull then my *Charmes,*
Till I doe lodge thee in my twined armes.
    No sooner had shee spake, but a black clowde[57]
With duskie curtains did them both enshrowde,
Where was begotten this Malignant Curr,
Who in this *Iland* hath made all this stirre.
    Full thrice three yeears within her cursed wombe,
He did remaine, ere he to light did come:
The long'd for houre is come, most strange to tell,
The *Furies* straight about their businesse fell;
Megera[58] midwife was to this strange Fiend,
For whose delivery all the *Haggs* attend:
Thunder and Earth quakes such a noise did make,
As if Heavens *Axletree* in sunder brake,
And either *Poles,* their heads together pash'd,
As all againe they had to *Chaos* dash'd:
Then was a noise, as if the Garden Beares,[59]
And all the Doggs together by the Eares,
And those in *Bedlam*[60] had inlarged been,
And to behold the bayting had come in.
    About by noon flew the affrighted *Owls*,[61]
And *Dogs* in corners set them down to howle,
Bitches and *Wolves* these fatall signes among,
Brought forth most monstrous, and prodigious young;
And from his height, the earth-refreshing Sun,
Before his houre his golden beams doth run
Farre under us, in doubt his glorious Eye

Should be polluted with this Progedy [*sic*].
A trembling fear straight on the people grew,
But for what cause there was not one that knew,
    Th' *Destinies, Furyes, Fates,* and all hells Crew
Came trembling in, and would this Monster view,
[p. 5] And long it was not ere there came to light.
The most abhorred, and most fearfull sight
That ever eye beheld, a birth so strange,
That at the view it made their looks to change:
Women stand off (quoth one) and come not neer it,[62]
The Devill, if he saw it, sure would fear it,
For by it's shape, for ought that I can gather,
The Childe is able to affright the Father:
'Twas like a *Dog*, yet there was none did know
Whether it Devill was, or Dog, or no.
    Scarce twice two yeers past o're, but quickly hee[63]
Excell'd his Mother in her Witcherie,
And in his black and gloomy Arts so skill'd,
That he even Hell in his subjection held;
Hee could command the Spirits up from below,
And binde them strongly, till they let him know
All the dread secrets that belong them to,
And what those did, with whom they had to doe.
    This Wizard in his knowledge most profound,[64]
Sate on a day the depths of things to sound,
For that the World was brought to such a passe,
That it well nere in a confusion was,
For things set right, ran quickly out of frame,
And those awrie, to rare perfection came,
And matters in such sort about were brought,
That *States* were puzzl'd almost beyond thought,
Which made him thinke as he might very well,
There were more Devills then he knew in hell.
    Now for to Act his part he doth beginne,
And tempt's the World to all abhorred sinne:
    To *Rome* he first resolves his course to steere,[65]
And quickly leaps into the Prelates Chaire,
Just 'bout the time some think when as Pope *Jone*[66]
Was head o'the Church, and troubled with the stone,
He cur'd her *Holinesse*, brought her abed,
And shew'd the *Romish Church* her Maiden head:
    But finding *Rome* already prone to Vice,
To *Pride, Vain-glory, Lust* and *Avarice,*
To *Murder, Rape, Idolatry* and more
Then he (though Devill) ever knew before,
[p. 6] For *Spaine* hee comes, just about Eighty Eight,[67]

And there a Fleet he Rigg'd for *England* streight,[68]
There did hee play his Water-prize with *Drake*,[69]
Who with Earth's thunder, made proud *Neptune* quake;
He taught this *Dog* to Duck, to swim, and dive,
Till scarce a *Spaniard* he had left alive;
But being vex'd, missing his aime at Sea,
He vow'd on Land revenged he would be,
      But Heav'n which ever did Protect that *Queene*,[70]
Debarr'd his malice, and repell'd his spleene;
Till *Jove* fetching her hence, gave her a Crowne,
More bright, more glorious, and of more renowne,
Who Reignes till *Time* hath date, or *Fame* hath breath,
Queen of true *English* hearts in life and death.
      Aurora's gone: Bright *Sol* is in his Throne,
Then dry your eyes, and cease for her to mourne:
This *Dogge* now casts about, tries all his skill,
To poyson, stab, or some new way to kill
Never yet heard of; The *Master-piece* of hell
Is now contriv'd that wants a Paralell,
The *Powder-Plot*, that would in one half houre,[71]
King, Prince, Peers, Commons, at one blow devower,
But then he failed too, the Eye of Heav'n
Descri'd the Plot, and Justice with an even
Impartiall hand, by the Decree of *Jove*,
Set free our Kingdom, and did them remove,
Gave them their just reward, sent them to Hell,
'Mongst better Devills then themselves and well.
      Our *Dog* is masterlesse; Could he but frame[72]
Himself to serve the Fav'rite *Buckingham*,
This cunning, slie, insinuating Elfe,
By him would work strange wonders for himself,
Then doth he Plot, contrive and cast about,
And Hell it self doth search, for to finde out,
If any way were left, he vow'd to [trie?]
Once more to bring this land to [Popery].
      Now dies that Noble *Scot*,[73] who[se manners?] tell,
'Twas thy Ambition made his carcasse swell.
Next, Prince *Henry*[74]—But here my *Muse* strikes saile,
A damp glide through [my soul, to what I aile?]
[p. 7] I know not, unlesse some powerfull Spell
Hath charm'd my head into a watery Well:
      "*Eyes weep out tears, tears weep out eyes in kindnesse,*
      "*Since he is dead, how best of all is blindnesse.*
A Match with *Spaine* must now be practised,[75]
Which soon will strike the nayle up to the head:

Oh, now it works, which makes his *Holinesse*,
Salute his hopefull *Sonne* with an *Expresse*,[76]
Answer'd with so much *Candor* to the *Chaire*,
As if Himself of it did stand in feare.
    The Match broak off with *Spaine,* our Noble *BOY*
Is yet to seek, and must finde out a way
By Poyson still, how that (O monstrous!) Hee
More home may strike at Sacred *Majestie*,[77]
Great Brittains KING, and *Europs* chiefest glory,
Scarce parallel'd in any *English* Story,
Must with *White Powder* given him in his drinke,
Cry out on him that made his Carcasse sinke.[78]
    O for a Bishop now, Come Little *Laud*,[79]
And usher in the *Babylonish Baud*,
This made him *Metropolitan*, when hee
Did move the *Duke* to goe toth' Ile of *Ree*,[80]
Poore *Rochell Ru'd* it, where by more then Chance,
England was made the scorne of conquer'd *France*:
But heaven by *Felton's* hand had so decreed,
He that shed all this blood, himself should bleed.[81]
    Now *Bishops, Coaps, Caps, Surplices* and *Crosses*,
Must needs *Religion-o're* these fattall *Losses*:
GODS Day must be Profan'd with *Sports* profane,[82]
Laud, White, and *Wren*,[83] like Tyrant-Kings must Reign:
Monopolies impos'd, and none goe free,
But those that lov'd the *Masse,* and *Popery*.
    Now *Tips* of *Ears*, and burning fiery scarres,[84]
Were all sad Symptoms of insuing Warres!
    The *Masse-Book* unto *Scotland* now must trace,[85]
Or else a *Bloody Sword* supplies the place.
    Now doth that sur-Reverend Piece of *Lust*,
That *Madam Pole-cat*, that was never just,[86]
Contrive and Plot, and wrack her whoary scull,
Urging her Daughter to make mischief full.
[p. 8] Now *Strafford's*[87] on the dismall Stage: 'tis hee
Must Act chief part in this red Tragedie:
    Now *Harry Je[r]min, Bristoll, Digby, Cott.*[88]
Must all to work, and see what they can Plot:
    Now *Bleeding Ireland* hath by Commission,
Brought th' Prot'stants to a sad condition:[89]
Two hundred thousand of them lately slaine,
The *Protestant Religion* to maintaine.
    'Tis time the King now leave his Parliament,
Let *Digby* weare his Crown, and give consent
To raise an Army Traytors to protect,

And his *Great Counsell* utterly reject.
  Now Prince of *Robbers,* Duke of *Plunderland,*[90]
This Dogs great Master, hath receiv'd command
To kill, burne, steale, Ravish, nay, any thing,
And in the end to make himself a King.
  Newcastle next, *Capell* the *Cow stealer,*[91]
And *Hastings* alias *Rob-Carrier,*[92]
Hopton, Hurry, Lunsford, that all doe Fight
For the true *Gospel,* and the *Subjects Right.*[93]
On *Ashton, Legge,*[94] and such as these doe stand
The Priviledge of Parliament and Land!
  And the *Known Laws,* that should good men protect,
Upheld by Rebells, that good men reiect,
  O *durum hoc*[95]! —Mine eyes burst out to thinke
How blinde he is, that can at these things winke.
  To tell you all the pranks this *Dogge* hath wrought,
That lov'd his Master, and him Bullets brought,
Would but make laughter, in these times of woe,
Or how this Curr came by his fatall blow,
Look on the Title page, and there behold,
The Emblem will all this to you unfold.
MORRALL.
The World's *the* Witch, *the* Dogge, *is the* Devill,
And men *th'* Actors, *that have wrought this evill.*
EPILOGUE.
He that can't get a peny me to buy,
May want a Pound, and a Malignant *die.*
FINIS.

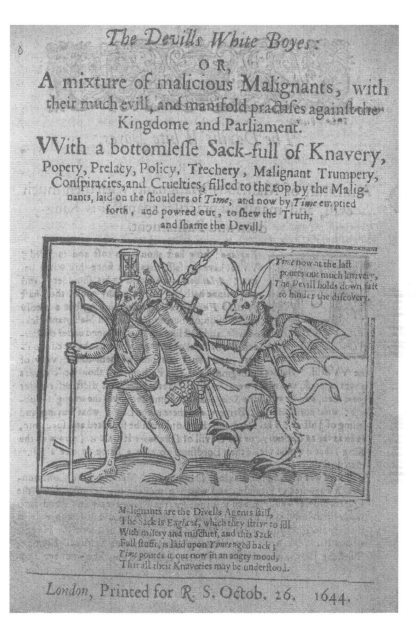

Figure 4.4 Title page, *The Devills White Boyes*, 1644.

The Devills White Boyes:
OR,
A mixture of malicious Malignants, with
their much evill, and manifold practises against the
Kingdome and Parliament.
With a bottomlesse Sack-full of Knavery,
Popery, Prelacy, Policy, Trechery, Malignant Trumpery,
Conspiracies, and Cruelties, filled to the top by the Malig-
nants, laid on the shoulders of *Time,* and now by *Time* emptied
forth, and powred out, to shew the Truth,
and shame the Devill.

Time now at the last
poures out much knavery.
The Devill holds down fast
to hinder the discovery.

Malignants are the Divells Agents still,
The Sack is *England,* which they strive to fill
With misery and mischief, and this Sack
Full stufft, is laid upon *Times* aged back;
Time poures it out now in an angry mood,
That all their Knaveries may be understood.

London, Printed for R. S. Octob. 26. 1644.

[p. 2] *The Devills White Boyes,*
OR,
A mixture of Malicious Malignants with their much evill, and manifold
practises against this Kingdom and Parliament.

O *England*! how hast thou been tost and tumbled? What have thy sufferings been since this warre began? *Atlas* beares the world on his shoulders, and
alas, sinne hath laid sorrow on thy back, thou hast been, O *England* a long
time nothing but a medly of confusion, of murder, plunder and Malignant
wickednesse, and hast like a Porter, groaned under the burden of a Sackful of
knavery, ease now thy tyred shoulders, and poure out some of them to the view
of the World. Before the beginning of this Parliament, thou wer't divers wayes
opprest, and many were thy greevances which thou didst suffer under great
men; and how did the *Star-chamber* domineere over the wrong'd Subiect?
what corruption and Bribery was there in the Law? what buying and selling of
Justice? This Lord, and that Lord must be sollicited and sued unto, even as far
as *Coventry,* or the Devill of *Dunsmore* HEATH[96] (now with the King) that it
would please their Lordships to take a Bribe to doe a poore man Justice.

There was nothing but Playing, Dancing and Masking; the Commonwealth was a tree of Pleasure, and whoring was the top branch, when the Queen-mother was here,[97] and it is thought, the Bishops ease and good fare, made them lusty, even to beget Bastards, which they could doe with ease in their studies; they lov'd pleasure better then Preaching, and were the Hogges of our Israel, that fatted themselves with the Acornes of Spirituall Livings; Then the Judges were the Kings Parrets, and cryed out, Ship-money, Ship-[p. 3] money,[98] but the Subjects regarded those Judges no more then Parrats or prating Sicophants; that with the Coblers Crow, were taught to cry, *Ave Cæsar, God save the King;*[99] Amen cry'd the people, and deliver him from such malignant Judges, that would make his Prerogative a Pick pocket; and a hand to squeese out the wealth of the Subject, according to the Princes pleasure, that so our King might like a forreign, whom I could name, be *Rex Assinorum,* a King of English Asses,[100] when the liberty of the Subject should be subject to the Tyranny of his Prerogative. These devices were then set on foot, and are now marching abroad on the Souldiers leggs in the Kings army: for what doth the Kings Army fight for? but first for an universall Tyrany, or unbounded Monarchy, that the free-borne *English* may submit themselv[e]ss to Royall slavery, in token whereof, the Schollers of *Oxford* not long before these warres began, made a Play called, *The Royall Slave,*[101] as if they had Prophesyed, that all *England* should be turn'd into a company of Royall slaves, and for this the Cavaliers fight, cut and kill the Kings Majesties Subjects, that they may conquer us into servitude, and (if they could) beat us out of our Name of Subjects, into the title of slaves, but theres no doubt, wee shall be able to baffle such knaves, that being pack't together, have shuffel'd in the King amongst them, and by their evill Counsell, have made the King like an incensed Lion against his people and Parliament. And what mad Lawes doe you imagine, if the Cavaliers were law-makers? It should be lawfull in the first place to kill any man for his money, if it were demanded, *cum privilegio,* that is by vertue of the Kings Prerogative. And the subjects should be turned into sub-jacks, every great man should have a Monopoly to maintain his pride and luxury, the Kings *Will* should be the liberty of the subject, and my Lords will, and my Ladies will, and my Lords Secretaries will, and my Lords great Horses will must be obeyed, so that *Jack* should be in Office, and every Courtiers will, even to *Will* the Scullion in the Court Kitching, should be a King, if the Malignants could have their will.

Then for Religion, we should have superstition, Organs piping,[102] Lawnesleeves[103] preaching, Bulls of *Bason* roaring,[104] and singing Anthems, Little young Levites preaching Morallity instead of Divinity, and cringing and complementing in the Pulpit; fat Benefices, and leane Sermons, Dunces that could onely read Service, and pray for faire weather, should be Country Curates, but 'tis no matter, this Religion would serve the Malignants, who are half Epicures, half Papists, and half Atheist, and a medly of mad wickednesse, they and the Devill have been in Counsell a great while, to devise a plot how to destroy all the honest Religious Protestants in *England*, and the Earl of

Strafford,[105] hee sits in Counsell every day about it with *Pluto*, *Ashteroth*, and the other Infernall Counsellors,[106] but this Devillish *Counsell-Table*, cannot yet, nor never shall [p. 4] be able to worke the ruine of the Protestants; No? yes the Cavaliers, the Irish, and Papists in the Kings Army will doe their endeavour, and with their swords mow them downe; theres *Digby*,[107] and *Cottington*,[108] and a great many Lords and Knights that are Politick Divills, that could instruct the King to undoe the Common-wealth in the times of peace, and cannot they play the Divell in the time of warre? yes, yes, no doubt, they enticed the King the head of the Parliament from the members, onely to save their own heads, and will not they incense the King to kill his true Subjects under the title of Roundheads? Come, beleeve it, they are wicked enough, how can they fail in their plotts? when experience tells us, that Papists are full of black Invention and hellish Plotts: what was the Gun-powder Plot, and *Straffords* plot; but what talke you of Plots? The Kings Majesty will have it so, and blinde men in Divinity have the best eyes; they preach, Obey the King, and dishonour God, but as for cruelty and cutting of throates I leave that to Prince *Rupert*, and will acknowledge that there was heeretofore no other purgatory but the Chancery. But what said my Court Lady at *Oxford*, I love the Romane Catholick Faith, for I would lie in bed and be religious, and confesse my sinnes, and live in pompe and pleasure, and know nothing but complementing in *French*, and praying in Latine, and hearing Masse, and when shee did goe to heaven, and [visite?] the Lady *Mary*, and all the Papists that are in heaven, which are very few, for they doe not live after the rate of going to Heaven, unlesse bloody murders, Idolatry, and killing of Kings be the way to Heaven.

These Malignants in my conceit are like those pictures which have a dubble aspect, one like a man, the other like a Devill, when they are to doe mischiefe by flattering the King, or making the countrey people rise in the Kings behalfe, then they put on smooth faces, and tell them of the Kings power and Prerogative, and that the Parliament is no Parliament, and therefore they may fight against it, that the King is wronged, when indeed no body wrongs him but his malignant Councellours, that they fight for the Protestant Religion, that is for Poperie, and to defend the Lawes, that is the Law of tyrannicall slavery, which the King would impose upon his subjects, and that as the Locust devoured the Land of Egipt,[109] so they might swarm againe and devour us as they did in *England* in the times of peace, when all the Law was in the hand of the Judge, and that hand must be filled with gold, or else no Law was to be had: but now for cunning wickednesse, which is the malignants other face, and wherin he resembles the Devill, consider him as he was in the shape of *Guído Faulx*[110] when he went with his darke lanthorn in his hand to set fire to the Gunpowder plot, and was taken in this Devills shape, and afterwards he and his Complotters were executed for traytors, but what a number of black malignants are there now in this Land, being a kind of smooth-faced machivilian Devills, [p. 5] some with flattering bellows blowing the coales of dissention betweene the King and Parliament; then there be horned malignant Devills that will roare, sweare, domineer, use nothing but Dammees, and Rammees, as the Cavaliers, who blaspheme Heaven and Earth, and are ready to sweare themselves a live into Hell; then there are Irish Devills as hot as fire, and as bloody as *Belzebub*,[111] these delight in firing of houses, in killing women and Children, in tearing the flesh off Protestants shoulders with hot Pincers, as they did in *Ireland*,[112] together with their horrible cruelties here in *England*, these are cruell Irish Divells, such as doe not lie idle in the Market-place, as the Divill did upon his Elbow, because he knew they would lie and sweare fast enough there, to damn themselves; but these Malignants are no Dormant Devills, but active and stirring to doe mischief; they proclaime his Majesties will, and their own counsell to be Oracles, and make the King beleeve that none have wit or understanding, but his Majesties Cavaliers, and his new borne Councellors, and that none are so fit to make Priests and Jesuites, as the *Oxford* Schollers; and that if his Majesty print but a plausible Oath, or a Proclamation, that all hee doth, is for the advancement of the Protestant Religion; his Majesty may doe what he will in favour of Papists, and follow their Counsells, as long as the Malignants can but brand the Protestants with the name of Brownist, Anabaptist, Separatist, or Round-heads, and then the Schollers of *Oxford* doe make Sermons before the King of the fidelity of Papists, and how farre they are to be preferred above Puritanes and Protestants, whom they accoumpt ireligious Traytors; but O King, be rul'd no more by wicked Evill Counsellors, but follow the advice of Scripture wisedome; If this Counsell, or this worke of the Parliament be of men, it will come to naught, but if it be of God, ye cannot overthrow it, least (happily) ye be found fighters against God [Acts 5:38–39]. Behold, O King, but the disposition of all these Eare wigs, that insinuate into your Counsells; can dissolute lawlesse Cavaliers defend good Lawes? Or can Papists and Atheists fight for the true Protestant Religion, that were as strange, as for Thornes to beare grapes, and Thistles to beare figgs, and as strange it were, that Papists and Athiests should bear arms, to defend the Lawes, the Libertie of the Subject, and the Protestant Religion, the Divell they will; no, they fight to errect here the Kingdom of Darknes and Popery, that spirituall ambition may domineere flat-cap,[113] and the four-corner'd Cap[114] may fill the foure corners of the world full of knavery, there should be then no schisme, but a constant Lubberisme in *England*, Bishops, Deans, Doctors, Dunces, and Lubbers,[115] that when they preach't (being very seldome) would speake with a hoarse low voice, as if two or three steeples (having plurallity of Benifices) stuck in their throat; and when young Wives and wenches came to Confession, how the *Frier* (like the Divell) would hugg them? would not this be a pretty medly of [p. 6] confusion; nay, right and wrong shall be all one, fetch me such a Subjects, head, 'tother subjects bed, and his table, nay plunder him to a Pewter spoone, if he will not submit unto the Kings Prerogative; but banish conscience, for miters and Bishops can't indure him, Papists Priests can devise an easie Religion for my Court Lady, that she may go to heaven on a bed of Roses; & never take the paines to come thither, she is troubled with a loosenesse in the bottom of her belly, and cannot sit out a long Sermon, nor make long Prayers, let her give a few scraps at her door, and a doal of

Puddings at her death, and Angels shall carry her to Pope *Jone*.[116] But let us let these shee-fooles alone, these shee-Papists and malignant women, that will talke themselves out of breath against the Parliament, but if they might have their wills, to beat and cuckold their husbands by act of Parliament, then, and not till then they would praise the Parliament.

But *Time*, since thou hast thus far discribed the Malignants, goe on with boldnesse, poure out the rest of thy Sackfull of knavery, make the Proverbe true, *speak truth, & shame the Divell*, who stands behind thee, pulling down the sack, to hinder the emptying of it; but out with the trumpery, the Knavery, the Popery, the Policy, the Malignancy, flattery, and all the close wickednesse and impiety that hath been laid upon the back of *Time*, doe it briefly, roundly and plainly, and shake out of thy Sack, all varieties of Knavery.

Well done *Time*, what comes out here first? *Inprimis*,[117] hundred-pound baggs of money, and these were for Bribes for my Lords the Judges; and for Symony to procure a Benifice for Master *Dunscombe*, a Levite of littell learning, and lesse Conscience, whose Bribe being taken, hee was admitted to the Parsonage. O this money makes the Common-wealth a common whore, that lies down, and let fooles ride her, and deride her, while Knaves thriv'd, and honest men went to wrack, and every *Jack* might be made a Sir *John*, for an hundred pounds, and to conclude, malignant hundred pounds have sent hundred thousands to the Divell.

What comes next, Malignant pounds of Candles, made only for Polititions, to give them light how to study Plots against the Protestants; the Bishop of *Canterbury*[118] burnt twenty pounds of these candles, in studdying how to bring in *Popery*; the Earl of *Strafford* studdyed always by one of these malignant Candles, till at last, the Divell puff't out both the light of his Candle, and the light of his life both together; It is known that *Diogines*[119] had a malignant candle in his Lanthorne, which gave him light to see how to rayle, and so Malignants, and all wicked men have some of these Candles, Prince *Rupert* never goes to bed, but the Devill lights him up a candle, that he may see to forget to say his prayers, and that he may not see his cruell plunderings; and one of these candles are continually burning before the Kings Majesty, which [p. 7] gives him[120] such a dim light, that he cannot see the way how to returne unto his Parliament[.]

Next comes out the Papists Reliques, beads, crosses, crucifixes, whips, papist bookes licenced by the Bishop of *Canterbury*, fire and faggots, with which they intended to have burnt the Protestants, as they did in the dayes of Queen *Mary*;[121] and our Queen *Mary*[122] thought to have seen the like bonfires in her dayes: Hold down the mouth of thy sack, *Time*, what great gray thing is that come out tumbling? Oh, 'tis one of the Fryers that liv'd at Saint *Jameses*, fatt and full of knavery and popery; hold, there's a Surplesse, and two payre of Lawn-Sleeves, a hood, a cope, and the poopish [*sic*] Service-boke that was sent downe to the *Scots*, and a paire of Organs, and a may-poole, and the skull of the Queen-mother,[123] with a number of papist skulls, that while they liv'd, were all Traytors to the Common-wealth of *England*.

What's heere, Serpents? such as *Cottington* and the rest of the Kings evill Counsellors; and look heere are Eeles, Court Eeles, that would slip into any place of preferrment, but it is knowne, that thunder doth break the bedds of Eeles, and since the thunder of warre began, these malignant Eeles are all run unto the King, and doe live in the fresh waters at *Oxford*, *Bristoll*, and other parts in the West Country.

Now comes forth Lawyers black-boxes, poore men brought these by their sides out of the Country to *London*, and returned againe with nothing but penury and papers; shake them out *Time*, for when these times were, the Divell and the Lawyer were alwayes full of businesse in the Terme time.

Whats heere? a Lions skinne, with a Foxes tayle to it, a very good Embleme, to shew that malignant Counsellours doe make use of the Lions power, to back their malignant plotts, and thus the King is abused by the malignants pollicy.

But oh horrible and monstrous, heer's a hand with a sword in it, full of hearts, that have been run through by the Sword, and upon the point of the sword is a Crowne, Oh I fear this sword doth too evidently point out the King, who hath been abused by his Evill Counsellors, his Cavaliers, and the Irish Rebells, who have run their swords through the hearts of many thousand Protestants, this is a bloody sight shak't out of the Sack of *Time*.

Here are more swords, all which have been guilty of *English* blood, not onely their hilts, but their blades are sanguin'd over, they look red, and blush, that friends and brothers, should with hearts of Iron, hard as their swords, kill one another; but now comes out of the sack two bloody hands, the one holding a sword, the other a Torch, and this doth signifie Prince *Rupert,* who is a bloody man of his hands, and doth shew continuall cruelty with fire and sword, as he did at Bolton in Lancashire,[124] and in many other places, which have suffered under this plundering Prince.

Heere comes out now a Box, full of Commissions to doe nothing; such as the Duke of *Buckingham* had when he went to relieve the Protestants in *Rochell*,[125] and *Sicill*, when he went *Cales* Voyage;[126] and then here's another box, with the Kings Armes upon it, and in it there's the Commission of Array, with a great many of the Kings Protestations, together with letters from the Queen, and how the Kings Cabbinetts of Jewells, being pawn'd, he hath nothing left but a box full of papers not of Poetry, but pollicy, and they must needs be strong lines, that are writ by a King and Queene, and their strong malignants.

Now comes out tumbling together Ship-money, Coxcombes for carpet-Knights, such as *Jermyn*[127] and *Endymion Porter*,[128] being new made Gentlemen, and now being malignants, are made I know not what: heere comes out Monopolies of white-soape, ragges, mary-bones, cardes, tobacco, and a pattent that should have been granted for pissing against the wall; monopolies and knaveries,[129] come out here.

Whats heere? Oh 'tis the Bishop of *Canterburies* new book, that he sent to the Scots, being sent to him from his Holinesse of *Rome*, and contrived by the Pope, but the mischief was, the bishop of *Canterbury* could not get a close cover for this booke, so that the Scots disco- [p. 8] vered his Popish purpose, and would rather see it burnt, then entertaine a leafe of it, to be read in their true reformed Churches.[130]

Hold, hold, heer'[s] a company of eyes and eares, and tongues poured out of the Sack of *Time*; why *Time*, wilt thou shame thy self, could there ever be a Time so wicked, that the *Star-chamber* should endeavour to pluck out the eyes of Religion, and to pick out the best men, to have them disgraced by cutting off their eares nay, and by cutting out their tongues, that is, by silencing Godly Ministers in the Diocesses where the bishops reign'd, this was true enough.[131]

But whats heere? *Oxford* Trumpery, and Knavery, Schollers flat-caps, and square-caps, Divines gowns which the Schollers lay down, and while they drink healths to the confusion of the *Roundheads*, they will cry; Lie there Divinity; these are pretty fellows to make Popish Priests of; it is known that *Aulicus* is one of these drunken fellows of *All soules* Colledge;[132] but here comes out more, namely Christ-Church Organs, surplesses, Beades, Crosses, Halfe-Crowns coyn'd out of *Oxford* Plate, Cuckolds hornes made by the Cavaliers, Books of Popery, of conjuring and all sorts of Malignant Pamphlets, long gownes, that cover the *Oxford* Levites, that have little Gospel in them, with speares, gunnes and Corslets and Helmets, which the Bishops and Schollers ware at *Oxford*, being better head pieces than their owne.

But oh what comes out now? the very worst of all, the bottome of bottomlesse Popery and cruelty, Heads, Armes, Leggs, feet, and whole quarters of men, women and children butcher'd by the Rebells in *Ireland*, and heere comes out tongs and Pincers wherewith being heated red-hot, they did pluck the flesh from the bodies of the Protestants; Daggers with which they stab'd the Protestants, and let them bleed to death in their sight, Gridirons whereon they roasted Protestants; with Halters, Clubs wherewith they knock out the braines of Protestants, long Knives where-with they ript Children out of their Mothers bellyes, and cut the throats of many thousand Protestants, Axes, wherewith they quartered Protestants, cutting some into small peices, but the burthen of varieties, of cruel-ties which *Time* hath born in *England* and *Ireland*, is insufferable, the Papists Plots and projects innumerable[,] the Malignants malice and pol-licy unchangeable; the Kings heart implacable, so that it would be a hard matter for *Time* to shake all Malignants out of his Sack, he is no small-coal-man, for his sack can never be emptyed, it having no bottom, but is as deep as the Sea of *Rome*, that have so many that help to fill it with knav-ery, as *Bishops, Malignants[,] rotten Lords, Cavaliers, Pint-pot Preachers, Judges, Lawyers, Country Knights, Malignant Majors of Towns, Bristoll, Cottington, Prince Robert[,] Mauris*,[133] *Lords of Cumber-land*,[134] *Bath, Southampton, Dorset, Northampton, Devenshire[,] Bristoll, Barkshire, Hopton, Capell*,[135] with the Lord *Digby*, and the Lord *Devill, the grand Malignant.*

FINIS.

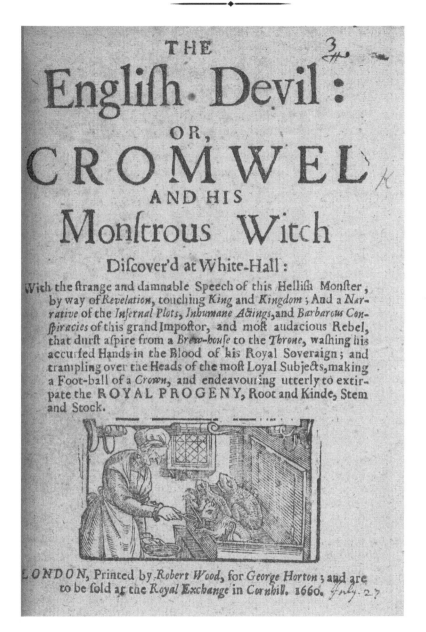

THE
Englifh Devil:
OR,
CROMWEL
AND HIS
Monftrous Witch

Difcover'd at White-Hall :

With the ftrange and damnable Speech of this Hellifh Monfter, by way of *Revelation*, touching *King* and *Kingdom* ; And a *Narrative* of the *Infernal Plots, Inhumane Actings*, and *Barbarous Confpiracies* of this grand Impoftor, and moft audacious Rebel, that durft afpire from a *Brew-houfe* to the *Throne*, wafhing his accurfed Hands in the Blood of his Royal Soveraign ; and trampling over the Heads of the moft Loyal Subjects, making a Foot-ball of a *Crown*, and endeavouring utterly to extirpate the ROYAL PROGENY, Root and Kinde, Stem and Stock.

LONDON, Printed by *Robert Wood*, for *George Horton* ; and are to be fold at the *Royal Exchange* in *Cornhill*. 1660.

Figure 4.5 Title page, *The English Devil*, 1660. The image depicts the stereotypical witch—an elderly woman with a pointed chin and hooked nose—feeding several familiars. The woodcut, or versions of it, seems to have been in circulation for at least eighty years: it appeared on sig. Av of the witchcraft pamphlet *A rehearsall both straung and true, of hainous and horrible actes committed* (London: [By J. Kingston] for Edward White, 1579).

Source: © The British Library Board E.1035.(3.).

THE
English-Devil:
or,
CROMWEL
and his
Monstrous Witch
Discover'd at White-Hall:
With the strange and damnable Speech of this Hellish Monster,
by way of *Revelation*, touching *King* and *Kingdom*; And a *Nar-*
rative of the *Infernal Plots, Inhumane Actings*, and *Barbarous Con-*
spiracies of this grand Impostor, and most audacious Rebel,
that durst aspire from a *Brew-house* to the *Throne*, washing his
accursed Hands in the Blood of his Royal Soveraign; and
trampling over the Heads of the most Loyal Subjects, making
a Foot-ball of a *Crown*, and endeavouring utterly to extirpate the ROYAL PROGENY, Root and Kinde, Stem
and Stock.

LONDON, Printed by *Robert Wood*, for *George Horton*; and are
to be sold at the *Royal Exchange* in Cornhill. 1660.[136]

[p. 3] *The English Devil*; Or, *The Bloody Traytor*, &c.

AS for that Hellish Monster, and damnable Machiavilian, that first gave
rise to our new-fangled Models of Government, we shall onely demonstrate
him to be the *Devil* of later Times, who Butcher-like made cruelty his profession, & was never better then when he had his Sword sheathed in his
Countrey-mens bowels; such an audacious Rebel was this *Oliver Cromwel*,
that durst aspire from the mean condition of a private person, to the Throne,
though he first wash'd his hands in the blood of his Soveraign: He represented the real Tragedy of a King and no King; whose mouth water'd after
that Title, but that he durst not assume it, having fought so long against it,
and was sworn to the deposition of all Kingship for the future. He, to raise
himself on the top of the Pyramid of honour, trampled over the heads of
the most Loyal Subjects of the Realm; made a foot-ball of a Crown, and
endeavoured utterly to extirpate the Royal Progeny, Root and Kind, Stem
and Stock: Nay, I may be bold to say, if that an innocent Babe had been
born with *Vive le Roy* in his mouth, he must have been food for his Sword,
as well as the first-born were for *Herods*.[137] It is credibly reported, that *Hugh*
Peters,[138] that spiritual *Dragooner*,[139] and *Nol*,[140] hatch'd this Government
as they were walking together in a field: *A brace of pious Devils!* The whole
Nation was enchained in a more than Ægyptian Bondage; who were compelled to submit to this Tyrant *Nol*, or be cut off by him; nothing but a word
and a blow, his Will was his Law; tell him of *Magna Charta*, he would lay
his hand on his sword, and cry *Magna Farta*. No Liberty was granted to

the Subject, unless it were that of the Conscience; and that too was denied the more Orthodox and Loyal Party. The People were [p. 4] rob'd of all Laws, Rights, and Priviledges, and sometimes of their lives; whilest he, like a Tyrant, insulted with a *Quis contradicet?*[141] The Citizens were so fleeced and pilled, that had this inhumane barbarous Wretch continued much longer, he had sent *London* into the Country a begging. To say *God save the King*, was a crime as black as any forbidden in the *Decalogue*:[142] but so long as that was prohibited publikely and privately, it was in vain to cry out, *God speed the Plough*, or expect any blessing from the Superiour Power. His infernal Plots and Machinations had wrought the utter ruine and desolation of the Country, had not Providence divine cut him off, to the general benefit and rejoycing of the Nation. *English* ground groaned with the burthen of this inhumane Tyrant. It was not enough that the *English* should be scourged, but the *whip* must lye before them; it is not sufficient that he should be the Author of all their Woes while living, but they must live subject to his Tyranny and Oppression, and like so many Mutes, condescend unto all his Actions by silence, not daring to mention the least dislike, though it thwarted their disposition never so much: *He was a Rod of their own making, and they were content to Untruss whilest he Whipt them.* In vain it was for the most accurate Wit to Plead Reason or Law against the Sword; the Tongue is too weak a Weapon for the Dagger. During the Usurpation of this same *Hellish Tyrant*, what a Chaos of confusion bespread the whole Nation? How was all the Land *Benegro'd*[143] with more than the Egiptian darkness of Persecution? The whole Countrey was inveloped in Clouds, and Ruine hung over the Heads of the People, by as slender a Thrid, as the Sword did over the Head of *Damocles* at the Banquet. The whole Land was Entombed in despair, and little or no hope of a Resurrection, till a Divine Hand wrought it by his long-expected Death: And it is the Cordial wish and Hearty desire of the Loyal *Pen-man*, that all his Majesties and the Kingdoms Enemies were as stately interred as he was. Had he deserved an Epitaph, We would have stretched hard but our Brain should have furnished him with one; but since he was so unworthy, We hold it as great a disparagement to our Quill to bestow a Copy of Verses on him, as he was a grief and trouble to the Loyal party of the Nation[.] And indeed, how can any Son of *Phœbus*[144] imploy his time so ill, as to salute his dead Corps with an Epitaph, that was so great an Enemy to them whilest living; Who had a real design to extirpiate all literature, and in[-]plunge us into as deep a Gulph of ignorance and prophaness as the Turk is cast into? He hated [p. 5] all Learning, and the Learned, because his Crimes were so black and horrid, that they went far beyond the mercy of the Book. He granted a tolleration for all Religions, because his own was to choose; and that he might not offend the Tender Consciences of his pretended Zealots and Favorites, who were true Vassels to the Lust and Villainy of such an Imperious Usurper. Honesty was so much out of fashion, that he that was Vertuous was a Malefactor, and deserved Death; for Knavery was *a la mode*; and you know the old saying, [*It*] *is as good to be out of the*

World, as out of the Fashion. An honest loyal Subject was as much hooted and pointed at, and judged as ridiculous an Object, as a *Spanish Don* in his Country Garb at *Paris.* An honest man was as strange a sight in *England*, as a Horse in *Venice*, or a Beggar in *Holland*, and he was as like to be preferred to his favour, as a Spurrier[145] was to Queen *Elizabeth.* But since he is in his Grave, We will not rake up his Ashes any further: if he can find any rest there now dead, who living I am sure had little or none in his Conscience (for he ever carried a Civil War in his Breast, of Fears, Suspicions, and Jealousies) he shall lye secure, for *we* intend to disturb him no farther.

After the death of this *Brittish Idol, Richard* the 4th. his Son peeped out; *who had no fault so great as that he had him to his Father*, for it was generally believed, he would be but Tenant to the Right Landlord, or the *Stuarts* Steward, to set all things in Order till he was restored. But, alas! he proved but a fortnights wonder; no sooner up, but down; his disposition[,] (if we may credit report) was the Womanish plot of Weeping-*Fleetwoods* Lady;[146] who stomached it that his preferment should be greater then her Husbands, though it proved to little purpose: And Indeed, it is seldome known that Females councel ever arrives to any better success; nor is there any reason that the *Distaff*[147] should be a companion for the *Scepter. A Kitchin was a great deal more fit for her than a Throne*, though she had Ambition enough to perswade her self that she deserved the name of a Princess. Yet had Richard iii[i] [been] Heir of his Fathers parts (*though it was well he was not*) he would have soon frustrated their designs, and came to as much heigth and greatness: But he had not enough of the *Rogue* in his Composition, to make up a *Damned Politician.* He was fitter to bear a *Hawk* on his Fist, than to hold a *Scepter* in his Hand. A sedentary, retired, Country-life, was far more suitable to his Temper and Disposition, than a Tumultuous City-life. He was altogether ignorant in that so much practised profession of peircing the *Lyon*[148] [p. 6] *with the Foxes Tail*; which no doubt he might have done, had he been as well read in *Machiavil* as his Sire was. He was not much read in *Politicks*, as appears by the small term of time that was allotted him to *play the Protector.* But no matter, it was well it fell out so, he is like to fare the better for it, in the judgement of the most censorious: Besides, it was what suited with his fancie (according to relation) better then all the Usurped Power and Authority of his Predecessor. *Exit Protector*, he was but like a *Pageant, a King in a Play*; he onely appears upon the *Stage*, makes a Legg, and takes his leave of you.

But what comes next? A Resolve here intervenes! No less then the Bloody Tragedy of OLIVER the *Traytor*, who to Unite firmly the Council of War to him, which consisted of a few able Head-pieces, to whom he laid himself open so far, as to shew them their profit and preferment in the designe, which United them fast to him, the other, who were soft Heads, and had a good meaning to do no evil, but to promote the Kingdom of Christ, and throw down Anti-christ, and then according to their duty, (as they were taught) to take possession of, and (as Saints) Reign over the Kingdom; *Cromwel* provided fit food to feed such fantasies, for he had provided a Monstrous Witch full of all deceitful craft, who being put into brave cloaths, pretended she was a Lady come from a far Countrey, being sent by God to the Army with a Revelation, which she must make known to the Army, for necessity was laid upon her: This Witch had a fair Lodging prepared for her in *White-hall*. Now having had her Lesson taught her before by *Cromwel* and *Ireton*, by whose order she was entertained, desired to have audience at the Council of War, for to them (she said) she was sent.

Cromwel and *Ireton* to beget the more attention and belief in the Officers of the Council of War, began to extoll the excellency of Revelation, and conceived that this Prophetess being a precious Saint, and having much of God in her, ought for to be heard, and that with all intention; because (said they) in such glorious dayes as these God doth manifest himself extraordinarily; and especially to his Saints, in chalking out their way before them, when they came into straights and difficulties; such as they were in at that time.

By this time the Witch was come to the door, and forthwith had admittance; where all the Officers beheld her strange postures, expressing high Devotion: *Cromwel* and *Ireton* fixing their [p. 7] Eyes upon her in most solemn manner (to beget in the rest of the Officers (who were ready to laugh) an apprehension of some serious thing) fell both of them to weeping; the Witch looking in their Faces, and seeing them weep, fell to weeping likewise; and began to tell them what acquaintance she had with God by Revelation, and how such a Day, such an Hour, after such a manner she had a Revelation, which she was to reveal only to them; and that was, That the glorious time of setting up Christs Kingdom was near at hand, and that Anti-christ must be speedily thrown down, and that they were the Instruments that were by God ordained to throw him down, and how they were about that great work, and that if they would prosper in it, they must first remove the KING out of the way, which they must do first by proceeding to Try him, and then to Condemn him, and then to Depose him, but not to put him to Death: This Relation I had from one that was strongly of the Armies party, but related this shamefull story with much indignation.

A *Lillonian* was taught at this time with Bribes to Print his opinion, which was much according to the opinion of his Sister Witch.[149]

Some of the Soberer and more Religious of the Officers being much startled at these Revelations, but not at all satisfied, repaired to some of the most Religious and able *Independents* to know their opinion of these things, and to defire advice what to do; they replyed (I am informed *Thomas Goodwin* in particular[150]) that since they had gone so far, they must now carry it on, though with the Blood of those that stood in their way, for if they now made a stop, farewel their Cause for ever: This was good in *Politicks*, but bad in Divinity: It was a true *Politick Aphorism* of *Machiavells*, but false Doctrine in the Divinity Schools; however they made use of this Doctrine to proceed in their designs, for the promoting of the *Independent Cause*.

By this time *John Lilburn*[151] and his party, who sate at *White-hall* to draw up their desires, had brought their business to some maturity, which was, as I conceive, inserted in the Paper called, *The Agreement of the People*, the sum whereof, was no other then this, to Throw down *KING, Lords*, and *Commons, as then established*, to Throw down the *Lawes, Inns of Court, Courts of Judicature, Church Government*, as also the *Universities*, and *Function of the Clergie*.

[p. 8] This Agreement being debated at the General Council, *Cromwel* (whose design was to set up another Government, and was then about it) opposed this Agreement, because it opposed his design; for though he sate in Councel with the General Officers, yet he consulted altogether with the Popish Faction, to set up a Government according to the Government of *Spain, (viz.)* by a Councel of State, and a High Court of Justice.

The General Councel of War was hereby divided about this Agreement of the people, and so equally divided, that onely one Voice carried it, or two at the most in the Negative, which gave ocaasion [*sic*] to Col. *Hewson*[152] to say, *How can we call this the Agreement of the People, when we our selves are divided about it? Cromwel* being now to shoot the greatest Gulf,[153] having now the Work to do, which he had been all this while by force and policy making way unto; he saw but two main rubs in the way, which he durst not meddle with in a boysterous *way*, and those were the Presbyterian Ministers of the Kingdom, who preached vehemently against the Treasonable practises of the Army. The other whom he durst not at this time meddle with, were those down-right dealers called Levellers: What he could not do by Flattery, he did by Threats; but could not in the least terrifie the Presbyterians, *who* declared against his wicked and open Rebellion, detesting those illegal proceedings of the Army, in offering violence to the Parliament, and going about to overthrow the King.

FINIS.

Notes

1 William E. Burns, "The King's Two Monstrous Bodies: John Bulwer and the English Revolution," in *Wonders, Marvels, and Monsters in Early Modern Culture*, ed. by Peter G. Platt (London: Associated University Presses, 1999), 188–189.

2 Joad Raymond, *The Invention of the Newspaper: English Newsbooks 1641–1649* (Oxford: Clarendon Press, 1996), 201–203.

3 Laura Lunger Knoppers, *Constructing Cromwell: Ceremony, Portrait, and Print, 1645–1661* (New York: Cambridge University Press, 2000; digitally printed version, 2009), 10.

4 Joad Raymond, "Henry Walker (fl. 1638–1660)," *Oxford Dictionary of National Biography* (Oxford: Oxford University Press, 2004).

5 For a discussion of judgment narratives and Beard's work, see Alexandra Walsham, *Providence in Early Modern England* (New York: Oxford University Press, 1999), chap. 2, esp. 65–75.

6 *A true and strange relation of a boy, who was entertained by the Devill* (London: Printed by J.H., 1645). Other narratives of judgment upon Cavaliers included *A blazing starre seen in the west at Totneis in Devonshire* (London: Printed for Jonas Wright, and I. H., 1642); *A wonderfull and strange miracle or Gods just*

vengeance against the cavaliers (London: Printed for Henry Hutton, 1642); and John Vicars, *A looking-glasse for malignants: or, Gods hand against God-haters* (London: Printed for John Rothwell, 1643; expanded ed., 1645).

7 Quoted in Raymond, *Invention*, 269.

8 Mark Stoyle, *The Black Legend of Prince Rupert's Dog: Witchcraft and Propaganda during the English Civil War* (Exeter, UK: University of Exeter Press, 2011); for a similar, though less detailed conclusion, see also Diane Purkiss, "Desire and Its Deformities: Fantasies of Witchcraft in the English Civil War," *Journal of Medieval and Early Modern Studies* 27 no. 1 (1997), 108. *Observations* is not reproduced in this sourcebook, but a transcription with helpful annotations can be found in Stoyle, 169–177.

9 Another version of the story was given in *Mercurius Civicus* (No. 18, 21–28 September 1643). The connection between these narratives is discussed in Stoyle, *Black Legend*, chap. 7, esp. 117–127.

10 *A Most Certain, Strange, and true Discovery of a Witch* ([London?]: Printed by John Hammond, 1643), 7. An alternative suggestion, posited by Stoyle, is that the author added this disclaimer to distance himself from the Parliamentarian authorities, who might have disapproved of the pamphlet either because of its implicit attack on the King or because of their "aversion to witch-tracts in general" (*Black Legend*, 122). This is possible; however, the disclaimer is unusual, and there seems no reason why the author/publisher would have felt *compelled* to add it.

11 For a discussion of Royalists' connection between rebellion and witchcraft, see the insightful discussion in Peter Elmer, *Witchcraft, Witch-Hunting, and Politics in Early Modern England* (Oxford: Oxford University Press, 2016), 90–100; quote at 97.

12 Most of the confessions made by East Anglian witches dealt with concerns more parochial than political, but some involved the Royalist war effort. For instance, an issue of *A Perfect Diurnall of Some Passages in Parliament* (21–28 July 1645), 830, as well as the pamphlet *Signes and Wonders from Heaven* (London: Printed by I.H., [1645]), 4, suggested the witches' executions would remove Prince Rupert's invincibility. See Malcolm Gaskill, *Witchfinders: A Seventeenth-Century English Tragedy* (Cambridge, MA: Harvard University Press, 2005), chap. 6, esp. 144–150.

13 1 Samuel 15:23 was a popular passage this year, with at least three other Royalist ministers invoking it in sermons preached in March, May, and August. Elmer, *Witchcraft*, 93–94.

14 Nath. Bernard, *Esoptron tes antimachias, or, A Looking-Glasse for Rebellion* (Oxford: Printed by Leonard Lichfield, 1644), 15.

15 *The Kingdomes Monster Uncloaked from Heaven* ([London: s.n.], 1643).

16 A reference to Henry Walker, a bookseller, preacher, and former ironmonger who had landed himself in trouble in the early 1640s for his critiques of the king. In 1642, Walker engaged in a heated pamphlet war with the Royalist "Water-Poet," John Taylor, in which the two lobbed scurrilous publications at each other. The present work, although not attributed to Taylor, was written in this context.

17 From "julep," a soothing, cooling drink.

18 Probably a mistake for "Arminius." Jacob Arminius (1560–1609) was a Dutch theologian whose views on the role of human free will in salvation conflicted with Reformed (or Calvinist) teachings on God's sovereignty, predestination, and fallen man's inability to save himself, and were extremely controversial in seventeenth-century England.

19 Original: "suller."

20 A small, private religious meeting. Since it usually consisted of members of an illegal religion, the word had a negative connotation, as demonstrated in this pamphlet.
21 From "Acheron:" in Greek mythology, one of the rivers of Hades, but later applied to Hell generally.
22 To drink deeply.
23 From the underworld river Styx in classical mythology; characteristic of Hell.
24 A reference to the parody of a sermon facetiously attributed to Walker in John Taylor's pamphlet *A seasonable lecture, or, A most learned oration disburthened from Henry Walker, a most judicious* Quondam *iron monger* (London: F. Cowles, T. Bates, and T. Banks, 1642). The copy of this pamphlet in the Thomason Collection has the annotation "Tobies Dog" on the title page.
25 Another sermon parody by Taylor, *A Tale in a Tub* (London: [n.p.], 1642). A "tub" was a colloquial term for a pulpit, and "tub-preacher" was used derogatorily of non-conformist preachers. Also in 1642 Taylor published his satirical *An apology for private preaching in which those formes are warranted, or rather, justified, which the malignant sect contemne and daily by prophane pamphlets make ridiculous*, in which he "justified" the supposed sectarian practice of literally preaching from a tub; the point was made pictorially by the woodcut of *A seasonable lecture*, which featured the preacher expounding on his text from a wooden cask.
26 A member of the Family of Love, a sect founded by the German mystic Henry Nicholis in the sixteenth century. Theologically, they were accused of such heresies as denying the Incarnation and divine providence and claiming to be sinless; morally and practically, they were associated in particular with sexual orgies among themselves, as suggested at the end of this pamphlet.
27 "Cracked:" impaired, morally flawed, or mentally unsound; possibly also bankrupt.
28 Original: "consideratious."
29 After the Separatist minister Robert Brown (c. 1550–1633). There was no coherent religious group of this name; rather, "Brownist" was equated with "sectarian" and applied derogatorily to those who wished to radically reform or else separate from the episcopal Church of England in favor of a more decentralized (congregational) church polity.
30 With the care of souls.
31 A corruption of "malmsey-nose," a nose enflamed by alcohol consumption (such as malmsey, a type of wine).
32 A "bilbo" was a type of sword and was also used for the kind of swashbuckling figure who might carry one.
33 "Hackney" and "jade" are both terms for common riding horses.
34 In order to procreate.
35 The copy in the Thomason Collection includes the annotation "Sept: 15."
36 Thomas Wentworth, 1st Earl of Strafford (1593–1641), was condemned by Parliament for treason and beheaded in 1641.
37 The capture and sack of Birmingham on April 3, 1643, by Royalist soldiers under Prince Rupert's command inspired several reactionary publications from the Parliamentarian press. The woodcut on the cover of one such piece featured Prince Rupert and his dog; the flaming city depicted in the distance was labelled "Brimidgham," as it is in this poem. See I.W., *The Bloody Prince* (London: [s.n.], 1643), frontispiece. For a Parliamentarian piece on the capture of Birmingham, see *Prince Ruperts burning love to England: discovered in Birminghams flames* (London: Printed for Thomas Underhill, 1643).
38 Annotation on the Thomason copy: "Sept. 28."
39 Middle letters blotted, but see note 4.

40 Roger Bacon (c. 1214–1292), a Franciscan friar and philosopher who left an ambiguous legacy; Thomas Bungay (fl. 1270–1283), a theologian and mathematician; and the apparently fictional Jacques Vandermast all appeared as magicians in the popular play *Friar Bacon and Friar Bungay*, which was first printed in 1594 and appeared again in 1630 and 1655. For the most recent edition from this pamphleteer's perspective, see *The Honorable Historie of Frier Bacon, and Frier Bongay* (London: Printed by Elizabeth Allde, 1630).

41 The story of Faust, who sells his soul to the Devil in return for the ability to do magic, was popularized by Christopher Marlowe's play *The Tragical History of the Horrible Life and Death of Doctor Faustus*. The work was first published in 1604, and different versions appeared in the following decades; see, for instance, the 1631 edition, *The Tragicall Historie of the Life and Death of Doctor Faustus* (Printed at London: for John Wright, 1631).

42 Original: "rried."

43 Original: "Wirch."

44 Robert Devereux (1595–1646), 3rd Earl of Essex, was commander of the Parliamentary forces in 1643. He won a victory against the Royalists at the First Battle of Newbury on September 20, a little over a week before George Thomason collected this pamphlet.

45 Mischievous.

46 A wooden plank.

47 Floated.

48 Killed; dispatched.

49 Gloss: "P. *Ruperts* sorrow."

50 Gloss: "His policie." Following the Royalist defeat at the Battle of Marston Moor on July 2, 1644, rumors circulated in Parliamentarian newsbooks that Prince Rupert had been forced to flee the scene and hide in a beanfield. A pamphlet published about a week prior to *A Dog's Elegy* featured a woodcut depicting not only the prince cowering ignominiously in the plants but his dog left dead amid the rifled baggage. *Ruperts sumpter, and private cabinet rifled* (London: Printed by Jane Coe, 1644), title page. See also Mark Stoyle, *The Black Legend of Prince Rupert's Dog: Witchcraft and Propaganda during the English Civil War* (Exeter, UK: University of Exeter Press, 2011), 135–137.

51 Gloss: "His Army Routed."

52 The four victorious Parliamentarian commanders. A combined English and Scottish Covenanter force under Lord Ferdinando Fairfax and Alexander Leslie, Earl of Leven, were besieging York in mid-1644 when Prince Rupert arrived to relieve the city. The Eastern Association army, under the overall command of Edward Montagu, Earl of Manchester, and with Oliver Cromwell in command of the cavalry, marched to Leven and Fairfax's aid and succeeded in defeating Rupert at Marston Moor. Lord Fairfax's son, Sir Thomas, also fought valiantly at Marston Moor and became commander of the New Model Army when it was established in January 1645.

53 Gloss: "His *Dogs* Progeny."

54 Gloss: "The property of *Witches*."

55 Gloss: "Her Spirit."

56 Prince Maurice of the Rhine (1621–1652) served his uncle Charles I's cause alongside his brother Rupert. At several points during the war he was rumored to have been killed; possibly the author had heard such a report.

57 Gloss: "The dog begotten."

58 In Greek mythology, one of the three Furies and the source of jealousy.

59 The Beargarden or Bear Pit in Southwark was so called for the bear-baiting entertainment hosted there.

60 The Hospital of St. Mary of Bethlehem in London was a facility for the mentally ill, and the colloquial form of the name, "Bedlam," had long been synonymous with madness.

61 Gloss: "Signs of prodigious births."

62 Gloss: "The dogges birth."

63 Gloss: "His cunning."

64 Gloss: "His depth of skill."

65 Gloss: "His first trick[e]."

66 In medieval lore, a woman named Joan was reputed to have disguised her gender and become head of the Catholic Church; her charade was revealed when she became pregnant and went into labor during a papal procession. The veracity of her scandalous story was debated by Catholics and Protestants in the sixteenth and seventeenth centuries, with Protestants employing it as proof of Rome's corruption. See, for example, Alexander Cooke, *Pope Joane A dialogue betweene a protestant and a papist. Manifestly proving, that a woman called Joane was Pope of Rome: against the surmises and objections made to the contrarie, by Robert Bellarmine and Caesar Baronius Cardinals: Florimondus Raemondus, N.D. and other popish writers, impudently denying the same* (London: Printed for Ed. Blunt and W. Barret, 1610).

67 Gloss: "The great *Armado*."

68 The writer credits Rupert's "dog" with the launching of the Spanish Armada, sent in 1588 in an ultimately unsuccessful attempt to invade England. The destruction of the fleet was invoked repeatedly by English writers as an example of God's protection of Protestant England.

69 Sir Francis Drake (1540–1596), a privateer celebrated for his raids on Spanish shipping and credited with the destruction of the Armada.

70 Gloss: "Queen *Elizabeth* many times miraculously delivered."

71 Gloss: "The Popish Powder-plot." In 1605, a group of English Catholics plotted to remove James I and his Protestant government by blowing up the House of Lords. Their treason was discovered before the plan could be put into action, and "Gunpowder Treason Day," November 5, was subsequently celebrated by English Protestants as a day of thanksgiving for God's deliverance.

72 Gloss: "The Dog turns Courtier." George Villiers, 1st Duke of Buckingham (1592–1628), was a courtier and favorite of James I and Charles I. His political influence was ascribed by some to the sorcery of the magician and astrologer Dr. John Lambe, whom Buckingham was known to consult. In 1628 Lambe was lynched by a London mob and Buckingham was assassinated. See Nathan Johnstone, *The Devil and Demonism in Early Modern England* (Cambridge: Cambridge University Press, 2006), 197.

73 The author's gloss identifies the noble Scot as the Duke of Lennox. Ludovic(k) Stewart/Stuart, 2nd Duke of Lennox and 1st Duke of Richmond (1574–1624) died of apoplexy, but his demise was viewed with suspicion by the likes of John Vicars; see *Prodigies & Apparitions* ([London: n.p., 1643]), 16.

74 The eighteen-year-old Prince of Wales, Henry Frederick, died suddenly in 1612 of a fever and his brother Charles became heir to the throne.

75 In the late 1610s and early 1620s, England and Spain attempted to arrange a marriage between the then-Prince Charles and the Infanta Maria, but negotiations foundered on the question of the Infanta's religion and of toleration for English Catholics.

76 Gloss: "The Popes letter."

77 Gloss: "K. *James* his death."

78 The Duke of Buckingham was believed to have poisoned James I in 1625; Johnstone, *The Devil and Demonism*, 197.

79 Gloss: "*Canterbury* ushers in popery." William Laud (1573–1645) was elected Archbishop of Canterbury in 1633. His attempts to reform the Church of England and to enforce conformity, in addition to his alleged Catholic sympathies, made him deeply unpopular with English Puritans; he was charged by Parliament with high treason in 1640 and was beheaded in 1645 after a long imprisonment.

80 Gloss: "The Ile of *Rue* voyage." In 1627, Buckingham led an expedition to La Rochelle and the Île de Ré to support the Huguenots in their conflict with the Catholic monarchy of France. The effort was a disaster and contributed to Buckingham's further decline in popularity back home.

81 John Felton, a soldier who had served under Buckingham, stabbed the Duke to death. Although he was executed for his action, some considered him a hero for removing the councilor from power. *ODNB*.

82 Gloss: "The *Declaration* for Sports on the Sabbath-day." Archbishop Laud's efforts to increase the beauty of church decorations and of clergymen's dress smacked to Puritans of Catholic extravagance and idolatry, while his 1633 reissuance of the Book of Sports, which allowed certain recreations on Sunday, offended those who saw all such activities as a desecration of the Lord's Day. These reforms were decried in the 1640 Root and Branch Petition; see in particular Articles XIV and XXI, *The first and large petition of the Citie of London . . . for a reformation in church-government* ([London: s.n.,] 1641), 8 and 10.

83 Francis White, Bishop of Ely (c. 1563–1638), and Matthew Wren (1585–1667), White's successor, were both proponents of the Laudian reforms and opponents of Puritanism. While White died prior to the war, Wren shared in Laud's fall from power: he was imprisoned in the Tower in 1642 and only released in 1660.

84 Gloss: "*Mr. Burton, Mr. Prynne,* and *Dr. Bastwick.*" Cases of sedition were tried before the Star Chamber, which issued harsh punishments to those found guilty of criticizing Church or State. These three men were Puritan critics of the regime who were charged with sedition in 1637 and had their ears cut.

85 Gloss: "*Scotlands* piety." Charles I's attempt to impose the Book of Common Prayer upon Scotland inspired a backlash from Scots who favored a presbyterian rather than episcopal church government. The ensuing conflicts became known as the Bishops' Wars (1639–1640).

86 Gloss: "Queen-mother." Marie d'Medici, mother of Queen Henrietta Maria, visited England in 1638 and remained until 1641. Her presence was perceived as part of a "Catholic revival" at court and thus played into the hands of the king and queen's Puritan critics; see the *ODNB* article on Henrietta Maria.

87 Thomas Wentworth, 1st Earl of Strafford (1593–1641), was charged by Parliament with encouraging Charles I to act without the Houses' consent and conspiring to bring in an army to force the recalcitrant MPs to accede to the King's wishes. He was executed in 1641.

88 Gloss: "Traytors, and papists, Whelps of the same litter." Henry Jermyn (1605–1684); John Digby, 1st Earl of Bristol (1580–1653); George Digby, Earl of Bristol (1612–1677); and Baron Francis Cottington (1579?–1652) were regarded by Parliamentarians as particularly dangerous members of Charles' Oxford council during the war.

89 When Irish Catholic gentry rebelled against English control in 1641, stories of the atrocities committed by the natives against English Protestant settlers quickly poured from London presses.

90 Gloss: "The Dogs Master." These were common names for Prince Rupert in the Parliamentarian press.

91 Gloss: "These and Irish Rebells, his Majesties *best Subjects.*" William Cavendish, 1st Duke of Newcastle upon Tyne (1593–1676), was a prominent Royalist general and commander-in-chief in the north. Arthur Capel, 1st Baron Capel

of Hadham (1604–1649), was appointed lieutenant-general of north Wales, Shropshire, Cheshire, and Worcestershire in 1643 but proved ineffective in his post. The appellation "Cow-stealer" appears to have caught on: see, John Vicars, *Gods arke overtopping the worlds waves* (London: Printed by M. Simons, and J. Macock, 1645 [1646]), 161.

92 Henry Hastings, 1st Baron Loughborough (1610–1667), served the king as high sheriff of Leicestershire from 1642. He was also accused of "robb[ing] many housekeepers" in *The Most Strange and Wounderfull apperation of blood in a poole at Garraton* (London: by I.H., [1645]), 4.

93 Ralph Hopton, 1st Baron Hopton (1596–1652), served in Royalist campaigns in both the west and the southeastern counties in 1643, and although he lost his independent command in 1644, he continued to play a significant military role. Sir John Urry/Hurry (d.1650) had joined the Parliamentarians after the war broke out, but in 1643 defected to the Royalists. Sir Thomas Lunsford (c.1610–c.1656), along with his brothers Herbert and Henry, served in the Royalist army; he was captured by the Parliamentarians after the Battle of Edgehill in October 1642 and was only able to rejoin the Royalists at Oxford in May 1644. See *ODNB* entries.

94 Both Sir Arthur Aston (c.1590–1649) and William Legge (1607/8–1670) were close associates of Prince Rupert, participating in several of his campaigns in 1643 and early 1644. See *ODNB* entries.

95 This is hard.

96 According to legend, the monstrous Dun Cow of Dunsmore Heath ravaged the Warwickshire countryside until it was killed by the chivalrous Guy of Warwick. Although it would be anachronistic for the author to talk of him receiving bribes or indeed of being present in Britain before the war, it is also possible that this is an allusion to Prince Rupert. In 1642, the pamphlet *Prince Roberts Disguises* had accused him of disguising himself as (among other things) an apple-seller in order to spy on the Parliamentarian forces encamped on Dunsmore Heath; this subtle suggestion of diabolic shape-shifting was then stated more baldly in *Observations Upon Prince Rupert's White Dog, Called Boy* (1643), which credited Rupert's disguises, perhaps facetiously, to "mysticall meanes" (p. 4). For a discussion of the connection between the two pamphlets, see Mark Stoyle, *The Black Legend of Prince Rupert's Dog: Witchcraft and Propaganda during the English Civil War* (Exeter, UK: University of Exeter Press, 2011), 39, 59.

97 Marie d'Medici, mother of Queen Henrietta Maria, visited England from 1638 to 1641 and was thoroughly unpopular with the English. See the note in *A Dog's Elegy* (p. 7) above.

98 The "ship-money" tax was traditionally levied directly by the King on maritime regions. Charles I's attempt in the 1630s to raise funds for England's wars by extending the tax to inland counties was condemned by Parliament as an abuse of royal power.

99 According to legend, a cobbler trained a crow to say *Ave Caesar victor, Imperator* (Hail Caesar, victorious commander) and attempted to sell it to Augustus following his victory over Mark Antony in 31 BC.

100 Several variants of this proverb exist; a contemporary version was that the Emperor of Germany was "rex regnum" (king of kings), the King of Spain "rex hominum" (king of men), the King of France "rex asinorum" (king of asses), and the King of England "rex diabolorum" (king of devils). See, for instance, Thomas Bayly, *The royal charter granted unto kings, by God himself and collected out of his Holy Word, in both Testaments* (London: [s.n.], 1649), 19 [of introduction].

101 A play produced for Charles and Henrietta Maria in 1636: William Cartwright, *The royall slave A tragi-comedy* (Oxford: Printed by William Turner for Thomas Robinson, 1639).

102 Organ music was condemned by some Puritans as an unacceptable holdover from Catholicism. In 1572, for instance, *An admonition to the Parliament* listed "organes and curious singing" as "proper to Popysh dennes," but not appropriate in truly reformed churches (p. 27).

103 A traditional part of bishops' attire.

104 A combination of Psalm 22:12 ("Many bulls have compassed me: strong bulls of Bashan have beset me round") with the papal bull, an official letter issued by the pope. The same play on words was used by Thomas Adams in his 1615 sermon on Genesis 25:27, "Politicke Hunting:" "Let the roring *Bull* be *hunted*; the Bulles of *Basan*, the Bulles of *Rome*; sent over by the Pope *ad interitum* [to destruction], either of us or themselves: For their end is not *implere Ecclesiam*, but *cæmiterium*; to fill Church yards with dead bodyes, not the Church with living soules." In Thomas Adams, *The sacrifice of thankefulnesse* (London: Printed by Thomas Purfoot, for Clement Knight, 1616), Part II, p. 80.

105 Thomas Wentworth, Earl of Strafford (1593–1641), was impeached by Parliament on charges of treason in 1640 and beheaded in 1641.

106 Pluto, originally the Greek god of the underworld, was often conflated in later tradition with the Devil, while Astaroth was believed by medieval demonologists to be a lesser (though powerful) demon.

107 George Digby, Earl of Bristol (1612–1677). A member of the Royal circle and a close confidante of Charles I, Digby's opposition to any compromise with the king's opponents made him unpopular with the Parliamentarians.

108 Baron Francis Cottington (1579?–1652), one of Charles I's senior advisors at the court in Oxford.

109 The swarm of locusts was the eighth plague inflicted by God upon the Egyptians: "they covered the face of the whole earth, so that the land was darkened; and they did eat every herb of the land, and all the fruit of the trees which the hail had left: and there remained not any green thing in the trees, or in the herbs of the field, through all the land of Egypt" (Exodus 10:15).

110 Guy Fawkes (c.1570–1606), best known for his part in the Gunpowder Plot. Fawkes' duty was to ignite the gunpowder beneath the House of Lords, killing James VI/I and his heir as well as the Protestant nobles, but he and his co-conspirators were arrested before they could implement their plan.

111 Beelzebub, synonymous with Satan or the Devil.

112 Cruelties allegedly inflicted by the Irish Catholics upon English Protestant settlers were graphically recounted in James Cranford's *The Teares of Ireland* (London: Printed by A.N. for John Rothwell, 1642), which used the events as propaganda to warn of the evils of papists and the dangers inherent in harboring them.

113 A round cap with a low, flat crown, worn by Londoners; also used as a euphemism for London apprentices.

114 One of the aspects of bishops' garb protested in the 1640 "Root and Branch" Petition, along with "lawne sleeves . . . the Cope and Surplisse, the Tippet, the Hood, and the Canonicall Coate." Article XIV of *The first and large petition of the Citie of London and other inhabitants thereabouts: for a reformation in church-government* ([London: s.n.,] 1641), 8.

115 A large, clumsy person; sometimes used of monks.

116 According to legend, Joan disguised her gender and became pope during the early Middle Ages. See the note in *A Dog's Elegy* (p. 5) above.

117 In the first place.

118 Archbishop William Laud (1573–1645) became the focus of Puritan ire for his attempts to introduce what were considered "popish" reforms into the Church of England. He was impeached by Parliament in 1640, although his trial was not held until March 1644; it concluded in early October, and Laud was beheaded in January 1645.

119 The Greek Cynic philosopher Diogenes of Sinope, who was reputed to have searched for an honest man in daylight with a lantern. The author may also be alluding to a 1641 satire that mentioned Diogenes in the context of Jesuits and the Gunpowder Plot: *Novembris monstrum* (London: Printed by F.L. for John Burroughes, 1641), 121.

120 Original: "mim."

121 Mary I of England (1516–1558), known as "Bloody Mary" for her persecution of Protestants.

122 Queen Henrietta Maria (1609–1669), whose ardent Catholicism and influence over the King made her one of the foremost targets of the Parliamentarians.

123 Marie d'Medici died in July 1642, having departed England about a year earlier.

124 On May 28, 1644, Royalist soldiers under Prince Rupert's command captured and sacked the Parliamentarian town of Bolton, Lancashire. The accompanying atrocities were broadcasted in such pieces as *An exact relation of the bloody and barbarous massacre at Bolton* (London: Printed by R. W. for Christopher Meredith, August 22, 1644).

125 In 1627, George Villiers, 1st Duke of Buckingham (1592–1628), led a force to La Rochelle to assist the Huguenots in their revolt against the Catholic monarch. The invasion ended in failure, increasing Villiers' unpopularity among English Protestants; he was assassinated in 1628.

126 Sir Edward Cecil (1572–1638) commanded an attack on Cádiz in 1625 as part of the Anglo-Spanish War. Like Buckingham's La Rochelle expedition, Cecil's efforts ended in a humiliating debacle.

127 Henry Jermyn (1605–1684), a courtier and close confidante of Queen Henrietta Maria, was created Baron of St. Edmundsbury in 1643.

128 Endymion Porter (1587–1649) was a groom of Charles I's bedchamber and a member of the Oxford Parliament during the war. His Catholic sympathies and his connection to the Villiers family, in which he began his career as a courtier, were unlikely to make him popular among the Parliamentarians.

129 Original: "knaveties."

130 Charles' attempt to introduce the Anglican Book of Common Prayer into the Scottish Church was resisted by Scots who preferred a presbyterian form of worship and church government, sparking the Bishops' Wars (1639–1640).

131 The Star Chamber, one of the king's courts of law, was used during Charles I's Personal Rule (1629–1640) to try cases of sedition. Its use of torture and the harsh penalties it dispensed to critics of Church or State earned it an evil reputation among Parliamentarians, for whom it became synonymous with tyranny. See the discussion in C.V. Wedgwood, *The King's Peace: 1637–1641* (New York: Book-of-the-Month Club, 1991), 143–144.

132 The Royalist newsbook *Mercurius Aulicus* was edited by (among others) John Birkenhead, a Fellow of All Souls College. Joad Raymond, *The Invention of the Newspaper: English Newsbooks 1641–1649* (Oxford: Oxford University Press, 1996), 26–27.

133 Maurice, Prince Palatine of the Rhine (1621–1652), Rupert's brother, also served his uncle Charles during the war.

134 Henry Clifford, 5th Earl of Cumberland (1592–1643), had died the previous year and his title become extinct; Prince Rupert was created Duke of Cumberland in January 1644, but as he is mentioned earlier in this line-up, it is unclear to whom the author is referring.

135 Henry Bourchier, 5th Earl of Bath (c.1587–1654); Thomas Wriothesley, 4th Earl of Southampton (1608–1667); Edward Sackville, 4th Earl of Dorset (1590–1652); Spencer Compton, 2nd Earl of Northampton (1601–1643), who had died the year before at the Battle of Hopton Heath; William Cavendish, 3rd Earl of Devonshire (1617–1684); John Digby, 1st Earl of Bristol (1580–1653);

Thomas Howard, 1st Earl of Berkshire (1626–1669); Ralph Hopton, 1st Baron Hopton (1596–1652); and Arthur Capel, 1st Baron Capel of Hadham (1604–1649).

136 "July 27" is handwritten after the printed year on the Thomason copy.

137 Matthew 2 recounts how King Herod, fearing the report that the new King of the Jews had been born in Bethlehem, ordered all male children in the region aged two and under to be killed.

138 Hugh Peter(s) (c.1598–1660), an Independent preacher closely associated with Cromwell and known for his support of the army leading up to the execution of Charles I. His active role in politics made him extremely controversial, and he was not granted a pardon after Charles II's restoration: he met his death on the scaffold in October 1660.

139 A mounted infantryman, so called for the "fire-breathing" musket he carried.

140 A nickname for Oliver Cromwell.

141 Who will contradict?

142 The Ten Commandments, given in Exodus 20 and Deuteronomy 5.

143 Darkened.

144 In classical mythology, Phoebus Apollo was the god of poetry.

145 One who makes spurs.

146 Lady Fleetwood was the title of Cromwell's eldest daughter, Bridget (1624–1662), who had first married the army officer Henry Ireton (1611–1651) and after his death was married to another officer, Charles Fleetwood (c.1618–1692).

147 A tool used for spinning and traditionally associated with women's domestic domain.

148 The last word on this page is damaged; the writer refers to the proverb that a fox's tail will serve to "piece out," or patch, a lionskin.

149 Perhaps a reference to William Lilly's short astrological prediction, *A peculiar prognostication . . . whether, or no, His Majestie shall suffer death this present yeere 1649* ([London: n.p., 1649). This work included dire possibilities for the year but did not actually answer the question posed in its title. Rather, Lilly prognosticated gloomy events in vague terms, writing: "We must expect the exile, vanishment [*sic*], imprisonment or death of some great King or Prince, shedding of blood amongst the common people, and greater persons; we must expect discords, mutuall dissimulations: the motions of a great Army, wars[,] murthers, firing of houses, theeves plundering, depopulations, miscarriage of women with child, sharp fevers, and universall sicknesse amongst men, by reason there will be a pestilent ayre, also an admirable change or mutation in the Common-Wealth; being forewarnd me thinks some might be forearmd, if the Parliament of England and Army invite Prince *Charles* home, and he refuse (as God forbid he should,) great things will assuredly be put in execution and may prove very fatall to the Prince, and so may produce that excellent mutation spoken of, and it were well advised if such counsell were given to the Duke of York [James, Charles I's second surviving son, later James II]." (p. 2)

150 Thomas Goodwin (1600–1680) was a respected nonconformist minister who worked toward the reordering of the church structure in England, being involved, for instance, in the Westminster Assembly. However, the writer may have meant *John* Goodwin (c.1594–1665), an Independent minister well known for his support of the army in the buildup to the execution of Charles and for his controversial political theories. For instance, he was a proponent of Pride's Purge and of the king's execution, justifying the latter after the fact in his work *Hybristodikai: The Obstructours of Justice* (London: Henry Cripps and Lodowick Lloyd, 1649). See *ODNB* articles for both men.

151 John Lilburne (c.1615–1657) was a political activist and leader of the Leveller movement. He had fought for Parliament, but also clashed with it, and especially

with the Presbyterian leadership, over his demand for greater religious toleration, social equality, and political levelling. His views were embodied in many publications, but the writer is here alluding to the Levellers' most famous manifestos, *An Agreement of the People* (1647–1649), which called for a radical reform of the political structure.

152 John Hewson (d.1660), an army officer who supported the execution of Charles, acting as one of the King's judges and signing his death warrant. Although he was one of those officers who clashed with Parliament in the controversies of the late 1640s, he was not a Leveller. See *ODNB*.

153 To sail through a dangerous passage, or, metaphorically, to attempt a dangerous undertaking.

5 Christian astrology

'Amongst the celestiall hieroglyphicks'

Introduction

As the period of revolutionary conflict heightened feelings of uncertainty, British pamphlets sustained the traditional conception of three possible sources of knowledge of the future: past experience, divine revelation, and astrological art/science. Indeed, the mainstream practitioners of astrology saw theirs as an art which understood divine revelation in God's handwriting among the stars and heavens, and astrologers placed great emphasis on the authority of previous astrological writers—we will see Latin quotations peppering their treatises to support their interpretations—and on examples of prior experiences that had followed particular astronomical alignments and events. Can we make a distinction between systematic astrology and extraordinary reports of prodigies and supernatural events? Such a division might reinforce the scholarly overemphasis on a distinction between a science of the heavens and the interpretation of signs. Our investigation of such texts is hampered further by the fact that astrology as practiced in the early modern period no longer exists as an intellectual category in the modern mind. The technically complex astrology with a well-developed astrological tradition offered a systematic and convincing way to explain the universe in the early modern period.[1]

Both regular, *predictable* motions and conjunctions of objects in the heavens and novel, *unpredictable* events were often seen as demonstrations of God's providence through nature. And, as we will see in this chapter, astrologers wrote both annual almanacs based on regular astrological motions and special pamphlets offering interpretations of extraordinary astronomical phenomena.[2] The English experience confirms observations about Reformation-era German astrology that in both practice and theory "the lines often blurred between a science of causes and a theology of signs." Even the most Biblicist authors who critiqued astrology "did not imply that one could or should ignore nature. Indeed most evangelical Biblicists were intensely awake to heavenly signs and natural wonders sent directly by God as warnings to a world unredeemable short of the final and eternal renewal."[3]

Thomas Dekker's *Looke Up and See Wonders* (see Chapter 2 this volume) clearly demonstrated the tensions across these blurred lines:

> Let us not be so daring as to pry into the closet of Gods determinations. His works are full of Wonders, and not to be examined: Let us not be so foolish, as turne Almanacke-makers and to Prognosticate, Prophesie, Fore-doome, or Fore-tell, what shall happen, faire weather or foule, to our owne Kingdome, or any other; scarcity, or plenty, Warre, or Peace, for such giddy-brayn'd Medlers, shoote their arrows beyond the Moone.[4]

The key thrust of the complaints against scientific astrologers, mocked by Dekker as "giddy-brained meddlers," centered on the question of prognostication. That God worked and revealed through nature was not questioned; it was rather an issue of how inquisitive into God's providence humans should be in making particular predictions. As Dekker concluded, "But let not us be too inquisitive what that purpose is: Enough it shalbe for us to see, and feare; to heare, and not meddle."[5] Some went even further in discrediting astrology by linking such prognostication to witchcraft. Indeed, the author of *The Divels Delusions*, the final pamphlet in this chapter, condemned astrologers, including "that impudent Prognosticator" William Lilly, along with the confessed witches who were very busy in their work with the devil.[6]

Even those novel, unpredictable signs in the heavens, however, merited careful scientific scrutiny accompanying moral prognostication. Yet, even astrologers themselves expressed awareness of the pitfalls of their own vocation. When, for instance, the famous 1618 comet appeared and was linked to numerous current events—from the Defenestration of Prague and its ramifications to the just-convened Synod of Dort—the English mathematician John Bainbridge published a pamphlet which included detailed astronomical descriptions with intricate mathematical calculations across each day of its appearance, followed by a second half of the pamphlet which offered "certain Morall Prognostics or Applications" of his mathematical descriptions. Bainbridge knew that many looked to such extraordinary astrological events with fear, but he argued against detailed prediction,

> God onely knows, and none, but He
> What is, what was, and what shall be.
> What this Comet doth in particular signifie is not possible to declare without . . . divine inspiration.[7]

The number of English astrological works lagged far behind those in Germany and on the continent, and royal monopolies in almanac-publication limited the extent of detailed political speculation in England until the 1640s.[8]

Through most of the early decades of the seventeenth century, English almanacs avoided political prognostication. John Booker, who developed an astrological practice in London answering clients' queries, became Britain's most famous astrologer through his annual almanacs which he began publishing in 1631.[9] Booker's *New Almanac* complained of official corruption and in 1633 predicted "wonderful change in the church," which got him arrested, jailed and fined. Moreover, in the aftermath of Booker's case before the court of High Commission, all future almanacs were to be licensed by either the Archbishop of Canterbury or the Bishop of London. By the Civil War of the 1640s as royal and episcopal censorship suddenly ceased, Booker was joined by numerous other almanac producers whose predictions took on decidedly partisan positions.

Booker's strong support of the Parliamentarian cause secured his 1643 appointment by Parliament as one of its two licensers of mathematical books. Thus, he ironically began the task of censoring almanacs, among other things. By 1644, the military turmoil of the Civil War had fully broken out in the popular astrology publications. Booker's almanac for 1644 seems to have begun this transition.[10] He limited his explicit political polemic to such standard fare as the anti-Catholic poem atop his monthly calendar for November, where, for instance, Booker predicted the purging of Catholicism from England.[11] Booker seems to have couched his more political prognostication in his Latin quotations from classical astrologers, where his English text provided merely astronomical descriptions and simpler weather prognostication. Indeed, during his prognostication "Of the Winter" after describing the retrograde position of Mars in opposition to Mercury as the Sun's ingress into Capricorn (marking the start of winter), Booker's quotation from the Arab astrologer Haly[12] without English clarification—"Cave ab homine trium literarum"[13]—fueled a firestorm of political polemic among the astrologers.

George Wharton, who had published his first almanac in 1641 under the anagramatic pseudonym "Naworth," had joined the Royalist camp and moved to Oxford.[14] In October 1643, Wharton completed his 1644 almanac (printed "by His Majesties command"), which, though limited in prognostication, was direct in condemning the actions of the rebellious Parliament and its army whose actions from 1642 and 1643 he detailed in each of his monthly calendars for the year.[15] His final three pages turned more polemical as he disputed Parliamentarian interpretations of the soon-emerging effects of the February 1642 conjunction of Saturn and Jupiter which predicted further war and the overthrow of the monarch. In contrast, Wharton repeated his account of the political effects of a November 1640 conjunction, predicting instead that the more recent conjunction was to be "fore-runner of a th[o]rough Reformation indeed, throughout this Realme; by a timely purging it of all sectaries, Brownists, Anabaptists, &c. And by bringing the Authors of this bloudy Warre to condigne punishment."

As he concluded, Wharton referred by name to "Master Booker" and "Hom trium Literarum" and accused him of meaning "REX: I must tell him, that intimation is as void of Reason as Loyalty." Instead of the King/Rex facing the fall, Wharton wrote, "But upon better and surer calculation . . . I shall desire you to observe what befalls (Homines trium Literarum) the Lord Say or Master Pym before Feb. 1644."[16]

Booker's short reply of January 1644 condemned both Wharton's astrology and his account of war. Instead of royalist victories, Booker described them as treachery, tyranny, slavery, and popery, and he accused Naworth/Wharton and those at Oxford of being the true rebels. "There was never so many Lyes heaped together in so short and few lines, since the word Almanack was used."[17] After claiming that Naworth corrupted the text to mean "Rex," Booker revised his name to be "No-worth, or a Man worth nothing."[18] Wharton composed an angry reply allegedly within six hours of having read Booker.[19] He began by condemning prognostication in the service of treason: "I find neither Conscience, Loyalty, nor Reason. The World knowes how long it hath beene deluded with your *Almanacks* and *Prognostications*." Wharton condemned Booker of "stuffing your Perfidious Pamphlets with Ambiguous Phrases, therby to beget new (or to increase the old) Feares and Jealousies amongst the People: (The onely prop now left to support your fading Faction.)"[20] After instructing Booker to "have a care of your neck,"[21] Wharton provided his own name-calling by ending with an anagram of Joannes Booker: "Sin on; be a rooke."[22]

In addition to the flurry of actual astronomical works that began to be published, the water-poet, John Taylor, jumped into the fray in support of Wharton. Mocking astrology itself as well as Booker, whom he termed "the Asse-tronomicall London Figure-flinger," Taylor indicated to Booker that "I have anatomized and skellitonized your railing Pamphlet and ridiculous Prediction." He then went on to lampoon the entire manner of astrological writing by throwing together a mock-prognostication including all of the planets and constellations with features often depicted in the almanacs:

> at the command of *Saturne* and *Jupiter*, the starres are malevolent pretending and portending revenge against thee for belying them, and calling and causing them to witnesse thy lying Conjunctions and traiterous expositions of them. *Aries* will brow-beat thee, with battering thy shamelesse *Head* and *Face*, and make thee Horne-mad. *Taurus* will gore thee through the *Necke*, and hunch thy Lyes into thy *Throat* . . . *Aquarius* . . . will dash and balderdash thee, ducke, sowse, pumpe and plunge thee, into the bottomlesse Gulfe of *Mare mortuum*; or if thou scape that, he will plague thee with Goutes and Crampes, and lastly hurle thee theadlong into the perpendicularity of the vast watry Region; where thou shalt irremediably and irrecoverably be crippled in thy feet, root and branch, *cap à pe*, top and tail by *Pisces*.[23]

It was in this climate that William Lilly, who would soon become the leading astrologer of the Civil War era, published his first almanac in April 1644.[24] Even Booker was apparently astonished by Lilly's initial manuscript because he licensed it only after demanding what Lilly later called "many impertinent Obliterations."[25] It sold out in a week, and when Lilly complained to some members of Parliament about it having been "defaced," he received an order to have a second printing as he saw fit. William Lilly published his annual almanacs until he died in 1681; from 1647 on, he published under the title *Merlini Anglici Ephemeris*.[26] Significantly longer than his competitors' almanacs, the text of one of Lilly's *Merlini Anglici Ephemeris* (for 1648) is included in its entirety in this chapter. The "English Merlin" was a dramatic success with his astrological prognostications relating to peace, war, and the decline (and later restoration) of the monarchy.[27] While he was not afraid to make bold pro-Parliamentarian predictions on their own, in the monthly prognostications of his earliest almanacs, Lilly couched his political predictions within the more acceptable natural astrology of weather predictions.[28] For instance, his prognostication for March 1647 predicted, "See the state of the weather, how uncertain it is towards the latter end of this moneth . . . the heavens, by their frowning weather, advise us to more unity."[29]

Although Lilly regularly pledged loyalty to the monarchy, his predictions and polemics made it clear that the unity he wanted was on Parliament's terms. In addition to his almanac, Lilly also published an interpretation of prodigies in the summer of 1644.[30] In his prefatory letter to the reader, Lilly wrote,

> I am a friend to Monarchy; but I hold it my native duty to adhere in purse, pen, and person to the now honourable Parliament at *Westminster*, the worthy Members thereof having for our good these three years and more spent their private fortunes, and weakned their healths, purposely to reduce our Common-wealth to its right temper; and to free me, thee, and the whole Kingdome from an approaching slavery . . . Reader . . . pray for his Majesties returne.

He described the strange apparition in the pale sky: numerous great flashes of lightning and then "a long yellowish apparition of somewhat in forme and shape almost like to a Serpent, incurvating a little at each end." After analyzing the constellations and stars through which the apparition was placed, Lilly offered his judgment of its meaning:

> Upon a suddaine and unexpected accident, the dissipation and dissolving of some mysterious close consultation and mischievous plot against our State and Common-wealth is portended; the disunion and disagreement of the Projectors amongst themselves, and all this in *[31] forraigne parts as well as in *England*: A renting in peeces or mutinous disturbance of

some Monarchy neare hand, or some *Austrian*[32] family or Principality, etc. A commotion of the meaner sort of people against some principall man, or Magistracy: Losse to *Spaine*; That we *English* with our Armies shall travers all the in-land Countries of this Kingdome, etc. This is all I either can or dare say.[33]

George Wharton published two almanacs for 1645. As in the past, he published under "Naworth," but this year he published a second almanac under his own name. In this second one, Wharton began the final page of his prognostication with a critique of Lilly's, the newest parliamentary astrological opponent, predicted effects of a recent eclipse, accusing him of misreading both the military events and the classical astrology authorities:

But here I cannot omit the Impudent and senselesse discourse of *William Lilly* (in a Pamphlet of his, styled *Supernaturall Sights and Apparitions, &c.* Licensed by that Licentious Libeller, *John Booker* concerning the Eclipse of the Summer . . . And yet forsooth this Pseudo-Prophet must preferre his owne opinion before the Judgement of all sound Astrologers that ever writ, neither quoting Author, nor rendring any reason but his owne Private Fancy for what he saith. But of this (and the like absurdities heretofore published) by *Booker, Lilly*, and others of their Brother-hood, I shall (God willing) take occasion hereafter to write more at large.[34]

Wharton took occasion to write more when the royalists began to march from Oxford in May 1645.[35] Based on the tables and celestial schemes and figures that he constructed from the time of the start of the march, Wharton's pamphlet provided an optimistic prediction of royalist success: "The severall Positions of the Heavens duly considered," he suggested, "doe generally render His *Majesty* and his whole Army unexpectedly victorious and successefull in all his Designes."[36] Lilly was already in the midst of composing his own treatise on the prodigious appearance of a triple sun on King Charles' birthday (November 19, 1644) when he encountered Wharton's astrological judgment on the King's march. Thus, while publishing his *Starry Messenger* (see Figure 5.1) on the meanings of heavenly apparitions, he appended a postscript in response to Wharton's pamphlet.[37]

In his prefatory letter to the reader, Lilly describes the current state of political factionalism, yet claims to:

write with no prepared gall, no not against Master Noworth of Oxford, who borrowes the grosse of his judgement in his last Almanack from my *Prophetick Merlin*, nor am I angrie, but pitty that woodden Doctour whether Atheist or Papist I know not, that swells with his owne ignorant fancy, and sayth, he can make it appeare, what I speake in behalfe of the Parliament, in point of Art ought to happen to their enemies; this is one of those purblind Prophesies.[38]

THE STARRY

MESSENGER;

O R,

An Interpretation of that strange Apparition of three
Suns seene in *London,* 19 *Novemb.* 1644. being the Birth
Day of King CHARLES.

The effects of the Eclips of the Sun, which will be visible in ENGLAND,
11 *August* 1645. whose influence continues in force, from *January,* 1646. to *Decemb.*
1647 almost two whole yeares; and cannot but be the fore-runner of some extraordinary mutation in most Common-wealths of *Europe,* but principally
in ENGLAND. With an *Answer to an Astrologicall Judgement,*
Printed at Oxford, upon his *Majesties present March.*

By WILLIAM LILLY *Student* in *Astrologie.*

L O N D O N,
Printed for *John Partridge* and *Humphry Blunden,* and are to be sold at
the Signe of the *Cocke* in *Ludgate Streete,* and the *Castle* in *Cornehill,* 1645.

Figure 5.1 Title page of William Lilly's *The Starry Messenger*, 1645.

His questionable claim against personal animosity to the side, Lilly did spend almost all of his forty-seven-page pamphlet on the effects of the triple suns and an eclipse. Lilly was keen to highlight the historicity of such apparitions by chronicling over thirty appearances of triple suns and moons over the preceding 1600 years, quoting astrological authorities to confirm prognostications of effects of the astrological movements he documented that year, and placing the general effects into their particular British (and European) political, religious, and military contexts of that year.

As he began his mathematical analysis of the strange apparition, Lilly posited a distinction between natural causes of regular events and such a supernatural sign. He argued that scholars could claim natural causes for the general ill weather around that time, even if it had occurred for many days together, but there was "no cause in Nature to induce a belief that the three Suns were occasioned from Nature."

> I am clearly of opinion, These Sights, as well as many others, were caused by those tutelary Angels, who, by Gods permission, and under him, have the Government of the *English* Common-wealth. They are sensible of those many impending Miseries now too plentifully amongst us. Their conference with man now, as in the days of old, very few attain unto, it being a blessing sought after by many, attained unto by few: And yet there are some of opinion, There lives in the world some, and of those some, a small Party in *England,* that know more then they utter, and, either by Vision, or verball Colloquie, have the knowledge of future events, yea, even from the blessed Angels.
>
> But alas, these are Riddles; I must adhere unto my Astrologie; and yet wish all happinesse to those good souls that either confer with their own *Genius,* whom some call, A good Angel; or with such other of those heavenly Ministers whom God in mercy affordeth them. And herein let no Reader mistake me; for I abhor Witches, or those *Necromancers* that raise the deceased out of their graves, or those Circular Priests now almost worn out of the world: My meaning is this, That I do believe there are many now living, to whom God, by his Angels, gives Revelation of things to come: And where and to whom God gives such a blessing, I believe that Saint may lawfully use the Talent God hath enabled him with.[39]

Such a prodigious sign, then, must necessarily be intended by God as a warning or revelation. For Lilly, the astrological art of interpreting such signs differed from witchcraft since God Himself had used signs in the Bible (such as the rainbow after the Flood in Genesis) and clearly wanted His people to take note of His works in nature, especially extraordinary ones.[40] "The Portent of this Prodigie is very great: The Angels are willing we should discern something, else why was it made visible? There was no necessity of it."[41]

Building on his burgeoning reputation, Lilly published his 800-page *Christian Astrology* in 1647 as a detailed handbook on the fundamentals of the practice of astrology and astrological prognostication. And its prefatory "Epistle to the Student in Astrology," which is included in this chapter, reveals that English almanac-makers continued operating with the confidence that mastery of this "heavenly knowledge of the Starres" confirmed God's providence and fostered public prediction. Clearly, as the British age of Revolution enhanced the disillusionment that many felt toward prediction, many of the published accounts turned more toward reports of prodigies as comments on past or current events.[42]

While some—like Lilly—were more willing than others to prognosticate on the basis of these natural phenomena, the range of pamphlets in this chapter and throughout the collection highlight the tensions in prognostication and allow analysis of ambiguity, wishful thinking, and humility (false or otherwise) in reading God's writing in nature into current and future political and social circumstances. We see such wishful ambiguity in Bainbridge's conclusion to his "Moral Prognosticks" regarding the 1618 comet:

> Whatsoever evil this new Comet may presage, the signe be to them that hate us, and the interpretation thereof to our enemies. But whatsoever good it can promise, the God of Heaven (who there placed it) confirme them all to his royall Majestie, and Great Britaines Monarchie.[43]

Or, as Dekker put it in his pamphlet in Chapter 2 (this volume): "forbeare to take the height of these false imaginary Sunnes; and fright not thy Countrey with thy over-daring, foolish, and vaine-glorious predictions." The irony here seems to be that people kept castigating astrologers for scaring their credulous countrymen (as in Wharton's response to Booker), but those astrologers remained pretty popular.[44]

Many of the astrological publications of the era are both longer than other pamphlets in this collection and technically complex in that they require a thorough knowledge of astrological terminology and thinking. In order to provide an uninterrupted presentation of popular astrological publications, this chapter includes a transcription of one of Lilly's annual almanacs in the entirety of its text (without its tables). His letter to the reader provides a bit more of a polemical context, followed by rather vague monthly predictions and then a longer discourse with more particular prognostication of special aspects, eclipses, and the like. Through all its components, one can note the essential intermingling of specific astronomic observations, mathematical calculations, appeals to astrological tradition and scholarship, and current political and military events (with some polemic thrown in for good measure). The other texts include more commentary on the art of astrology than demonstrations of it in practice. Excerpts from the prefatory material to Lilly's *Christian Astrology* provide brief descriptions by and about Lilly on the purpose and value of astrology. The introductory letters in Johnsen's

Anti-Merlinus offer an overview of lines of criticism he would take in his book *Anti-Merlinus*, which disputed both Lilly's astrology and his prognostications in his 1648 publications. Finally, the account of the witchcraft trial and confessions in *The Divels Delusions* presents an indication that astrology and prognostication maintained associations with the devil and witchcraft in some quarters.

The astrological symbols of planets, signs, aspects, and conjunctions have been left in the texts so that readers can become aware of the technical complexities and skills necessary to practice astrology in this early modern tradition. Even though space does not allow explanation of the technical astrological terminology in this collection, we encourage readers where possible to consult Lilly's 1647 *Christian Astrology*, which provides an introduction to the various terms and methods used by these authors.

	Planets		Signs		Aspects
♄	Saturn	♈	Aries	✳	Sextill (60°)
♃	Jupiter	♉	Taurus	□	Quartill (90°)
♂	Mars	♊	Gemini	△	Trine (120°)
☉	Sol/Sun	♋	Cancer	☍	Opposition (180°)
♀	Venus	♌	Leo	☌	Conjunction (0°)
☿	Mercury	♍	Virgo		
☽	Luna/Moon	♎	Libra		
		♏	Scorpio	℞	Retrograde motion
	Nodes	♐	Sagittarius	⊗	the Part of Fortune
☊	Head of the Dragon[45]	♑	Capricorn	deg.	degrees
☋	Tail of the Dragon[46]	♒	Aquarius	Asc.	Ascendant
		♓	Pisces		

CHRISTIAN
ASTROLOGY
MODESTLY
Treated in three Books.

The *first* containing the use of an Ephemeris,
the erecting of a Scheam of Heaven; nature of
the twelve Signs of the Zodiack, of the
Planets; with a most easie Introduction
to the whole Art of ASTROLOGY.

The *second*, by a most Methodicall way, Instructeth
the Student how to Judge or Resolve all manner of Questions contingent unto Man, *viz.* of Health, Sicknesse, Riches, Marriage, Preferment, Journies, &c.
Severall Questions inserted and Judged.

The *third*, containes an exact Method, whereby to
Judge upon Nativities; severall wayes how to rectifie
them; How to judge the generall fate of the Native by the
twelve Houses of Heaven, according to the naturall
influence of the Stars; How this particular
and Annuall Accidents, by the Art of Di-
rection, and its exact measure of Time
by Profections, Revolutions, Transits.
A Nativity Judged by the Method preceding.

By WILLIAM LILLY Student in Astrology.
Omne meum, nil Meum: Nihil dictum, quod non dictum prius.[47]

LONDON:
Printed by *Tho. Brudenell* for *John Partridge* and *Humph. Blunden*, in
Blackfriers at the Gate going into *Carter-lane*, and in *Cornhil*, 1647.

An Epistle to the Student in A s t r o l o g i e.

MY Friend, whoever thou art, that with so much ease shalt receive the
benefit of my hard *Studies*, and doest intend to proceed in this heavenly knowledge of the *Starres*. In the first place consider and admire
thy *Creator*, be thankfull unto him; be thou humble, and let no natural
knowledge, how profound or transcendent soever it be, elate thy mind to
neglect that *Divine Providence*, by whose al-seeing order and appointment

all things heavenly and earthly have their constant motion; the more thy knowledge is enlarged, the more doe thou magnifie the power and wisdome of *Almighty God*: strive to preserve thy self in his favour, for the more holy thou art, the more neer to God, the purer *judgment* thou shalt give. Beware of pride and self-conceit; remember how that long agoe, no irrationall Creature durst offend man the *Macrocosme*, but did faithfully serve and obey him, so long as he was master of his own Reason and Passions, or until he subjected his will to the unreasonable part. But alas, when iniquity abounded, and man gave the reins to his own affection, and deserted reason, then every Beast, Creature and outward harmfull thing became rebellious to his command: Stand fast (oh man) to thy *God*, then consider thy own noblenesse, how all created things, both present and to come, were for thy sake created, nay, for thy sake God became Man: Thou art that creature, who being conversant with *Christ*, livest and reignest above the Heavens, and sits above all power and authority. How many pre-eminences, priviledges, advantages hath God bestowed on thee: thou rangest above the Heavens by Contemplation, conceivest the motion and magnitude of the *Stars;* thou talkest with Angels, yea with God himself; thou hast all Creatures within thy dominion, and keepest the *Devils* in subjection: Doe not then for shame deface thy Nature, or make thy self unworthy of such gifts, or deprive thy selfe of that great power, glory and blessednesse God hath alotted thee, by casting from thee his feat,[48] for possession of a few imperfect pleasures. *Having considered thy God, and what thy selfe art, during thy being God's servant; now receive instruction how in thy practice I would have thee carry thy self.* As thou daily conversest with the heavens, so instruct and forme thy mind according to the image of Divinity; learn all the ornaments of vertue, be sufficiently instructed therein; be humane, curtius, familiar to all, easie of accesse; afflict not the miserable with terrour of a harsh judgment, direct such to call on God to divert his judgments impending over them; be civill, sober, covet not an estate; give freely to the poor both money and judgment; let no worldly Wealth procure an erronious judgment from thee, or such as may dishonour the Art. Be sparing in delivering judgment against the Common-wealth thou livest in; avoyd law and controversie: In thy study be *totos in illis*,[49] that thou mayst be *singulus in arte*.[50] Be not extravagant, or desirous to learn every *Science;* be not *aliquid in omnibus*:[51] be faithfull, tenacious, betray no ones secrets. Instruct all men to live well, be a good example thy selfe: love thy owne native Country: be not dismaid if ill spoken of, *conscientia mille testes*,[52] God suffers no sin unpunished, no lye unrevenged. Pray for the Nobility, honour the Gentry and Yeomanry of *England*; stand firme to the commands of this Parliament; have a reverent opinion of our worthy Lawyers, for without their learned paines, and the mutuall assistance of some true spirited Gentlemen, we might yet be made slaves, but we will not; we now see light as well as many of the *Clergy*. Pray, if it stand with God's will, that Monarchy in this Kingdome may continue, his

Majesty and Posterity reign: forget not the *Scottish* Nation their mutuall assistance in our necessity, their honourable departure: God preserve the illustrious *Fairfax* and his whole Army, &c. let the famous City of *London* be ever blessed, and all her worthy *Citizens*.

WILLIAM LILLY.

———————◆———————

MERLINI ANGLICI
Ephemeris 1648.

No positive, but a naturall Astrologicall
conjecture of the most materiall
affaires of *England, Scotland*
and *Ireland.*

Monthly Observations throughout
the whole Yeer.
Observable Predictions concerning the
casuall occurrences of *Germany, Spaine,*
Italy, France, and States of *Holland.*

By William Lilly, Student
in Astrology

En quo discordia cives
Perduxit Miseros![53]

LONDON:
Printed by T.B. for *John Partridge* and *Humphrey*
Blunden, in *Blackfriers* at the Gate going into *Carterlane,*
and at the *Castle* in *Cornhill.* 1648

[p. 1 of unnumbered front matter]
To the Reader.
To the whole Kingdom of England, Scotland
and Ireland.

IN *a most distracted season, as unto the humours and fancies of men, and*
expectation of the times, doth Anglicus *appear: it's observed, he never becomes*
publike, but at what time emergent occasions and eminent State-actions or
Consultations are upon the Theater of the English Common-wealth, *and at*
what time mens minds are greatly impregnated in expectation of some grand
Catastrophe, *as even now they are. A little before the publishing of his* Starry
Messenger 1645, *mens minds did droop exceedingly, Cordials being more fit*
at that time then Purgers,[54] for Leicester *was lost, his Majesty in the head of a*
considerable Army, our Army wandring with uncertain hopes, the Londoners
were amazed, and I beleeve the Parlia. dubious of future successe: the very day
of Knaisby *fight* Anglicus *peeps out with his* Starry Messenger, *promises better*
things, viz. the regaining of Leicester, *and the fatall routing of all our enemies,*
their flight into the west, Cornwal, *&c. yea of scurrilous* Wharton *and his*

*galloping knapsack, wherein some say that silly Prophecie of so glorious a
Martch was pickled up: the most honourable Sir* Tho. Fairfax *and his uncon-
quered Army (guided by God) obtained this victory: In* Octob. 1646, *the
whole Kingdome were amused, doubting the integrity of the* Scottish *Army,
and the fidelity of that Nation,* Anglicus *he in words at length, and not ambig-
uously, speaks in the affirmative for the honour of that Nation:* Speak & write
what thou canst (most absurdest of men *Noworth*) have not that Nation, to
their everlasting honour, verified my predictions, and deluded thy malicious
scandals imposed upon their Souldiery? they returned according to Covenant,
seasonably delivered us our Towns and Arms, what could they do more? *In
the beginning of* May 1647 Anglicus *sets forth the* Worlds Catastrophe,[55] *and
his judgment Astrologicall upon the three Suns seen in* Shropshire, *admonish-
ing the Kingdome of what immediately did appear, and what must succeed for
almost two yeers: to the Book it self he refers the Reader, wherein there is
involved many high and great mysteries concerning the very times: In that*
Catastrophe *he appears most confidently for the integrity of the present Army;
let the veriest Viper of all his enemies contradict, if they can, any thing he
spoke in behalfe of the Army, &c. But Master* Anglicus, *what shall become of
us now? the people generally repine and murmure, the Army* [p. 2] *is unsatis-
fied, the Citizens melancholly, the Clergy consulting to no purpose, his Majesty
invironed with armed Troopers, the Court (such as it is) full of Malignants,
many Cavaliers, mixed with the Army, the Army divided, the Agitators and
Officers not agreeing: some affirme, his Majesty and Army are accorded: It's a
very lye, if* Wharton *swear it: Others, and they no little fools, say,* That the
intentions of the Parliament and Army run invisibly into a unity, and at last
will jump in one and the self same *Center*, both intending one and the same
thing; so say I: *and that a few weeks will produce a strange and admirable*
Catastrophe, *very unexpected unto many, now lull'd asleep: Many say his
Majesty will signe the Propositions when presented; others say the contrary: I
say if he doe signe them, he is* Mortalium prudentissimus.[56] *God direct his
heart, and guide ours, and instruct us all in our severall enterprizes, to undertake those acts which may prove for the peace of the Kingdome,* Amen. *Many
expect a present Thunder to break forth amidst us, that is in plain tearms, they
would have us cut out anothers throats, or divide to undoe us, and then smile
at our folly and plunder the City, But it shall appear to our malicious enemies,
neither the Army or we are such asses, as having beaten all that resisted, now
in conclusion to bumbast our selves, viz. Souldier against Souldier, Round-
head against Round-head, Citizen against Citizen; oh how the Devill would
smile at this, and poor* Wharton *grin and mump: God blesse the City from
divisions, and preserve it from fire and trechery. Its not the least of mens fears
the returne of the* Scottish *Army: such men have no eyes.* Ha; I should be sorry
that prudent people uninvited by Parliament, should againe come amongst us;
for if they returne againe voluntary without the Parliaments commission, they
may come into the Kingdome (it's true) with sound bodies, but they shall
returne home over *Tweed*,[57] limping, halting, lame, with bruised bodies and

empty carriages: but the nation is more provident and noble, and have yet no invasive design against us. *Againe, many stand to this very day Newters, and wish confusion to all parties; some would have the Army disband, others that the Parliament might dissolve; some wish* London *levelled to the ground (these many and no small ones), others wish his Majesty may reign, some desire nether he or Posterity should rule; some are for Anarchy, others for Democracy:* Anglicus *is yet for Monarchy, as most consonant to* English *constitutions. We will leave his Majesties Cause,* [p. 3] *his protection and restoring unto God, his person to the care of both Kingdomes and the Army, hoping they will act according to the Covenant, wherein we of the Commonalty are also engaged. Much cause there is the Country-man should repine and grumble, having an hard cruell Landlord, who grinds him to powder; an honest Souldier to feed upon his Provision, and yet not a farthing of Taxes lessened, during these his unsufferable pressures, of which I hope our State will take timely considera-tion. Many distrust the Army, of whom I now freely speak thus much, That the whole Kingdom hath had the benefit of the Souldiers hard Martches, in season and out of season, their dangerous and bloody fights, their hungry, weather-beaten and irksome sufferings, their extraordinary and miraculous undertakings and victories; and yet now many repine and think them not wor-thy of their wages, or security for it, but could be content to send them into* Utopia[58] *or* Terra incognita[59] *to go seek their Pay; but our Parliament have more care and better thoughts of them. These men have performed the Kingdomes service, secured the Citizens persons at home, and their fortunes abroad, and generally in their deportments (notwithstanding their extreame poverty) have so soberly demeaned themselves, as to this day they are rarely accused of any eminent rapine, theft, plunder, or other abusive disorders, sub-ject to a male-contented and necessitous Souldiery. The very Law of nature informs us, that it is necessary we eat, else we cannot subsist; and what hath this very Army had more, or at present do enjoy more then bread and meat, naked bodies and empty purses, yet doe they most willingly offer allowance for their free quartering when we shall pay them their arrears.* Saturday Aug. 7. 1647. *that Paragon of war his Excellency Sir* Tho. Fairfax, *and most of his valiant Commanders and whole Army martched through the very heart of the City; did any Mercer in* Cheapside[60] *lose an inch of Taffetie,[61] or any* Costermonger[62] *a Pippin[63] by any of the Army? nor hath a souldier hitherto been quartered in the city; every man therein sits under his owne Vine, and yet is discontented at what he knowes not, whilest the poor Country-man is enslaved to all and every necessity. Yet behold, say some male-contented Citizens, the Army obstructs all.* A few words I speak to the Kingdom of England. *Backslide not, or become* Apostata *unto this Parliament or their valiant Army; they are Gods Instruments: Providence cannot be deluded, or the Decrees of God lessened. The dissolution of this Parliament, is the resolu-tion of thy very bowels into* [p. 4] *tears, murthers and confusion: the Armies disbanding totally, is the assured forerunner of a new and more bloody war: For, being curious in the search of thy welfare, Loe, I beheld a wicked Angel setting a price upon the lives and fortunes of our Worthies in Parliament, and he importuned audaciously, that all their friends, both Citizens, and Souldiers, might together with them be destroyed, slaine and eternally perish: But the Angels love no deeds of darknesse; for this designe was contradicted by their Guardian-Angel, and then my eyes were for a time shut:* Conformity *may,* Tumults *can never re-estate his majesty. Scaricity of Bread approacheth, the Plague will wander through many of thy Provinces, but it's beyond my knowledge if the devouring Sword harme thee this yeer. I was then desirous to know something concerning the honourable City of* London, *whose welfare I so much esteem, and whose Citizens I doe so cordially respect: for a time I was in much perplexity, for where men love, they also fear, so did I: slumbering I thought a voyce delivered articulatly these words:* Oh London be then passive; *many deluding and dividing Angels are emitted and mixed with thy naturall sons, they have assumed power over thee* 1033. *dayes,* 268. *of those are past, more are not. Hereat I was much astonished, opened my eyes, and behold a very fierce Angel with a sharp sword, mortall and destructive appeared, and hovered over thee; he shook his sword at thee, would have also drawn it; the Saints prevailed, the Angel was rebuked, &c. Amongst the Coelestiall Heroes, no preposterous Councels take place, the day of thy visitation is not so neer: doe thou heale and apply Balsome to thy bitter divisions: by prayer prevent the approaching Plague; thousands of ungodly desire thy ruine: thou art among the number of those designed for slaughter and pillage.* But to my task. *Whose envy doe I fear? am not I my selfe a parcell of the publick? if I have not thousands of pounds to lend the State, I have a million of good wishes for their prosperity; I shall have the teares of many, and a sheet to my grave; not an Alderman scarce so much, for the heirs of rich Parents seldome mourn, &c. a present rupture amongst the Commonalty and in the City would be pleasing to many; let fools nourish their ill conceptions, and live upon shadowes; the endeavours of many unadvised people are not wanting to contrive and help forwards a miserable combustion amongst us: it's affirmative in* Astrology, *that there will not be any such notorious distractions, as to engage the Kingdom in blood,* Amen, *or the City of* Lon- [p. 5] *don to a fury. Let me not live, if any earthly thing should be more welcome unto me then to live under Monarchy, yea under his Majesty, and I now expresse myself unto the quick, that I desire his Majesty should be restored, (but herein I submit to the decree of the almighty) and leave the manner how it must be done to the wisdome of the two Parliaments of* England & Scotland. *Again, I now speak positive truth, according to the rules of that art, which hath been seconded with prosperous success, viz. That his Majesty nor friends by underhand practices or any surmizes of connivance with the army, or any their Officers, can ever advance any designe tending to his restitution, theirs or the Kingdomes good, &c.* sic est in fatis,[64] &c. *Some would have the whole army disband: Friend be not partiall, I tell thee, he that contributes a penny to disband it, will lose a pound by the bargain, yet am I no Souldier. Am I not assured, it's for the good of the whole nation the army stands: are thou well affected, thou shalt need fear no menacing of the contrary party: hast thou been in armes against us, performe thy just payments; be not seditious, thou mayst from hence live securely. Verily to the dis-affected* English *I say, if once again they flye out, then skin for skin. My God! how much do I wish an everlasting oblivion of those two grand nick-names* Round-head *&* Cavalier? *we are National Brethren, in the name of God let us live lovingly and forget preceding injuries: after this time* Wharton *shall write untill dooms-day ere I mention the poor animall. Our unseasonable divisions render us forgetfull of our duties to God; for of what effects can the prayer of an Episcopall Clergy-man be, who prays cordially without doubt that his Maj. may come againe to rule; but the poor man hath a Coloquintida*[65] *in his devotions, viz Lord restore his Maj. provided he restore us to our Bishops lands, Deaneries, &c. and our sequestred Benefices? he that is on our side, he praies largely, that peace may be restored, his Maj. re-seated, yet intentionallie he must first be assured to enjoy the Benefice, Office he at present hath, &c. or else he puts in his verdict against his Majestie, and stumbles his friends with intricate contradictions to no purpose, wave self-ends on all hands, and then in the twinckling of an eye his Maj. and Parl. will accord, be enjoying his due Regalitie, we our native birth-rights. In this work, his Maje. being mortall, must act his part, & every Member of both houses theirs, for they are but men; the Souldier, the Citizen, the Presbiter, the Independent must leave all self-ends and follow Christ, and become poor: a hard* [p. 6] *task. In words we mention* self-denying,[66] *but in actions who is free from* self-doing; *we prohibit by laws to steal, & yet most men theeve and pilfer from the Common-wealth: let us not suffer the quarrell to be* world without end, *and say also* Amen: *In fine, I say, we must adhere to the Parliament, and not affront them as of late; and this is the readiest means for cure of our present distmpers, and speedy re-setling his Maj. But I am wandred almost into a Pulpit, unto which I never had fancy, I return to my proper sphear, desiring every Reader of this yeers* Anglicus, *to give it a favourable censure; its not doubted but some will find ten thousand errors therein: let them say what they please, write what they can, no man in the world dotes lesse on his owne poor brats then* Anglicus *doth, they being produced to light in great deformity: with generous souls his failings may happily find seasonable excuse this yeer, sith* Anglicus *was performed whilst his fancy was over-burdened with intricate meditations made use of in his* Introduction. *Let God doe his pleasure with me, let the world censure my writings, and mine enemies speak large sentences against me, the integrity of my owne heart is onely knowne unto God and my self, wherein for a full satisfaction I say, that the good of the Publick first invited my pen to action, without prejudicate opinion of Monarchy, Episcopacy or of any particular injury offered me by any other; and when I shall return to earth, and must expect to be no more remembred, it shall even at that instant be a cordial to my conscience that I loved Monarchy, took part with the* English *Parliamant against oppressions; flattered no man, honoured my own Nation, never received Bribe, or was partial, or willingly enforced a judgment contrary to Art, but ever retained,* mentem sanam in corpore sano.[67]

William Lilly.
Octob. 23: 1647
Without Temple-Barre at the corner
house over against Strand-bridge.

[Lilly ends his prefatory material with two pages that include a recom-
mendation for Booker's Almanack and a description of his own recently
published *Christian Astrology*. The next 48 pages are Lilly's monthly observations. Each month begins with three pages of daily tables—"The daily
motion of the Planets and ☊," "The Lunar Aspects & The Planets Mutuall
Aspects," and a calendar with holidays and some sunrises and moon features—and concludes with a page of "Observations." The complete texts of
the monthly observations are reproduced here.]

Januaries *Observations.*

WIDOWES and *Orphans* send up their Tears and laments to Heaven,
Petitions & *Cryes* procure no money or pitty from men. We are distressed for
Money, the *Commonalty* payes most unwillingly; the *Souldier* cryes out for
his Pay: what do our *Superiors* all this while? *O Lord God!* how cunningly
are the Actions of these days carried? with what fair pretences? what Missives,
Messages, Treaties or Letters passe frequently? The *Kingdom* expects a good
accompt of this Moneths promises, *Parturiunt Montes*:[68] we tug & labour
to undo our selves. The *Northwest* of this *Kingdom*, & some other parts are
highly discontent, much afflicted, ill satisfied, a small occasion would stir up
a *Lyon* among them: Many are the *Petitions* presented this Month; would
God the *Parlia*. had Treasure to satisfy every one. The month begins wth cold,
snowy, misling *weather*, more frost succeeds, wholsome gales of *wind* then do
follow, & several *Ships* arrive to the *Merchants* content. About the 3^d week
expect a condensed, troubled *ayre*, & such thick *clouds*, as shall disperse in several parts much snow, or many showrs, to the *Country-mans* great prejudice.
The consultations of the *Scot.* nation are much enquired after, and we hear of
them more then is true; their consults are not yet mature. Me thinks we hear of
an angry *Souldier* at home; but alas! who pitties? who sends *mony* & *cloths* to
the poor, but wel-deserving *Irish Souldier?* Now remember valiant *Inchequin*[69]
and honorable *Jones*,[70] men infinitely deserving; if the *weather* retard not,
you shal hear those noble *Souls* are active. At home we feare some turbulent
results, & justly we may; *Remissionem frigoris cum aura leni expectemus.*

Februaries *Observations.*

THE Southern winds or *South-west* blow fair, and the frost or cold is more
remisse. Plausible words or promises are good cheap, but *pious actions*
succeed not. We are lul'd asleep, & hope wel: but observe, a distempered
people break out, cry out & u[p]braid their *Superiors* wth breach of trust.

Heres none or little agreement; ô the fury of an enraged people, like a whirl-wind, is ready to make irruption into the bowels of her oppressors! How long, O God, wilt thou suffer us to be miserable? Most worthy *Jones, Inchequin, Coot*,[71] and honest Col. *More*,[72] behold the *Stars* inform me, that it is fit you act against the villain *Irish*, for now division, poverty, famine, scarcity approacheth neer them; you or some of you are promised very much, yea this moneth, if the season with you permit, I need not direct the part of Heaven, Providence will doe it for you. How scurvily we disagree? what can be expected from this selfnesse but confusion of the *authors?* crosse, malapert[73] Petitions, scandalous Informations, pernitious Pamphlets undo our *State,* appear plentifully even to their faces. An appearance of many or some eminent men to be questioned or committed. The Souldier is still angry, the Country-man highly displeased, the Citizens at a stand, impregnated but not yet delivered. The eight day □ of ♄ & ♂ snow or rain, *ventorum concursus cum nivibus*: 14. *die*[74] more cleer, but yet rainy or snowy, afterwards fierce winds and various turbulent weather; towards the latter end of the month unseasonable & high winds, occasioning some losse at Sea on the *Southwest* parts of this Kingdom, &c. I nothing like this Moneths actions, nor may I speak home.

Marches *Observations.*

OUR *Parlia.* or Governours of the Affairs of this Kingdom, are wearied with multiplicity of action. News from the North arrives, so also from *Irel.* both appear to be good, yet little pleasing to some Detractors. Matters are carried very occultly, & some actions of moment are smothered: here's great plodding and stickling to raise parties, many are dispersed into severall parts of this Kingdom, to hawk matter to undo their fellow-Subjects, for there's but one King, and *England* endures no more. 20 *die* □ of ♄ & ♀ *auram humidam ac ventosam minatur, aliquando vehemens fiat ventus, pluviasque cum tonitribus commiscet, fiat etiam nonnunquam Septentrio.*[75] We are crossed by petty, absurd fellowes, who grow potent and would dominere, but our *Senators* scorn to buckle: our Souldiers elevate their conceptions; the whole *Kingdom* stands in amazement. Now the *Scot* is feared: then doubtfull newes from severall places afflicts us. How wicked are the minds of men who labour our confusion? behold the *Scot* is honorable: what! twice in one month comfortable newes from our *Irish* Commanders! blessed Souls are yee: If from hence no check runs to *Dublin* how fair an accompt may this wasted Kingdom expect from the present Commanders. The painfull Country-man is promised a good seasonable Seed-time, yet the Weather inclines more unto moysture then drinesse. But what have I to doe with the Weather? civill high matters, grand deliberations are approaching, *Aut Caesar aut nihi!*:[76] this moneth begins the dance, a yeer hence may end it.

Aprils *Observations.*

GOD is very mercifull to us, if for many days together we smart not with unseasonable gusts of wind, storms, hail, sudden tempestuous weather, to our great discontent. Our *Grandees*[77] or many of our principall Gentry and Officers dissent, disagree, like not the publike proceeds on foot. A *Populous* people there are who cannot obey, or know how to command, are now ill disposed, mutter and tacitly repine, fear is more prevalent with them then there is cause. Behold on a sudden what hopes of a fair reconcilement we have! God grant a true understanding betwixt our great ones and one great one, and then full happy are we generally. I protest *Scotland* if thou doest affront or intrench upon us, as the unadvised would have thee, we shal be sure of victory. Good & not good, ill and not ill is signified to the *Londoners,* whom I mention not so oft as perhaps is expected. Live *English Parlia.* fear not the male-contented, thy *Angel Protector* is very potent, his name is not *Michael,* yet is he powerfull: *Ventos frigidiores expectemus, nebulasque cum rore cadentes:*[78] Why doest thou frown ô *Londoner?* thou art but a portion of *England*; be not seduced with, or by the tyrannicall Divine. Welcome sweet Messenger from *Ireland,* what newes doest thou bring? Famine, mortality, & most horrible division is now there, great deserting each other; poor bestiall Kingdome, thy *Angel* is a sluggard, but the *English* Angel is active. Hark, the preparation of the *French* arives amongst us, but to little purpose. The death of one *Grandee* approacheth. Scorn and dislike doth now begin to take place upon the heart of one of the tallest *English* Cedars. When we can agree, then we will send assistance to the noble *English* in *Ireland.*

Mayes *Observations.*

THE Souldiers shift their Quarters, demeane themselves with much civility, and addresse to their Superiours for Moneys. Strange things are whispered; people fear a sad disaster unto some great one, they swell with expectation of the issue: Removes are frequent; the world is round. *Nocturnas pluvias expectemini; efficitur aer pluviosus, & aliquando aestuosus.*[79] *Venice, Venice,* thy *Guardian-Angel* groans to support thee longer; will no warning serve thee? The *French* hold up their heads, are numerous, yet must act no high exploits. Our active Gallants play their parts in *Ireland,* while the dirty *Irish* now and then peep out with a ragged Regiment; there's more words come from the *Pope* then Crownes, yet have they some slender hopes; but unawares our men attaine an honourable day of them; some losse we must expect. We abound with multiplicity of lyes and fraudulent reports; Oh the endeavours that are used to undoe us by mis-understandings! but Providence discovers very materiall things for our good this moneth, or neer it. We may fear the *Plague* or some pestilentiall Disease to be now at hand.

Many pious Senators with wisdome perswade a disconsolate or grieved people to patience. Loe! I feare mischiefe is at hand to a person of quality; and many opposers appeare to disturb our greater proceedings. Thunder, Lightning or some sudden furious Hail-stormes about the third week. Offices of honour conferred on some: Happily the City may be more contented, she might if she harboured not serpents amongst her children. A not visible Eclipse augments misfortune upon the noble *Spaniard*, and draws vengeance from heaven on some where it hath been long expected to fall: Children are not alwayes blessings. The Eclipse of the ☽ neer the true *Aphelium* of ♄, shewes matter of consequence to some, if their eyes could be opened. I can speak no evill of the *Scottish* Nation, sith the Heavens give me no information: *Ergo*,[80] let us not mistrust; for if not seriously provoked, we shall find them Brethren as formerly: *In the name of God, amen.*

Junes *Observations.*

NEER the months beginning here seems disagreement about Petitions, or an ungentle Message. The *Londoners* begin to be high, yet not sufficiently confident; they fear the Sicknes, not wholly without cause: verily if themselves are not froward no ill is ment them. The Stars whisper a tumult, or a melancholy people fear disturbance. Words or Petitions are not at present pleasing to our State, engaged in greater affairs: I hope we may expect a day of thanksgiving for a *victory* over the *Irish*, which seems not obtainable without the death of an eminent Worthy on our side. *Dubia aeris constitutio, moventur venti Occidentales.*[81] It's very probable we shall have thunder, lightning, and a strange face of heaven for many dayes. We are necessitated for moneys, whilst severall rumors come from the North, little pleasing; not long after true and sure newes comes from *Scotl.* in which Kingdom matters are now variously handled; the results wherof we earnestly long after, for we seem plunged, or almost mired in our home-resolutions: we consult of many things, conclude nothing, are in fear of the angry Souldier; yet there are good men and wise amongst us, who cordially reconcile a sturdy people, apt to take an occasion to disturb themselves and Commonwealth. Here seems an accusation or impeachment brought against a prime man. A second eclipse *Solar* not visible; absolutely we shal have newes from the North, the effects will appear in those parts, *Nil desperandum Christo Duce*;[82] the heavens intimate & give warning of a violent Commotion, or declare the minds of the Commonalty & Souldier extreamly exasperated. God blesse *London* from Sicknesse and casualties neer about these times; *mane occidit arcturus circa 16. die,* ♂ ☉ & ♀ *die proximo, mutationem aeris affert arcturus*[83] ☉ & ♀ shew much moisture, or much thunder; the month concludes with manifest expectation of some notable accident; I am fearfull a great person is neer a great piece of treason or trechery, *Sed quae non prosunt singula multa juvant.*[84]

Julies *Observations.*

THE malevolent Planets ♄ and ♂ separate slowly, nor are they yet without the limits of the □ of ♃; great are the actions of these moneths; the consultations of the times are in excesse; little moderation is used; mercy is wanting to the distressed sick people: Christians perish; a Sicknesse wanders far & near, the mischief now raging is like to be permanent for our divisions are fomented by supream connivance: the wooden *Clergy* act their parts, the Souldier is not wanting, his poverty enforceth him, but the quarrell is not among petty people, the *Cedars* shake. There are yet a peaceable people amongst us, who by prudence and moderation regulate our despairing conditions: how many meetings have we? or what pains do the honest hearted take to pacifie a giddy multitude. High desires may arrive from the North; our State, if the heavens deceive me not, are in an honourable condition, are not much disturbed in their resolutions. Good Sir, be not so peremptory, a religious party little fear the threats thou bringest. Why cannot the *Citizens* thrive and be pleasant? a time is now approaching, which imports felicity unto them: remove, remove the male-contented, beleeve the Clergy but a little; let them preach Doctrine, but no State-policy. The *French* have now pleasing intelligence, a Victory is neer unto them; nor are we destitute of what contents us from our *friends* in several parts of *Irel.* If an Angel were President in the present *Parl.* he must seek matter to please a stiff-necked people; who neither know how to command but with pride, nor to obey without distaste. When all matters seem reconciled, behold there arrives very boisterous Petitions, or surly words, or tart aspersions are divulged; whereupon succeeds much melancholly and sadnes in many peoples hearts; many fearing an irruption into the *Northern* parts, whilst we are not in perfect unity in the *South* and City.

Augusts *Observations.*

NE *timeatis fratres, sed attendite;*[85] the day of judgment is not at hand, but verily matters of greatest consequence are neer agitation, both with us in *Engl.* and all over *Europe.* I love thee *Spain,* but now beware of an imminent trechery, be careful of thy Officers this moneth; the Planets and their intelligences speak as if this moneth would produce a very great fight at Sea, and much action betwixt the *Turk* & *Venetian,* as also with the *Swede* & *Germane. Austrian* family be not timerous, the effects of the Comet in 1618. is now almost extinguished, after which thou oughtst to flourish yet a while. But at home, why have we so many envious enemies, wishing ill to those have preserved us all? O the sad condition of Magistrates! behold how the wicked backbite, & spue out viperous language against them. Here appears very great division and great destraction seems to be neer; if the influence of the *Caniculars*[86] was not now extinguished by their late setting, I should fear a generall dog-raging madnesse amongst us, we do so snarl at one another.

News arrives from the *Southwest,* nothing welcome or pleasing; it at instant seems the forerunner of some mischief, but a few days informs us the matter is not so hainous. If no suppression be of irregular pamphlets about this time here do most wretched ones appear, much to the dishonour of the *Parlia.* If we can agree amongst our selves in *Irel.* which I hope we shall, it's not the least or the worst news I expect from thence; *Circa hoc tempus, apparet ventus procellosus, turbidus, grandinosus, impetuosus, violentus, qui aedificia evertit, naves destruit, arbores sternit, & plaustra onerata percellit:*[87] Thunder also and lightning is like to be; afterwards mens minds are set upon mischief, and the crosse influence of heaven stirs up much secret malice amongst us, so doth it in *Ireland* amongst the naturals, by means whereof we attain either a victory absolute, or somewhat of much moment.

Septembers *Observations.*

THE uncomfortable aspects of the preceding moneth, may be the instruments of much good to ensue in this: If the fate of *Monarchy* be not inevitably decreed for suppression in these Kingdoms of *Engl. Scotl.* and *Irel.* or if the immediate hand of God be not at present against it, I then conceive his Majesty or many great persons are very neer a restauration to former dignities. As I was ever a faithfull lover of Monarchy, and of his Majesty as my Soveraign, so am I still, and shall continue; our *Parl.* and the just rights of the *English* involved in them, entirely preserved. Me thinks, at lest, we are promised fair, God almighty give his Majesty what is due unto him; and to us of the Commonalty our native Birthright without impeachment: Let's have no jugling, but let us understand one another rightly, and then is my soul full of hopes that the consultations of this moneth shall exceedingly tend to the good of the whole Nation, and many heavy impositions lessened, or quite taken off from the Commonalty: ♂ ♃ & ♀ *ventos movet ab occasu, adventantem hyemem minatur Spica Virginis occidens vesperi cum 10. grad.* ♎.[88] The *Londoners* now have no such molestations, but that they may with much freedome elect their *Lord Maier;* concerning whose election I find no great stickling; without doubt ♀ is elected, let him enjoy it, the man is discreet and wel-spoken, &c. From beyond Seas, we hear the *French* are Rampant, and the *Emperour* is not unfortunate; the *Venetian* brags but a little of this moneths actions; formidable actions in the *west-Indies:* The *Portugals* rather keep their owne in those Countries by trechery then manhood: Truly I wish the *Hollanders* good successe, which they many now expect, yet all is not well handled there by their Officers: those provident people must expect a period of their greatnesse, yet this age must not see it.

Octobers *Observations.*

THE affairs of the *English* Commonwealth continue in a peaceable & quiet condition, no present distractions doe I foresee. From the *West* arrives newes at *London,* which in my judgment portends us good, yet are we doubtful, & a little afflicted with mistrust, but time reveals the very truth, to our exceeding content, the matter is materiall. *Aer inconstans producitur, flatus ventorum magnus adest.*[89] The *Southw.* wind is high, the Merchant fears Westward: be of good comfort adventurous soul, thy losse is not so great, I hope none at all: ♀ *intrans* ♏ *subitas tempestates cum vento & pluviis multis movet:*[90] we may expect rain or showrs in abundance. If God almighty suffer the influence of his creatures to take effect, farewell stinking *Irish Rebell,* for by this time, or in this month, our worthy Souldiers make thee run, while we possesse thy habitations and thy fertil fields, with what wealth thou cruelly extortedst from our murthered Country-men. Industrious *Hollanders* you may expect a victory over the West-India *Portugals* in *Brazil,* your Ships bring plenty of Returns, to the Merchants great advantage. At home I fear we have some verball scuffling, or doubt a trechery or plot; indeed there is mischief intended, but the Actors will timely be discovered, we shall not suffer by it, for they will be deservingly rewarded. From what part *Northward* comes this Messenger? what ill tidings brings he? either such a thing, or eminent persons are accused and informed against: □ ♂ & ♀ *ventos Occidentales movet:*[91] towards the latter end of the moneth[92] we are molested with peremptory demands, or prick-eard fellowes would domineer over their betters; woodden-witted men they are, neither obeying God, loving their King, or caring for the Parliament, or that Committee which in intervals must be respected. The moneth concludes well, with good words and actions, an universal welfare is expected.

Novembers *Observations.*

HOW sweetly this moneth begins, how mournfully it ends! (if God by his divine providence divert not the malevolent influence of his creatures the *Stars.*) Want of money, clamors for arrears, suits about preceding damages and trespasses generally afflict us; would this were all. Mens stomacks are full of revenge and anger: the winds rise high, the Seas roar and swell, & laments of *Europe* are many for the impoverished Merchant. Our *Citizens* are in the number of men, losse they must expect. Cold frosts, or a penetrating sharp ayre afflicts the *Northeast* parts of this Kingdom, enforcing the poor Farmer to begin the winter early. Justice seems to question Offenders, and they not of inferiour rank: can nothing but discord undo us, and must we now unseasonably begin? we are mad or besotted with the nationall sin of this Kingdom: Division. Many theevish pranks and horrible robberies in houses in this City, and upon the High-ways, are this moneth committed; some steal publickly, others rob the Republick privately, both ought to be hanged. Will our Magistrates and Superiou[r]s never unite? shall the Devil ever grin at their perpetual discord? and must we of the Commonalty suffer eternally? A sad time I fear approacheth to some, to one, to more, to a family, nay to many; I hope our *Senators* will be wary, there are that

hunt and sneak in corners to mischief them. I see great dissenting of opinion in our *Grandees,* and their serious consultations frequently interrupted
by private and secret practices. Of the *Lunar Eclipse* this moneth I intend
to write apart in the generall judgment of the yeer. What pains is taken
to do his Majesty disservice? how the pragmaticall insulting Priest acts his
part preaching Policy more than Religion: ungodly men, you cannot prevent Providence by Tyranny; I doubt some will be impeached for Murder
or Treason, &c. God's mercy is great amidst his judgments, for his peaceable Angel miraculously lessens much of the evill intended: and why? many
honest souls of the *Lay-people* (few of the *Clergy*) stand in the gap and
overcome God by prayer.

Decembers *Observations.*

A Second *Eclipse,* this of ☉ not visible, yet above the earth, here will effects
succeed, and they not mean ones; God acts by his Messengers. Here are ten
digits eclipsed; some *King* or *Prince* loses a branch or an arm of his Regality.
Clandestine consultations on foot, the actions of the month superlative,
requiring a more prophetick and divine Pen, then poor innocent *Anglicus.*
*Tranquillissima tempestas nobis evenire solet circa Brumale Solstitium,
aliquando sine ventorum flabris, cum hyems aspera & aliquomodo serena
est, terraque gelu maximo constringitur, ut nihil fere vaporum è terra educi
potest;*[93] discontented *Citizens* mutter and repine, I fear the strict *Clergy*
have a hand in fomenting their rage. More discord is evident and many sad
complaints arrive from the Souldier and the Country-man, both in great
necessity; the Souldier for his pay, the Farmer for better weather. It's probable our Parliament will be moved to indignation concerning certain passages
acted against them, for treasonable plots are hatching to divide or destroy
them: the not suppression of illiterate Pamphlets doe much prejudice their
Honours. This yeer is now ending, tranquility seems to conclude it, the blessing of God going along with the cordiall intentions of our *Senators.* God
almighty restore his Majesty, blesse the Parliament and the whole Kingdome
of *England,* their Councels, their Armies; God defend our *Irish* friends, that
have so many times acted valiant things this yeer. I submit my predictions to
divine Providence; I hold no fatall necessity: I love the modest Divine where
ere I find him; I hate the wrangling Prebyter: I love the Army for the good we
have received from them, so also the *Scots:* if the one or other doe ill, I am
then convertible: God blesse with long life my assured friend in the North,
and all his Family. *Nives cum ventis occidentalibus producunt posteriores
aspectus hujus mentis.*[94]
    [13 pages of tables omitted]

[p. 1]
The generall Contingencies of ENGLAND,
SCOTLAND and IRELAND *Astrologically*
predicted for this present yeer 1648.

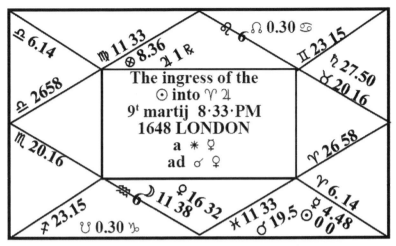

The ingress of the
⊙ into ♈ ♃
9ᵗ martij 8·33·PM
1648 LONDON
a ⚹ ♀
ad ☌ ♀

Hercle, restat regnum aliud, piis
Cœlo sub amplo, bestia cum cadet
Dandum, potestatisque summæ
Jus, pede sub dominante Christi
Stratis Tyrannum verticibus.

Figure 5.2 Lilly's General Contingencies for 1648 opened with this Scheme of the Heavens, 9 March 1648, marking the entry of the Sun into Aries, captioned with Latin poetry.[95]

THE malevolent influence of that prodigious *Comet* in 1618. so fatall to *Germany* and most Kingdomes of *Europe*, being now by the divine permission of almighty God, transmitted by his ministring Angels beyond our *English Horizon* unto more remote parts, we must expect and search out some neerer causes, and later *Coelestial Configurations* to direct our present Conceptions, for better discovery of such generall affairs as may happily be of speciall concernment to our beloved Mother *England*, her Sister *Scotland*, and our rebellious Servant the Kingdom of *Ireland*. A most difficult labour we undertake, for if we write meerly in *Astrall termes* and *language*, we edifie very few; and we straine a [p. 2] judgment from the Intelligencees or Presiding Angels, we are then lesse understood and by some suspected; if we deliver our intentions in vulgar termes, we are wholly mistaken in many things, our sense perverted, and our sentences so variously applied, & unto such a sinister construction, as we were never guilty, no not in thought; the consideration whereof had so discouraged our pen, that we never had any further intentions of entring upon the publike stage again in this annuall way of Judicature: but God who by his divine[96] Providence disposeth all our humane actions, & who of late extended great mercies unto us, hath once again, even from a desperate and forlorne condition, raised & elevated our *Astral* conceptions, & stir'd up in us these subsequent judgments, which we now emit into the mercilesse world, to be slanderously or ignorantly traduced. This present *9. March 1648.* we have the distempered effects of those *Parelii* or three Suns, visible *April 3.* last, yet forcibly operating, and not determined: we are also subject at this present to the influence good or evill, of that last □ of ♄ & ♃, *Sept.* 30.ult. but in effects are declining, & we are approaching to receive our share and portion of that heavenly influence which God shall suffer the second □ of ♄ & ♃ now imminent this 29. of *March* instant, to shour down upon us, for it will work violently. The 27^{d}. 34. min. of ♉ is this yeer the *Profectional* ascendant of their last ☌, upon which very degree, and almost minute ♄ by his *transit* doth now this 9. of *March* passe; ♃ being by progresse arrived to the first deg. of ♍, in partil dexter □ to the radical place of *Mars* in that ☌; and if we enquire for the very *Profectional* Sign of the ☌ it self, we shall find it 25^{d}.46'. of ♌, unto which very deg. the bountifull Planet ♃ this yeer by his *transit* doth not arrive, proceeding *Retr.* in ♌ but to the 29. deg. thereof, meeting not-withstanding before his egresse out of ♌, yea even in that very degree with a △ dexter of ☉ *Apr.* 8. following our present ingresse: from these configurations at present (as being our *Basis*) must we naturally, and according to Art extract our ensuing judgment for this present yeer 1648. wherein God direct us.

What our judgment was upon the *quadrature* of *Saturne* and *Jupiter, Septemb.* 1647. you shall here have related *(verbatim)* out of our *Propheticall Merline,* pag. 108.[97] [p. 3] *upon the first quadrature of* Saturn *and* Jupiter *Sept.* 30. 1647. ♄ *then arriving to the place of* ♂ *in the* ☌, *and* Jupiter *to a* □ *of* ♂ *by transit; the peregrination of* Jupiter *in that Signe not hindring by a double debility in Sign and house,* viz. *if there were then no underhand-dealing, jugling, shirking and dissembling fellowes in request, we might hope well, and that with some trouble we should sensibly taste the fruits of Peace, or have a glimpse of it: but whether the hypocriticall Religious Saints, or the disturbed Trade of an impoverished people produce nothing; or above all this, the much lamented and untimely death of a gallant, and not to be paraleld* Generall, *or brave Field-Officer put us in confusion, I know not: here's much time spent to no purpose; but it being not the first time foul actions smother over deceitfull pretences, I leave all to God; let the Sun shine upon the Author this yeer,* & omnia bene.[98] These were our predictions; let the Kingdome it selfe explaine our sense and meaning without mis-application. We come now to deliver that judgment wch naturally ariseth from the positures and configurations preceding, upon the ☉ his entrance into the first point of ♈: the figure erected here for our Meridian of *London* hath ♎ 26.58. ascending; which because it is a movable Sign, according to the judgment of some, shall give us judgment but of three moneths affaires, *viz.* untill the ☉

enter the Sign ♋: the words of *Bonatus*, fol. 527. are these: *Si quidem ascendens fuerit signum mobile, non durabit illa revolutio, nisi usq; ad introitum ☉ in ♋, & tunc oportebit te aequare ad omnes quartas anni, eritq; dominus primae quartae ille cuius fuerit dominium in introitu ☉ in ♈, &c.* when the Signe ascending is movable that *Revolution* endures but untill the[99] ☉ his entrance into ♋, & then you must erect figures for the other three quarters of the yeer. He shal be Lord of the first quarter of the yeer who hath dominion at ☉ his entrance into ♈, &c. and so of every Planet who is Lord of the figure in the *Solstitial, Autumnal, Hybernal* quarter. *thus he.* But I take it to be thus understood, that when in any *annual revolution,* the beginning, middle or greater part of a movable Signe possesseth the *asc.* that when we ought to change and vary our figure four severall times, as he directs; but when the latter degrees of a movable Sign ascend, & there remains but two or three within the house, I then justly affirm, [p. 4] and with reason maintain, that the Lord of the subsequent Sign shall more properly governe, and be called Lord of the ascendant, then that Planet who solely hath dominion but of two or three degrees; and therefore in our Schem, I do say that ♀ shal have some signification of our people & the Governours of our *English* affaires; but ♂ who is most potent of all the Planets, and Lord of ♏ the succeeding Signe, shall most powerfully and significantly represent them and their actions; which as they are like to be various, so of very high concernment, and will be managed by our *worthies* of Parliament with much moderation, justice and integrity, to their owne eternall honour, and perpetuall good of the whole *English* Nation, and of this let the Commonalty of *England* be most assured, &c. I have no desire to be copious, or to enlarge a judgment beyond Art; the onely scope of a *Revolution* being as *Bonatus* saith, *Per Revolutionem annorum mundi,*[100] *scitur quid in illo anno sit futurum de bono aut malo, utrum annus sit tranquillus on importunas, & utrum sint guerrae futurae an non; qualis sit status regum, principum vel magnatum, similiter & populorum, atque vilium & religiosorum, etiam uniuscujusque in suo esse, uniuscujusque generis universaliter secundam hominis ritus, quid de terrae nascentibus sit futurum, utrum ex cis abundantia vel penuria expectetur, quodque ex cis sit carum aut vile,* pag. 489.

We know by the Revolution of the years of the world, what manner of accidents shall happen in that yeer, whether good or evill, whether the year will be peaceable, or if warres will ensue therein, yea or not; what shall be the condition of Kings, Princes & Noble-men as also of the common sort of people, or of low and poor degree, of the Religious, yea, of every man in his kind, and of every other thing universally, according to the property of man therein; what encrease we may expect from the fruits of the earth, whether from thence plenty or scarcity may be expected, and what manner of Commodity will be cheap, what dear, &c.

In this manner did the *Ancients* proceed in their judicature, which method we now intend to follow, sith we are in peace, and have no open enemy, though a million of private ones.

Forasmuch then as ♎ the Signe ascending is movable, *mu-* [p. 5] *tans & cambiens res*;[101] we may probably conjecture, that there is a great change or mutability of humane affaires approaching, especially concerning the Ric[h]es, Priviledges, Lawes and Customes of this Kingdome of *England*, and whole Commonalty therein included; and as the Signe possesseth both the cusps of the first and twelfth houses, so it imports the great willingnesse of many noble soules to draw our disordered matters to a faire and seasonable conclusion; and it doth also decipher the clandestine practices of others, and they no small ones, to prolong our home-bred differences: and the Stars informe us, that these unequal distempers, or unsetled results, seem to be on foot much about or very neer the time of the beginning of this yeers Revolution: but in regard ♀ hath no great continuance of her dominion in the *Vernall* quarter, but leaves her rule unto ♂, who enters upon his command about *May*, and that then the dominion of the succeeding part of the yeer is in a manner wholly committed unto him, clandestine practices shall now faile, and businesse shal be fairly and judiciously carried; and as then the remainder of the yeers actions may be deduced from ♂, who then regulates the ascending Signe ♏, being fixed, we may not doubt, but that from a troubled and long continued *Series* of doubtfull distempers, we shall about those times arrive to a most setled condition, and enjoy our Customes, Trades and Priviledges in quietnisse and contented security: *This* is generally intended to the Countryman in all parts of the Kingdom, as well, if not more then to the Citizen.

Seeing ♀ is partly Lady of the ascendant, and ♂ in the house of ♃, and ♃ in the tenth house; as also that ☽ who usually hath representation of the common condition of man-kind (*nam Sol pro Magistratis, Luna pro subditis, viz.* the ☉ is for the Magistrate, the ☽ for Subjects or common people) sith I say she is not unfortunate, but is applying to ☌ of ♀, we have great reason, according to Art, to hope well, and to expect God's blessings, and to live in assurance that the Commonalty of this Kingdome shall doe well, and every one at his own house, and in his Vocation and calling live quietly and secure. Verily this is no fiction of our owne, but the opinion of those reverend Professors that studied this Science long before us, from whom *Ori-* [p. 6] *ganus* fol. 522. drawes this inference, and confirmes our opinion.

In anni & quartarum Revolutionibus aut thematibus Lunationum, si Luna, sive firma & potens, sit in angulo, vel succedente domo & Dignitatibus suis, sive debilis & cadens extra Dignitates, applicuerit benefico alicui Planetae Jovi vel Veneri, significabitur status populi fortunatius quo lucra eidem accrescent & abundabunt necessaria, & si applicuerit Veneri, erit hilaritas, gaudium & frequentia connubiorum.

In the Revolutions of a yeer, and quarterly ingresses, or of the severall Schemes of Lunations, if the ☽ whether she be fixed or powerfull in an angle or else in a succedant house, and in her owne Dignities; or if she be weak, or cadent, and not in any of her Dignities, and yet shall apply to any benevolent Planet, whether it be *Jupiter* or *Venus*, the state or condition of the

Commonalty shall be signified succesfull and fortunate; in which yeer they shall encrease their Estates, and shall abound in all manner of necessary provisions; and if that *Fortune* unto whom the ☽ shall apply be *Venus* (as now it is) the common people shall much rejoyce, be frolick and very cheerfull, and freely suffer their Sonnes and Daughters[102] to marry, so that upon a sober consideration hereof, if we may confide in the words of our Author, it's not onely like to be a good yeer in the generall, but such a one as wherein every poor Country-man is promised very faire: yet because ♀ doth apply to the □ of ♄ in the eighth house, *Plurimi morientur*, many aged men shall in this yeer dye, more then usually in another yeer they are wont, and these of the vulgar people, or people who daily labour in earthly Commodities.

But if any shall object, That *Mars* is the most considerable Planet, not onely in the *Vernall* ingresse, but also in all other quarters, and Lunations of the yeer, and therefore we may justly[103] suspect him the fore-runner of more War or bloodshed.

Unto this I say, That he doth not alwayes signifie War in every Revolution or quarterly ingresse, although he chances to be most dignified; for we must warily pronounce judgment upon such a posature, for it's considerable, whether the generall influence[104] of all the other Planets doe concurre with him and [p. 7] or whether the ascendant of the King promise any such matter, whether the King or principall Ruler or Rulers of that Common-wealth have any malevolent Directions coincident with that malevolent Revolution, &c. or whether the effects of any preceding Eclipse or comet did pronounce War, and is then in force.

What ♂ signifieth. As ♂ is posited in our Revolution, he doth not premonstrate Wars, Slaughters or so grand Commotions as our eyes have beheld; he as now posited in the Heavens, threatens us with sad discontents, back-slidings in Religious matters & Ceremonies, great disconsolation amongst the *Clergy*, and high demands or results amongst the *Schismatical*, the setling of, or a strong endeavour to settle the just Laws, Proceedings and Customes of the people: & it doth signifie, that these disgusts generally are not to happen amongst the inferior people, but amongst the principall *Gentry* of every Country, and greatest Citizens of every City, and in plain terms, amongst our greatest *Statesmen*, or such as do regulate the affairs of our *English* Common-wealth. I write thus much to undeceive any of our Nation, that being not well versed in the fundamentals of *Astrology*, might be misled either[105] by the erronious fancy of their own judgment, or blind mistakes of such an asse as *George Wharton*, and so might be timerous of new broyles to arise amongst our selves in this Kingdome, which my heart utterly abhors. I have authority to countenance my opinion, for if we beleeve *Haly*, fol. 360. he informes us, that ♂, as posited in our Scheme, shall not prejudice us; his words are, *Semper in revolutione, cave, & respice Martem, quia si bonus fuerit, & in bono statu, melius succedet negotium vassallorum regis & exercituum*: In every Revolution, be well advised in giving judgment, and have respect to the place of *Mars*, for if he be well qualified, and in a good state, the affaires of the King's Subjects and their Armies shall well succeed. An assured testimony it is, that our Common-wealth of *England* shall not in this present yeer be molested with Warre, or much grieved or offended with the Souldier, so that the Country-man and honest Farmer may with quiet and contented minds serve God, follow their daily employments, and may also live secure from plundering or [p. 8] any rapine or oppression of his Superiours, or of the Souldier. But if it be con-ceived our judgment herein is partiall (because we ever affect the Parliament, and some malevolent spirits think otherwayes) then I say the *Arabick* learning in this point may much advantage us, which runs thus, as *Haly* saith, fol. 364. *Nota quod Planeta qui est Dominus & Significator anni, quando invenitur in aliquo signorum, significat secundum proprietatem ipsius Planetae, & secun-dum ipsius proprietatem loci in quo versatur de domibus figurae, & secundum statum, & ejus fortunam & infortunia; quia per fortunam & bonum statum, significat bonum & meliorem successum & gaudium, &c. & si quando Mars talis fuerit, significat quod homines vincent homines inimicos suos, & erunt tuti & muniti ab occasionibus, &c.*

Observe that Planet who is Significator of the yeer, and in which of the twelve Signes he is found, be assured he shall signifie according to the propriety of that Planet, Signe and house of heaven wherein he is posited, and accord-ing to his state, fortune or infortunatenesse, for that Planet well fortified shall signifie good successe, joy and gladnesse, &c. and if at any time ♂ shall be so posited or qualified in a Revolution, it imports the Commonalty shall overcome and destroy those men that shall become their enemies, and themselves shall remaine safe and saved harmlesse, or protected from all sinister occasions: for as I said before, unlesse a generall Calamity be impending upon a Kingdome or Country, the sole position of ♂ in Essentiall dignities in any Revolution cannot portend War. We have him now singularly qualified, by his existence in a good house of Heaven, and in the house of a peaceable Planet, and also applying unto a ✳ of ♄, who is Lord of the fourth, as if we might with more confidence expect an end of our long sufferance, then a new Hurliburly or War.

For further confirmation of our preceding judgment, let us have recourse to the Profectional figure of the last ☌ of ♄ ♃, we find ♀ therin to have great dominion, the latter degrees of ♉ her house ascending; we also have ♂ who is Lord of ♈, *Englands* horoscopicall Signe,[106] in ♏ his owne house; and if we consider the ascendant upon the ☌ of ♄ and ♂ in ♊ the 28. of *June* this yeer, we shall find it about four degrees of ♏, very neer to the [p. 9] Profectional degree of ♂: By all wch positures, and from all the preceding & subsequent Configurations, I conjecture according unto naturall causes, that we shall not this yeer be afflicted by any Forreigner, either *Scottish* (for they are too honourable) or *French* (for they will have work enough at home) or *Danish*, &c. for certainly the prevalency of our Kingdoms Planet imports no cause of feare unto us of any invasion; and verily so powerfull he is, that it may deter the advance of any nation whatsoever amongst us, *Deus enim dedit Angliam Anglis usque ad diem judicii,*[107] *&c.* having delivered our concep-tions upon the generall fate of *England,* as to the probability of War or Peace, we now come to diflect every Planets particular signification, as posited in the Revolution, and from thence will enlarge as occasion shall offer.

As to the particular person and fate of his Majesty, I have now very few words to say, he being not at present in armes against the Parliament: his Significator is very properly this yeer ☉, posited in the fift[h] house, ♀ separating from him, and ♃ by a retrograde motion applying to his △, both of them *in terminis ultimis signorum*:[108] this configuration promiseth him faire, argues that he is or may be neer some Treaty or unity with his people; it fully and perfectly concludes it not: for the good of the Kingdome I wish a setled peace; that wandring Gypsie *Wharton* is as farre mistaken in his partiall judgment upon ☉ his being in the sixt[h], as when he prophesied of a Running Martch at *Oxford,* for he saith in his scandalous impudent Prog. *Rex perveniet ad pristinum suum Dominium & renovabuntur res*:[109] God grant he may doe so; but this positure of Heaven is negative as unto that judgment, ☉ is in the sixt[h] in W.*[harton]* his Figure, *Si ☉ fuerit in sextae habebit Rex illo in anno tristitiam,*[110] *Haly 378.* But let us proceed, and heare the opinion of *Haly* in other matters, pag. 371. *At si ♃ in Decima infortunatus fuerit, erunt justiciae communitur in omnibus hominibus illius climatis, & habebunt honorem & mercedem & pietatem a suis regibus & Dominis, & lucrabuntur cum ipsis, ac eis facient utilitatem;*[111] so that here seems an equal distribution of justice by the Parliament and their subordinate Ministers in the severall parts of this Kingdome unto the people, and much honour unto [p. 10] them for their so great justice and piety in ordering the affairs of this Common-wealth; but as to that high & mighty restoring beforementioned, heres not one fillable for defence of that opinion. We find ♄ L.[ord] of the 4th posited in the 8th, the cusp of the 4th is in the Terms of ♄, the Sign is his house, and he posited in the 8th, *Quando ♄ fuerit in octava domo, accident mortes in animalibus quae sunt de natura illius signi, si quidem fuerit quadrupedum, morientur animalia, si fuerit in signo humano morientur, homines antiqui & senes:* When in an annual Revolution we find ♄ in the eighth, there wil be a dearth or scarcity of such creatures as that Sign represents wherin he is; if he be in a Sign representing four-footed Beasts, there will be a scarcity of such Cattle: if he chance to be in a humane Sign, which represents generally man-kind, it's an argument of the Plague, or of the death of many ancient people: As here he is posited in our figure, he threatens the Husband-man with losse as to his greater Cattle, or some scurvy disease unto them, whereby he shall receive much losse and damage, and these Cattle should be Horse and Oxen. And indeed in regard ♄ is this yeer to meet with the ☌ of ♂ in ♊, an aery Signe, it's like to be a very sickly yeer, and it is also probable, the Plague will disperse it selfe into many parts of *England*, and will be violent for a time in the City of *London*, so also in the Western parts or North-west of this Kingdome; we may justly fear that there may be many distractions and very great discontents, great scarcity of Grain and Corn, so that a small famine in the more mountain Countries of *England* may be feared: ☌ of ♄ and ♂ in ♊ foreshewes scarcity of

Provision for man, & great distractions amongst men; *Cum duae Infortunae conjunguntur, & ☽ ♄ in latitudine, erit fames & mortalitas;* When the two *Infortunes* are in ☌, and ☽ hath the same latitude w^ch^ ♄ hath, a Famine and Mortality succeeds, But why this ☌ that be so fatal and ominous to the City of *London*, & stir up the effects of an Eclipse which appears not until five moneths after, or why that ☌ shall procure unto the *Cavaliers* such esteem from the *Londoner*, it's verily Utopian and Malignant *Astrology*, and neither naturally deduced or to be deduced from that positure of ♄ and ♂, or any other that I know of. This I tell the City of *London*, had an Army of the most reformed *Cavaliers* passed through the [p. 11] City instead of those of his *Excellency*, the Citizens would ere this have been sensible of such misdemeanours in them, as in the least measure they cannot impute unto any of those hopeful soules under Sir *Thomas Fairfax* his command: But in these matters I am willingly content to be silent, having received so great civilities from many gallant Gentlemen, who have been engaged in his Majesties quarrel; what I speak is of the vulgar Souldier, and such ill bred and necessitous fellowes as *Noworth* who followed the cause on foot, and never engaged but once, and that in a poor Hog-stye, where he was well cudgeld, for mistaking a Pig for the learned *Campanella*,[112] &c. ♃ in the tenth in ♍ an earthly Signe, is an argument that Corn will be deare, and the Clergy little satisfied, rather highly male-contented. Again, *Si Mars applicat Saturno, de tertio, significat laborem & damnum in causis hominum, & damnum in redditibus regum & eorum factis, ac discordiae & labores quae accident inter homines ratione legis,* Haly *f.* 391. In that yeer, when in the Revolution you find that ♂ applieth unto ♄ by ✱ aspect, he doth then signifie labour and travell unto man-kind, damage in the Revenues of Kings, and impediments in their actions, & many controversies amongst men in regard of the Law, or for Priviledges and Customes, or it more properly imports, in regard that ♄ is Lord of the fourth & posited in the eight[h], that there will arise innumerable Law-suits & unreasonable quarrels about Lands, and the Inheritances of men, detained for some time from them; but forasmuch as ♀ is in the 4th, its the opinion[113] of *Haly*, *finis illius anni erit melior & felicior suo principio:* that although the yeer began somewhat boisterously, and many verball contentions may be therein, yet are we assured that the end of the yeer shal conclude with much more content then it began: but *Wharton* being sorry it should be so, runs on with his Judgment of *Halie's*, as impertinently & malitiously as may be; Haly 373. *Si ☽ fuerit in quarta & signum fuerit infortunatum erit fortiter populus obsessus, & accident ei careeres & anxietates graves.* If ☽ be in the fourth[114]: & the Sign therof infortunate (perhaps the people, saith *Wharton*) the word is *fortiter*, the common people will be much straiened. The Sign of the fourth is ♒, ☽ & ♀ is therein; if the Sign it self be not fo[r]tunated by ♀ I am mistaken, and must learn ignorance of the [p. 12] poor sneaks; but this by way of catechizing, &c. Of the Kingdome of *Ireland*, upon which the sad influence of ♄ in ♉ will fall in great abundance; as also the miserable effects of the □ of ♄ and ♃

March 29. 1648. I say thus much, That there will arise in that Kingdome so great and fierce Wars, so great and horrible dissention in all matters, betwixt the great men and the popular sort: there will be such unheard-of discord, and divers such unmercifull and unusuall quarrels and heart-burnings amongst the principall Citizens of every or most of the Cities of that Kingdome, that in many of them the Sonne shall be against the Father, the Wife against the Husband, the Servant against his Master, one Neighbour against another, this Country betrayes the next, this Noble-man his Neighbour, this Castle surrendred today, another by treason the next; for the sword of Gods destroying Angel is now drawne forth at length and is falling upon that devillish people to devour them.[115]

The Signe ascendant of that Kingdom is afflicted by the presence of ♄, and is also posited in the eighth from thence, *Litigia causa Petitionum haereditatum, seu reliquiarum mortuorum, & causa Petitionum antiquarum rerum, & contristationem causa mortis, & significat res quarum dolor & angustia seu tristitia diu durabit:* Many shall be their sad complaints about losse of their Inheritances, and the Estate of their deceased friends; many dissembling Treaties shall they offer to our English Generals, and Commanders of our Forces; many and grievous complaints shall be amongst themselves by reason of the death and miscarriage of their Kinred, engaged in this rebellious quarrell; but the scorne, repulse and contempt which they shall receive from our noble English, shall be such and so great, that the Irish shall unfainedly accurse the authors of their present calamities, for of their sufferings they or their children shall see no end: having therefore been otherwise promised by that *Manapian*[116] Astrologer, and the very scorne of Art Scribe *Wharton*, they begin to curse both the one and the other, the *Manapian* for an asse, and *Noworth* for a fellow of no judgment or honesty, but a meer Changeling.

Of the Kingdome of *Scotland* I have little to say, but that *Janus*[117] with two faces lives amongst many of that Nation; for [p. 13] after a few moneths there seems much tergiversation[118] in many of that people; but yet I doe find the good hand of God will direct the Nationall Councell of that people: so that from hence we may expect all actions correspondent to nobility and wisdome; in which good mind I doubt not but their Angel-protector will in this yeer preserve them, for in very deed, I neither see any probability of their returning into the northern Counties, or that they have any will or intention to harme us. *O utinam!*[119] from my heart I wish our owne Nation of *England* may prove as constant for the good of our Kingdome, as that discreet and frugall people are for theirs. I might further enlarge this Discourse, and write of the Eclipse in *November* visible in *England*; but because the effects thereof shall not manifest themselves untill 1649. I do now forbear, intending Godwilling to begin an easie method in the next yeers A N G L I C U S, for judging Eclipses.

[The final 13½ pages of the almanack conclude with a listing of "Beneficiall Aphorismes:" 7½ pages of "The last fifty Aphorismes of PTOLEMEY" and 6 pages of "The Astrologicall Aphorismes of HERMES."]

———————◆———————

Anti-Merlinus:
OR
A CONFUTATION
of Mᵣˑ *William Lillies* Predictions for this year 1648. comprised in two Bookes:

One of which he cals *Merlinus Anglicus*,
or *An Ephimeris*: The other his *Prognostication*
of the Occurences in *England*,[120] clearly prove-
ing his predictions in both Bookes to be groundlesse,
absolutely void of Art, full of contradictions, Treason,
falsehood, and such a ridiculous piece of foolery, as an
Artist would blush to owne, especially pretending (as
he doth) to ground his predictions upon Cacodemologie,[121] or conference with Devils, and lapsed Angels, as
well as on Astrologie, an Art lawfull and laudable.

As Also the Authors own opinion, not only concerning what we may expect from the
present Treaty, and the principall Occurences of the remaining part of this present year, but also his positive
judgement touching the event and finall determination
of this Civill War, Succinctly set downe, together with
his reasons in Art therefore.

By *H. Johnsen* Student in Astrologie.

Printed in the Year, 1648.[122]

[The Epistle Dedicatory, p. 1]
To His Highnesse the Prince
of Wales.

Great Sir,

THAT I approach so faire a shrine, with so coorse an offering; accuse not my unworthinesse, but your owne worth which like the load-star,[123] is pleased to attract even the coorsest mettall, to make knowne its power. And indeed to whom else, *(save to your Highnesse)* should I Dedicate this *worke* of mine, sith it was compiled *for your dear Fathers sake, my most Gracious Soveraigne?* the necessity of the times even requiring it of me, as a testimony *of my unfeigned love* unto my native Country, and to its onely father, to whom 'tis turned *Apostate* yea a *parricide.* A taske indeed *not of much labour, yet of exceeding danger,* in such times as these; I doubt not but your Highnesse knowes full well, that *but to speake truth in England in these dayes,* is now no lesse then *capitale crimen.* I would therefore most willingly, if I could, have *declined this taske,* which I long forbore, expecting its *performance,* by some [Dedication, p. 2] *abler hand;* but no man would ease me of that *labour.* I held it therefore my duty to my *God,* to my *King,* to my *Country,* to admonish all such, who through misguided *zeale* or otherwise, engaged against our *Soveraigne,* either in this or the former *War,* to repent betimes,[124] and to make their speedy attonement, both with the one, and the other: or else to let them know, that their *destruction* draweth nigh; that *Astrologie* is now cleare and positive therein; that Mr. *William Lilly* perswading them to the contrary, and encouraging them, with the assurance of successe, is a false *Prophet,* all which I doubt not *(God willing)* but to prove so clearly by the rules of *Art;* and to confute him so manifestly, that any man (though but of indifferent capacity) shall be easily able to discerne his *predictions,* to be meere *forgeries, lyes, and delusions,* mine to be grounded *upon Art, and nature.* Sir Christopher Heiden, *a famous Scholler of this Kingdome, in his defence of judiciall Astrologie,*[125] proves this *Art* to have been *deduced from God to Adam, to Sheth, to Abraham,* that in all Ages, *Emperours, Kings, and men of the greatest ranke,* have not onely been favourors thereof, but *Students* also therein. I am therefore the more encouraged to present *your Highnesse* with a piece of this nature, not doubting but *your Highnesse* will easily beleeve, that the *Stars* have influence upon all *sublunary bodies:* doubtlesse *omniscient God,* never made [Dedication, p. 3] any thing in vaine, and consequently did not create, all those *glorious lampes of heaven,* to bespangle the firmament: *the Scripture tels us;* that they were made for *signes,* and for *tokens,* and for *dayes,* and *years*; nay it goes further, and plainly affirmes, that the *Stars in their course fought against Sisera* [Judges 5:20]; as I doubt not, *but your Highnesse* shall perceive them to doe, against *yours and the Kingdomes* Enemies. I have strong, yet humble *hopes,* (let them not be accounted *presumptions*) that *your Highnesse* will be *graciously pleased,* to give these my *labours,* an *acceptance,* answerable to the *ambition,* wherewith he offers them, who is,

Your Highnesse most obsequious

and ready servant.

[p. 1] To the Reader.

Reader,

ASTROLOGIE *is an Art I love, and I may lawfully do so:* Cacodemologie *I extreamely hate, for all men ought to abhor it. I list not with* Mr. Lilly, *to enquire into the* name, nature, or potency *of the the* guardian Angel *of this, or any other* Kingdome *in the* Universe, *nor care I to know, whether he be active or a sluggard.* The *is to taste of that forbidden fruite, wherwith our* grand Parents *teeth were set on edge* [Genesis 3]: *for my part, I had rather know nothing at all, then by unlawfull Arts.* Were *there not a lawfull Art, whereby a man might foresee future accidents, I should never desire an abil-ity to predict any thing.* That Astrology *is an Art lawfull enough, there is no* man that is compos mentis,[126] *will I thinke deny; and the validity thereof, I dare maintaine against all opponents, and yet that is a crabbed learning I will not deny. I am verily perswaded, and that not without cause, that the* Devil *himselfe, knowes*[127] *very little of future accidents, otherwise, or fur-ther, then he finds them legible, in the* aspects, and configurations of that starry vo- [p. 2, To the Reader] lume *of heaven, why then should any man be so curious, nay so madde as to desire to know that by the* Devill, *which he himselfe may know without him, and lawfully from the same Art? I deny not, but the Devil is the subtilest Astrologian in the world; his angelicall nature, and long experience must needs perswade us thereunto: but is he not withall the father of lies? the* word of God *affirmes him so to be, and* Mr. Lillies predictions *for this year confirmes it; for if it be possible they out-doe the Devill himselfe for lying: such a ridiculous piece of folly, fool-ery, and contradictions, an* artist *would blush to owne.* It is his owne axiome, and a very good one, that qui inter multa falsa, pauca miscet vera, non est ei in recitando dicta ejus, quicquam tribuendum: *he that lies com-monly, and speakes, or writes, but now and then, a truth, is neither to be trusted, nor to be beleeved. I shall easily assent to* Mr. Lilly, *calling such* Malignant Prophets, *with this* axiome *he lashes* Mr. Wharton, *for one onely mistake, and that a small one too; I meane comparatively small, in regard of his owne* folio[128] *failings: for the substance of what* Mr. Wharton *predicted, was doubtlesse true; and* Mr. Lilly *will find it so to be, and I to his cost I feare.* Upon the Conjunction with *Saturne* and *Mars,* in the eighth house, near oculus tauri,[129] *he predicted the utter overthrow of the Parliament: thus far I am confident he was right enough, but the time of this their overthrow he assigned, to* [p. 3, To the Reader] *be about the end of* June *last; and in this he failed I must confesse: nor had he reason to affirme it, for the* Conjunction of those two Planets, *was but then newly past; did not yet begin to operate; their effects continue many* moneths: *and long before the effects of that* Conjunction cease; the Moone comes to be Eclipsed, and in Gemini too, near the body of Saturne, in the seaventh and eighth houses of heaven; *and if this doe not totally overthrow them (pro-vided that the King and they agree not before, by a Personall Treaty) I shall for ever after question the truth of that Art, which I so much love: the valid-ity whereof, I never yet found cause to doubt of. At least I shall exceedingly question, my owne judgement therein: the greatest fury & force, both of the Conjunction, & the Eclipse also, will be over by the* end of June *next; and therefore my hopes are strong, and* my grounds in Art I am sure are good;

that by that time, most of our troubles wil be overblown; yet perhaps not fully ended, *for some few moneths following.* For this so small a mistake in Mr. Wharton, *he cals him* Malignant Prophet, the *scorne of Art, change-lings, &c. but* qui alterum incusat probri ipsum se intueri oportet,[130] *he that is so busie to pick holes in the coates of others, had need have more then an ordinary care of his owne words and actions.* M. Lillies axiome could not reach Mr. Wharton; *for he committed not many, but one; not a grosse, but a small mistake; I say* comparatively small, *in re-* [p. 4, To the Reader] *spect of those* grand falsehoods, *those almost* innumerable contradictions, *those many* Treasons, *and* forgeries, *committed to the* Presse *this year,* by Merlinus Anglicus. *I will here give you but a glimpse of his* failings and feignings *this year, anon*[131] *I shall set them out in more lively colours; and* marshall *them together, and as near as I can, into ranke and file. Did he not in divers places of his* Ephimeris predict peace this year? and absolutely affirme, that *this would be a year of* joy, and merryment, not of Martiall exploits, *in this our Kingdome?* Nay did he not basely, and malitiously scandalize Mr. *Wharton,* for predicting War? *whither spake true? yet* Mr. Lilly *cals him* manapian[132] Astrologer; *and this* Utopian, *and* malignant Astrologie. *Did not* Mr. Lilly *affirme, yea confidently also, that the* Scots *would not assist the* King this year against the Parliament? *no nor any other* Kingdome *else?* he saith, behold the Scots are honourable, and have no invasive designe against us: *nay, he saieth farther,* that they, who are of this opinion, that the Scots wil invade us, have no eies: *I shal willingly leave it to the* Readers *judgement, who deserves most to ride* blind bayard.[133] He addes *afterwards, that he can speake no evill of the* Scottish Nation, *sith the* heavens *give him no information; but after he h[e]ard that they were come, contrary to his* prediction, *he could scarce invent any* Oyster-whore language,[134] *bad enough to revile them with.* Againe he saith, that [p. 5, To the Reader] *some thinke that the* Parliament Souldiers, will some of them dissert the cause, *and fight* Round-head against Round-head, Citizen against Citizen; which yet he affirmes will not come to passe: *and yet we all know, this and more was true enough;* Ergo, Mr. Lilly *said false, and therefore is no son of* Merlins: *Is not I pray the* Fleet[135] revolted to the Prince? *have there been no* knocks at all this year in London? *is not this Round-head against Round-head, Citizen against Citizen?* He saith of Ireland, *that this year, there will be in that* Kingdome, *such notorious, and so great distractions; such fierce and cruel Wars, that of their sufferings, they, and their Children shall know no end.* Loe, they are quiet in that Kingdome; no such thing at all hath hapned. *Very little Blood (if any at all) hath been shed in that place:* behold, they are willing, yea, and ready also to assist His Majesty, our most gracious Soveraigne. It seemes *this year, that his fancy was overburthened* (as himself confesseth) with very intricate meditations; *fine white and yellow meditations: doubtlesse the* Parliament *cash which he hath got, for a reward of his Treason and Treachery, has had strong influence upon his giddy crown, to fill it, With such strange* Chymeraes:[136] *and certainly it were madnesse in any to belch out such horrid Treasons against his* Soveraigne: *such viperous, and false aspertions, against his friends, such encomiums*[137] *to his enemies, the* Independents, *and their Army, who have not onely* [p. 6, To the Reader] *rob'd their' gracious* Soveraigne *of His native b[ir]thright, revil'd His Wife, and Children, with most foule and false aspersions; but have Imprisoned, and enslav'd His person also; slaine and rob'd His Loyall Subjects, set all His Kingdomes on a flame; if he were not well rewarded by his great Masters, for so great Treason: It is now well knowne to all men, that have eyes to distinguish chalke from cheese, white from black, light from darkenesse, that their intentions, (notwithstanding their faire pretences for the Kings Honour, the subjects Liberty, and the reformation of Religion) have been solely to enslave their Soveraigne, to raign themselves, and like* Ph[o]enixes, *to revive their bankerupt fortunes, out of the Kingdomes ruines: and how far they have accomplish'd these their aimes, there is no discreet, and honest man in this whole Kingdome, but evidently now perceives: how have they pillaged, rob'd, and plundered the whole Kingdome? to what vast summes, have they raised their owne tottering fortunes? how have they preferred to places of highest trust, and greatest gaine, such as have stoutly endeavoured to raise them to this height, either by sword or penne? this undeniable position being granted, as perforce it must; it will also follow, that* Mr. William Lilly *deserves the Van,*[138] *in this list of* Traytors, *and consequently hath been therefore well rewarded. For doubtlesse* Fairfax and Cromwell, *could hardly have led the Kingdome by the nose thus long, had* [p. 7, To the Reader] *not* Merlinus Anglicus, that Welchified, London, Incubus,[139] *entered the sceane, and prevailed as much upon the minds of giddy-headed men, with his screech-owles quill, as they upon their bodies, with all their Armies, Engines, Weapons, and subtile machinations. For people are, and were ever too to apt to be seduced by any, who but pretend to Astrologie,* Aecromancy,[140] Chyromancy:[141] *especially if they tell them that the things they predict are from God, or revealed by some Angel, they will easily beleeve almost whatsoever such a one shall assert: for bring them but once to beleeve, that there is validity in the Art, and learning in the* Artist, *they come on of their owne accords, to beleeve what such an Artist affirmes to be true, and infallibly to happen: although 'tis certaine, that the stars doe but encline, cannot enforce. And most men loving preferment, and estate in this world, more then their God, or their* King, the Lords Anointed, *will easily make shipwrack of their duty to the one, of their Allegiance to the other; if once they beleeve they shall be loosers by either.* They will argue thus: *whatsoever God hath decreed, shall come to passe, cannot be avoided by any industry of man; nay it were madnesse in any to attempt it, and lost labour if he did, but* Mr. Lilly *hath affirmed, and with a* sic est in fatis;[142] *that the* Parliament *shall overcome the* King, *and His adherents, and therefore it were madnesse in them, to cast away their dearest lives, and their estates to boote, in the* Kings *quarrell, sith all is but lost labour.*

[p. 8, To the Reader] *Thus have many a thousand in this Kingdome been hobgoblin'd into Rebellion, against their lawfull Soveraigne.* If this will not prevaile, he hath yet another baite for the devouter sort of men: he saith, that the Parliament and Army are Gods Instruments, *Ergo*, saith he, (and they believe it to excellent logick, yea, and very good divinity too) you ought to adhere to the Parliament, and not affront them, as of late. *A speciall concluding argument indeed; but good M. Lilly, is not the Divell too Gods Instrument? makes not God sometimes use of him, as we do of a Hangman to execute his pleasure? must we therefore adhere to the Devill? no certainly. I cannot sufficiently wonder at the madnesse of men, in suffering themselves to be so long deluded, by meere falsehoods ande forgeries; even such as are to be discerned by every eye, if they wink not on purpose; but this was alwayes, the fashion of the world, to believe falsehood easily; hardly to believe the truth.*

> Tunc etiam fatis aperit Cassandra futuris
> Ora dei jussa, non unquam credita Teucris.[143]

But that the Kingdome may be no longer deluded by such a cheating sycophant: *I am resolved to enter the Lists,*[144] *against this* demigorgon,[145] *this* hel-sent fury, our junior Merlin: *not doubting, but to confute his sophistry by reason; his Astrologie, by Astrologie, his Cacodemology, by the word of God; and by that time I have th[o]roughly uncased him,* [p. 9, To the Reader] *I doubt not but he will appear to all the world, more ridiculous then the* Apes of India, *that mockt the* Macedonian Army.[146] *I desire not to derogate any thing from M. Lillies abilitie in the art of Astrology; I am verily perswaded, that he is a good proficient therein; and understands rightly, a great part thereof: but he that wilfully, and purposely shuts his eyes, that he may not see, deserves to be lasht with many stripes. I protest ingenuously, I never had any intenions of shewing my self in Print, upon this subject, till I saw M. Lillies Ephemeris for this year, which was not till* June: *and then I was in a manner compelled to this taske, for either I must write a confutation, or some body else; or else the Kingdome must be still deluded, gull'd, and cheated with forgeries and lies: and* Astrologie *(an art which I extreamly love) be condemn'd therefore. Before I had fully perfected my confutation of his* Ephermeris, *he puts forth his judgement upon the* parelii;[147] *and conjunction of* Saturne and Mars: *which as soone as I had perused, I found it so full of Contradictions, Treason, Falsehood, and such a ridiculous piece of foppery; as the eye of man, nor that greater of the world, scarce ever yet beheld, which made me conclude, that* Master Lilly *had now even sold himself to work wickednesse, which put me on to write a Confutation of both his said Bookes, with all the speed I could. In the doing of which, it cannot be expected, but that he vaunting so much as he doth, of his own abilities;* [p. 10, To the Reader] *as to call those who contradict him,* Manapian Astrologers, *the scorne of the Art, Changelings,*

&c. *that when I finde him tripping, I should bite him a little with my cynick tooth: when I finde him feighning, or failing, if I lash him soundly with my Satyrs Whip.* My Love *to my* Country, *my Allegiance to my* Soveraign, *my Respect to* Art, *and my just detestation of all such* vaunting and Machi[a] vilian Traitors, *challenge of me, and must receive from me, no lesse, no lower satisfactin: I had no other sinister motives to induce me thereunto; as hatred, malice, envie, &c. and so he unfeignedly protesteth, who is*

Thine in his best endeavours,
H.J.

———————◆———————

THE
DIVELS DELUSIONS
OR

A faithfull relation of John Palmer *and*
Elizabeth Knott *two notorious* Witches
lately condemned at the Sessions of Oyer
and Terminer *in St.* Albans.

Together with the Confession of the aforesaid
John Palmer *and* Elizabeth Knott, *exe-*
cuted July 16.

Also their accusations of severall Witches *in*
Hitchen, Norton, *and other places in the*
County of Hartford.

LONDON
Printed for *Richard Williams* Stationer at Sʳ. *Albans,*
Anno Dom. 1649.[148]

[p. 1]
A Letter sent from S. *Albans* to a friend in the Country concerning the
Tryall, condemning and execution of *J. Palmer* & *Elizabeth Knott,* two
notorious *Witches.*

SIR,

According to your earnest desire, I have taken the best care I could to satisfie you, concerning the *Witches* lately tryed, condemned, and executed at
Sʳ. *Albans:* It had been very difficult to convince me of that which I find
true, concerning the wiles of that old Serpent the Divel, for the supporting
of his dark dominions, which appeares in the subtile trade hee drives for
the enlarging of his territories; by strengthning of himself upon the weaknesse of his subjects, relapsed men and women.

I shall the more clearly give you to understand what you desire concerning these two, by name, *John Palmer* and *Elizabeth Knott* of *Norton,*
within the Liberty[149] of St. *Albans,* if you please to pardon the method
whereunto I shall reduce the severall kinds of *Witches.*

First I find that man at his best estate was created with excellent beauty
of knowledge in his mind, [p. 2] which his own unhappy mutability together
with the Divels suggestion, hath folded up in darknesse and obscurity; whereupon being impatient to be coop't up within the narrow scantling[150] of his
own intellectualls, I see him very busie with the Divel; and rather then keep

his station, hee will make tryall what the Divel can do for his advancement in knowledge: I find those that dealt with curious arts in *Acts* 19. 19. fitly comprehended under this kind: I know not whether to reduce *Marsh* of *Dunstable*,[151] whom *Palmer* confesseth to be the head of the whole *Colledge* of *Witches*, that hee knows in the world: This *Palmer* hath been a *Witch* these 60 years, (by his own confession) long enough to know and give in the totall summe of all the Conjuring conclave, and the society of *Witches* in *England*. This *Marsh* hath so long gratified the Country people with his Conjurations, that time and ignorance stiles him a good *Witch*, or a white *Witch*; I suppose you easily grant that the Divel is never blacker, and more to be abhorr'd then when hee transforms himself into an Angel of Light. S^r. I easily believe that if *Marsh* was brought to his tryall, hee might confesse as much of his brother *Lilly*,[152] as *Palmer* hath of him, that impudent Prognosticator, and bold *Balaam*.[153]

This I conceive to be one occasion to the god of this world, in tempting and deluding those who are led captive by him, namely an inordinate desire to [p. 3[154]] know more then his maker hath thought fit for him to know.

Secondly I find an other occasion whereupon the Divel offers his service so officiously, which is envy, who seeing a predominancy in the irascible faculty, hee is never behindhand in the proffering his service for the attempting what ever hee tempts them to. I find *Manasses* the King, by the piously learned to be reckoned under this kind, concerning whom tis said, 2 *Chron.* 33. 6. That he used enchantments, and dealt with a familiar spirit, and not long after we find that hee made Jerusalem to run down with bloud from one end to another, as an effect of his envious disposition: Yet vers. 12, 13. The father of mercies was intreated of him, upon his humiliation and repentance.

By the plain confession of *Palmer* it may certainly be guessed that the Divel took advantage of him i[n] this breach, and brought him into [bonds] upon this ground; in as much as hee was (as hee said) of a fretfull and revengfull nature, and not being able of himself to aveng himself of his adversaries hee [ad-]joyned himself to the Divel, and wrought [much evill] in the eyes of the Lord: upon his [compact] with the Divel, hee received a flesh-brand, [or mark upon the] side, which gave suck to two familiars, [the one] in the form of a dog, which hee called *George*, and the other in the likenesse of a woman called *Jezabell*, when the [p. 4] Divel first made this mark he drew his bloud and caused him to write his mark upon the ground with his own hand therewith; his trading in this horrid and abominable practice of *Witchcraft* was (as hee confessed) betwixt the space of 50 and 60 years, the hurt which from time to time hee had done was very much; and this I account his prime pranck that he notoriously seduced *Elizabeth Knott* his kinswoman, to consort with him in his villany who hath assented to him more especially in the death of one Goodwife *Pearls* of *Norton*, whom *Palmer* said hee would do nothing to occasion her death unlesse this *Elizabeth Knott* would assent: whereupon they presently agreed to frame the picture of the woman (*Pearls*) in clay, which was forthwith laid upon the fire, and duly raked up in the embers; while it was consuming and mouldring away the woman lay in miserable torments, when it was quite consumed the woman immediately dyed: and this hee confessed to be done by him, and his kinswoman out of revenge which he ought her, for hanging a lock upon his doore, for the not paying of his rent: At another time to satisfie his revengfull humour hee killd an horse of Mr. *Cleavers* by sending his familiar: and this *Elizabeth Knott* bewitcht a Cow of *John Lamans*, by sending an evil spirit unto her, which was in the likenesse of a *Catt*, but had no hand in the death of any thing, save the death of Goodwife *Pearls*. The [p. 5] familiar which she entertained came to her about three weeks before the said Cow was bewitched at twelve of the Clock in the night, and the familiar promised her, that she should have her desire in any thing she would desire, except money: and the reason why she bewitched the Cow of *William Laman* was, because she demanded money which was due to her, from the said *Lamans* wife, and it was denied her. We understand also from this *Elizabeth Knott* that when she was cast upon the water her familiar sucked upon her breast, but after she came out of the water she never saw it any more.

It would be tedious to reckon up the multifarious exploits of this old Witch *Palmer*; for *Knott* his kinswoman was but a novice, in comparison of him, and as I conceive had made no direct Covenant with the Divel, as *Palmer* had.

A little before his execution he confessed to *Sampson Clark*, the Keeper of the Prison, that falling out with a young man, hee transformed himself into a Toad, and lying in the way where the young man came, he kick't it, immediately *Palmer* complained of a sore shinne, whereupon hee bewitched the young man for many years to his great woe and torment.

That you may further understand what society hee had on your side the Countrey, with such as were in-bond to the Divel, I shall signifie to you what hee confessed before his execution: In *Hitchin*, he reckons [p. 6] two, *Mary By-chance* and *Widdow Palmer*: In *Norton John Salmon* senior. *Joseph Salmon*, and *Judeth* his wife. *John Lamen* senior and *Mary* his wife, *John Lamen* junior. *Mary* the daughter of *John Lamen* senior[,] *Joan Lamen* the daughter of the aforesaid *John Lamen*: and the wife of one *Mayes* in *Weston*. And at the place of execution he confessed two more, *Sarah Smith* and *Anne Smith* servants, the one to Mr. *Beamont*, the other to Mr. *Reynolds*.

There is a third ground whereupon the Divel takes advantage by his delusions to beguile men and women, and that is by a diligent observation of their concupiscible faculty, whereby they are inordinate in their desires after money and gain, which the God of this world is very free to promise, but as one of his slaves confessed, she never wanted, (that is) any misery or affliction, after she had contracted with him.

I am in hast but rest, yours
B. Misodaimon

FINIS.

Notes

1 For a helpful reconstruction of the astrological mentality that grew out of a thorough study of William Lilly's writings and activities, see Ann Geneva, *Astrology and the Seventeenth Century Mind: William Lilly and the Language of the Stars* (Manchester: Manchester University Press, 1995).

2 Bernard Capp, *Astrology and the Popular Press: English Almanacs 1500–1800* (Ithaca, NY: Cornell University Press, 1979); Patrick Curry, *Prophecy and Power: Astrology in Early Modern England* (Princeton, NJ: Princeton University Press, 1989).

3 Robin Barnes, *Astrology and Reformation* (Oxford: Oxford University Press, 2016), 90, 118–119.

4 Thomas Dekker, *Looke Up and See Wonders A miraculous apparition in the ayre, lately seene in Barke-shire at Bawlkin Greene neere Hatford. April. 9th. 1628* (London, 1628), 17–18.

5 Dekker, *Looke Up and See Wonders*, 19, "the wranglings of Schooles, is not so unpleasing, to ignorant standers by, as our contentions and quaeres about this business, should be to God . . . to apprehend what our weakness can, and to admire the depth which we cannot read."

6 B. Misodaimon, *The Divels Delusions* (London, 1649), 2. For a survey of early modern arguments about the value of astrology, see Don Cameron Allen, *The Star-Crossed Renaissance: The Quarrel about Astrology and Its Influence in England* (Durham, NC: Duke University Press, 1941).

7 John Bainbridge, *An Astronomicall Description of the late Comet from the 18. of Novemb. 1618. to the 16. of December following. With certain Morall Prognosticks or Applications drawne from the Comets motion and irradiation amongst the celestiall Hieroglyphicks* (London: Edward Griffin, 1618), 30.

8 Capp, *Astrology and the Popular Press*, 70ff. Compare Barnes, *Astrology and Reformation*.

9 Bernard Capp, "Booker, John (1602–1667)," *ODNB*.

10 John Booker, *Mercurius Cælicus sive Almanack et Prognosticon vel Speculum Annia Nativitate. J.C. 1644* (London, 1643).

11 "This moneths fift[h] day, shall never be forgot,/ The Powder-treason, or the Papist's plot/ To blow up King and Parliament; still we see./ And still we find, they work more treachery / Against poore england: But the doome's at hand / To purge the Romish rout, out of the Land."

12 Abu'l Hasan Ali ibn Ridwan Al-Misri (c.988–c.1061), often cited in the West as Haly Abenrudian, was an Egyptian astronomer who wrote a commentary on Ptolemy's *Quadripartitum*.

13 Beware of the man of three letters.

14 Bernard Capp, "Wharton, Sir George, first baronet (1617–1681)," *ODNB*.

15 G. Naworth [i.e. George Wharton], *Naworth. 1644. A New Almanac, and Prognostication for the Year of our Lord and Saviour Jesus Christ, 1644. Being the Bissextile or Leap-year. With a brief Chronologie of the most remarkeable occurrences since the beginning of this Rebellion* (Oxford, [1643]).

16 Wharton's "men of three letters" were both leading parliamentary figures. Lord Say (William Fiennes, Viscount Saye and Sele) was a nobleman who led the regiment that had occupied Oxford and whose religious Independent attitudes (including his appointment to the Westminster Assembly of divines) raised particular Royalist ire. John Pym's leadership of the Commons, from his role as one of the "five members" to negotiations with Scots to resist the King, made his death on December 8, 1643, a happy fulfilment of Wharton's prophecy.

17 John Booker, *Mercurius Cœlicus; or A Caveat to all the people of the Kingdome, that now have, or shall hereafter happen to read the counterfeit and most pernicious Pamphlet written under th name of Naworth* (London, 1644), 2.

18 Booker, *Mercurius Cœlicus*, 6.

19 G. Naworth [e.g., George Wharton], *Mercurio-Coelico Mastix, or, An Anti-Caveat To all such, as have heretofore had the Misfortune to be Cheated, and Deluded, by that Grand and Traiterous Imposter of this Rebellious Age, John Booker. In Answer to a frivolous, and senselesse Pamphlet of his newly printed at London, and by him Intituled Mercvrivs-coelicvs* ([Oxford], 1644).

20 Naworth, *Mercurio-Coelico Mastix*, 1–2.

21 And he continued prophetically, "for I have calculated your destinie . . . Your death is not like to prove Naturall."

22 Naworth, *Mercurio-Coelico Mastix*, 14. The anagraming and name calling continued. In Booker's March rejoinder, "George VVarton" became, among other things, "A huge rot'n Rogue" and "Hang ô true Rogue"; John Booker, *A Rope for a Parret, or, A Cure for a Rebell past Cure* (London, 1644), 6.

23 John Taylor, *No Mercurius Aulicus; but some merry flashes of intelligence, with the pretended Parliaments forces besiedging of Oxford foure miles off, and the terrible taking in of a mill, instead of the King and citie. Also the breaking of Booker, the asse-tronomicall London figure-flinger, his perfidious prediction failing, and his great conjunction of Saturne and Iupiter dislocated* ([Oxford], 1644), 7–8. Booker responded to Taylor in his *No Mercurius Aquaticus, but a Cable Rope Twisted for John Tayler, the Water-Poet* (London, 1644). Toward the end of his next vitriolic attack on Booker and his astrology later in the summer, Taylor anagramized his own name as "O harty Lion"; John Taylor, *John Taylor being yet unhanged sends greeting to John Booker that hanged him lately in a picture, in a traiterous, slanderous, and foolish London pamphlet called A cable-rope double-twisted* ([Oxford?], 1644), 7. Another fully satirical portrayal of the astrological predictions and polemics can be seen in the pamphlet by the pseudonymous Timotheus Philo-Bookerus, *Mercurius vapulans, or, Naworth stript and vvhipt. In answer to a most base and scandalous pamphlet, called Mercurio Coelico-Mastix, or an anti-caveat, &c. Sent abroad from Oxford, under the name of G. Naworth. In opposition to Mercurius Coelicus, or a caveat to all the people of the kingdom; lately penned by Mr. John Booker* (March 1644); he continued the anagramizing by ending with "Georgius Naworth: 'Tis a Whoring Rogue" (8).

24 Patrick Curry, "Lilly, William (1602–1681)," *ODNB*. Harry Rusche, "*Merlini Anglici*: Astrology and Propaganda from 1644 to 1651," *The English Historical Review* 80, no. 315 (1965), 322–333.

25 William Lilly, *William Lilly's History of His Life and Times, from the Year 1602 to 1681. Written by Himself in the Sixty-sixth year of his Age, to His Worthy Friend, Elias Ashmole (Published 1715)* (London: reprinted for Charles Baldwyn, 1822), 103–104.

26 An ephemeris is a table showing the (predicted) positions of a heavenly body, usually daily, for a given period.

27 His almanacs sold 18,500 copies in 1648 and almost 30,000 in 1649 (the first to include his woodcut portrait on the front). By the 1650s Lilly's almanacs were being translated into Dutch, German, Swedish, and Danish. Curry, "Lilly, William."

28 Geneva, *Astrology and the Seventeenth Century Mind*, 57–58, argues that Lilly was a commited parliamentarian, if not republican, from his early publications, but with an eye to practical politics (a possible royalist victory, especially before Naseby) and patronage in his consultations, he encoded his strongest anti-monarchical subtext in astrological terms.

29 His February weather prediction had been more explicit in the connections between weather and political unity: "toward the latter end, [the weather will be] very serene and wholesome; at what time the heavens intimate more unity amongst us, and our counsellours more concurring for the benefit of the sub-jects of this Nation. His Majesties friends fail him, and now our Parlia. seem to advise and determine upon honorable and grand designs; and it's apparent to the whole world, their words and intentions are as full of loyalty, as their enemies of treachery, scurrility and malice to their Native Country."

30 William Lilly, *Supernaturall Sights and Apparitions Seen in London, June 30. 1644 interpreted. With a Mathematicall Discourse of the now imminent Conjunction of Jupiter and Mars, 26 July, 1644. the Effects which either here or in some neere Countries from thence may be expected* (London, 1644).

31 Marginal note: "*Merline* is almost inclined to believe some that wore a Crown were dying at time of this strange sight: or in some jeopardy of loosing their Scepter. A wise people inclining to great indiscretion if not their undoing."

32 The Austrian Habsburgs had been involved in the Thirty Years War (1618–1648) in the Holy Roman Empire.

33 Lilly, *Supernaturall Sights*, 7.

34 George Wharton, *Wharton. 1645. An Almanack and Prognostication for that Year* (Oxford, 1645), final two pages.

35 George Wharton, *An Astrologicall Judgement Upon His Majesties present Martch: Begun from Oxford May 7, 1645* (Oxford, 1645). A transcription of this pamphlet is available at http://name.umdl.umich.edu/A65580.0001.001.

36 Wharton, *Astrologicall Judgement*, 8–9.

37 William Lilly, *The Starry Messenger; or, An Interpretation of that strange Apparition of three Suns seen in London* (London, 1645). See figure 5.1 of the title page; a transcription of the text can be found at http://name.umdl.umich. edu/A88290.0001.001.

38 Lilly, *Starry Messenger*, page 5 of unnumbered prefatory material.

39 Lilly, *Starry Messenger*, 11.

40 Lilly, *Starry Messenger*, 1, has an approving quotation from a recent book by Dr. Thomas Browne, specifically from within several sections of that treatise dealing with miracles, oracles, the Devil, witchcraft, and magic: "I doe thinke that many mysteries ascribed to our owne inventions, have beene the courteous revelations of Spirits; for those noble essences in heaven beare a friendly regard unto their fellow-natures on earth; and therefore beleeve that those many prodi-gies and ominous prognostickes which fore-run the ruines of States, Princes, and private persons, are the charitable premonitions of good Angels, which more carelesse enquiries terme but the effects of chance and nature." Thomas Browne, *A true and full coppy of that which was most imperfectly and sur-reptitiously printed before vnder the name of Religio medici*, 2nd ed. (London: Printed for Andrew Crook, 1643), 70.

41 Lilly, *Starry Messenger*, 19–20.

42 William Lilly, *Christian Astrology modestly treated of in Three Books* (London, 1647), first page after table of contents: Yet, though he viewed the "heavenly knowledge of the Starres" as a learned science that can be mastered, he nonethe-less urged his students to remain humble and not allow pride to dim their view of divine providence. Lilly had already made a name for himself, but we might question his modesty as he also expressed in his prefatory note "To the Reader" that although he was not yet forty-six years old and had only been "studied this Science" for the past fifteen years (six of which he was not in London) "yet I know I have made more Schollers in this Profession, then all that profess this Art in England" (To the Reader, p. 3).

43 Bainbridge, *An Astronomicall Description*, 42.

44 Lilly's autobiobraphy recounted that he was "sufficiently abused" in 1646 on both religious and political grounds: "The Presbyterians were, in their pulpits, as merciless as the Cavaliers in their pamphlets;" *William Lilly's History of His Life*, 135.

45 Where the moon crosses the ecliptic from south to north.

46 Where the moon crosses the ecliptic from north to south.

47 (It is) all mine (and) nothing mine: nothing said, that has not been said before.

48 The 1659 edition reads "fear."

49 Totally in it.

50 Single-minded in art.

51 Something in everything.

52 Conscience is a thousand witnesses.

53 From Vergil's *Eclogues/Bucolics*, Eclogue 1 ll. 72–73: "Oh, where has civil discord brought our fellow citizens?"

54 Of medicines or beverages, cordials invigorate the heart, revive or cheer; purgers removed bad fluids or humours.

55 Lilly published his seventy-one-page *The World's Catastrophe, or, Europes many Mutations untill, 1666. The fate of Englands Monarchy untill its Subversion. Government of the World under God by the seven Planetary Angels; their Names, Times of Government. An exact type of the three svns seen in Cheshire and Shropshire, 3.April 1647. Their signification and portent, astrologically handled . . . To which is added, a whip for Wharton* (London: Printed for John Partridge,and Humphrey Blunden, and are to be sold at the Cock in Ludgate-street, and at the Castle in Cornhill, 1647).

56 The most prudent among mortals.

57 River Tweed marks part of the border between England and Scotland.

58 Any imaginary or mythical place, imagined as existing in some remote location on earth; term coined by Sir Thomas More as the imaginary island in his *Utopia* (1516).

59 Unknown land.

60 A mercer was a retail tradesman of high social status, dealing particularly in textile fabrics; Cheapside was a London street with one of the main market districts in the city.

61 A thin, fine fabric, often silk or linen.

62 An apple or fruit seller who sells in the street from a handcart.

63 A sort of sweet apple.

64 It is fated.

65 The colocynth or Bitter-apple or gourd furnished a purgative, cathartic drug.

66 Parliament had passed the Self-Denying Ordinance in 1645 which said that no member of the House of Commons or House of Lords could hold a military command.

67 A healthy mind in a healthy body.

68 From Horace (parturiunt montes, nascetur ridiculus mus): The mountains are in labour and will give birth to a ridiculous mouse.

69 Murrough O'Brien, first earl of Inchiquin, went over to the Parliament side and was appointed Parliament's Lord President of Munster in 1645, from which position he led the Protestant faction against the Irish rebels. See Patrick Little, "O'Brien, Murrough, first earl of Inchiquin (c. 1614–1674)" (*ODNB*).

70 Welsh Parliamentarian John Jones had become a colonel of horse by 1646. In the fall of 1648, Jones was given authority to raise troops to put down John Owen's Royalist revolt in Wales. He thereafter attended the trial of Charles I as a commissioner and was one of the 57 regicides signing the King's death warrant. See Stephen Roberts, "Jones, John (c. 1597–1660)" (*ODNB*).

71 Charles Coote, first earl of Mountrath, was one of the Protestant agents in a delegation to Oxford to attempt to convince Charles to send supplies to western Ireland to fight the Irish rebels. When the royalists rejected them, Coote declared support for the Parliamentarians and became the Parliament's Lord President of Connaught in 1645. He became vice-admiral of Connaught in 1647. See Patrick Little, "Coote, Charles, first earl of Mountrath (c. 1610–1661)" (*ODNB*).

72 Parliamentarian Colonel Samuel More was the major commander of the West Midlands region. He and his garrison had tenaciously defended Hopton Castle in 1643 against Royalist forces over fifteen times larger; his entire garrison except More was executed when they surrendered, creating a propaganda controversy in which Parliamentarians depicted Royalist butchery. See Conal Condren, "More, Samuel (1594?–1662)," (*ODNB*).

73 Presumptuous, impudent.

74 The winds encounter the snows: 14th day.

75 20th day the quartill aspect of Saturn and Venus cool, moist, and windy threatens, wind sometimes become violent, and rain mixes with thunder, becomes also sometimes northerly.

76 Either Caesar or nothing!

77 High ranking army officers; had been negotiating with King Charles and attempting to maintain discipline over the more radical Agitators.

78 We expect frigid winds, mist and dew fall.

79 Expect rainy night; the air becomes rainy and sometimes very hot.

80 Therefore.

81 Doubtful nature of the air, the westerly winds are stirred up.

82 Do not despair under Christ.

83 Arcturus sets in the morning around the 16th day, conjunction of the sun and Mercury, the next day Arcturus effects a change of air.

84 But what is not useful alone, helps when there are many (Ovid).

85 Fear not, brothers, but pay attention.

86 The dog-days, the hottest part of the summer, immediately preceding and following the rising of the dog-star Sirius (or Procyon), typically in July and August. The popular belief was also that this was the season in which dogs were most likely to go mad.

87 Around this time appear boisterous, stormy, powerful, violent winds, mixed with hail, which ruins buildings, destroys ships, scatters trees, and overturns laden carts.

88 Moves the winds from the west; Spica Virginis, westerly in the evening with 10 degrees in Libra threatens the arrival of winter.

89 Changeful air is produced; great breaths of wind accompany.

90 Venus entering Scorpio, it produces unexpected storms with wind and much rain.

91 Moves the west winds.

92 Original: "moueth."

93 The most tranquil season usually comes to us around the winter solstice, sometimes without gusts of wind, when there is bitter and somehow clear frost, and the earth is bound in the greatest ice, so that almost no vapors can be drawn up from the earth.

94 Snow with wind to the west produces the subsequent appearance of this judgment.

95 The poem here is an excerpt from a late sixteenth-century German poet laureate Paul Schede Melissus; his Ode XIII "To Johannes Opsopoeus, Doctor from Bretten, on the Prophets and Sibyls" was published in his *Melissi Meletematum Piorum Libri VIII* (Frankfurt, 1595), 58–60 (here 59): "Surely another kingdom remains to be given to the blessed under magnificent heaven when the

beast shall fall, and also the authority of all power when the heads of tyrants are under the dominating foot of Christ."
96 Original: "diviue."
97 In 1644, Lilly published his *Englands Propheticall Merline, Foretelling to all Nations of Europe untill 1663. the Actions depending upon the influence of the Conjunction of Saturn and Jupiter, 1642/3.* The following quoted passage is verbatim (with spelling differences) except for two changes: the original pamphlet reads "to a square of Saturn" (rather than Mars here) and "smooth over" (rather than smother).
98 All is well.
99 Original: "the the."
100 Original: "mnndi."
101 A moving and changing thing.
102 Original: "Danghters."
103 Original: "justla."
104 Original: "iufluence."
105 Original: "eithet."
106 Lilly identifies the planets and signs associated with countries and cities, diseases, animals, body parts, etc. in Book 1 of his *Christian Astrology*; here, chapter XVI.
107 For God has given England to the English until the day of judgment.
108 In the farthest boundary of the sign.
109 The King will come to his former rule and things will be renewed.
110 If the sun is in the sixth, the King will have grief in the year.
111 And if unfortunate Jupiter is in the 10th house, there will be justice commonly to all men in that region, and they will have dignity and pay and loyalty from their own kings and lords, and will prosper with them, and make use of them.
112 Italian philosopher and astrologer Thomas Campanella (1568–1639).
113 Original: "opiinon."
114 Original: "fourrh."
115 See Johnsen's *Anti-Merlinus* (p. 219 in this volume) for initial criticisms of Lilly's failed predictions of Irish violence and Scottish calm in 1648.
116 *A New Almanack for the Year of Our Lord 1646* was published in Waterford, Ireland, by "A Manapian." Among its Royalist and Catholic sentiments, its calendar highlighted January 10 by the Remarkable Event "The commencement of the Parliamentarian Opposition to King Charles; that most pernicious anarchical Rebellion of the Roundheads of England, 1641;" for October 23, it identified the 1641 Irish uprising, "The happy union of the Catholics, *eo die.*" M.J. Hurley, "An Old Waterford Almanack," *Journal of the Waterford & South East of Ireland Archaeological Society* III (1897), 169–172. This "Manapian Almanack" prompted John Booker's angry publication, *A bloody Irish almanack, or, Rebellious and bloody Ireland, discovered in some notes extracted out of an almanack, printed at Waterford in Ireland for this yeare 1646.* George Wharton responded with *Bellum Hybernicale: or, Ireland's warre astrologically demonstrated . . . The ignorance, malice, mistakes, errors, insolencies, and impertinencies, of Iohn Booker . . . discovered, corrected, refuted, and retorted: and the author further vindicated, from his, and Master Lilly's former frivolous, false, and malicious aspersions, throughout the whole discourse* (1646).
117 Roman god with two faces, looking to past and future.
118 To turn one's back, abandon a cause.
119 O, I wish!
120 William Lilly, *An astrologicall prediction of the occurrances in England, part of the yeers 1648. 1649. 1650. concerning these particulars, viz. 1. The effects depending upon the late conjunction of the two malevolent planets*

Saturn and Mars. 2. What successe may be expected from the present intended treaty between his Majesty and the Parliament. 3. The standing or falling of this Parliament, and the army under the command of his Excellency the Lord Fairfax. 4. Our imminent disturbances generally handled, together with many contingencies to the whole kingdom, London especially. 5. The product of the Scots army: with some observations upon Duke Hamiltons nativity. 6. What may succeed the apparition of three suns in Lancashire, seen of many, the 28. Febr. last. By William Lilly, student in Astrologie (1648)

121 Demonic magic, conversing with demons.
122 October 21, 1648 handwritten on Thomason copy.
123 Guiding star.
124 While there is yet time.
125 Christopher Heydon, *A defence of iudiciall astrologie in answer to a treatise lately published by M. Iohn Chamber. Wherein all those places of Scripture, councells, fathers, schoolemen, later divines, philosophers, histories, lawes, constitutions, and reasons drawne out of Sixtus Empiricus, Picus, Pererius, Sixtus ab Heminga, and others, against this arte, are particularly examined: and the lawfulnes thereof, by equiualent proofes warranted* (1603).
126 Mentally competent.
127 Original: "knnowes."
128 The largest paper size of a book.
129 Aldebaran, the eye of Taurus.
130 The one who accuses another of improper conduct ought to look to himself (Plautus).
131 Straightaway.
132 See note 116 in Lilly's 1648 *Merlini Anglici*.
133 A blundering, foolish horse that sees no peril. See, for instance, Chaucer's "Canon's Yeoman's Tale" in *The Canterbury Tales*.
134 Oyster-wench, oyster-wife, oyster-woman was a woman who sold oysters; often portrayed as loud, uncouth, and indecent.
135 In the summer of 1648 nine warships joined a mutiny against Colonel Thomas Rainsborough and were put at Prince Charles's disposal as a new fleet.
136 In Greek mythology, a fire-breathing monster with a lion's head, a goat's body, and a serpent's tail.
137 A high-flown expression of praise.
138 The foremost or leading position.
139 A demon who descends upon persons in their sleep.
140 Aeromancy is divination by air, weather, or things in the air (as birds, clouds, etc.).
141 Divination by inspecting a person's hands.
142 It is fated.
143 From Vergil's *Aeneid* (II.246–7), "Even then Cassandra, who, by the god's decree, is never to be believed by the Trojans, reveals our future fate with her lips."
144 To join combat or a contest, such as jousting.
145 A terrible god or demon associated with the underworld.
146 Alexander the Great launched his campaign into India in 326 BC.
147 A mock sun or multiple suns. This is a reference to Lilly's second book of 1649 which includes a triple sun and conjunction. Lilly also discussed triple suns in his 1645 *Starry Messenger*.
148 Annotation on Thomason copy: "July 19."
149 A precinct distinct from neighboring territories and possessing some autonomy.
150 Rule of measurement.
151 Marsh of Dunstable was an astrologer who, according to the writer and antiquary John Aubrey, admitted "that he did his business by the help of the blessed

spirits" rather than by scientific skill; clearly the author of this pamphlet credits Marsh's work to the operation of less benign spirits. John Aubrey, *Miscellanies Upon Various Subjects*, 4th edition (London: John Russell Smith, 1857), 161.

152 Parliamentary astrologer William Lilly referred briefly to Marsh in his autobiography; William Lilly, *William Lilly's History of His Life and Times, from the Year 1602 to 1681. Written by Himself in the Sixty-sixth year of his Age, to His Worthy Friend, Elias Ashmole (Published 1715)* (London: reprinted for Charles baldwyn, 1822), 121–122.

153 Balaam was an Old Testament soothsayer hired by the Moabites to curse the people of Israel, although he ultimately pronounced blessings on them instead; see Numbers 22–24.

154 This page has several damaged sections; they have been reproduced as nearly as possible, with uncertain words or sections of words marked by brackets.

6   Sectarians and recusants
'Recant . . . those dangerous errors'

Introduction

The conflict over religion in the early modern era was not merely between Catholicism and Protestantism; it was also a battle between more "mainstream," established confessions and those radical groups perceived by their detractors as having gone beyond the pale of orthodoxy. To many Protestant Englishmen and women of the mid-seventeenth century, religious tensions were growing keener and sects were proliferating at an unprecedented rate: in addition to Catholic recusants, whose loyalty to the government was habitually regarded as suspect, adherents to the Church of England had to contend with Presbyterians, Independents, and a host of smaller, and potentially more troubling, groups like the Anabaptists, the Quakers, the Ranters, and the Family of Love. Some of these pressed for a revision of the structure of church government and rejected certain traditional Anglican rites, such as infant baptism; others repudiated foundational doctrines like the Trinity, rejected the authority of scripture, or claimed new revelation from God. In still other cases the teachings that made a group unorthodox were neither well defined nor well understood, and general terms like "Brownist" and "Adamite" might be used with no specific sect in mind but merely to convey the negative image of separatists, heretics, blasphemers, or licentious livers.

A few writers at least could turn their anxiety over the rise in sectarianism into scathing humor: the ubiquitous John Taylor, for instance, both criticized and poked fun at "the swarme of sectaries, and schismatiques" in many of his works.[1] Others, however, published more serious works in an attempt to combat wrong teachings which had, as one writer put it, "crept into the very bowels of this Kingdome, striving to shake the whole foundation and to destroy both Church and Kingdom."[2] Broadsheets like the *Catalogue of the severall sects and opinions in England* (1647) alerted godly readers to the range of dangerous errors abroad, giving them a simple reference work to consult as they went about among "the unquiet spirits of a lawlesse generation;"[3] newsy pamphlets meanwhile recounted murders committed by sectaries, conveying the clear message that such crimes were the natural outworking of the individuals' theological errors.[4]

Yet the pamphlets in this section reveal that "natural" crimes, even those as heinous as homicide, were not the only ones outsiders feared from or associated with religious groups: heresy could also be linked to witchcraft. Unsurprisingly, given that Protestants believed the Roman Church to be not only corrupt but motivated by demonic forces, this threat was typically associated with Jesuits and recusants.[5] While during the war partisans of both sides expanded their rhetoric to link their *political* opponents with the forces of Hell, it was already traditional for pamphleteers to churn out satires that commented on religious issues and reflected fears of Catholicism, or "popery," by depicting the pope in conference with Satan. This was useful in critiquing such elites as the Archbishop of Canterbury, William Laud, but the demonic association was considered no less valid for more pedestrian figures, or what one might call run-of-the-mill recusants. Thus, for instance, *A Declaration of a Strange and Wonderfull Monster* (1646) linked the threat of witches and 'underground' Catholics when it observed that "no parts in *England* hath had so many Witches, none fuller of Papists" than the county of Lancashire, which had indeed witnessed several witch-trials in the preceding decades.[6] More bluntly, *A Relation of a Strange Apparition in an Ale-house* (1641) depicted a group of Irish Jesuits "conjur[ing] with their Beads (as I may so call it)" and summoning up the Devil, albeit accidentally.[7] As religious groups multiplied, however, the association with witchcraft likewise grew to include such radical movements as the newly-emergent Quakers, whose secret assemblies, claim to experience new revelation, and violent shaking under the purported influence of the Holy Spirit all left them uniquely vulnerable to such accusations.[8] The 1650s saw a number of witchcraft cases involving Quakers, such as the one discussed in *Strange & Terrible Newes from Cambridge* (1659), when two Quakers were accused of bewitching a woman into a horse and riding her to one of their meetings. The matter was dismissed in court and the pamphlet drew a sharp rebuttal, *A Lying Wonder Discovered* (1659), illustrating not only debates over religious sects but the controversy surrounding witch-trials and the frequent difficulty of obtaining a conviction. Nevertheless, the central premise would have had merit to some readers: to conclude that those who purveyed religious lies might also be working with the father of lies through occult means was not inherently unreasonable, and the association was a strong one.

Even without the threat posed by witchcraft, however, unorthodox teachings remained a menace that members of different confessions sought to combat in print as well as from the pulpit. One clergyman, Thomas Edwards, contributed to the effort in the 1640s with a three-volume work evocatively titled *Gangraena*, which combined Edwards' refutations of specific theological errors with accounts of judgments like that which had allegedly fallen upon a Separatist couple in 1645. In his telling, after the woman had "resolved . . . that if ever she had any more children, they should never be baptized" in accordance with the rites of the Church of England, she bore two stillborn babies, one "perfect" and the other headless.[9] Monstrous births, in fact, had long been a common theme in both treatises and popular judgment narratives, as they were "the extreme forms of the promise that private sins—particularly those sins ignored or protected by a faulty conscience—would be exposed."[10] Contemporaries recognized, at least in theory, that such births sometimes occurred through no fault of the parents, and some writers took pains to insist that the prodigies to which they drew attention "embodied a generic warning" rather than being "a variety of retributive justice directed against their begetters;" yet in many cases, especially those involving families of suspect religious confessions, the child's specific deformities did become a mirror of the parents' errors.[11] In both *A Strange and Lamentable Accident . . . at Mears-Ashby* (1642) and *Strange Newes from Scotland* (1647), women who rejected Anglican baptismal rites for their children were punished by bearing deformed babies, while the blasphemous mother in *The Ranters Monster* (1652) gave birth, not to the Messiah she claimed she would but to "the most ugliest ill-shapen *Monster* that ever eyes beheld."[12]

Such causational narratives were straightforward but not impeccably theological, as Alexandra Walsham points out of judgment narratives more generally: in addition to assuming unbiblically that God's ways of executing justice were quick and predictable,[13] they nearly always suggest a "theologically questionable" correlation between oaths or other forceful language and a literal outcome.[14] Thus, in *A Strange and Lamentable Accident*, *Strange Newes from Scotland*, and *A Declaration of a Strange and Wonderfull Monster* (1645) one finds the pregnant mother declaring her wish to bear a headless child rather than submit it to baptism (in the first two cases) or have it grow up to be a Parliamentarian (in the third case), then bearing a headless child who embodies her words. By contrast, but no less didactically, *The Ranters Monster* results in an inversion rather than an exact version of the mother's words.

Whatever their theological shortcomings, however, these narratives graphically demonstrated the evils of heresy and the importance of doctrinal accuracy on matters ranging from the rites involved in baptism to the identity of Jesus Christ. As Julie Crawford has argued, such publications were a form of "Protestant casuistry" which

> explained, with God's voice and in marvelous form, the answers to controversial matters of practical theology. Stories of monstrous births . . . were cases of conscience that intended to provide clear guidelines for religious and moral behavior through marvelously judgmental stories.[15]

The same point could accurately be made of narratives involving witchcraft, terrifying appearances of Satan, or other forms of judgment visited upon those of questionable religious views. The narratives in the following pamphlets were not the only arguments put forward to prove the illegitimacy of sectarian beliefs or to encourage men and women to follow true teaching; rather, they served as supporting evidence, visible and dramatic illustrations of heretics' sins and God's judgment.

———————◆———————

A
RELATION
OF A STRANGE
APPARITION
In an Ale-house next doore to the *White
Horse*, against *Somerset-House* in the Strand;
Where a company of Papists were at their
Exercises: as is conceived the Devill in an
ugly black shape disturbing them, and tea-
*ring the Rugge, and scattering it in
pieces up and down the Roome.*

WITH A RELATION
Of a Judgement that strangely fell upon
one at Mr. *Mundayes* House in *Little Brittaine*;
who whilst he was cursing of Mr. *Burton*, Mr.
Prinne, and Doctor *Bastwick*, his eares fell
a bleeding, to the amazement of the beholders.

LONDON
Printed for *Richard Smethrust*, 1641.

[p. 1] A STRANGE APPA-
rition at an Alehouse next doore
to the *White Horse* against Sum-
merset House in the
Strand.

CERTAIN Jesuites or Papists, being met together at an Alehouse in the
Strand, neare the White Horse over against Sommerset House; they were at
their Exercises in an upper Chamber, three stories high, they were most of
them *Irish*; who whilest they were at the exercise, with what zeal, I shall not
need to relate, because it is too well known what Popish zeal is.

But see how exactly they conjured with their Beads (as I may so call it)
for without all doubt it was either the Devil or some strange Monster, that
disturbed them from the Devill.

There was in the roome where they were a bed, and under the window
against the beds feet, stood a back Chaire of Red leather.

And after their long and loud acclamations, or [p. 2] Popish exercises,
there appeared amongst them a strange Monster: or if you will the Devill
in the shape of a Monster, all as black as pitch, as bigge as a great Dogge;
which appeared in a most horrid shape, to the affrightment of all the company; which disturbed the company exceedingly; then they crost themselves,
and applyed them to their Popish Customes.

But the black Fiend leaped into the Chaire that stood by the window, at the beds feet, and there roused it self up; which made them all to quake and tremble. It put them out of the tale of their Beads, and made them to run some one way, and some another, and set the whole house in a distraction.

Amongst the rest, one of them (an *Irish*-man) drew out his Rapier, and with a great rage began to scuffle with this strange Monster: and between hope and fear ran desperately at him; but it leaped down from the Chaire in a furious[16] manner, and immediately got upon the bed, which was covered with a green Rugge.

This Fiend toare the Rugge all to peeces, and threw it up and down the roome: and many peeces of it was found upon the floore. And those that were then present were so amazed hereat, that they knew not how the vision vanished, or what became of it; one of the servants of the house ranne forth of the doore to a neighbours, quaking and shivering at what she had seen: but one of them, seeing her in such a fright, laboured to perswade her that it was a dogge: Lord blesse me from such [p. 3] dogges (quoth she) but they could not soon pacifie her, to mitigate her fear.

Neighbours hearing of it, enquiring concerning it, the people of the house report it to be a mighty Cat: the Papists report it to be a dogge: but multitudes of people have resorted thither, to enquire of it; and to talk with the people about this vision which so disturbed them.

A
RELATION
Of a strange Judgement at the
House of Master MUNDAY
in *Little Brittaine.*

Two Gentlemen were talking together about news, and such like discourse at the house of one M^r. *Mundayes* in *Little Britaine,* who at the last fell into Discourse about Religion. Then they fell into discourse of M^r. *Burton,* M^r. *Prinne,* and Doctor *Bastwicke,*[17] and of their sufferings: the one of them applauding them for honest godly, religious men, and such as suffered [p. 4] patiently; and were faithfull witnesses of Jesus Christ, commending them to be such as he verily thought were the Children of God.

But the other answered: Oh you are deceived man, they are Scismaticall Fellows; it is no matter if they were hanged: a company of base *Brownists,*[18] as we are troubled with a company of them; they are base dissembling fellows.

Oh! I pray you, said the other, be not so hot, I beleeve that they are such as are reall honest men, and such as have stood for Christ from their very heart, as witnesse may testifie.

But the other answered (cursing them) and all such Puritans (as he called them) If *Burton,* quoth he, had had a Bishopricke, and had beene made a Bishop, (quoth he) he had never found fault with that government.

No, quoth the other man, you are mistaken; what he did or any of them, I am verily[19] perswaded that they did out of conscience, and that they were men truly fearing [p. 5] God; oh the weeping eyes that beheld them when they lost their eares, and the tender hearts that pittied them then, and ever since; methinks it grieves me to thinke of it: Push (quoth the other, swearing a bloody oath) It were no matter if they had beene hanged, base scismaticall Jacks, to trouble the whole Kingdome with their base opinions, and he concluded that saying with bloody, and fearefull Curses.

Whereupon, on an instant, he began to sweat, and to be faint, and taking out of his pocket, an hankercher, to wipe his face and his head, a strange Judgement fell upon him, his eares fell a bleeding, and thereby his handkercher was all bloody with wiping of them; which wrought a strange amazement to all that stood by.

Oh! therefore, let every one beware how they curse Gods people; for the righteous God judgeth justly, and will avenge himselfe on those that rise up against him, and his distressed Saints.

FINIS.

Figure 6.1 Title page, *A Strange and Lamentable Accident that happened lately at Mears-Ashby*, 1642.

A
STRANGE
And Lamentable accident that happened lately at
Mears-Ashby in Northamptonshire. 1642.

Of one *Mary Wilmore*, wife to *John Wilmore* rough Mason, who was
delivered of a Childe without a head, and credibly reported
to have a firme Crosse on the brest, as this ensuing Story shall relate.
Hor: *Miranda cano*.[20]

Printed at London for *Rich: Harper* and *Thomas Wine*, and are to bee sold
at the Bible and Harpe in Smithfield. 1642.[21]

[p. 1] A strange and lamentable Accident that happened lately at Mears-
Ashby in Northamptonshire.
1642.

THIS Kingdome once glorying in the flourishing title of Olbion: which is
as much as happinesse and tranquility (*tam Eccles. quam Respub.*[22]) but
now being clouded and maskt with various distractions, as are apparantly
knowne and made manifest to the whole world, in so much that she is made
a laughing stocke, and a scorne to all Nations, may now with the Publican
cry, *Lord have mercy on me a sinner* [Luke 18:13]: or with *Eccebolius*,
chiefe Captain of the Apostates, who in *Constantines* time tooke[23] upon him
the note of a zealous Christian: in the reigne of *Julian* he became a Pagan;
Julian being dead then he would become a Christian: but be- [p. 2] ing sensible of his mutability and inconstancy, prostrated himselfe flat upon the
ground at the Porch of the Temple, crying with a loud voice, Tread on me,
tread on me, for I am unsavoury salt.[24]

I feare me we have too too many of these unfavourable and wheeling
Rotundities frequent among us, but I pray God it happeneth not to them
as it did to *Julian* Uncle to *Julian* the Apostate, for their contemning and
slighting Gods holy ordinances, who coming into a Church at Antioch, pro-
faned the Lords Table by pissing upon it, saying in scorne, that the Divine
Providence tooke no care of outward ceremonies. But not long after divine
Justice found him out, for being taken with a disease that rotted his bowels,
his excrements leaving their wonted passage, ran through his throat and
blasphemous mouth in as stinking a manner, as the poysoned trash and beggarly rudiments are fomented now adayes from the impudent mouthes of
unlearned and ignorant Teachers, the event of whose pernicious and illiterate doctrine will lead me to this ensuing story of Gods wrath and judgements
to over curious and nice[25] zelots of our times.

[p. 3] In Mears-Ashby in Nottinghamshire,[26] one *Mary Wilmore* wife of
John Wilmore, rough Mason, being great with childe, and much perplext in

minde, to thinke that her childe when it pleased God she should be delivered, should be baptized with the signe of the Crosse: The Minister of the Parish being a very honest and conformable man, not suiting with the vaine babling and erroneous Sycophants, as there are too too many thereabouts inhabiting, desires her husband to goe to Hardwicke, a Village neare adjoyning to one Master *Bannard* a reverend Divine, to know his opinion concerning the Crosse in Baptisme: whose answer was, That it was no wayes necessary to salvation, but an ancient, laudable, and decent ceremony of the Church of England[.] Which answer being related to her from her husband, it is reported she should say, I had rather my childe should bee borne without a head, then to have a head to be signed with the signe of the Crosse.

Haply this woman through her weaknesse, or too much confiding in the conventicling Sectaries, *Qui quicquid in buccam venerit blatterant:*[27] might thinke she did well, supposing as shee was taught by them, the Crosse in Baptisme to bee a pernicious, popish and idolatrous ceremony: yet see *Uzzah*, 2 *Sam*. 6.6,7. I *Chron*. 13.9,10. *vid. Judg*. 8.27. though thy intent in doing a seeming [p. 4] good action be never so good, yet if thou have not warrant for not so doing, thou and thine action may happly perish together, as the sequell of this story will declare. It pleased God about a month after, shee was accordingly delivered of a Monster, *Rudes indegestáque moles*,[28] a child without a head, to the shame of the parents, in not having that part whereon it might have been markt with that token whereof it should never after have beene ashamed.

What strange judgements of God have we seene, saith *Pollychronus*,[29] in the times of revolters? as we may see in the third yeare of Queene *Elizabeth* of ever blessed memory, when as in *Moore* and *Geofferey*, two of the divells agents, publisht their prodigious and hereticall tenents, to the allurement of many faithfull and constant beleevers: the yeare after was many monstrous births. A man childe was borne at Chichester in Sussex, the head, armes, and legs whereof were like Anatomy, the brest and belly monstrous big from the navell, about the necke a great coller of flesh and skin growing, like to the double ruffes and neckerchiefes then in use,[30] and many more like accidents, *Qua nunc norandi non est locus*.[31] Good Lord therefore which hast made and fashioned us, and as there is one Lord, one faith, and one baptisme, one God and Father of all [Eph. 4:5–6], even so Lord grant that wee may joyntly agree in love, [p. 5] and that there remaine amongst us a godly consent and loving concord, and that nothing bee done in contention and vainglory: and suffer us not to exercise our selves in the works of the flesh, as hatred, emulations, contentions, heresies, seditions [Gal. 5:20], needlesse and unprofitable questions [Titus 3:9], which tend to rebellion and discord, breeding ungodlinesse, and make dissention: breake thou the bonds of Sathan, and the malice of those who extinguish the bond of peace.

By *John Locke, Cleric.*

FINIS.

A DECLARATION,

Of a strange and Wonderfull MONSTER:

Born in KIRKHAM Parish in LANCASHIRE (the Childe of Mrs. *Haughton*, a Popish Gentlewoman) the face of it upon the breast, and without a head (after the mother had wished rather to bear a Childe without a head then a Roundhead) and had curst the PARLIAMNET.

Attested by Mr. FLEETWOOD, Minister of the same Parish, under his own hand ; and Mrs. *Gattaker* the Mid-wife, and divers other eye-witnesses : Whose testimony was brought up by a *Member* of the House of Commons.

Appointed to be printed according to Order : And desired to be published in all the Counties, Cities, Townes , and Parishes in England : *Being the same Copies that were presented to the Parliament.*

London, Printed by *Jane Coe*, 1646,

Figure 6.2 Title page, *A Declaration of a Strange and Wonderfull Monster*, 1645.
Source: RB 122034, The Huntington Library, San Marino, California.

A DECLARATION,
Of a strange and Wonderfull MONSTER:

Born in KIRKHAM Parish in LANCASIIIRE (the Childe
of Mrs. *Haughton,* a Popish Gentlewoman) the face of it upon the breast,
and without a head (after the mother had wished rather to bear a
Childe without a head then a Roundhead) and had curst the
PARLIAMNET [*sic*].

Attested by Mr. FLEETWOOD, Minister of the same Pa-
rish, under his own hand; and Mrs. *Gattaker* the Mid-wife, and divers
other eye-witnesses: Whose testimony was brought up by a *Member* of the House of Commons.

*Appointed to be printed according to Order: And desired to be published
in all the Counties, Cities, Townes, and Parishes in* England:
Being the same Copies that were presented to the Parliament.

London, Printed by *Jane Coe.* 1646.[32]

[p. 3] A
DECLARATION OF A
Strange and Wonderfull
MONSTER:
born in *Kirkham* Parish, in *Lancashire.*

This wonderfull manifestation of Gods anger, against wicked and prophane
people; we shall lay open thus.

1   In declaring where it was done.
2   Upon whom.
3   What is supposed might be the cause.
4   What proofs there are to make it appear to be a truth.

In the first, we have discovered the County, Parish, and the House.
In the second; the woman her parentage, her husband, and religion.
In the third, her course of life, and her speeches.
[p. 4] In the fourth, that it is confirmed, both by relation and testimonials
under their own hands, who were eye witnesses.

First, the Dukedome of *Lancashire* is the County where this Monster was
brought forth; the County it self lyes North, bordering upon the West of
York-shire, and Derby-shire, and by the Irish Sea. The people that live there,
are a mixt Number; some precious godly people; but for the most part very
bad: No parts in *England* hath had so many Witches,[33] none fuller of Papists,

and they were the chiefe Instruments in seeking to have that wicked Book of Allowance for Sports on the Lords Day to be published, and it was set forth by their procurements,[34] and the godly people amongst them have suffered very much under their reproaches and wicked malice.

This Monster was born in the Town and Parish of *Kirkeham* in that County, which is in *Amoundernesse* Hundred, between *Preston* and little *Morton*, within three miles of *Clifton*, on the West side of *Lancashire*, within some three miles of one point of the Sea, and some six or seven miles of the main; a Parish which God hath blessed with good Ministers, and some godly people (though but few) in it; who by the malice of wicked and prophane Wretches, have been much abused heretofore.

This Gentlewoman (for so she is both by Birth and Mariage) was delivered of this Monster at her Husbands house in *Kirkeham* Parish aforesaid, and about a mile from *Kirkeham* Town, where the Midwife being sent for came to her, and delivered her in that house, the Child (or rather Monster) was born, but dead, and there it was shewed, and from thence caryed into the Church-yard a day or two after, and there buried: after which, some (in Gentlemens habit) were seen to go in; supposed to be Popish Priests and Fryars: and thus you have the place where this Monster was brought forth.

Secondly, for the woman that bore it, she is a good hansome, proportionable, comely Gentlewoman, young, and of a good complexion, of a merry disposition, and an healthfull Nature, well personed, had her conditions been suitable.

For her Parents they were of a very bitter disposition against godly people; Papists they were both, and divertive[35] against honest [p. 5] protestants, For her mother she would usually call honest men Roundheads and Puritans, and Hereticks, many gentlemen did much use her house, which were suspected to be popish priests[;] her husband (which was this womans father) was called Mr. *Browne*, who lived in the parish of *Kirkham* also: And amongst other reproaches and scornes which her mother cast upon religious people she took her Cat; and said that it must be made a Roundhead like *Burton*, *Prinne*, and *Bastwicke*;[36] and causing the eares to be cut off; called her cat Prynn (instead of Pusse) both then and after she hath often said, that she hoped to see the Church flourish againe (meaning the Popish Church) and all Roundheads subdued; and she hath done much for the releife of poore Papists in those parts.[37]

The young woman, viz: Mistris *Brownes* daughter, who bore this monster, was married by one Master *Haughton* a papist also; for none else were admitted to come suiters to her, This Master *Haughton* then lived at *Grimshall* in the same Countie, but after they were married dwelt sometimes in a village neere *Kerkham*[ ]in the same parish where her mother lived, Mr. *Haughton* is a gentleman descended of an ancient family, wel known in those[ ]parts and not altogether of such a bitter spirit as those he matched with, he hath been a gentleman wel bred, only in a popish way educated.

The woman he married was a notorious papist, and would many times hold a notable discourse with her neighbours about her religion, she was not onely borne of popish parents, but bred, and brought up with them, and educated in the popish Religion having many popish pictures, and Crucifixes, and[ ] other popish trumpery wherein she much delighted; and if she were at any time reproved for the superstitious fooleries she so affected, she would speak much in defence thereof, and was alwayes very obstinate, and would expresse much invection against those godly protestants and others that reproved her.

3[.] Now for the course of life which the woman lived, who bare this monster, it hath been much spent in popish devotion; and some[t]imes in company with her neighbours the gentlewomen and Farmers wives that lived about her, she was one very zealous amongst papists, and friendly amongst neighbours, onely when her Religion was touched, she expressed much passion.

[p. 6] She hath been often heard to curse against Mr. *Prinn*, Mr. *Burton*, and Doctor *Bastwick*, and the Roundheads. Also to revile the Parliament, and say that shee thought that the King and the Bishops were the righter part of us; she hath been heard to wish, that she and hers might never live to be *Roundheads*, nor *Separatists*, and that she hath praid to God, that she might never live to see any of hers such; and that the *Puritans* and *Independents* deserve all to be hanged: and many such like expressions would often fall from her.

Amongst the rest, one speech of hers was most notorious, and hath rested in the memory of some Gentlewomen, and others that heard her when she spake it; that being in company with her, they fell to discourse of the present miseries of the Kingdome, by these warres; and some spoke against the *Cavaliers*, and the *Papists* in the Kings Army; Whereupon this Mrs. *Haug[h]ton* said little lesse against the *Roundheads* and *Independents*, and she said the King was in the right against them; she was replyed to, that those called *Roundheads* were honest men, and in the r[i]ght way of walking, and living like the people of Ged [*sic*], and sutable to the profession of Christians: And withall wishing, if it pleased God, that she had her eyes opened, and was such a Roundhead. No saith she, I had rather have no head, nor life: I nor any of mine, I hope will ever be such. Answer was made her, that her children if she had any, might (if God so please) have their eyes opened; and see that good which she is ignorant of. Mrs. *Haughton* made answer again in these words: *I pray God, that rather than I shall be a Roundhead, or bear a Roundhead, I may bring forth a Childe without a head*. This was a fearfull saying, and taken notice of by divers of her neighbours that heard her speak it. And this many who know it, do apprehend, might be a great meanes to provoke God to shew such a testimony of his displeasure against her, by causing her to bring forth this Monster, whose Picture is in the Title-page of this Book.

4. Now for testimony of the truth of this, we shall give it you in Order thus: Her Neighbours who heard her speak the aforesaid words, have been with Mr. *Fleetwood* the Minister of the Parish of *Kirkham*, [p. 7] where she was brought to bed of this Monster, and where it was buried also, and it was told to some of the Committee of the County what had happened, and that she had spoke those words. And after that she was with childe, and delivered of the Monster, one Widdow *Gattaker* the Midwife, formerly wife to Mr. *Gattaker*, sometimes Vicar of the said Parish; she being a godly woman, could not be eased in her minde, untill she had discharged her conscience in making it known to Mr. *Fleetwood*

the Minister aforesaid; That she had brought the said Mrs. *Haughton* to bed of a Monster, which had no head; declaring her opinion, that she verily believed that it was the hand of God upon her, for those imprecations she wished upon her self, as is before exprest: The Minister he spoke of it to others, and so did the Midwife also, which made it to be spread up and down the Country, so that it came to the eares of some of the Committee;[38] And for the further satisfaction of the truth thereof, Collonel *More* an honest godly Gentleman, a Member of the House of Commons, and one of the Committee being there, it was desired he should send a Letter to Mr. *Fleetwood* the Minister of the Parish, to know the certainty of it, whether it was truth or not; which Letter was writ, and by him sent accordingly. And Mr. *Fleetwood* receiving the said Letter, sent for the Midwife about it, and she still confirmed what she said before, yet for better satisfaction, Mr. *Fleetwood* caused the grave to be opened, and the childe to be taken up, and laid to view, and found there a body without an head, as the Midwife had said; onely the childe had a face upon the breast of it, as you may see in the portraicture.

The Certificate was shewed before divers of the Committee, and by Collonel *More* a Member of the House of Commons, brought up to *London*, and shewed to divers of the House; who have commanded it to be printed, that so all the Kingdome might see the hand of God herein; to the comfort of his people, and the terrour of the wicked that deride and scorn them.

[p. 8] **A Copie of a Certificate under the hand** of Mr. *Edward Fleetwood* Minister of *Kirkham* Parish in *Lancashire*, concerning the Monster brought forth by Mrs. *Haughton* a Papist, living in that Parish.

As we must tell no lye, so we should not conceal any truth; especially when it tends to Gods glory: There was a great Papist and of great Parentage, within the Parish of Kirkham, *and his wives mother being of the same Religion, did usually scoffe and mocke the Roundheads, and in derision of Mr.* Prinne, *and others, cut off the the [sic] Cats eares, and called it by his name. But behold an example of the justice and equity of God in his judgements: As* Adonibezeck *was repaid in his own kinde [Judges 1:7]:* Haman *hanged upon the same Gallowes he had prepared for* Mordecai *[Esther 7:10], and* Pharaoh *and all his Hoste drowned in the Sea into which he had thought to have driven the Israelites [Exod. 14], And likewise one of the Popish Prelates, who said he would not dine before* Ridley *and* Latimore *were burnt, was burned in his own enttrails.*[39] *So (much what) alike, it fell out with this mans wife, a Popish creature, who being great with childe, when the time of her delivery came, she brought forth a Monstrous childe without an head, ugly and deformed, the portraicture whereof (as near as we could delineate) is here described, and my self,*

EDWARD FLEETWOOD, Pastor;
With the Midwife, and others who saw the Childe taken out of its grave;
   Witnesses hereof.

FINIS.

Strange Newes from

SCOTLAND,

OR,

A ftrange Relation of a terrible and
prodigious Monfter, borne to the amazement
of all thofe that were fpectators, in the Kingdome of
Scotland, in a Village neere *Edenborough*, call'd
Hadenfworth, Septem. 14. 1647. and the words
the faid Monfter fpake at its birth.

Printed according the Originall Relation fent overto
a great Divine hereafter mentioned.

Figure 6.3 Title page, *Strange Newes from Scotland*, 1647.

Strange Newes from
SCOTLAND,
OR,
A strange Relation of a terrible and
prodigious Monster, borne to the amazement
of all those that were spectators, in the Kingdome of
Scotland, in a Village neere *Edenborough*, call'd
Hadensworth, *Septem*. 14. 1647. and the words
the said Monster spake at its birth.

Printed according [to] the Originall Relation sent over to
a great Divine hereafter mentioned.[40]

[p. 1] STRANGE NEWES
from SCOTLAND.

In *Hadensworth*, neere *Edenborough*, (for so the Village was called) as it
was certified by the Minster of the Parish, (a man of gravitie, and good
estimation amongst his neighbours, and of good repute generally; as also
by the Church-wardens of the same Parish, and other people of good
qualitie and esteeme, and the Relation sent hither to a friend of his, one
M. *Obadiah Slingsby*, a pious and a painfull[41] Minister of Gods Word)
was borne a Child, or rather a Monster, (I think *Lærna* nor *Ægyptian Nyle*
ever produced the like[42]) with two heads, growing severally, somewhat
distant one from the other, bearing the similitude of man and woman, the
one face being all over-growne with long haire, the other more smooth
& more [p. 2] effeminate, the eares of both long, (like as the Poets fancie
Mydas his ears, who was Judge between *Pan* and *Apollo*[43]) standing bolt
upright, in shape and length much like unto an Asses; the Eyes standing in the middest of the Fore-head (they having but one a piece) cannot
unfitly bee paralelled with that horned Monster *Polyphemus*, spoken of
by *Homer*, which *Ulysses* extinguisht the sight of, by thrusting a Fire-
brand into the Eye[44]) [*sic*] they being bigge and round, like unto Sawcers:
His Body shap'd, [(]or rather having no shape) round like the truncke of
a Tree or Barrell: The Neckes to support this horned structure (I meane
the Heads) were strong, sinewie and short, like to a strong neckt Bull:
The Armes had their growthes from severall places; being of great dimensions, but very small, having annexed to their wrists great Tallons, like
to a Griffins. From the Secret parts (which shewed it to bee both Male
and Female) downewards, all hairie, like your Satyres, or Sylvane Gods:
The Legges long and cloven, like an Oxes Foot, and out of the knees, or
upper part of the legges, brancht out hands, shap'd and coloured like a
Monkeyes: In short, all the parts about it were monstrous and ill-shapen;
insomuch, that it strooke into a quaking terrour all those that were eye-
witnesses of this [p. 3] horned production, some betaking themselves to

their prayers; others, that wanted faith and confidence to pray, to flight, and the rest standing amazed, as if they had beholden *Gorgon* (a Monster that had this propertie annexed to her, that whosoever chanced to cast his eye upon her, was suddenly metamorphosed into a stone[)].

At the birth of this Monster, Nature seemed to bee disquieted and troubled; insomuch, that the Heavens proclaimed its entrance into the World with a lowd peale of Thunder, seconded with such frequent flashes of Lightning, that it was credibly beleeved of all (whose sences were not ravished from them with the sudden apprehension of feare) that the latter day was now come upon them; in the height of which confused noyse; the Monster (with a hoarse, but lowd voice) was heard to speake these words, being ever after silent, *I am thus deformed for the sinnes of my Parents.* The Mother, what with the extremitie of the paine and horrour of the sight, after some few expressions, gave up the Ghost; the words shee used before breath left her body, were these, *Good people* (sayes shee) *pray for mee as I shall doe for my selfe; this Judgement is questionlesse fallen upon mee for my sinnes, which are many and grievous, for I have often wisht this or some such like judgement might befall me, (which might* [p. 4] *not onely be a terror to my selfe, but all other that [sh]ould behold it) rather then any Child borne of my body should receive those Christian Rites which by the Lawes and ancient Customes of* England *and* Scotland *were given Children at the Font, at their Baptisme: And I confesse, that I did vehemently desire (being seduced by Hereticall factious fellowes, who goe in Sheepes cloathing, but are naught but ravening Wolves) to see the utter ruine and subversion of all Church and State-Government (which too many in these times have desired, as the late unhappie differences can testifie) and to be an eye witnesse of the destruction of the Ministerie, who were not of our faction; all which ungodly wishes (I am confident) have occasioned this horrid judgement to be so heavily inflicted upon me: Therefore I desire you (deare friends) as you tender your being here, and your well-being hereafter, if any here amongst us be guiltie of the same sinnes (as I feare they are too generall) to recant in time those dangerous errors, calling to God for mercie, and making your peace before your sinnes call to Heaven for vengeance, lest this Sceane be continued from me to you, and so to your posteritie, till at length this Nation be pestered with as many Serpents as*—But before shee could put a Period to her Speech, Death put an *Exit* to her dayes.

Thus ended the Tragedie of this afflicted Woman: I would to God it might (as I hope it may) serve as a meanes to dehort[45] those peo- [p. 5] ple, who, though for the present they labour not with the same Births, (yet too many, I feare, with the same Disease) whose out-sides though they appeare not so horrid to the Eye as this mishapen Monster, I feare their in-sides are hung Round with all sorts of crying sinnes. Let such take this dying Womans counsell into their considerations before it be too late, calling to Heaven for Mercie, before their sinnes call to Heaven for Judgement.

FINIS.

Printed at London by *E. P.* for *W. Lee,* 1647.

THE
RANTERS
MONSTER:
Being a true Relation of one MARY ADAMS,
living at *Tillingham* in *Essex*, who named her self the Virgin
Mary, blasphemously affirming, That she was conceived with
child by the Holy Ghost; that from her should spring forth
the Savior of the world; and that all those that did not believe
in him were damn'd: With the manner how she was deliver'd
of the ugliest ill-shapen *Monster* that ever eyes beheld, and afterwards rotted away in prison: *To the great admiration of all
those that shall read the ensuing subject; the like never before heard of.*

London, Printed for *George Horton*, 1652.

Figure 6.4 Title page, *The Ranters Monster*, 1652.

THE
RANTERS
MONSTER:
Being a true Relation of one MARY ADAMS,
living at *Tillingham* in *Essex*, who named her self the Virgin
Mary, blasphemously affirming, That she was conceived with
child by the Holy Ghost; that from her should spring forth
the Savior of the world; and that all those that did not believe
in him were damn'd: With the manner how she was deliver'd
of the ugliest ill-shapen *Monster* that ever eyes beheld, and afterwards rotted away in prison: *To the great admiration of all
those that shall read the ensuing subject; the like never before heard of.*
London, Printed for *George Horton*, 1652.[46]

[p. 3] Strange and terrible News from Essex; being a true Relation of the
most impious life, and blasphemous actions of one Mary Adams, who
named her self the Virgin Mary, and said that she was conceived with
child of the Holy Ghost: but being cast into prison, soon after she was
delivered of the ugliest ill-shapen Monster that ever eyes beheld.

IN the County of *Essex* at a place called *Tillingham*, there lived one *Mary
Adams*, who said that she was the Virgin *Mary*, and that she was conceived
with child by the Holy Ghost, and how all the Gospel that had bin taught
heretofore, was false; and that which was within her she said was the true
Messias; for she obstinately and very impiously affirmed, that Christ was not
yet come in the flesh; but that she was to bring forth the Savior of the World,
and that all those that did not believe in him were damn'd: For which blasphemous words, and [p. 4] wicked opinion of hers, Mr. *Hadley* the Minister
caused her to be apprehended, & cast into prison, until the time came that
she was to be delivered; At which time, when the Midwife and other good
women of the Parish came to her, they did their best endeavors to bring her
to a safe deliverance, but could not prevail, so[47] that there she lay in exceeding great misery for the space of 8 dayes and nights; and upon the ninth day
about 7 of the clock in the forenoon, she was delivered of the most ugliest
ill-shapen *Monster* that ever eyes beheld; which being dead born, they buried it with speed, for it was so loathsome to behold, that the womens hearts
trembled to look upon it; for it had neither hands nor feet, but claws like
a Toad in the place where the hands should have been, and every part was
odious to behold.
    And as for *Mary Adams*, which had named her self to be the Virgin
Mary, she rotted and consumed as she lay, being from the head to the foot
as full of botches, blains, boils, & stinking scabs, as ever one could stand
by another. But her latter end was miserable, for the women that was about
her, seeing there was no hopes of her life, desired her to pray, and to ask

forgiveness for her sins, she answered, *That her heart was so hardened in wickedness, that she had no power to repent*; but desired one of the women to lend her a knife to pare her nails, which when she had made use of, she laid the knife aside till such time the women were gone, and afterwards ript up her bowels with the same knife.

This *Mary Adams* was descended of good parentage, and for many yeares deported her self both in a civil life and conversation, being a great frequenter of the Church, and a most excellent pattern of true Holiness, till at last she fell off from these divine and glorious principles, to the most Heretical and undeniable way of *Anabaptisme*; and to the [p. 5] end that she might become a dear sister, and one of their society, desired to participate with them in their watry Element, and accordingly her former zeal to the divine Ordinance was extinguished and washed away, by being re-baptized, or dipped: But before the expiration of many moneths she began to learn a new Exercise, and revolted from the *Brotherhood*, to be one of the *Familists of Love*; but she had not long embraced that *Venerable Sect*, but she began to desire a further change, and immediately after turned *Ranter*, holding an Opinion, *That there was no God, no Heaven, no Hell; but that the Creation came by providence*, with divers other Diabolical and blasphemous Tenets; amongst the rest, she said, *That [W]oman was made to be a helper for man, and that it was no sin to lie with any man, whether Batchelor, Widdower, or married; but a thing lawful, and adjured thereunto by Nature.*

This example may sufficiently serve as a *Caveat to all true Christians, that they presume not to offend their Heavenly Maker in such a high degree*; And the truth of this matter is affirmed by

Mr. *Hadley*. Minister
James Townsworth, Andrew Farmer } Church-Wardens.
Richard Gittins. Constable
James Woodhouse, John Smith, John Walton, } Collecters.
William Jackson, Gilbert Pickering, Thomas Watson, } Headboroughs.

[p. 6] Another sad president I cannot but instance, which is an evident demonstration of the life and death of one *John Rogers* a Carpenter, who upon the 4. of *Jan.* being the Sabbath day, told his wife, that he had a piece of work in hand that he promised to make an end that very day, swearing that he would be so good as his word whatever followed after. His wife hearing him say so, endeavored to disswade him from that presumptuous sin of Sabbath-breaking, and told him that God would bless his labour the better all the week after, and that he would find it better both for his soul and body, for that he remembred to keep holy the Sabbath day: To which her husband replyed, *That he that was born to be drown'd should never be hang'd.* Furthermore he said, *That if he were ordained to be saved, he should be saved, how wickedly soever he led his life; and if he was ordained*

to be damned, he should be damned, though he lived never so godly a life:
And so taking up his Tools at his back, went to his work, as he said he
would do, having no other company but his Apprentice boy along with
him; so when he came where his work was, he drew forth his Ax, and as
he was hewing of a piece of Timber, the Ax glanced, and cut him on the
leg, whereby he fell down backwards, crying out that he had kill'd himself;
which when his Apprentice perceived, caught him up, and held him by the
arm, desiring him to go back again home with him, and he would do his
best indeavor to guide him along on the way: No Villain, quoth he, I will
never go home what ever betide me, neither shalt thou live to carry news
what is become of me: so putting his hand in his pocket, pulled out a keen
knife, swearing that he would kill the boy; At which words, the boy being
afraid what would be done unto him, let go his hold, and ran away; and
coming home told what his Master had done: Whereupon his wife called
six of[48] her neighbours to go a- [p. 7] long with her to see what was become
of her husband; but when they came to the place where he was they found
him lying on his back not quite dead, having with his[49] knife stab'd himself
in 8 several places; some of his guts lying two yards from him: his neighbours did their endeavors, but could not bring him home alive. The Lord
in his mercy keep us all from vain opinions, hardness of heart, and from
desperate deaths.

Here followeth another sad example which was done *Jan.* 7. in the
County of *Yorke*, at *Rippon*, where lived one M. *Clerk*, who having a poor
Tenant 4 miles off, that was behind hand of his Rent 7 *l.* & od [i.e. 0 *d.*]
monies, took course of Law against the poor man, and threw him, his wife,
and 3 children out of the hous[e] on a bitter cold snowy day, they poor
soules not knowing what to do, or whither to go for succor, and that poor
lodging and houshold-stuff which they formerly had was kept from them:
neither could the cries of the poor woman and her children any wais prevail
with their greedy and covetous minded Landlord; but the more they sought
to perswade him, the worse he was: At last there came some of the chiefest
men of the Parish to perswade him that he would let them stay in his house
a little time longer, til such time as they could procure some other place to
dwell in. To which he answer'd, That he had rather make a Den for Devils
of it, then that the poor folks should dwell there any longer: and therewithall, he wisht that he might never depart out of the world in the right mind,
if he would let them have one peny worth of their goods to succour them
in their need. But mark what came pass; This M. *Clark* took horse and rid
speedily away; but before he came home, his horse threw him in the street,
and fell upon him, and with the fall bruised him so grievously, that the
bloud issued forth of his mouth, insomuch [p. 8] that for two hours space
he was not able to speak: But at the last when he came to his speech he
raved and raged like a madman, crying out, that his sins were so great, and
so many, that they could never be forgotten; and so in a sad and despairing
manner he departed the World that very time, in the sight of many of his

neighbors, not having so much grace as to say, *Lord have mercy upon me,* when he departed the World.

One thing I had almost omited, which is very remarkable, *viz.* That when the aforesaid *Mary Adams* was in prison, she used many Imprecations against the *Independents*; saying, *That rather then she would bring forth the Holy Ghost, to be a Round-head, or Independent, she desired that he might have no head at all.* O horrible blasphemy! What an Age do we live in? God in his mercy be our guides, and blesse, keep, preserve, and defend us, all the dayes of our appointed time.

FINIS.

Strange & Terrible
NEWES
FROM
CAMBRIDGE,
being
A true *Relation* of the *Quakers* be-
witching of *Mary Philips* out of the Bed from her Hus-
band in the Night, and transformed her into the
shape of a Bay Mare, riding her from
Dinton, towards the *University*.

With the manner how she became
visible again to the People in her own Likeness and
Shape, with her sides all rent and torn, as if they
had been spur-gal'd, her hands and feet worn
as black as a Coal, and her mouth slit with
the Bridle Bit.

Likewise, her *Speech* to the *Scholars*
and *Countrey-men*, upon this great and wonderful *Change*,
her Oath before the Judges and Justices, and [t]he
Names of the *Quakers* brought to Tryal on *Friday* last at the Assises held at *Cambridge*. With
the Judgment of the *Court*.
As also, the Devils *snatching of one from his Company, and
hoisting of him up into the Air, with what hapned
thereupon.*

London, Printed for *C. Brooks*, and are to be sold at the
Royal Exchange in *Cornhill*, 1659.

[p. 3] *The* Quakers *Tryal on* Friday *last, at the Generall Assises held at*
Cambridge.

AS the Wings and Motion of *Time*, are usher'd into the Universe with
various Changes; so is the Creature transformed daily from his Rational
Intellects, to an irrational sensuality of Dumb Creatures. O monstrous!
What Christians become Beasts; what a sad Age do we live in? Woful
Experience makes it deplorably evident: Iron sides, in Iron Times, suits well
with a true Christians Qualifications; but Satanical Delusions in Backsliders
from the Truth, carries a Badge of Infamy, aswel against the Glorious
and Invisible Creatour, as against His admired Works of Creation: Such
Atheistical Spirits, are the *Original Rise*, from whence the ensuing subject

takes its Discourse; and true it is, that the Judgments of God upon Witches and Inchanters, are clearly manifested by Scriptural Examples, where the Lord saith, *Thou shalt not suffer a Witch to live*, Exod. 22.18. *There shall not be found amongst you one that useth Divination, or an observer of Times, or an Inchanter, or a Witch, or a Charmer, or a Consulter with Familiar Spirits, or Wizards, or a Necromancer. For all that do these things are an abomination to the Lord*, Deut. 18.10, 11, 12.

Many such like Instances, may here intervene by way of similie to the people called Quakers; and as [p. 4] *Constantine* forbad all to ask Counsel at Witches, or to use the help of Charmers, *upon pain of Death*; so shal I admonish all people from adhering to *Sorcerers*, which like so many *Mushrooms* (in this Age) spring up in an instant, deviating from the Truth, and fancy a New Light, proceeding onely from the Prince of Darkness; as manifestly appears in the case of *Mary Philips*, who falling from the Church of *England*, entred into the Society of *Robert Dickson*, and *Jane Cranaway*, two unrefined Quakers; but after some few weeks expired, she declined their ways, utterly renouncing them, and detesting their actions; insomuch, that they adjudged her to be in a Reprobate Condition, and not worthy of an Earthly Being; but rather a transfiguration from the Glorious Image she was created in; which (poor Soul) she was soon divested of, even in the Night, as she betook her self to rest with her Husband, being bewitched or inchanted out of the Room where she lay, and transformed into the perfect shape of a Mare, and so rid from *Dinton* to a Town within four miles of *Cambridge*, where a Company of seeming Quakers were met: But upon the aforesaid Inchanting-Witches alighting off, and hanging the Bridle upon the Pails, the snafflle (or Bitt) came out of her mouth, and miraculously she appeared in her created Form and Likeness, to the great astonishment of the Neighbours, who beheld this unexpected change with abundance of admiration; and upon the Womans declaring of her self, and the state of her Condition, she went along with some Officers to the Meeting, and coming into the Room, she pointed to the two Quakers, saying, *This is the Man and Woman that bewitcht me*: Whereupon they were apprehended, and carryed before a Justice, who committed [p. 5] them to safe Custody, there to remain till the Assises, which on *Thursday* last began at *Cambridge*, and on *Friday* they were brought to Trial, where the Woman that was bewitcht made Oath against them, and shewed her hands and feet, which were lamentably bruised, and changed as black as a Coal, her sides being also exceedingly rent and torn, just as if they were spur-gal'd, and her smock all bloudy: Evident signs of her sad sufferings; yet utterly denied by the prisoners, who at last were cleared, notwithstanding the Grand Jury finding the Bill of Indictment.

But to demonstrate more plainly, That there are Magicians and Witches, is evident by these two ensuing Examples;[50] to wit, *Cleomedes* a great Magician in *Rome*, having practised the death of many little Children, the Parents of them at last sought revenge on him, who to shun their Fury, shut himself close up in Coffer: but when they had broke it open, the Devil had carried away the Magician.

The Governour of *Mascon*, a great Magician, as he was at diner with some company, was snatched away by the Divel, hoisted up into the air, and carried three times about the Town, to the great astonishment of the Inhabitants, to whom he cried for help, but all in vain.

Thus it is evident, that as there are *Magicians* and *Witches*; so are there divers of the sons of *Adam* reaching out their hands to the forbidden Tree, and catching at the fruit of it; yea, this off-spring of *Eve* longing for the greenest Apples, the precocious knowledg of Events, and New Lights, before they come their just and perfect ripeness of maturity. And true it is, that there are some who can find no satisfaction, no Sabbath, no quiet in their present state, and therefore [p. 6] they would fain know what the next day, what the next year, what the next age will bring forth; in the highest prosperity they fear a mutation; in the lowest ad versity [*sic*] they are impatient for a change; and hence it comes to pass, that futurity is the mark at which all level the arrows of their aspiring thoughts. As for instance, the Jews who had the *Urim* & *Thummim*, and Prophets of God to enquire of, yet ran a madding after Wizzards, and such as had familiar spirits, had their false Prophets by hundreds;[51] yea, and sent to *Baalzebub* the God of *Ekron*, an Oracle of the Devils, to enquire; as in the life of *Ahaziah* will appear [2 Kings 1].

With how frequent and costly sacrifices did the *Græcians* adore their Oracle-giving Deities, purchasing an answer with a *Hetacomb*,[52] and with the bloud of a hundred dumb beasts conjuring their dumb Devils, before the sullen Fiends would vouchsafe to answer them?

To pass by the several kinds of madness expressed in *Geomancy*, by Circles in the Earth; *Pyromancy*, by Fire; *Hydromancy*, by Water; *Necromancy*, by the Ghosts of the Dead, we shall descend, and treat your view, to another Inspection of the New Lights of these Dark Times; which appears[53] so visible, that they may be discern'd as far as *Norwich*, where a highflown Spirit, on Sabbath day last was a sevennight, took the impudence to pull down his breeches on the Communion Table, and laid there his most odious and nasty burden: But observe and tremble at the Divine Vengeance; he was suddainly tormented with the griping in his guts; and lamentably roaring out, died within the space of an hour or two. Will any [p. 7] man now say, that this is a Generation of men indued with New Lights: Surely no; for what is more obvious, than the proceeding of these Lights from the Prince of Darkness.

And as there are some, who by their inchanted black Ribbons, tyed about the Creatures left Wrist, gain many Proselytes; so there are others who deny the Lords Day, charging the Ministry of *England* to be Antichristian, and yet seem to be strict in the ways of Holiness. I shall not therefore set bounds to other mens knowledge, nor circumscribe them within the Circle of my own Ignorance; they may have Dawnings, where

I perceive no Star-light: yet take this along with you, that God often in Text-hand declares his Mind, in a Comet, a Blazing-star, and other fiery Apparitions; and not by the vain-bablings of *Magicians* and *Sorcers*; Who may fitly be compared to the great Conjurer that *Picus Mirandulæ* writes of in his time, *viz*. That promising a certain Prince he would present to him the siege of *Troy*, with *Hector* and *Achilles* fighting together as when they were alive: But as he was about his Conjurations, the Devil carried him away that he was never heard of after.[54]

To conclude, As the Jews and Heathens formerly, so many of the Quakers in these days, have been tampering about Futurities, how lawfully I cannot say, and pretend a Vision seen in the Air, betwixt *Kingston* and *London*, figuratively presenting the dividing of the City and *Southwark*; and of the Cities devolving and extinguishing in smoak.

[p. 8] But doubtless, the best way is to acquiesce in Gods revealed Will; for He will have his Children in some sense entertain Fortune by the day, choosing gradually and leasurely to discover the thoughts he hath concerning them, that he might keep them in a waiting and obedient[55] posture, in a posture of dependance and expectation; not that I would have them with *Anacreon* cry out, *Give me to day, let who will care for to morrow;*[56] or with the *Stoicks* lazily expect the blind stroak of a conceited unavoidable Fate; but using all lawful and probable means, endeavour their Countries, and in it their own future good.

FINIS.

A Lying Wonder
DISCOVERED,
AND
The Strange and Terrible Newes from
CAMBRIDGE
proved false.

Which false News is published in a
Libel, Concerning a wicked slander cast upon a
QUAKER, but the Authour of the said
Libel was ashamed to subscribe his
name to it.
ALSO
This contains an answer to *John Bunions*
Paper[57] touching the said imagined witchcraft, which
he hath given forth to your wonderment (as
he saith) but it is also proved a Lye and
a slander by many credible witnes-
ses hereafter mentioned.

LONDON,
Printed for *Thomas Simmons* at the Bull and Mouth
near Aldersgate, 1659.

[p. 3 (incorrectly numbered 2)] Whereas one *Margret Pryor* of *Long Stanton* in *Cambridge* Shire, who hath been taken notice of by several of her neighbours to be a lewd vain woman, of evil conversation, that hath ben seen uncivilly to behave her self, often times in prophaneness and drunkennesse; She hath brought a slander upon some of them called Quakers, in accusing one of them with bewitching her into a Mare, and saying that two of the Quakers did ride upon her when she was a Mare, four miles from the place where she lived, to a banquet, she said, they were at, which thing she having wickedly muttered abroad, some in their hatred against the people of God did instigate the woman to proceed against these whom she thus accused, (as she confessed) to have them Indicted for witches, which was nigh two years after the time that she said she was so ridden; Whereupon some of the Justices at the Sessions having the hearing of this complaint against the Quakers, the two of them accused, and the woman that was their accuser were called to make their appearance before Judge *Windham* at the Assizes at *Cambridge*, holden the 28. of *July*, (so called, in 1659) and then she the said *Margaret Pryor*[58] brought the same accusation aforementioned against one Widdow *Morlin*, but she said she quitted *William Allen*, whereby the Judge saw her lies and confusion, in her saying that (on the 20 of *November*, in the year 1659)

Widdow *Morlin* took her out of bed from her husband in the night, and that she put a bridle into her mouth, and transformed her into a bay Mare, and rode upon her to *Maddenly* House, where she said they hung her on the latch of the door, and that they went in to the Feast, where she said they had Mutton, Rabbets and Lamb. In all this story she was plainly discovered to be an impudent Liar, to say that they had Lamb at that time of the year, in *November*, or that she being a Mare (as she said) could distinguish of these meats; This is like *John Bunions* Relation, who saith, that she (the said *Pryor*) said she could see who they were a feasting, that they, as they sate at the table did shine so bright [p. 4] as if they had been Angels; and that she heard them at the feast talk of Doctrine, which was a shame for him to have uttered, that a horse could understand what was like Angels, or understand Doctrine; Ye may see *John Bunions* faith, what he hath believed and published to make people wonder at such Lies; and the said *Pryor* hath accused several honest people of good report with being at that feast, whether [*sic*] she said she was ridden; And she told us that it was an evil spirit that took her out of bed, and made her a horse, and yet hath accused Widow *Morlin* with doing it, whom one of her neighbors confessed to the Judg was always counted an honest woman; and moreover *Jo. Bunion* saith in his Paper, that she (the said *Pryor*) told him that she was a bay horse, and yet she told the judge that she was a Mare. So see her Lies, one while saying she was a horse, as she told us, another while saying she was a Mare: and one while saying that it was an evil spirit that made her a horse, another while that it was Widow *Morlin*.

And the Judge said, seeing it was a year and almost three quarters before she did complain, (after she confessed she was so dealt with) he asked her whether or no she was not forced to complain; she answered, she was compelled by a Warrant from the Justices, and forced by them to binde Widow *Morlin* over, and prosecute against her at the Assizes (which Justices were *James Thompson* and *Dudley Pope*)[.] So it appears some were partakers of the womans iniquity, in putting her on to proceed upon such an absurd slander. The Judge asked the said *Pryor* if her hands and feet were not gauled, and if she was not dirty with their riding on her; she answered, her feet were a little sore, but her hands were not sore, neither was she dirty, which doth contradict his words who set out the said Libel, Called *Strange and terrible newes from Cambridge*, for there it is said that she shewed her hands and feet, and that they were lamentably bruised, and changed as black as a coal; so that here both the Accuser and the Libel writter are found Liars, confuting one another, she saying her hands were well, though they were her fore feet, and he saying they were lamentably bruised: The like story she told us, that though her hands were her fore feet when she was a horse (as she said) yet her hands ailed nothing, but her hinder feet were all on a [p. 5] gore blood, which is not at all usual; for horses that travel are the soonest beaten and gauled on the fore feet; but this Lie is like the rest of her accusations. The Judge asked the said *Pryor* How it came to passe that she was not ridden no more; She answered, That she burnt elder bark and her own hair, and the Widow

Morlin came to her house, she said, and after that had no more power over her; The Judge replyed and said to the said *Pryor* the accuser, That she was the Sorsorer, and had used sorcery by her own confession, and said he did perceive *Pryor* to be a whimsycal woman, and was set on by some to do the Widow wrong, seeing she complained a year and nigh three quarters after she said the thing was done to her; and the Judge said he perceived it a meer dream, and a phantasie; whereupon he seeing this said Impudent accuser so in confusion, and so unsavory, slighted her complaint, and the Jury of life and death acquitted the two persons that were accused (in a quarter of an hours time) that were so defamed and slandered by that impudent wicked woman aforesaid, and the Judge commended the Jury for their justice in clearing them. And though she the said *Margret Pryor* did for some time go to the quakers meetings, yet she was never owned by them as one of them, neither do we understand that ever she was come in the least measure into that innocent life which the Quakers are in, whom thus she, and them, that put her on in her wickednesse, have sought to render odious; but her folly was so far made manifest, and her slanders appears so grosse and absurd, that many are ashamed to give the least credit to it. And note, that this said woman told some of us that she was so bewitched as aforesaid after that she left the Quakers, and went to the Church to hear the Minister, which is a shame for any Minister of *England* to own such for their Converts as she is, and to tell of Christians becoming beasts, as in the Libel from *Cambridge* its told; and we know that if such Priests as knew of the said *Pryors* accusation (before the trial) had been clear from her prosecuting of it, they would have stopt her from proceeding (as the Priest of the Town might have done if he had been honest) and the said *Pryor* when she was questioned by the Judge how she came by money to prosecute in the said business, she said she had [p. 6] money lent her, but did not declare of whom she had the money, nor who was the chiefe in setting her on to prosecute.

And as for that said Libel aforesaid, its stuffed with lyes, and confusion, so that it was no marvel that he that wrote it was ashamed to set his name to it, yet his Priest like language we know to savour of the Priests enmity, and he that set it out God will judge him for his impudency and wickednesse, though he hath hid his name, who was so impudent as to accuse the said *Quakers* so publickly with being inchanting witches after that they were acquitted and cleared by Law; which accusation is no lesse crime then accusing Judge *Windham* and the said Jury with favouring and owning witches, in suffering them to live, contrary to Law; and so he hath brought a grosse aspertion and slander both upon Judge and Jury, and upon the people of God.

And werein the said Libel, it is said that she (to wit the said *Pryor*) *was rid from* Dinton *to a town within four miles of* Cambridge, *and that upon the witches alighting off and hanging the bridle upon the pales, the snaffle or bit came out of her mouth, and miraculously she appeared in her created form, to the great astonishment of the neighbours who beheld this unexpected change.*

To which we say that these are grosse lies, and contrary to the womans own confession, who spoke not of *Dinton* (for there is no such town in *Cambridge* shire) nor of being hung on the pales, but on the latch of the door, neither is her name *Mary Phillips*, as is expressed in that libel; neither did ever any of her neighbours behold such a change in her, as to see her either changed into a *Mare* or out of her shape; Let her neighbours be tryed, and see if any of them will grant to any such thing, and let them prove him a lyar that hath dispersed these absurd slanders abroad.

And where its said in that libel, *that her sides were exceedingly rent and torn just as if they were spur-gald, and her smock all bloody.*

To which we say that its a great disgrace and shame to Priests professors and Schollars, that such grosse dirty stuffe should ever be reported or given credit to by them in *Cambridge*, or elsewhere; for beside the falshood of this report, see how grosse it is to tell of *the womans sides being rent and torne, and her smock being bloody*, who also told us, *that her smock was all on a muck sweat, with their riding on her*, as if when she was a mare or horse (as is [p. 7] reported,) she could wear her smock; what, can a horse be ridden in a womans smock? Oh! grosse delusion and folly, that ever *Cambridge* should be so dishonoured, as to have such newes as these proceeding from any of the learned in it; Oh! what a sad thing is it, that those that should be teachers are given up to such stronge delusions, as to believe such lies, but where the well head is corrupt, and dirty, it cannot send forth pure water.

And now to thee *John Bunion* who goes up and down to preach and lookest upon thy self higher then the Priests and many others, In that thou hast also dispersed a paper abroad against the *Quakers*, of what the said *Margaret Pryor* said to thee of her being a horse & ridden upon, thou hast shamed thy self in believing such lyes which thou hast given forth, to render the innocent odious, and to make people wonder like the beast, with thy lying wonder; and thou callest the woman *Good-wife Pryor* (who hath pretended she was bewitched) and thou saist, *she was Rid*; what, thou a preacher to people and so given over to believe lyes, and false dreams which thou hast told, like the false prophets whom God was against? *Jer.* 23.32. and thus thou hast slandered the *Quakers* from the report of a wicked lewd woman, who in the envy and delusion of the devil, hath gon about to vindicate her fals dreams and slanders whereby to murther the innocent; and hast not thou been an incourager of her in this horrible wickednesse, in giving such credit to her, and getting her lyes to publish? And what, will *John Bunions* hearers own him in such reports as these? who hath believed that a woman through witchcraft may be made a horse? which is such a foolish and unsavoury thing, as we never have read of, that ever was acted among all the Magicians or witches of *Egypt*, nor that ever such a thing was known to be among the *Egyptians* when they were the most plagued of all.[59]

And such as imagine the Devil by the power of witchcraft can change a man or woman into the substance and forme of either horse or mare, they would make Gods decree alterable, by which man was set in his own proper place above the beasts; and such would make the Devil a creator, and set him in Gods place, for there is a vast difference in the substance and form of a man or woman from the substance and forme of a horse; Therefore mans substance must be added to, by creating and adding more sub- [p. 8] stance to him, or else he cannot become an horse. But I hope few will believe such grosse delusions as this, which *John Bunion*, and other professors and Priests have believed and reported, as those that are themselves bewitched, who thus are filling up the measure of their iniquities against the innocent, as they did against Gods people of old, who said, *Report and we will Report* [Jeremiah 20:10]; -- and said Christ, *they shall speak all manner of evil of you falsely, for my Name sake* [Matthew 5:11], which suffering we partaking of, we bear it in patience waiting till the Lord avenge our cause against all the witches, Sorcerers, false dreamers, deviners, and slanderers who are our enemies, and against them all we bear witness, and know that the Lord doth excuse and clear us, and washeth away the shameful reproaches and dirt which the wicked casts upon us.

And we know that these said slanders against the *Quakers* are much manifest in *Cambridge* shire to be false, though some of the Priests and *John Bunion* in his witchcraft doth seek to delude and make people wonder, with such prophane and vaine bablings against the innocent as mentioned (which are to be avoided) and their iniquities will be upon themselves, upon whom these scriptures are fulfilled, see *Rom.* 3.28, 29, 30. *and 2 Thes.* 2.10,11.

That this is a true relation aforesaid we whose names are hereto subscribed are witnesses, who were at the hearing and examination of the particulars herein mentioned,

James Blackley Alderman
John Smith Sen.
Robert Letchworth
George Whitehead
John Harwood

Cambridge the 8th of the 6th moneth called *August* [*sic*], 1659.
THE END.

Notes

1 See, e.g., John Taylor, *A swarme of sectaries, and schismatiques* ([London: s.n.], 1641 [1642]).
2 *Religions lotterie, or, The churches amazement* (London: Printed by T.F. for F.S., July 20, 1642), title page.
3 *A Catalogue of the severall sects and opinions in England and other Nations. With a briefe rehearsall of their false and dangerous tenents* ([London]: Printed by R.A., 1647).
4 See, for instance, *Bloody newes from Dover* ([London: s.n.,] Feb. 13. 1647) and *Strange news from the north: or The sectaries sacrifice* (London: Printed by J.M., 1648).

5 For a discussion of the charges of witchcraft levelled by Protestants at Catholics, and vice versa, see Stuart Clark, *Thinking with Demons: The Idea of Witchcraft in Early Modern Europe* (Oxford: Oxford University Press, 1997), 533–537.

6 *A declaration of a strange and wonderfull monster* (London: Printed by Jane Coe, 1646), 4.

7 *A Relation of a strange apparition in an ale-house* (London: Printed for Richard Smethrust, 1641), 1.

8 Peter Elmer, "'Saints or Sorcerers': Quakerism, Demonology, and the Decline of Witchcraft in Seventeenth-Century England," in *Witchcraft in Early Modern Europe: Studies in Culture and Belief*, ed. Jonathan Barry, Marianne Hester, and Gareth Roberts (New York: Cambridge University Press, 1996), 145–179. See also Charlotte-Rose Millar's discussion of the Quaker-witch association in popular pamphlets in *Witchcraft, Emotions, and the Devil in Early Modern England* (Routledge, 2017), 163–169.

9 Thomas Edwards, *The first and second part of Gangraena* (London: Printed by T.R. and E.M. for Ralph Smith, 1646), 4 [of Part II].

10 Julie Crawford, *Marvelous Protestantism: Monstrous Births in Post-Reformation England* (Baltimore, MD: The Johns Hopkins University Press, 2005), 113. Monstrous births have been more fully analyzed by early modern scholars than most other forms of prodigies, with Lorraine J. Daston and Katharine Park's seminal essay "Unnatural Conceptions: The Study of Monsters in Sixteenth- and Seventeenth-Century France and England," *Past & Present* 92 (1981), 20–54, helping to inspire many insightful works in the subsequent decades. For a taste of this work, see, in addition to Crawford's study, Jennifer Spinks, *Monstrous Births and Visual Culture in Sixteenth-century Germany* (London: Pickering & Chatto Publishers, 2009); David Cressy, "Lamentable, Strange, and Wonderful: Headless Monsters in the English Revolution," in *Monstrous Bodies / Political Monstrosities in Early Modern Europe*, ed. Laura Lunger Knoppers and Joan B. Landes (Ithaca, NY: Cornell University Press, 2004), 40–63, and *Travesties and Transgressions in Tudor and Stuart England: Tales of Discord and Dissension* (New York: Oxford University Press, 2000), chapter 2; and Dudley Wilson, *Signs and Portents: Monstrous Births from the Middle Ages to the Enlightenment* (London: Routledge, 1993).

11 Alexandra Walsham, *Providence in Early Modern England* (New York: Oxford University Press, 1999), 194–203, quote at 198.

12 *The Ranters Monster* (London: Printed for George Horton, 1652), title page.

13 Walsham, *Providence*, 69.

14 Walsham, *Providence*, 84–85. Walsham is speaking specifically of curses, which "implied an ability on the part of human beings to summon and manipulate divine power which was at odds with the idea that God preordained and actively brought about each and every event" and did not simply act upon "His creatures' whim or command." The principle holds true for monstrous birth narratives in which parents (especially mothers) pronounced a 'curse' on their unborn child out of erroneous religious beliefs.

15 Crawford, *Marvelous Protestantism*, 21.

16 Original: "furions."

17 The men are discussing the fates of Henry Burton (1578–1648), William Prynne (1600–1669), and John Bastwick (1593–1654), each of whom attacked Archbishop Laud's 'High Church' reforms through sermons or print in the 1630s. As Charles I was head of the Church of England and supportive of Laud, their criticisms brought the three men into conflict with the government; they were arraigned in 1637 on charges of sedition and sentenced by the Star Chamber to heavy punishments, including having their ears cut off.

18 After the Separatist minister Robert Brown (c.1550–1633). The term was applied generally during the seventeenth century to those who wished to radically reform or, barring that, separate from the episcopal Church of England, and to establish a more independent (congregational) church polity.

19 Truly.

20 Either *Miranda* or *Mirando*; the first would be correct. "I sing of wonders."

21 The annotation on the Thomason copy adds "Aug. 23."

22 In the Church as much as in the State.

23 Original: "to oke."

24 The narrative of Ecebolius is recorded in Book III, chapter XIII of the fifth-century church historian Socrates Scholasticus' *Historia Ecclesiastica*.

25 Fussy, overly precise or fastidious.

26 A mistake; Mears-Ashby is in Northamptonshire, as it is correctly identified on the title page.

27 Who blather whatever happens to come into their mouths.

28 From Ovid's description of the creation of the world in his *Metamorphoses*, I.7: *rudis indigestaque moles*, "a rude unordered mass."

29 Probably a reference to Ranulf Higden's fourteenth-century chronicle, the *Polychronicon*, which included descriptions of many fantastic wonders.

30 A 1562 broadsheet used a woodcut and ballad to inform readers of "a monstrous chylde, born at Chychester in Sussex." Unlike the parents in the present pamphlet, those in the ballad were characterized as "of honest & quiet conversation;" the monstrous birth was thus presented as a sign of "the great abuse and vyce" in England generally and as a call for repentance in each individual reader, rather than as a judgment aimed against any one transgressor. "Repent, amende both hygh and lowe," the author, like John Locke, urged, "The woorde of God embrace / To lyve therto, as we should doe / God gyve us all the grace." *A discription of a monstrous Chylde, borne at Chychester in Sussex* (London: by Leonard Askel for Fraunces Godlyf., 1562).

31 Benjamin Guyer, who includes a transcription of this pamphlet in *The Beauty of Holiness: The Caroline Divines and Their Writings* (London: Canterbury Press Norwich, 2012), 54–56, changes *norandi* to *notandi* and translates as, "Now is not the place where they must be observed" (56 n.4). In other words, while Locke has many other examples he might use, he does not consider this pamphlet the appropriate place to discuss them.

32 The Thomason copy has the annotation "march 3," with "1646" crossed out and "1645" written in beside it. The printer has begun the new year (1646) with January 1, whereas Thomason continues to use the Old Style, in which the new year does not begin until March 25.

33 Lancashire was the location of the Pendle and Samlesbury witch-trials of 1612, as well as a witch-scare in 1633–1634 that was popularized in Thomas Heywood and Richard Brome's play *The Late Lancashire Witches* (1634).

34 Archbishop William Laud's 1633 reissuance of the Book of Sports, which allowed certain recreations on Sunday, offended those who saw such activities as a desecration of the Lord's Day. See, for instance, Article XXI of *The first and large petition of the Citie of London . . . for a reformation in church-government* (London: s.n., 1641), 10.

35 Amusing or entertaining, but in this context, probably has the more negative connotation of mockery or scorn, in the sense of poking fun at the "honest protestants."

36 Lawyer William Prynne (1600–1669), doctor John Bastwick (1593–1654), and minister Henry Burton (1578–1648) were foremost in the Puritan attack on the Church reforms introduced by Archbishop Laud. The three were imprisoned in

1637 on charges of sedition and sentenced by the Star Chamber to have their ears cut; although all survived their punishment, they were viewed as martyrs by their compatriots and came to represent the Puritan cause.

37 The tale of Mrs. Haughton's mother and her earless cats may have already been notorious, as it was recounted earlier in the 1640s by both William Prynne himself and the Presbyterian poet John Vicars. For a discussion of the story's evolution, see Julie Crawford, *Marvelous Protestantism: Monstrous Births in Post-Reformation England* (Baltimore, MD: Johns Hopkins University Press, 2005), 140.

38 Original: "Commitree."

39 John Foxe recounted the martyrdoms of Nicholas Ridley and Hugh Latimer, burned at the stake during the Marian regime, in his famous *Actes and Monuments*, and also appended a comment on the fate of the "papistical monster" Stephen Gardiner, Bishop of Winchester. On the day Ridley and Latimer died, Gardiner "sat down with a joyful heart to dinner;" he was immediately "seized with illness" and died after fifteen days of misery. John Foxe and William Byron Forbush (ed.), *Fox's Book of Martyrs: A History of the Lives, Sufferings, and Deaths of the Early Christian and Protestant Martyrs* (Grand Rapids, MI: Zondervan, 1967), 237–238.

40 The Thomason copy includes the annotations "7ber [September] 24" and "1647;" see also imprint information at the end of the pamphlet.

41 Diligent, conscientious.

42 Lerna, located in southern Greece, was the home of the multi-headed Hydra confronted by Hercules, while scholars and mapmakers of the Middle Ages considered the Nile to be the source of a wide range of monstrous creatures. Chet van Duzer, "*Hic sunt dracones*: The Geography and Cartography of Monsters," in *The Ashgate Companion to Monsters and the Monstrous*, ed. Asa Simon Mittman with Peter J. Dendle (Ashgate, 2012), 401.

43 According to the fable, King Midas was cursed by Apollo with a pair of donkey's ears when he dared to insist that Pan's music was better than Apollo's own.

44 Recounted in Book IX of Homer's *Odyssey*.

45 To advise or counsel against (an action, etc.).

46 Thomason copy includes the annotation "March 30th."

47 Original: "fo."

48 Original: "hf."

49 Original: "kis."

50 These examples are from chapter XXI of Thomas Beard's *The theatre of Gods judgements* (London: Printed by Susan Islip, 1648; 4th ed.), 73 and 74–75. Beard's popular work, an augmented translation of the original French text by Jean Chassanion, first appeared in 1597 and went through several editions.

51 In the Old Testament, the Urim and Thummim were set in the high priest's breastplate. Although their precise nature is unclear, passages indicate that God communicated His will through them (see, for instance, Numbers 27:21). The author may be thinking of King Saul, who asked counsel of the Lord but was not answered "by dreams, nor by Urim, nor by prophets," and went instead to the Witch of Endor (1 Samuel 28:6–7); additionally, he may have in mind the rebuke to the Israelites generally for consulting witches rather than God (Isaiah 8:19–20).

52 Misprint for "hecatomb," a public sacrifice of 100 oxen practiced by the Greeks and Romans.

53 Original: "appeass."

54 Recounted in Beard, *The theatre of Gods judgements*, 75.

55 Original: "obebient."

56 The fifth-century BC poet Anacreon was known for his epicurean themes. His works had recently been translated into English by the classics scholar Thomas Stanley, and the author may have had in mind a line from Ode XV: "All my care is for to day; / What's to morrow who can say?" Thomas Stanley, *Poems, by Thomas Stanley Esquire* (London: Roger Norton, 1651), 11.

57 Baptist preacher and author John Bunyan (1628–1688), best known for his allegory *The Pilgrim's Progress*, wrote several works in the 1650s refuting Quaker theology. No copy of a document in which he affirms the story of witchcraft in Cambridge survives, and its existence was dismissed by nineteenth-century biographies as preposterous: "No one can believe that John Bunyan gave credit to such a tale," editor George Offer concluded in 1862. "His reply [to the accusation] was . . . 'God knows that I am innocent'" (George Offor [ed.], *The Whole Works of John Bunyan, Accurately Reprinted from the Author's Own Editions*, Vol. I [London: Blackie and Son, 1862], liv). More recent historians are less dismissive; see, for instance, Richard L. Greaves, *Glimpses of Glory: John Bunyan and English Dissent* (Stanford, CA: Stanford University Press, 2002), 118, and Greaves' biography of Bunyan for the *ODNB*.

58 Marginal note: "Least any should be mistaken touching that Margaret Pryor, note that there are others of that name Pryor in the same Town that are not of her relation: For they fear the Lord."

59 In Exodus 7–12, Moses performs miracles (which the Egyptian sorcerers replicate) and God inflicts plagues on Egypt for the pharaoh's refusal to release the Hebrews from slavery.

7 The removal of the King
'Innocent blood calls for vengeance'

Introduction

On January 30, 1649, having been condemned to death at a controversial trial in the preceding days, Charles I was beheaded on a scaffold outside the Banqueting House at Whitehall. The popular response was almost universally one of shock. The decision even to try the king had been divisive, and now that the deed was done, many who had once supported Parliament—and, indeed, some of those who would continue to support the government in the coming months and years—were stunned by what was nothing less than a monumental departure from tradition. To Royalists, meanwhile, it was the terrible culmination of years of rebellion. Outwardly, as C.V. Wedgwood observed, "tears and silence were the rule, not [hostile] demonstrations,"[1] but in the world of print Parliament's opponents capitalized on both the enormity of what had been done and the widespread unease that accompanied it. The most influential of their works was the *Eikon Basilike*, published less than two weeks after Charles' execution, which purported to be a compilation of the King's reflections and devotions in the days leading up to his death. That Charles wrote all or any of the book is uncertain, to say the least, but "in 1649 it was accepted with gratitude and reverence by the Royalists as the King's authentic record of his troubles, his patience and his faith. It created the vision of King Charles the Martyr in which they needed to believe."[2]

It was also a very powerful polemical vision, one which was taken up in other, less prestigious works as well. As Jason Peacey has demonstrated, the government attempted, during the weeks surrounding the trial and execution, to broadcast news of these polarizing events in a manner favorable to itself,[3] while Amos Tubb has drawn attention to the government's two-pronged approach: shutting down critical presses and saturating the market with works supporting the regicide.[4] Yet despite this effort, Peacey has argued that Parliament's campaign for public opinion was a failure, since accounts of the trial and execution actually fed Charles I's cult.[5] Practically, there may have been widespread cooperation with the existing government; nevertheless, in January 1649 and the years to come,

Royalists continued to memorialize their fallen leader in the ever-popular *Eikon*, in verses, in elegies—and in the kind of providentialist literature that had previously been the almost exclusive purview of Parliamentarians.

Two of the most sensational and subversive of these works appeared the year of the regicide. The understandably anonymous *A Miracle of Miracles* (1649) relays a story that seems to have become widespread in the immediate aftermath of the execution and which appeared in no fewer than three pamphlets that year.[6] The work described, "to the comfort of the Kings friends, and astonishment of his Enemies," the miraculous properties of a handkerchief which had been dipped in Charles' blood and used to heal a girl of the skin disease scrofula, or "king's evil." Such claims were all the more impactful in light of the traditions attached to the disease: medieval and early modern kings were expected by their subjects to touch victims, thus conveying grace and healing while also demonstrating their identification with even the lowliest of their people.[7] For Protestant intellectuals like King James VI/I, the touching ceremony was problematic and perhaps superstitious; nevertheless, the custom was continued, and Charles I touched many during the war and especially after his defeat and imprisonment—including, perhaps, individuals who supported that imprisonment.[8] Paradoxically, "as Charles's political powers diminished, his thaumaturgic ones were thought to increase."[9] From the belief that the King's touch could cure scrofula to the belief that a cloth imbued with his blood could do the same was a simple step; but as Stephen Brogan has pointed out, it would have been even more controversial than the touching ceremony (itself not above suspicion) because of the difficulty of detaching the object from associations with relics and Catholicism.[10]

By contrast, the pamphlet *Vox Infantis* (1649) steered clear of questionable objects but dealt instead in the no-less contentious (though highly popular) business of prophecy. Like astrology and other forms of providentialist literature, ancient and purportedly ancient, prophecies were widespread; what is especially intriguing about this pamphlet is the intersection of prodigy and prophecy, for rather than simply conveying a prediction from, say, Merlin, it told of a baby found in a field who had prophesied the downfall of those who had condemned Charles I, as well as the return of Charles II to sit in triumph on his ancestral throne. This main narrative was preceded by some of the other wonders that had occurred in recent years to dissuade England from its path of sin, such as a celestial battle in 1648 and a rain of blood in the portentous year of 1649; in this instance, however, the prodigies had a Royalist cast, rather than the Parliamentarian one they had so often worn in earlier years. Likewise, on the eve of the Restoration a decade later, *The Five Strange Wonders* (1659) saw the eponymous prodigies as warnings to the present tyrannical government and spoke of signs that boded ill "for those that shall assume the Royal Dignity without Authority" (p. 5). These and other such narratives skillfully linked the prodigy genre with the prevalent belief that the monarch was anointed by God to rule, and that rebellion against him—especially rebellion that went to the extreme of trying and beheading him—constituted a sin against God and the natural order. Where prodigies had been employed to critique the king's political and religious policies and to lament the nation's failure to fully reform and shake off the vestiges of Catholicism, they now graphically symbolized God's judgment upon a land whose subjects had rebelled against the ruler He had set over them. As *The English Devil* (1660), transcribed here in Chapter 4, put it: the English people during the Interregnum could not or would not say, "God save the King," and until they did so, they cried in vain for God to bless their ploughs. The political situation and the physical world were interlinked.[11]

The Royalist use of prodigies to critique those who resisted the monarch can, however, be overstated. For instance, Jerome Friedman has argued that concern about rebellion dominated popular literature throughout the years of the Civil Wars and that Royalists always commanded the authoritative position when it came to propaganda.[12] Yet it has hopefully become clear that it was usually the opposition who dominated the press—a point stressed by Peter Elmer, who notes that during the Personal Rule in particular, "providentialism . . . was monopolized by those most critical of Charles' regime."[13] Moreover, even after the monarchy had been abolished, Royalists were not alone in observing prodigies, neither did all such events that went to print carry an explicitly pro-Stuart message (as Friedman has suggested). While the regicide provided fodder for opponents of the government, the twists and turns of the following decade also provoked discussions of prodigies from those who made their political allegiances less overtly known. Such is the case with Ellis Bradshaw's *A True Relation of the Strange Apparitions Seen in the Air* (1650), in which he interpreted two unusual rainbows as a condemnation of those who had "laid aside their Covenant-Engagement" (p. 1) and lamented at length the many differences in opinion over matters both political and religious. Although he was clearly dissatisfied with the current situation, he left his own political preferences unstated, and the work suggests, if anything, more inclination to support the government than otherwise. Later that same year, when the Scots, England's former allies, signed a treaty with Charles II and an invasion of England seemed imminent, the pamphlet *Strange Newes from the North* (1650) reminded readers of old and reported new prodigies in the northern counties, "the Lord warning us as it were thereby, not only of our late troubles, but of the continuance thereof" (p. 1). His solution, however, was not for England to repent of regicide and bring the Stuart heir back to the throne; on the contrary, he insisted that the government apply itself with greater rigor to securing the North against the Royalist threat.

Prodigies, then, were as equivocal as always, capable of being interpreted on the one hand as signs of divine wrath for the execution of the King, and on the other as admonitions for the republican government to watch its back and secure the nation's borders. Nevertheless, it is true that in the loss of their leader and their fall from political power, the Royalists after

1649 paradoxically commanded a better position from which to exploit the continued occurrence of signs and wonders. Prodigies had been employed over the last several decades to critique the intertwined political and religious policies of the (monarchical) government; now that the government was that of Parliament and, later, Oliver Cromwell's Protectorate, supporters of the would-be King Charles II continued the oppositional tradition through miracles, portents, and prophetic infants. Later, when the monarchy was restored in 1660, opponents of the new Stuart order would likewise take their opposition to the press with the influential *Mirabilis Annus* pamphlet series—and the tables, at least as far as prodigies were concerned, would again be turned.[14]

————◆————

Vox Infantis.
OR,
THE PROPHETICALL CHILD.

*Being a true Relation of an Infant that was found in a
Field, neere* Lempster, *in* Herefordshire, July 16.
1649.

*That did Declare and Fore-tell of many Strange things that
Shall ensue in* England and Ireland, *within the space of
three yeeres.*

Concerning the Crowning of CHARLES *the second
King of* England, Scotland, *and* Ireland; *His
great Victories, with the Destruction of this present*
Parliament *and* Army; *and many other passages touching the Death of our late King.*

*This Relation is Attested to bee True, as appeares by the
hands of severall Witnesses annexed to the Booke.*

LONDON, Printed in the yeere 1649.[15]

[p. 1] STRANGE NEWES
OUT OF
Hereford-shire.

THE workes of the Lord are wonderfull! And the Heavens declare his
handy worke: Before the day of Judgement Signes shall appeare in the
Firmament, and Wonders upon the face of the Earth; Nation shall rise
against Nation, and Kingdome against Kingdome, there shall bee Famines[,]
Pestilences and Earthquakes in divers places: False Prophets shall arise,
Rebellion, Murther and Desolation in all places; Factions, Schismes and
Heresies in the Church; and Distractions, Feares and Oppressions in the
Common-wealth. Are not all these Judgements fallen upon us? For the
nationall Sinnes of this Kingdome are these things come to passe? Who
lookes upon these bloody and unnaturall Warres which have continued the
space of seaven yeeres amongst us? Where the most flourishing Kingdome in
the Christian World, is now become the *Theater* of Misery, and a Spectacle
of Lamentation; where Brother hath slaine his Brother, and the Sonne hath
not spared to sheath his Sword in the Bowells of his Father[.] *England*! The
Glory of *Europe*, is now become the [p. 2] Scæne or Stage of Rebellion,
Blood and Murther. A Den of Vipers. A Cage of Uncleanenesse; and a

Nursery of all Sects and Schismes. The Subjects of the most virtuous Prince that ever swayed the Scepter in this Kingdome, have made it no Sinne or Guilt to Sacrifice the Blood of their Soveraigne to their ambitious Fury.

How many forerunners of these our Calamities and Sorrowes have beene heretofore Declared and Predicted, to forewarne us of the Evils to come; but wee have rejected and contemned them as Erronious and Ridiculous, but our sufferings have made us sensible what our Sinne and security hath brought upon us.

I shall, for your better information, particularize some of the most remarkable Miracles and Wonders that have appeared in these latter times.

As for instance; At *Bradford*, in *York-shire*, in the yeere of our Lord one thousand six hundred forty eight, there appeared in the Ayre the visions of two severall Armies, in Batalia skyrmishing one against another, with Colours flying, the sound of Drumms were perfectly heard, and the noyse of Musquett-Reports, which continued the space of three houres; to the admiration of many hundreds that were Spectators, and shortly after it vanished.

Againe, neere *Skipton* in the same Countie, not farre from *Denton* (where the Ld. Generall *FAIRFAX*[16] was born) in the yeere of our Lord one thousand six hundred fourty nine, it rayned blood, of which my selfe was an Eye-witnesse, in the company of many more.

In the same yeere (at six of the clock in the morning) being in *June*, two Sonnes appeared, and continued visible the space of two hou[re]s.

What inordinate Thunders, Tempests and Earth-quakes hath beene of late yeeres; great and impetuous Winds, and stormy weather, losses at Sea, with great Inundations on the Land.

[p. 3] At *Dublin* in *Ireland*, in the yeere of our Lord one thousand six hundred fortie, Another wonderfull sight in the Sky, where thousands of Byrds, called *Sterlings*, did meete neere the City, like two Armies, and fought; untill many were killed, and fell in great multitudes on the Earth.

The like was neere *Scarborough*, not farre from *Rippon* in *Yorkeshire*, in the yeere one thousand six hundred foury-foure, where thousands of Crowes, called Rookes, did meete and fight in two bodies, untill an innumerable company were killed and fell upon the ground.

In *Norfolke*, in the yeere of our Lord one thousand six hundred forty five, a Childe was borne, who presently spake some certaine things that should ensue in these times, and lived not above two houres.

In *Buckingham-shire* in the yeere one thounsand six hundred fourty nine; A Child was borne (neere *AEsbury* [Aylesbury]) that declared some strange passages, which should happen in this Kingdome, and lived not above three dayes, but dyed.

But I shall forbeare to mention any more in this Nature (because I would not seeme tedious to the Reader:) And now to the Relation of this strange and miraculous Wonder I promised you, which is Attested by many sufficient eye Witnesses there present, that will averre and manifest this Relation for a Truth, against the incredulous and unbeleeving times.

On *Monday July* the sixteenth, one thousand six hundred fourty nine, neere *Lempster* in *Hereford-shire* (hard by a Village called the *Hope*, not farre from *Corfe-Castle*) Certaine Workemen or Mowers, that went to cut downe Grasse or Hay, in a very large and spacious Field containing above threescore Acres, and being at their laborious Worke (betwixt the houres of ten and eleven) they heard the Crying of an Infant or a young Child, which they imagined to bee in the middle of the Field; but pausing a little while with giving attention to it, not without admiration; they concluded unanimously, or all of them, to goe to the place from whence they heard the Voyce, and comeing [p. 4] to the place in the middle of the Grasse or Field, they found a young Child, which was wraped up in Swadling Clout[h]s, and to their Judgements appeared not to bee above a quarter of a yeare old: standing thus amazed with their eyes fixed upon the Child, at last resolved to take it up, and to make some of the chiefe of the Towne acquainted with this Accident. But one of the Mowers or labouring Men (having never a Child at all,[)] replyed hee would take it home as his owne, the rest of them having made it knowne to the Towne, the Child was brought to a house, where the Inhabitants round about flocked together to see this Child; after every ones Censure was past upon this Infant, they provided some sustenance for it, suspecting it was hungry, which was Milke and Flower boyled in it (which that Countrey calleth Pap;) the Child eating very heartily of it, and being therewith satisfied, begun to speake to all the People there present, and told them that it was the best meate hee did ever eate, which Miracle in an Infant so young, bred admiration and astonishment in all the Spectators.

This Child told them further, That the Warres of *England* should continue three yeares longer, and that *Charles* a young King, whose Father was put to death by seventeene of his Subjects that Conspired his death long before, who for Acting such a bloody Tragedy shall come to untimely ends, not any of them shall dye in their Beds; saying also, that Innocent Blood calls for vengeance; and that which they spilt in the first Moneth,[17] shall in the same Moneth prove their destruction, and His Sonne bee restored to the Crowne of England.

Againe, this Child further related; that the Kingdome of *Ireland* shall Proclaime him King of His Fathers Realmes; and bee the landing place from all his Troubles and Exile: and after that, hee shall Conquer *England* againe, and shall destroy his and his Fathers enemies, and bee a great and Powerfull Prince: Then shall this land Flourish againe: And in that Field where hee was found shall bee a great and Bloody Battell fought, greater then any yet hath beene in this Kingdome, where the young King, CHARLES, [p. 5] *the Second* of that name, shall get the day, and win the Field.

The People and Inhabitants thereabouts, hearing these sayings, proceeding from an Infant, were struck into great amazement, and after the Child had done speaking, they resolved how to provide for him; but he Answered again, take no care for Me; and withall desired they would carry Him to the place where they found Him, which, according as hee

Commanded them, they did: And being brought to the place they laid him downe, hee thanked them, and wished them all to love one another, and relieve the oppressed, and succour the fatherlesse and the widow, feare God and hee will blesse your Labour, bee no time servers, meddle not with them that are given to change; observe these sayings, your reward shall bee in Heaven: My time is set; I have no more to say, but now shall leave you[.] Uttering these words, *Glory bee to God on high, peace on earth, &c.* and so vanished away.

Some of the Inhabitants doe believe it to bee an Angell sent from Heaven; some are of opinion, that it was a Child newly borne, and left there by the Mother, unto whom God gave Power and Strength to reveale his Will; but it hath left a deepe Impression in the hearts of some of them. This Copy was taken by one that was both an eye and eare witnesse of these sayings and predictions, which this Infant revealed to all. His time of abode and continuance with us was about three houres.

This Relation was Communicated from *George Colly* of *Hope* neere *Lempster*, to a friend in *London* to bee published in Print, desiring three hundred Copies to bee sent him to bestow upon friends.

The Witnesses that attest this Relation to bee Truth in every Particular; are, *Sampson Jones* Gent. *Henry Shipman, Richard Williams, John [. . .]*[18]

————◆————

A
MIRACLE
OF
MIRACLES:

Wrought by the Blood of
King CHARLES the First
Of happy memory,

Upon a Mayd at *Detford* foure miles
from *London*, who by the violence of the Disease
called the *Kings Evill* was blinde one whole yeere;
but by making use of a piece of Handkircher
dipped in the Kings blood is recovered of her sight.

To the comfort of the Kings friends, and astonishment
of his Enemies.

The truth hereof many thousands can testifie.[19]

LONDON,
Printed *Anno Dom.* 1649.[20]

[p. 2] *A Miracle of Miracles.*

LOVING Countreymen, this is a briefe and faithfull Relation of a Mayd dwelling and living now in *Detford*, foure miles distant from *London*, daughter to M^ris *Baylie*; which mayd being about the age of fourteen or fifteen yeers, hath long time been grievously tormented with the disease which is called the *Kings Evill*,[21] which evill continued its force so long upon her, that it putrified and corrupted, not onely the unseen parts of her body, but her face and her eyes, in so much that she became blinde therewith. Her mother being a carefull and loving woman, having more regard to the welfare of her childe, then she had to the wealth of the world, endeavoured (as farre as her Purse or pains would extend) to do her good. But alas, all that ever she could do was but lost labour, only through Gods great mercy she kept the Girle alive, though her pains every day increased more and more. Yet notwithstanding this, M^ris *Baylie* sought to many skilfull folks, hoping in time to have some remedy for her daughter; amongst others, she imployed one M^r. *Stipkins*, a man of very good knowledge [p. 3] and understanding in the practice of Surgery, being very well approved of for his skill both in the City of *London* and many parts of the Countreys adjacent: This Mr. *Stipkins* often frequented Mistris *Baylies* house in hope to cure her daughter of the Evill; but all he could doe would little prevaile, though for a time, while he was present, she found some ease, yet when he was gone from her she became as bad or worse then she was before; so that all the help that man could do could

not cure her disease: wherefore those that were neighbours dwelling neere unto
her perswaded her mother even to give over, and let God work his will with her;
& some others that ministred to the Damsell, bid her, serve God and be content, and prepare for Heaven, for there was no likelihood of long remaining in
this World. And thus was the poore silly soule past all hopes of recovery, being
discomforted with words, blind of her sight, forsaken by the Physicians, and left
off by acquaintance. But yet for all these doings the Lord provided for this poore
creature such a miraculous blessing, whereby to preserve her life, and cure her
blindnesse, the like was never known since our Saviour Christ and his blessed
Apostles lived on the Earth, as will appeare by this following Discourse.

[p. 4] *Here followeth a true and faithfull Discourse concerning the
daughter of Mistris* Baylie, *who had been a long time possessed of the disease called the* Kings Evill: *and how at last she was cured by a Handkircher
that was dipt in the Kings Blood that day he was beheaded.*

IT is an old saying and a true, that when men and women are at weakest,
then is God full as strong, and the same God he was before; as may appeare
by these examples which are here set down. Though the three Children (we
read in the Scripture) were cast into a fiery Furnice, the Lord sent an Angel to
deliver them out. Though *Daniel* was cast into the Denne amongst Lyons, yet
God provided so for him, they had no power to hurt him [Dan. 6:22]. Though
Jonas was cast into the depth of the Sea, the Lord sent a Whale to bring him to
Land [Jon. 1:17, 2:10]. Though *Job* was tormented and buffeted by the divell,
the Lord restored him to his former estate [Job 42:12]. Though *Paul* suffered
shipwrack, yet the Lord suffered him not to be utterly lost [Acts 27]. Though
the man spoken of in the Gospell was borne blinde, which no man could cure,
yet the Lord Jesus Christ could curse him by working a Miracle upon him, by
annoynting his eyes with Clay, whereby he re- [p. 5] ceived sight [John 9:1–7].
Even so hath the Almighty Lord of Heaven restored this poor forlorn Mayd of
Detford to her sight again, by way of Miracle, and thus it was:

It hapned, by Gods appointment, that one Master *John Lane*, now living in
London in the *Old-Change*, a Woollen Draper by profession, hearing of the
misery that M^ris Baylies daughter was in, he having a Handkircher about him
which had been dipped in the Kings blood on the day that he was beheaded.
This Mr *Lane* gave her a piece of the same Handkircher, which the mayd
tooke, and applied to her sores, and wiping her eyes with the bloody side of
the Handkircher, hath through Heavens providence recovered her eyesight,
and is become lusty and strong, and able to doe any thing abroad and at
home, as is fitting for one of her age and growth to doe, and many hundreds
of people come daily to see her both from *London* and other places; and all
that ever saw her in her sicknesse, and sees her now in health, do confesse that
it is a work the Lord hath done, whereby his Name might be glorified, and the
Kings death thought upon. And those that desire to know further of the matter, may both see and talke with the Mayd at her mothers house at *Detford*.

[p. 6] And now beloved Christians, let us consider what a precious Jewell
we lost, when we parted from our Kings life; whose Blood after his death was
of such a valuable vertue, that it made the blinde to see, by no other meanes
but by stroaking and applying the Handkircher to the soarnesse of the places

where her griefe lay, which she did morning and evening. And though, by Gods good pleasure this one poore creature hath recovered her life by his death, yet there are many thousands that stand in great need of helpe for the same Disease, which never can be cured, for want of a King that can safely say, *I touch, God heals.* Now there are some that will say, why doe not all them that are troubled with the *Kings[ ]Evill,* make suit & get some of the Kings Blood to cure them? the answer is, that it is not to be had for love nor money; for where any is, they either keepe it secretly, or if it be known, they will not part from it. But it fared better with such poor distressed souls while the King lived, for he was so gracious, that when there were a numberlesse company of poore distressed people, he would appoint them a time to give them a visit, and be as good as His word; and when His patients came into His presence, He scorned not to touch the poorest creatures sores, [p. 7] and handle their wounds to doe them good, while the corruption of their Diseases ranne upon his Princely fingers, and by the virtue of the same they had their perfect cure. Where is the man to be found that now can doe so? surely not alive in *England.* Here are them left that can kill the Kings friends; but here are none that can cure the Kings Evill.

And now I hold it not amisse to speake something of the happy estate that we lived in while the King lived, and how our fortunes are crost by His death; and this shall be done by way of comparison. First, suppose there were a rich man living, as *Job* was at the first, having many children, plenty of servants, store of Corne on the ground, and Cattell in the field, and flocks of sheep feeding on the pleasant mountaines: would it not greatly grieve this rich man to part with his children, to forg[o]e his riches, to be turned out of his habitation, to be cast in prison, and to have his servants banished out of his sight? Even so fared our Soveraigne Lord King *Charles,* His Wife was banished, His Children dispersed, His Servants disinherited, His goods taken from Him, and at last His Princely Head brought to the Block, which well may make the heart of every Christian tremble to think on.

[p. 8] In the holy Book of God is written thus, *Touch not the Lords Anoynted, nor doe my Prophets no harme.* And in I *Pet.* 2.17. we are forewarned, to *feare God, and honour the King.* Exod. 22.20. *Thou shalt not speake evill of the King.* Eccles. 10.20. *Curse not the King in thy thought.* But alas, how far is the feare of God hidden from our eyes! How many times hath *Charles* the first, the Lords Anoynted been, not onely toucht, but buffeted, kickt and spurnd at? How many seditious persons have been suffered to speake evill against his Majesty, and with spitefull tongues and slanders scandalize and abuse him to his face? yea, how many thousand envious Matchevils have not onely cursed him in their thoughts, but openly said, they hoped to wash their hands in His hearts blood? And last of all, instead of *Feare God, honour the King,* they have forgotten their duty to both.

To conclude, he was a *Salomon,* for wisdome; a *David,* for courage; and a *Job,* for patience. He was a forgiver of injuries, a lover of Religion, a hater of lewdnesse, a friend to his enemies, a maintainer of the Truth, Defender of the Faith, a protector of his Subjects, and a help of the poor. The Lord in mercy send that no worse come in. [*sic*] His place now he is gone from us.

FINIS.

STRANGE NEWES

From the *NORTH*.

CONTAINING

A True and ·exact Relation of a great and terrible
Earth-quake in *Cumberland* and *Weſtmerland*, With the miraculous Apparition of three glorious Suns that appeared at once. And o-
ther wonderful Appearances that happened in *Yorkeſhire*, of divers bodies
of armed men marching, and riding through every Town for twelve miles
compaſs about *Malton*, with the ſtrange accidents that befel the Cattel
therabout through fright thereof, to the admiration of many thouſand beholders. Together with, the Charge againſt *Charles Howard* Eſquire High
Sheriff of the County of *Cumberland*.

Uerefied by ſeverall Gentlemen of known and approved credit.

LONDON, Printed by *J. Clowes* and are to be ſold at the *Royal Exchange*
and without *Cripplegate, June* 11. 1650.

Figure 7.1 Title page, *Strange Newes from the North*, 1650.

STRANGE
NEWES
From the *NORTH.*
CONTAINING
A True and exact Relation of a great and terrible
Earth-quake in *Cumberland* and *Westmerland*. With the miraculous Apparition of three glorious Suns that appeared at once. And o-
ther wonderful Appearances that happened in *Yorkeshire*, of divers bodies
of armed men marching, and riding through every Town for twelve miles
compass about *Malton,* with the strange accidents that befel the Cattel
therabout through fright thereof, to the admiration of many thousand beholders. Together with, the Charge against *Charles Howard* Esquire High
Sheriff of the County of *Cumberland.*

Verefied by severall Gentlemen of known and approved credit.
[Figure: *depiction of Tynemouth Castle*]
LONDON, Printed by *J. Clowes* and are to be sold at the *Royal Exchange*
and without *Cripplegate, June* 11. 1650.

[p. 1] STRANGE
NEWES
FROM THE
NORTH.

SIR,

I Have often mentioned in my letters to you, the many and marvelous signs
and sights, which before and since these Warrs, have been seen in these our
Northern parts, the Lord warning us as it were thereby, not only of our
late troubles, but of the continuance thereof; if by righteous judgements
our Governors do not appease his anger, I formerly related to you how
shortly after the *Scots* march into *England* in aide of our Parliament, it
rained blood, and covered the Church and Church-yard of *Bewcastle* in
Cumberland, of three Suns seen there the day before *Edg-hill* battle, and
a little before *Hambleton* with his Army came into *England*, two Armies
[p. 2] were in Yorkshire, seen in the aire vissibly, discharging and shooting one against the other; and seemingly after a long fight, the Army which
rose out of the North, first vanished. This last Winter in the North we have
had very strange and fearful storms, with much thunder and lightnings;
But to admiration that of the 18. of *January* last was most remarkable, in
the night time the storm began very fearfully, Armies and Armed Troops,
(in every town for twelve miles compass about *Molton* in Yorkshire) were
heard to ride and march through the Towns; their Cattle and beasts in these
Towns, were so frighted with the storm, as most of them broke out of their

pastures, some breaking their necks and some their legs, in this madding fit, some run away four miles, some more, who when found and brought home, were so wild and heated, as if they had been chased with a hundred mastive Dogs; one Oxe where he lay in a stake-yard lame, and not able to rise without the help of man, in this storm broke out, and the next day was found lying above a mile from the place he was in the night before, and was brought home on a sledge; for a month after the the [*sic*] storm, the beasts thereabouts run madding about, and would not be kept in their Pastures, people were so astonished therewith, as for a long time they had little other discourse then of the strangness of the storm. I see a Relation of three Suns, lately seen about *Manchester*; but sure it is, that in the beginning of *March* last, there were seen at one time in *Cumberland* and *Westmerland*, three glorious Suns, to the admiration and great astonishment of many thousands of the beholders.

And further, upon the 11. of *April* last about 5. of the clock in the afternoon, in the Counties of *Cumber-* [p. 3] *land* and *Westmerland*, we had a general Earth-quake; the people were so frighted therewith, that they forsook their houses, and some houses were so shaken, that the Chimnies fell down; Some may doubt and question the verity of these things, be confident I have related nothing but what I know to be true, and have had from men of known and approved credit. These things I thought good to communicate to you, as I have done before things of like nature; for news we have little in these parts, only great fear of the *Scots* invading us again; I could wish our honorable Parliament and Councel of State, as they are very sensible of the ensuing threatned troubles, and for prevention whereof, as they have increased their forces: so they would be pleased, to make diligent inquiry of all in Magistracy, how they stand affected to the Common-Wealth under this present Government, especially in these our bordering Counties, which will be a dore to let in, or kepe out any enemy from *Scotland*. Here the honest party are much cast down, our Justices of the Peace do countinance such Ministers as be against the Engagement, and Mr. *Baldwin* the Lecturer of *Penreth* and other Ministers there, have had sundry privat meetings, and do work privatly against the subscribing the Engagement, if somewhat be not speedily done herein, all our County will be against the Engagement. Our new Sheriff of *Cumberland*[22] the most powerful man of the County, we find he hath been in Arms, both in the first and second War; and now hath for his Agent and Councellor, one *Lawyer Fallowfeild* a profest *Papist*, and now said to be a Priest; and the other day came from the *Irish* Rebels (as I hear) in *Ireland*. How in the last War our Sheriff behaved him- [p. 4] self, by the Charge and proof before the Commissioners for Sequestrations in *Cumberland* against him wil appear, a Copy thereof being come into my hand I send you, desiring it may be published for publick good. It were good the Councel of State would take notice of those, who recommend such dangerous persons to so great offices of trust; by this means honest men are still kept under, and till such be removed out of these places of trust, we are never the more secure for all our great successes and victories; for our enemies though they have lost their swords in battle, yet by regaining the sword of authority, are in hopes to recover their former estate, and bring us under them; in the mean time, by their ill Government they do disaffect the people, and bring them in dislike of the present Government, and oppress the honest party, and will be ready as formerly, to invite a forraign enemy, and at home raise tumults and insurrections upon any opportunity; therefore I pray improve your interest & credit, that such with[ ]us as have been in Arms against the Parliament, may no longer continue in such great places and offices of trust, and I shall as opportunity serves from time to time, let you know the state of our County, in the mean time, I bid you farwel.

Penreth 30. *May T.C.*
1650.

[p. 5] *The Charge against* Charles Howard *Esquir*
High Sheriff of the County of Cumberland,
Exhibited to the Commissioners *for*
Sequestrations in Cumberland.

THAT the said Mr. *Howard*, having a Commission to be a Col. for the King in the last war, which he did confess was as large as any man had, did by vertue therreof, send out his warrants to the several Constables of *Gilsland* for three several musters; Requiring, all men above sixteen, and under threescore to appear before him at *Brampton,* And the Constables to present their names upon *Thursday* the 10. of *August*, 1648. and the fourteenth, and the sixteenth day of the said moneth following at the several days, the said Mr. *Howard* came to the abovesaid place, accompanied with many Soldiers in Arms, under his command, and gave order for freequarter[23] for his Soldiers; And that the Constables should Leavy monies to pay for the horses he took in every place.
Proof to this Article,
Tho. Milburn.
Tho. Bell.
Anthony Hevyside.

Secondly, That the said Mr. *Howard*, took 10. horses in *Hayton* parish for the said service, and proportionably in other parishes within *Gilsland* according to the purvey.
Tho. Bell abovesaid,
Anthony Heviside.

Thirdly, That the said Mr. *Howard*, did declare openly at the said Musters, that the men and Horse so levyed, was for the Kings service; And that he was to meet the Prince with his men at *Barwick* Satturday the 19. of *August* following.

Tho. Milburn.
Tho. Bell.

[p. 6] Fourthly, The said Mr. *Howard* sent a Letter to ten Cavileers that had horse and Arms, quartering upon *Leonard Hodgson* Constable of *Hartleburn* in *Northumberland*, That if they would ride in his Troop to *Barwick* as Reformadoes, they should have Command as places fell; and they should come to *Francis Grames* of the Stone house in *Gilsland*, and there abouts they should have quarter till they marched to *Barwick*.

Proof to this Article
Leonard Hodgson.

Fifthly, The said Mr. *Howard*, repared several times to the enemies Garrison at *Carlile*, and walked abroad with his Arms.
Richard Hutton.

Sixthly, At two several Musters by warrant from the said Mr. *Howard* in the first Article mentioned, the said Mr. *Howard* had made his speeches to the Country, his Soldiers drew their swords and cryed, a King a King.
Thomas Addison.

This Charge was presented to us, and the several witnesses names to every Article, that will make good the same.
Tho. Craister.
John Musgrave.
John Priscoe.
Thomas Laughorne.

FINIS.

———◆———

A TRUE
RELATION
Of the Strange
APPARITIONS

Seen in the Air, on *Monday* 25. *February,*
in and about the Town of *Bolton* in the Mores,
in the County of *Lancaster* at mid-day, to the
amazement of the Beholders.

Being a LETTER sent from
ELLIS BRADSHAW
OF THE
Same Town, to a Friend in *London,*

WITH
OBSERVATIONS
Thereupon, what probably they may signifie, and
what Use may be made thereof.

LONDON,
Printed for *Tho. Brewster* and *Gregory Moule,* and are to
be sold at the three Bibles in the *Poultry,* under *Mildreds* Church, 1650.[24]

[p. 2] *SIR,*

There hath appeared to us such visible characters of the Infinite power here,
of the mighty, miraculous, and clear Demonstration of the hand of God,
which as visible signes of his invisible Power, and of his Will and Decree, he
hath held forth to us perspicuously[25] and apparantly in the open sight of all
beholders, that did but lift up their eyes to behold the same in the azure Skie,
that the like hath not been seen in any Age, that is as yet recorded in any
History that I have ever read or heard of, either here, or in any Kingdom:
And though, it may be, that the same was visible as well with you, as in
our horizon, yet because we know not how far it appeared, as it did unto
us, I could do no less then write the Relation of such strange Apparitions,
in regard the publishing thereof, if you think it convenient, might greatly
tend to the glory of God, and the good of all those that desire to observe,
and to consider the operations of his mighty hand, which he holdeth forth
as a warning to us, of some great thing that he is about, and hath fully
determined to bring to pass within a short time, even in this our Nation, if
not in this our County, to whom this Apparition was miraculously visible.

However it appeared, or whether it appeared or no unto other people, for we cannot tell; and therefore if it be no news nor strange unto you, it may well excuse me for writing of it, that if it be news you might know it first, and so declare it first, if you think good, as I shall here relate it, and descant[26] upon it, what it may possibly signifie, according to my apprehension.

The thing was thus, Yesterday being *Munday, February* 25. 1650. being our Market day at *Bolton* in the Mores in the County of *Lan-* [p. 3] *caster*, betwixt ten and twelve of the clock, and much of that time there appeared to us, yea to all in the Town, or in the way thither, that look so high, A white Circle, compassing directly from the glorious Sun shining in his strength, (the Skie being clear, and not overspread with clouds, or mist, &c.) straight into the North, as it were of a levell height, with the height of the Sun, compassing round to the Sun again, as if it had been a wall, and the Sun a Postern in the side of it. And besides the true Sun, there appeared also a great way distant on either side the Sun, a bright place in the aforesaid Circle, not unlike in greatness to the true Sun, but not so bright nor formable,[27] but rather red and changeable, especially at its vanishing; like part of a bright Rainbow, or as we call them, Weather-Galls, though far brighter, and more clear and splendrous to all beholders when they were at brightest. There appeared also in the Northern parts of the same Circle, two other likewise, which like bright places of the same colour, but not so bright and splendrous: All which four were set directly in the white Circle, like so many Postern Towers in the walls of a City, a great way distant each from other[.]

There appeared likewise directly over our heads, two fair Rainbows in the clear Skie, the one tending with either end of it, towards the two bright places, that were next to the Sun, though they did not reach them. And the other tending with both its ends, as directly pointing to the other two places, that were in the Northern parts of the white Circle, that shined also as hath been said; So that these two Rain-bows, that were directly over our heads, tended with their backs together, and their ends directly one from the other; the one Southwards, and the other Northwards; the one as inclining to embrace the Sun, and the other to embrace the North Pole.

All these visible Apparitions continued a great while, some say two hours, but of the certain time I am not certain, for I saw them not at first: but I saw them vanish by degrees away, beginning in the North; for the North-side of the white Circle began to vanish first, and then the two bright places in the North of the Circle did also first vanish before the other, and so also did the North Rainbow, and then by degrees the other also, so that the nearer to the Sun, was the longer visible, not only of the Rain-bows, but of the bright places, and of the white Circle.

From all which visible appearances, if I may not seem over-bold [p. 4] and presumptuous, being but such a man: I shall desire to descant, and conclude thus far, as my own apprehensions, what these things mean, or at least, what use we had best to make of such strange visions and signs in the

Heavens, as are so frequently seen in these days of ours in our own horizons, and by our own eyes.

And first then, in my apprehension, These visible Apparitions are held forth to us, as admonitions of some great displeasure, and of wrath kindled, that must be executed in its time and season.

And that especially against all such, who have laid aside their Covenant-Engagement, whereby they were united each to other, and joyntly bound in their places and callings, even to the Lord himself, to seek and indeavour a full Reformation both in Church and State, according to the word of God, and not to their own inventions, nor as might best serve for their own interests, nor the interests of others, either Civill or Ecclesiastick: For in so doing, we lay aside our Covenant and the Interest of God, who hath hitherto saved us from our common Adversaries.

And therefore, it is observable, that these two Rainbows were not set in the Skie directly upwards in the usuall manner arch-wise, but they were both in appearance to us as laid aside, like two fallen arches, and that with their backs together, so that their four ends were at the furthest distance each from others that they possibly could be; Which may well signifie, that if such who have Covenanted shall desert each other, in regard of mutuall assistance, against the common Enemies of Reformation, they utterly cast down their supporting Arches, and lay aside their Covenants, so that in respect of the Ends of our Covenant-Engagement, they utterly frustrate their mutality, and set them directly at the furthest distance each from other that they possibly can.

For our Covenant-Engagements were chiefly intended for the supportation, strengthening, and incouragement of one another, for else we had not needed any express Covenant, being already bound in duty unto God, and each to other, before we entred into such Engagements, even by the Law of God, which is the Law of Love, and obligeth deeply unto mutuality in all lawfull things.

And I hope no man will say that ever any Rainbow was set in the Skie, but it something concerned Covenant-Engagement betwixt God and man, for there is no other end Recorded in Scripture;[28] and therefore I dare conclude, that it being always set by the hand of God [p. 5] by way of *Memento* both to himself and us; We ought to consider these visible mementos and admonitions, and bethink our selves ere it be too late, and not turn our backs each from others; for any self-respects, or private Interest, turning our ends, through self-ends, to their furthest distance from mutuality, in our common cause, to wit (a throughout Reformation.) but to draw if possible to a neerer distance in our publike ends; and that our Covenant-Engagement might not make us two; but unite us together according to its end, and make as one. That so it might be represented by the sign of the Covenant, to wit by one Rain-bow, and that also, set directly upwards as a supporting arch, and not so unnaturally by two parts or pieces of a Rain-bow, and those laid aside, as writhen[29] about and wrested asunder each from the other, at the furthest distance that can be devised by the art of man: for just so we are, as, if time would permit, I could shew at large; for there is division, and that most sad and lamentable, even amongst those who are not only brethren in name and profession, but in nature also, yea even truly spiritual, and Christian brethren, and that of the very chief of the most eminent in the Church of God, insomuch that it is to be feared, if they take not warning by these visible Characters, but remain stubborn, and obstinate therein, it will end in blood, and that of one another; of which these are warnings to all that will observe.

There is cause that those divisions of Ruben should cause sad thoughts of heart.[30]

One cals that perjury, and Covenant-breaking, which another counteth but the necessary keeping of their Solemn Covenant, in bringing Delinquents to condign[31] punishment.

One cals that murther, which another accounts a Judicial execution of a grand murtherer.

One counts it a breaking off the Parliament, which another accounts but a necessary restraint from inslaving of the Kingdom, which is their (Lord) as some affirm.

One proclaimeth a message from the Lord of Host[s], which another saith is a cleer inhibition of his express command, *Numb.* 35.16, 17, 18, 19. to wit, that the revenger of blood himself, shall slay the murtherer, when he meeteth him: see also, *verse* 20. 21. and 30, 31, 32, 33.

One seemeth zealous for pious Reformation; and another thinketh that he doth but fast for strife, and debate, and to smite with the fist of wickedness.

[p. 6] One cals that Tyranny, Oppression, Cruelty, Wrong, Persecution, *&c.* Which another thinks but a necessary loosing of the bands of wickedness, and an undoing of the heavy burthens, and freeing of the oppressed; yea a breaking of every yoke, as *Isa.* 58.6.

Some are consulting with the Kings of the earth, and the Rulers thereof, against some men whom they think are plotting to insnare, and bind them to their own wils.

Whereas others think, that such consultation is against the Lord, and against his anointed; saying, *Let us break their bands asunder, and cast away their cords from us*; And that he that sitteth in Heaven doth but laugh at them, yea that the Lord himself, hath them in derision. Expecting confidently that yet ere long he will speak unto them in his wrath, and vex them in his displeasure, seeing he hath set his King upon his holy hill of *Sion*, according to *Isa.* 14.20, & to 28. Some advise the Kings and great men upon earth, to stand it out stifly, in the maintenance of their Cause, and not to stoop nor submit their Royal Power, and Royal Authority, to the wils of men; who plead for liberty from all tyrannical oppression, or bondage whatsoever, either Civil or Ecclesiastical; And that all might be forced, will they nill they, to such form of Government, as they themselves in conscience, shall think most just and agreeable to the Scriptures.

But others advise them, to be so wise and learned, as to kiss the Son lest he be angry, and they perish in his wrath; especially now, when it is a little kindled; yea that they should serve him with fear and rejoyce trembling, *Least he break them with a Rod of Iron, and dash them in pieces like a Potters vessel*, as Psal. 2.

Some advise them to serve the Lord, and to Govern, and Rule over his Church and people, in the old manner and form of Government. But others advise them to bring their glory and honor to the New Jerusalem, and to submit their Scepters to the Scepter of Christ, the Scepter of whose Kingdom, is a Scepter of Righteousness, and he the King of kings, and Lord of lords.

One affirms that the oath of Allegiance bindes us chiefly to the defence and maintenance of the persons of Kings, more then their authority, and rather ought to destroy his authority, then not defend his person. And another saith, that his authority ought chiefly to be maintained, yea though directly against both his life and estate; and that we were tyed by our oath of Allegiance to his Just Authority, and not abstractively to his person only, as when acting contrary in a [p. 7] destructive manner, to his Just Authority; And that our Allegiance is no further lawful, then relative to the Kingdom, whereunto even he himself was tyed in Allegiance.

And again that Allegiance, if relative, bindes no further then according to the Laws of relations, and that relations are contractive, and the root of all obligations; which whether natural or otherwise, yet when one party shall seek the destruction of the other, the other may justly claime a recess, so far at le[a]st as absolute preservation requires.

One alledgeth our Protestation, that part of it especially which is for the defence of the Kings person, and for the power and priviledge of Parliament.

But another alledgeth that the sentences are complex, and do take in with them, the Kings honor, and estate, the defence of the power and priviledges of Parliament, the lawful Rights and Liberties of the Subjects, as well as the person of the King.

So that if the person of the King be engaged against the Priviledges of Parliament, and Liberties of the Subjects, yea or the Parliament themselves plead priviledges, against the lawfull rights, and liberties of the Subjects, the protestation cannot be obligatory, unto inconsistences. The lawful rights and liberties of the subjects, being the great end both of the King and Parliament, which they ought to seek, and therefore must prostrate both King and Parliament, they having not so much as their being, muchless priviledges against the lawful rights and liberties of the subjects; So that by the protestation, the greater being (of duty) to be always preferred before the less; If either the person, or the King, or the priviledges of Parliament, stand as a Lyon to devour and destroy the Rights and Liberties of the Subjects; we are bound to know neither King nor Parliament, but rather the people, who are the root of them both, so that it were better they both should perish, then the whole body and bulk of the people.

Again one saith, that our Covenant bindes us to our old form of Government, by Kings, Lords and Commons; and that by Kings Hereditarily, whether they be wise or foolish, so that we must have no other, but such, fool or tyrant, or what ever he proves that shall be heir to the crown.

But another thinks that if we be so bound by our vow and Covenant or Allegiance either; we have therein done as rashly and unlawfully, as those that bound themselves with an oath, neither to [p. 8] eat nor drink, till they had kill[ed] *Paul* [Acts 23:12]. And therefore such an unlawfull vow, is better broken then kept, seeing it can never be proved from Scripture ground; but that though Kingly Government in it self be lawful, yet to oblige a Nation, to Hereditary Government, be they wise, or foolish, can never be proved to be either wise, or lawful in the sight of God, nor any rationall man, if men once may chuse and have power in their hands, through the providence of God, But ought to shake of[f] such necessary bondage, when they can get power, else they are guilty even of self-destruction, through their own counsels.

And thus our Covenant-Engagement, is parted into two, like the two Rain-bows, and is wrested, and turned for every mans end; so that the true ends, are removed quite to the greatest distance that possibly can be one from another, and will end in blood, unless we repent and reconcile these things, and study the things that may make for peace, and for love and concord, as we ought to do: Which the Lord grant that we may do in time, ere it be to[o] late; So he prayeth who is your loving friend and brother in the Lord,

Ellis Bradshaw
Tuesday this 26. of
Feb. 1649.

FINIS.

———————◆———————

More WARNING yet.
BEING
A True Relation
OF
A Strange and most Dreadful
APPARITION
Which was seen in the Air
By several persons at *HULL,*
the third day of this present *Septemb.* 1654.
NAMELY,
Two Great Battels
Fought in the Air:
One Army coming from the East,
AND
Another out of the North-West.
With the maner of their Engagement and
VICTORY.
Enclosed in a Letter[32] from a Godly-Learned Minister of the
Gospel in the said Town of *Hull,* who having diligently
examined the truth thereof, sent it up to be published.
Printed at *London* by *J. Cortrel*; and are to be sold by *Richard Moone,*
at the seven stars in *Paul's* Church-yard.[33]

[p. 1] More Warning yet.

Upon the third day of this present month *September,* a day not only remarkable for two notable & famous Victories which the *English* had over the *Scots,* the one at *Dunbar,*[34] the other at *Worcester;*[35] but observable also, as to be the day appointed for the sitting of this *Parliament:*[36] between nine and ten of the clock at night, there was seen by *James Cook* Corporal, *Thomas Blossome,* and *Edward See,* all souldiers belonging to the Garison of *Hull,* [p. 2] this strange and unwonted apparition.

These being (at the time before mentioned) on the top of the *North-Blockhouse,* having the Watch according to order, on a sudden the skie seemed to be of a fiery colour, and to cast forth many streams. Whereupon, *Thomas Blossome* observing the strangeness of the thing, began to tell the other two, how he had seen the very like appearance a little after the sitting of the first *Parliament*; and after such fiery streams, a great Battel of horse and foot appeared in the air. He had not ended his Relation, but in the *East* appeared a huge Body of *pike-men,* several Parties marching before, as a *Forlorn-hope.*[37] Never saw they in their lives an Army (to their thinking) in better equipage. Suddenly they beheld in the *north-west* another Army, the which seem'd unto them to march towards the *Eastern* Army with extraordinary speed.

And first, there was the representation of some Skirmishes between Parties of each Army, as the *Forlorn-hope*. Afterwards both Bodies did engage, and furiously [p. 3] charged each other with their Pikes, breaking thorow one the other backwards and forward, in such dreadful sort, as the beholders were astonished thereat.

Besides, such was the order of the Battel, as the *Wings* of each Army came in, to relieve their Bodies: And each had their *Reserves*, who accordingly came in: so that for an half quarter of an hour, there was a most terrible Fight. But to their thinking, the Army which came from the *East* had the worst.

It is here to be noted, that both these Armies seemed to be of a *Red* colour.

Within a little while, there appeared another Army from the *north-west*, greater then the former, which marched directly to the place where the former Battel was fought.

This Army was *black*: and here they perceived horse as well as foot.

[p. 4] And now begins another Battel far exceeding the former for fierceness and cruelty. From the *black Army* there went off Muskets and Cannons, insomuch that they clearly discerned the fire and smoke thereof. This Battel was between the *black* and the *Eastern red Army*, being, as they apprehended, the Reserve of the former Army which came forth from the *north-west*.

These two Armies thus engaged, brake thorow one another, forward and back ward; but the *black* seemed still to have the best.

But before both *Bodies* met, there were several Skirmishes of *Parties* between the *black* and *red*, as in the former Battel. And when both Armies did encounter, they saw such fire and smoak, as if a dozen Cannons had been discharged together.

A little beneath these Armies, not far from the earth, upon a *black cloud*, appeared Horse-men, and amongst them they could perceive nothing, but rising of fire and smoak, and a multitude of *spears* as it were standing upright.

This latter Battel continued a little [p. 5] longer then the former, the *black* driving the *red* before them, till all the *red* vanished out of their sight. And the *black* remained; who in a little time after, departed, and were not any more seen of them.

*

READER,

WHAT Interpretation thou wilt make of this Apparition, I know not; neither shall I adde any thing of mine own to the Relation: Onely take notice, (and believe it) it is no Fiction nor *Scar-crow*, but a thing real, and far beyond what is here reported: for the Spectators (such was their astonishment) could not recollect so much as they saw, afterwards to make a true report of.

[p. 6] D' *Alva* being ask'd whether he had seen the *Blazing Star* which appeared at that time; made answer, That he had so many earthly employments lying on his hands, as he had neither time nor leasure to look up, to see what God was doing in the heavens.[38] I wish it be not so with too many at this time.

God speaketh once, yea twice; yet man perceiveth it not. Job 33. 14.

FINIS.

———————◆———————

The Five strange
WONDERS,
In the *North* and *West* of
ENGLAND:
AS
They were communicated to divers
Honourable Members of *Parliament*, from several Countrey Gentlemen
and Ministers; concerning the strange and prodigious flying in the Air of
a Black *Coffin* betwixt *Liecester* and *Nottingham*, on *Sabbath* day last
was a fortnight, with a flaming Arrow, and a Bloody Sword, casting forth
streams of Fire, to the great wonder and astonishment of many Hundreds
of People that beheld the sparkling and glittering Rays, as far as *Newark*
Beaver, *Loughborough*, *Melton* and divers other places: With a *Conjectu-*
ration thereupon, what these dreadful Signs from Heaven, may denote and
signifie to the People on Earth this present Summer.

Likewise, the great and wonderfull
Warlike Prodigies, which appeared over *Marston-Moor*, near the *City* of
York, between two fiery or flaming Pillars. And the three Monstrous
Creatures found in three Eggs, laid by one Hen bought in *Exceter* Market
one Night, wherein was found a *Serpent*, a *Cockatrice*, and a *Toad*. Together with the opening of the *Skie* in a fearful manner over *Standish* town
five miles from *Gloucester*, and the appearing of a terrible fiery shaking
Sword from the Heavens, with its Point downward towards the Earth; as
also the colour thereof, and what proceeded from it, running along the
ground.

Attested by an Eye-Witness; and entred upon Record, in the Original
Mirrour, or Loo-king Glass: *And for more general satisfaction, presented*
to the view of the three Na-tions of England, Scotland, *and* Ireland.
London, Printed for *W. THOMAS*, 1659.

[p. 3] *The Worlds New Wonders;*
OR,
The Fiery and Flaming Prodigies, in the North and West of *England*.

Many of the People of God who live in such backsliding Times, wherein
publike dangers are approaching, being conscious to their own infirmities,
and weakness, are many times much perplexed with the fears and apprehensions of ensuing perils (especially upon the appearing of such strange
Prodigies in the Skies, even in these latter dayes:) and through weakness of
Faith, much question, Whether they be able to undergo such Conflicts, and
endure such Temptations, as many despised Creatures of this Earthly Fabrick

formerly have done? Or whether the power of God doth so eminently appear in these latter Times for his Church and Children, as in precedent Ages, and in the first primitive times of the Gospel it did? But certainly the Name of God is wonderful still: His glorious Arm is not shortned, that it cannot save; nor his Ear heavy, that it cannot hear [Is. 59:1]: So that we may assure our selves, that he will preserve us from, or support us under, or deliver us from the rage and subtilty of the grandest Serpents, notwithstanding the various Changes, and unparallel'd Revolutions, either in State or Common-wealth: For observable it is, both of the ancient and modern Times, that the greatest Prince who ever reigned in Tyranny, had (at the last) a final subversion in defamation and misery; and those that think to palliate their black and wicked Designs, under the specious pretences of Religion and Liberty, must know, that the time is near, of their disguising, and the Stalking-horse[39] discovered, under the Name of Gospel and Reformation: For as the Comets appeared before the death of *Manasses* King of *Judah*, for his cruel Tyranny against the good Prophet *Esay*,[40] so doth the prodigious Exhalations in the Air (in this our Age) denote the great Fall of those who shall usurp the Peoples Liberties; and as three Suns and a fiery Dart, were seen in the Heavens before the death of *Dioclesian* the Tyrant,[41] so likewise appeared very strange Prodigies, upon the change of a great and high Potentate, who by the good hand of Providence was timely removed and taken from us.

[p. 4] Amongst the rest, that which is most observable, is, the Dismal sight in the Air, on Sabbath day last was a fortnight, prodigiously reprepresenting [*sic*] it self from one of the clock in the forenoon, till about a quarter and a half after three, in the perfect Figure and Form of a black Coffin, with a fiery Dart, and a flaming Sword flying to and again, backwards and forwards, towards the head of the said Coffin, which was with great wonder and admiration beheld by many hundreds of People between Liecester and Nottinghamshire; the lustre whereof, at its breaking, was of so large an Extent, that the streams thereof were seen glittering and sparkling as far as Newark, Beaver, Nottingham, Loughborough, Melton, and divers other Countrey Towns, and parts adjacent; to the great astonishment of the Inhabitants.

And very observable it is, that the fiery Dart, or Arrow, during the time that the Coffin lay havering and flying up and down in the Air, seemed as it were to charge each other, and with such clashing, and streaks of fire, as the like is not to be parallel'd in any Age; but upon the dissolution of the Coffin, abundance of streams of fire proceeded from it, which appeared so conspicuous, That the Heavens seemed to receive its Light and Serenes from its illustrious influences: But no sooner were these serene and bright Rays clouded and eclipsed by the black and louring Clouds, but the great splendor of the fiery streams, proceeding from the Sword and Arrow, immediatly took their center within their own Region and Horizon, and were seen no more from that day, &c. The truth hereof is attested from the hands of several Gentlemen of quality, and Reverend Divines, to divers honourable Members of Parliament, persons of great worth and integrity, and several conjectures (possibly) may be made thereupon: But that the Coffin denotes Mortality, too sad and woful Experience we have in these our days, both in city & countrey; and probably the other two Signals from Heaven, may represent a War or Famine: But the Lord of his infinite mercy divert these sad and just-deserved Judgments from falling upon these Nations, notwithstanding the great confederacie of her potent Enemies, and grant, that there may be redintegrate[42] imbracings, and renewings of love between the People and their Representative, as being far better for all the Plants of this Common-wealth to be watered by the [p. 5] sweetest Dewes and showers of Heaven, than by the most liberal hand of any person whatsoever, which is always consummating.

The next thing that presents it self to publike view, is, the great fleak [i.e. flake] or sheet of fire, which appeared in the Skie over the Town of *Oukam* In *Rutland*, on Sunday was fortnight, the manner thus: About four of the clock in the afternoon, as people were coming from the Church, great sparklings, and illustrious Rays were seen to descend from the Firmament and immediatly after a great sheet or fleak of Fire appeared, which at the last flew quite down the Town, to the sign of the Crown, where it centr'd, burnt, and extinguished. *A sad Omen for those that shall assume the Royal Dignity without Authority.*

In a word the next Prodigie that we shall here insist upon is, another Exhaliaton [*sic*] in the Air as full of wonder as admiration, as evidently appears, by the testimony given by the *York shire* Carriers, who affirm, that about the beginning of this moneth two Fiery Pillars were visible seen at Noon-day over *Marston Moor*,[43] about five miles from the City of *York*; the brightness whereof extended as far as *Wakefield, Wetherby, Pontefract, Sandwich, Doncaster, Leeds, Hallifax,* and divers other places; and between these two Pillars intervened several armed Troops and Companies in the Battail array, presenting each other with several Vollies, and after some Dispute, the Northern Army vanquished the Southern Army: which being done, the two Pillars vanquished.[44]

What this portends, no man can conjecture aright: but it may be supposed, the two Pillars represent his Highness and the Parliament, and the Northern Army the Forces of this Common wealth, vanquishing their Enemy, and maugre[45] the Designs of all Forreign and Popish Confederates. Who need not in the least be feared, if the mutual closings and claspings of redintegrate affections and endearments be insisted upon between the Supream Authority and People[,] and each member of this Common-wealth, to return to his duty and proper station, and firmly to unite together, for the recovery of our long-lost Liberties, and dear-earn'd Priviledges.

[p. 6] And as there appeared a fiery Meteor in the Air near Bristow, on the South side of the City, for divers nights together, in form long, with fiery streames shooting out East and West; which was the week before the beheading of the late King *Charles*: So have we had sundry other Mutations, since those dismal and gloomy days; as fiery Comets, Blazing Stars, Warlike Troops, and visible Bands of Foot, which caused great admiration to many hundred Spectators at Newmarket-Heath, on *Tuesday* last was seven night, where many of the Inhabitants thereabouts were much astonished, especially at the dreadful noise of Drums beating, and Trumpets sounding, which caused as great astonishment, as wonder; by reason they saw no Warlike Bands visible at present: Yet no sooner had this Eccho possess'd them with various Ruminations, but immediatly they began to discern several Warlike Troops and Companions, arraying themselves in Battalia; and after some pickeering,[46] and vollies presented between several[47] Parties, as it were Forlorn Hopes,[48] the two main Bodies joyned Battel, disputing very puisiantly,[49] and with great vigour. During this Engagement, there seemed to be an extraordinary Light, and glittering of Swords, and Men in Armour, which continued for the space of half an hour; and then the one seemed to vanquish the other, taking their pursuit towards the City of *London*.

And as this was no small terrour to the Beholders, so was the succeeding Thunder as great a Wonder to the Spectators, who after sundry great Claps from an Angry God, even like unto an Enemies Warning-Piece,[50] presented to the Earth a mighty Thunder-bolt, much like unto the Shell of a great Granado;[51] which was taken up and carried to Justice *Foster*'s house nea[r]e adjacent, where it now lies, and is there to be seen at this day; as it was affirmed by Captain *Neilson*, the *Norfolk* Post, and some others, who came to *London*, and lodged at the Sign of the Ram-Inne, in West-Smithfield.

It is observable, That not long after this Wonder from Heaven, had presented it self to the Inhabitants of the Earth, but a bright Star of a great Magnitude, was seen glittering and sparkling up and down, even like unto that in the West; whose Lustre was of so large an Extent, and appeared so conspicuous, That although the Air was dark, yet bright and serene were the glorious Rays which streamed forth by its great splendor, as if the Heavens received all its Serenes[52] from its illustrious influences. This Star was seen for the space of two Nights constantly about ten of the Clock: yet in several Forms; as sometimes like a fiery Dragon; sometimes like a flaming Sword; and sometimes in an Oval Form, casting forth a round flame as big as a bushel, and divers sparkling Coales.

[p. 7] As these prodigies portend no little wonder; so doth Beheaded Dr. *John Hewytts* Ghost,[53] produce as great admiration, amongst many; who by its pleading[54] and crying, calls for Justice; which to some seems already executed; and begins thus; saying he is by Birth a Freeman of England, and that it is the undoubted ancient inseparable Birthright, Privilege, and Inheritance of every English Freeman both by the Common Laws, Franchises, Great Charters, Statutes and Usages of this Land, ratified from Age to Age by the Votes, Resolutions, Declarations, Judgements of the High Court of Parliament, and other publike Courts of Justice: That no Freemen of England may or ought to be taken or imprisoned, or disseised, or disinherited of his freehold, Libertyes, or Free Customs, or to be outlawed, exiled, or any way destroyed, or put[55] to death, upon any accusation whatsoever, but by the lawful Judgment of his Peers, or by the Law of the Land, upon Inquest and

Presentment by the Oaths of 12 good and lawful men, upon good and probable evidence and witness. And that if any thing be done to the contrary of the Premises, it shall be void in Law, holden for errour, and nought.

An Exact Relation[,] touching the descending down from Heaven great Fleaks and sheets of fire, neer Coventry and Litterworth.

On the 24th of this instant March, 1659. By several persons of worth it was certified, That about the beginning of this Moneth, great Apparitions and wonderful Signs and Lightnings of Fire were seen in the Air; and a Flaming Flake of Fire, about the bigness of an ordinary Sheet, were seen at the Market-Town of Litterworth in Leicestershire, taking its flight towards Cotsbich Grounds, where it descended to the Earth, and immediatly extinguished, without doing any harm; although many hundreds of the Countrey People beheld the same, to their great wonder and astonishment. The like also appeared at a Town in Warwickshire, called Non-Eaton, about 7 miles from Coventry, where a great Sheet of Fire were seen hovering and flying in the Air about the 7th instant, towards the Evening; and after some time flying up and down, at last took its descent down into the Church-yard, where a great company of Boyes were playing, falling just amongst them; yet did no harm, not so much as a hair of any of their heads perishing: for no sooner was it come to the ground, but it immediatly extinguished likewise, although it seemed of a light flame upon its falling down. What these strange Signs and Wonders portend, no man knoweth: yet this conjecture may fitly be applyed, That it denoteth great Changes, Alterations, and Mutations, in several Nations: for it is observable, That sundry Examples of divers Prodigies, are still fresh in the Memory of Man; As the raining of Blood in the North, presently after the Scots came into England, to assist the Parliament, which covered the Church and Church-yard of Bencastle in Cumberland. And the day before Edge-Hill fight three Suns were seen in the North.[56] God divert his heavy Judgments from falling upon these Nations.

[p. 8] To conclude, in the next place, be pleased to observe, that amongst the greatest of Wonders, that shall arise from the forementioned Prodigies: this may be fitly ranked amongst the most strangest of them, *viz.* That about a fortnight agoe, a Woman buying of a Hen in *Exceter-market*, with a resolution to kill her the next day, put her over night in a Coop, and the next morning comming to take her out, found that she had laid three Eggs, which made her exceedingly astonished; insomuch, that acquainting some of her Neighbors with it, they advised her to break them, which she did; and in the first discovered the perfect sign and shape of a *Serpent*, dead: in the second, a *Cockatrice;*[57] and in the third a *Toad*: both which last, seemed to stir at the first, but immediately died. These may fitly signifie the Death of an old *Serpent*, the surviving of a *Cockatrice*, and a resemblance of the most unworthy Actions of many in Authority, whom we leave for true Justice to rectifie. Desiring rather, that each member would endeavour to sail in the Ocean of Security to the desired Haven, than split against the Rocks of Ambition and injustice.

Thus having given you an account of these strange Prodigies which hath lately happened in these our dayes, give me leave to wind up the truth of all, with one President or Example, that hapned upon the 30 day of *Jan.* in the year 1650. which was thus, Upon St. *Andrews* day, a little before, or about Sun-rising, the Skie opened in a fearful manner, in the *South-West* over *Standish*, a Town five miles from *Gloucester*, and there appeared a terrible fearful fiery flaming Sword, with the hilt upwards, towards the Heavens, the point downwards to the Earth; the Hilt seemed to be blue, the Sword was a great length, shaking hither and thither, and comming lower towards the Earth. There was a long flame of fire towards the point, sparkling, and flaming in a fearful manner, to the great astonishment of the Spectators, who were many. At last the H[e]aven closing, the Sword vanished, and the fire fell to the Earth, and ran upon the ground.

This is entred upon Record, by an Eye witness, and published for generall satisfaction to the Nations.

FINIS.

Notes

1 C. V. Wedgwood, *A Coffin for King Charles: The Trial and Execution of Charles I* (New York: Book-of-the-Month Club, 1964), 229.

2 Wedgwood, *A Coffin*, 240.

3 Jason Peacey, "Reporting a Revolution: A Failed Propaganda Campaign," in *The Regicides and the Execution of Charles I*, ed. Peacey (Basingstoke, UK: Palgrave, 2001), 161–180.

4 Amos Tubb, "Printing the Regicide of Charles I," *History* 89 no. 4 (2004), 500–524, esp. 507–509.

5 Peacey, "Reporting a Revolution," 176–177. Tubb seeks to qualify this conclusion, observing that while in the long term Parliament's propaganda campaign failed to win the hearts of the people, in the *short* term it was remarkably successful at dominating the press; "Printing the Regicide," 524.

6 In addition to *A Miracle of Miracles*, it was related in *A letter sent into France to the Lord Duke Buckingham His Grace of a great miracle wrought by a piece of handkerchefe, dipped in His Majesties bloud* and *A second letter to the lord duke of Buckingham*. See Stephen Brogan, *The Royal Touch in Early Modern England: Politics, Medicine and Sin* (Woodbridge, UK: Boydell & Brewer, 2015), 94–95.

7 Touching for scrofula is discussed in, e.g., Marc Bloch, *Les Rois Thaumaturges* (1925), translated into English as *The Royal Touch: Sacred Monarchy and Scrofula in England and France* (Montreal, Canada: McGill-Queen's University Press, 1973); Keith Thomas, *Religion and the Decline of Magic: Studies in Popular Beliefs in Sixteenth- and Seventeenth-Century England* (Oxford, UK: Weidenfeld & Nicolson, 1971; reprint Penguin Books, 1991), 227–242; and Brogan, *Royal Touch*. On developments in touching for king's evil during the Stuart period, see especially chapter 3 of Brogan.

8 Brogan, *Royal Touch*, 92–93.

9 Brogan, *Royal Touch*, 91.

10 Brogan, *Royal Touch*, 95.

11 *The English Devil: Or, Cromwel and His Monstrous Witch* (Printed by Robert Wood for George Horton, 1660), 4.

12 Jerome Friedman, *The Battle of the Frogs and Fairford's Flies: Miracles and the Pulp Press During the English Revolution* (New York: St. Martin's Press, 1993), 34, 255, 259 and passim.

13 Peter Elmer, *Witchcraft, Witch-Hunting, and Politics in Early Modern England* (Oxford, UK: Oxford University Press, 2016), 86.

14 For a discussion of polemical prodigy works during the Restoration and the government's official, and unofficial, response, see William E. Burns, *An Age of Wonders: Prodigies, Politics and Providence in England 1657–1727* (Manchester, UK: Manchester University Press, 2002), chap. 1, esp. 19–45.

15 Annotation on Thomason copy: "Aug: 2ᵈ 1649."

16 Thomas Fairfax, 3rd Lord Fairfax of Cameron (1612–1671), was one of the foremost cavalry generals and the commander-in-chief of Parliament's New Model Army during the war. Unlike most of his compatriots, Fairfax opposed the execution of the King, which is perhaps why the pamphleteer decided to invoke his name.

17 Charles I was beheaded in January 1649.

18 The final page of the pamphlet is missing and is replaced with a page from the July 25–August 2 issue of the Royalist periodical *The Man in the Moon, Discovering a World of Knavery Under the Sunne*. The author reported on the situation of the "young King" in Europe and added, in a lamentation similar to this pamphleteer's, "What a shame it is for English-men, that they should have no more love or natural Affection to their Native Prince, and rightful Soveraign, but to expose him to the Courtesie of Strangers, whilst they stand adoring two or three *Golden Calves* of their own making!" John Crouch, *The man in the moon, discovering a world of knavery under the sunne; both in the Parliament, the Counsell of State, the army, the city, and the country. With intelligence from all parts of England, Scotland, and Ireland* (Number 15: July 25–August 2, 1649), (London: s.n., 1649), 130.

19 Annotation on the Thomason copy: "this is verry true."

20 Annotation on Thomason copy: "July 5th."

21 It had long been held in England and France that the royal touch could cure the skin disease scrofula, which was thus traditionally known as "king's evil."

22 Charles Howard, 1st Earl of Carlisle, was appointed high sheriff of Cumberland after the Civil War, despite having been charged in 1646 with supporting Charles I. Charges of disloyalty to Parliament were also brought against him in March 1650, and though he was cleared and allowed to continue in his post, *Strange Newes* indicates that anxieties about such former Royalists were not easily allayed. See the *ODNB*.

23 Original: "quarrer."

24 The Thomason copy has "1650" crossed out and "March 5 1649" as a hand-written notation, reflecting the collector's use of the Old Style calendar (which officially begins the new year on March 25) as opposed to the publisher's New Style (which begins January 1). Note the use of 1650 at the beginning of the ensuing 'letter,' but 1649 at the end.

25 Clearly; without ambiguity.

26 To make observations, typically at some length.

27 Shapely.

28 See Genesis 9. Following the destruction of the earth in the Flood, the preservation of Noah and his family, and God's promise never again to send such a watery judgment, God places a rainbow in the sky as a sign of His covenant.

29 Twisted out of natural shape; contorted.

30 A paraphrase of Judges 5:16: "Why abodest thou among the sheepfolds, to hear the bleating of the flocks? For the divisions of Reuben there were great searchings of heart."

31 Appropriate.
32 Original: "lettet."
33 Annotation on Thomason copy: "7ber [September] 12" and "1654."
34 The Battle of Dunbar (September 3, 1650) was part of the English campaign against the Scots, who had declared Charles II their king following the execution of Charles I. It ended in victory for the English under the command of Oliver Cromwell, who considered it "one of the most signal mercies God hath done for England and His people." Oliver Cromwell, "Letter CXL: For the Honorable William Lenthall, Esquire, Speaker of the Parliament of England: These," in *Complete Works of Thomas Carlyle: Oliver Cromwell's Letters and Speeches with Elucidations*, Vol. 2, ed. Thomas Carlyle (New York: P.F. Collier & Sons, 1901), 139.
35 Fought a year after Dunbar, on September 3, 1651, the Battle of Worcester was another victory for Cromwell and the last major conflict of the English Civil War.
36 The First Protectorate Parliament began its term on September 3, 1654 and sat until January 22, 1655, when it was dissolved by Cromwell.
37 The corps of skirmishers set in the front of an army to begin an attack.
38 The story of Henry IV's conversation with the Duke of Alva was mentioned in Thomas Brooks' sermon *Gods delight in the progresse of the upright*, preached before the Commons in December 1648 and published in 1649 (by M.S. for R. Harford). Brooks warned against "an inordinate love to the things of this life" and used Alva as an example: "I remember its storied of *Henry* the fourth of France, asking the Duke of *Alva*, whether he had seen the Ecclipses, he answered, He had so much businesse to do on earth, that he had no time to look up to heaven. A man whose heart is engaged to the love of the world, will finde so much to do in the world, that with that wicked Duke, he will have no time to look up to heaven for strength, to walk in heavenly and holy ways against opposition" (p. 31).
39 A horse trained to allow a hunter to conceal himself behind it while approaching his prey, thus enabling him to come within easy range without startling away the quarry; also refers to a canvas screen made in the shape of a horse and used for the same purpose.
40 King Manasseh of Judah was known for the wickedness of the early years of his reign, including his idolatry and patronage of sorcerers. Although the story is not recorded in the Biblical canon, tradition ascribes to him the murder of Isaiah, ostensibly having the prophet sawn in half for daring to reprove him for his sins.
41 The Roman emperor Diocletian was notorious for his intense persecution of Christians in the early fourth century.
42 Renewed; restored to a perfect state.
43 Marston Moor was the site of a Parliamentarian victory during the First Civil War (July 2, 1644), at which Royalist forces were routed by a joint English and Scottish army.
44 Undoubtedly a mistake for "vanished."
45 To defy or get the better of an opponent.
46 Skirmishing.
47 The 'a' is inverted.
48 A "forlorn hope" was a body of skirmishers set in the front of an army to begin an attack.
49 Aggresively.
50 A signal gun discharged to warn of danger. The metaphor is used by other writers to refer to prodigies and apparitions; see, for instance, *Irelands Amazement, Or the Heavens Armado* (London: Printed for John Thomas, 1642) and John Vicars, *Prodigies & apparitions* ([London?]: Are to be sould by Tho. Bates . . . & by Ralphe . . ., 1643]).

51 A grenade, or small explosive shell.

52 Original: "Screnes;" see p. 4.

53 John Hewitt, an Anglican minister and royalist, was arrested in April 1658 for his involvement in a plot to overthrow the Cromwellian government and place Charles II on the throne. Like Charles I at his own trial, Hewitt refused to recognize the authority of the court or to lodge a plea; and, like Charles, Hewitt was found guilty and beheaded (June 8). His case was made posthumously in the press by his associate William Prynne, from whose work the pamphleteer is copying (*Beheaded Dr. John Hewytts ghost pleading* [London: [s.n.,] 1659]). See also the entry for Hewitt in the *ODNB*.

54 Original: "plcading."

55 Original: "pur." This sentence quotes article 39 of Magna Carta.

56 Both the rain of blood in Cumberland and the three suns at Edgehill were also repeated in *Strange Newes from the North* (London: Printed by J. Clowes, June 11. 1650), 1.

57 A serpentine creature associated with the basilisk, which was fabled to kill with a glance and was hatched from the egg of a cock, not a hen.

List of pamphlet locations

(Note that many of the pamphlets survive in multiple copies. For this list, just one location is given for each pamphlet.)

Anti-Merlinus: Or, A Confutation of Mr. William Lillies Predictions for this Year 1648 (1648)
[The British Library, E.1171.(3.)]

Christian Astrology (1647)
[Cambridge University Library, N.3.53]

A Declaration of a Strange and Wonderfull Monster (1645)
[The Huntington Library, CA, RB 122034]

The Devills White Boyes: Or, A mixture of malicious Malignants (1644)
[Houghton Library, Harvard University, MA, *EC65.A100.644d3]

The Devils Last Legacy (1642)
[The Huntington Library, CA, RB 321482]

The Divels Delusions (1649)
[The British Library, E.565.(15.)]

A Dogs Elegy, or Rupert's Tears (1644)
[The British Library, E.3.(17.)]

The English Devil: or, Cromwel and his Monstrous Witch (1660)
[The British Library, E.1035.(3.)]

The Five Strange Wonders (1659)
[The Huntington Library, CA, RB 16166]

A Great Wonder in Heaven (1643)
[The British Library, C.21.b.10.(41)]

Irelands Amazement, or the Heavens Armado (1642)
[The British Library, E.181.(41)]

The Kingdomes Monster Uncloaked from Heaven (1643)
[The British Library, 669.F.8.(24)]

Looke Up and See Wonders (1628)
[The Huntington Library, CA, RB 31532]

A Lying Wonder Discovered (1659)
[The Huntington Library, CA, RB 439253]

Merlini Anglici ephemeris (1648)
[The Huntington Library, CA, RB 146681 v.5 (1648)]

A Miracle of Miracles (1649)
[The Huntington Library, CA, RB 16195]

More Warning Yet, Being A True Relation of a Strange and most Dreadful Apparition (1654)
[The Huntington Library, CA, RB 146941]

A Most Certain, Strange, and true Discovery of a Witch (1643)
[The British Library, E.69.(9.)]

The Most Strange and Wonderfull apperation of blood in a poole at Garraton (1645)
[The British Library, E.303.(22.)]

Motus Mediterraneus; or, A True Relation of a Fearefull and Prodigious Earthquake (1626)
[Bodleian Library, Oxford, UK, Arch. A e.49 (6)]

The New Yeares Wonder (1643)
[The British Library, E.86.(23.)]

Prodigies & Apparitions, or Englands warning piece (1643)
[The Huntington Library, CA, RB 148141]

The Ranters Monster (1652)
[The British Library, E.658.(6.)]

A Relation of a Strange Apparition in an Ale-house (1641)
[The British Library, E.180.(19.)]

Sad Newes from the Eastern Parts (1646)
[The British Library, E.344.(16.)]

Signes and Wonders from Heaven (1645)
[The Huntington Library, CA, RB 16199]

A Strange and Lamentable accident . . . at Mears-Ashby (1642)
[The British Library, E.113.(15.).]

Strange and Terrible News from Cambridge (1659)
[The Huntington Library, CA, RB 15117]

Strange Newes from Scotland (1647)
[The Huntington Library, CA, RB 447805]

Strange Newes from the North (1650)
   [The British Library, E.603.(3.)]

A Strange Wonder or, The Cities Amazement (1642)
   [The British Library, E.136.(4.)]

A True Relation of the Strange Apparitions Seen in the Air (1650)
   [The Huntington Library, CA, RB 16161]

The warnings of Germany By wonderfull signes (1638)
   [The Huntington Library, CA, RB 60364]

Vox Infantis (1649)
   [The Huntington Library, CA, RB 26224]

Index

(full pamphlets are designated by their document number within their chapter, e.g. 1.i)

Index of scriptural references

[chapter number in brackets]